'The project of this book', writes the author in his Preface, 'is to investigate how poetry and the figure of the poet are represented, discussed, contested within the poetry of ancient Greece.' Dr Goldhill seeks to discover how ancient authors broached the question: From what position does a poet speak? With what authority? With what debts to the past? With what involvement in the present? Through a series of interrelated essays on Homer, lyric poetry, Aristophanes, Theocritus and Apollonius of Rhodes key aspects in the history of poetics are discussed: tale-telling and the representation of man as the user of language; memorial and praise; parody, comedy and carnival; irony, masks and desire; the legacy of the past and the idea of influence. Detailed readings of major works of Greek literature show how richly rewarding and revealing this approach can be. The author makes liberal use of critical writings from areas of study other than Classics and focuses on problems central to contemporary critical debate. His book is uniquely placed to bring together modern and ancient poetics in a way that is enlightening for both. The work is written as much for the serious scholar of literary criticism as for the Classicist, and all Greek is translated.

THE POET'S VOICE

THE POET'S VOICE

ESSAYS ON POETICS AND GREEK LITERATURE

Simon Goldhill

Lecturer in Classics in the University of
Cambridge and Fellow of King's College

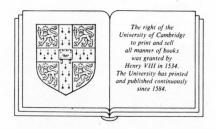

The right of the
University of Cambridge
to print and sell
all manner of books
was granted by
Henry VIII in 1534.
The University has printed
and published continuously
since 1584.

CAMBRIDGE UNIVERSITY PRESS

Cambridge

New York   Port Chester

Melbourne   Sydney

Published by the Press Syndicate of the University of Cambridge
The Pitt Building, Trumpington Street, Cambridge CB2 1RP
40 West 20th Street, New York, NY 10011, USA
10 Stamford Road, Oakleigh, Melbourne 3166, Australia

First published 1991

Printed in Great Britain at
the University Press, Cambridge

British Library cataloguing in publication data

Goldhill, Simon
The poet's voice: essays on poetics and Greek literature.
1. Poetry in Greek, to 500 – Critical studies
1. Title
881.0109

Library of Congress cataloguing in publication data

Goldhill, Simon.
The poet's voice: essays on poetics and Greek literature / by
Simon Goldhill.
    p.   cm.
Includes bibliographical references.
Includes index.
ISBN 0-521-39062-1. – ISBN 0-521-39570-4 (pbk.)
1. Greek literature – History and criticism.   2. Poetry in
literature.   3. Poets in literature.   4. Poetics.   1. Title.
PA3015.P62G65   1991
880.9'001 – dc20   90-1862   CIP

ISBN 0 521 39062 1 hardback
ISBN 0 521 39570 4 paperback

AO

Contents

vii

Preface

I do not want to simplify
Or: I would simplify

By naming the complexity
Adrienne Rich

The project of this book is to investigate how poetry and the figure of the poet are represented, discussed, contested within the poetry of ancient Greece. It is a vast subject and some markers of my procedure may prove helpful at the outset. There are three major strands of analysis that link the studies that follow. First, I set out to chart how the (self-) representation of the poet's voice implicates a wide series of questions about authority in language, access to knowledge, and the representation of humans in society. (For an adequate study of the poet's voice cannot be limited to describing the institutions of poetic production within a culture or to collecting the passages of ancient writing where poets are portrayed or the performance/writing of poetry is explicitly discussed.) Second, I explore how an awareness of other poets' poetry – an awareness displayed in parody, allusion, rewriting – is a fundamental dynamic of the construction of the poet's voice within a literary tradition. Third, my arguments return to the varied problems that arise from poetry's focus on its own workings – the self-reflexiveness inherent in such poetic self-representation. These three interrelated topics, which could be termed the problems of representation, intertextuality and self-reflexiveness, form an integral part of trying to discover the position from which the poet's voice speaks – and together connect the separate studies of this book.

The subtitle, however, *Essays on poetics and Greek literature*, has been chosen for two particular reasons. The first is to stress that this is not a history of Greek literature (nor even does it cover all the aspects of the problems I have just outlined). Each chapter takes a particular, delimited set of questions and a particular, delimited set of texts. Chapter 1 focuses on the relation between the hero as a teller of tales and the poet as a teller of tales in the *Odyssey* to discuss the representation of man as user of language. Chapter 2 puts together the *Iliad*, the *Odyssey*, some lyric fragments and Pindar's *epinikia* to consider the development of what is a crucial aspect of the ancient perception of the poet's role – praise, celebration, memorial. Chapter 3 turns to the public poetry of the fifth-century democracy of Athens and in particular to the comedy of Aristophanes to look at parody and the carnivalesque as foundations of the comic poet's voice. The fourth and fifth chapters turn to poetry from the Hellenistic archive: epigonal poetry, after the rise of the prose genres of history, philosophy, science. The fourth chapter selects some poems of Theocritus to investigate ideas of framing, multiplicity of voices and desire. And the fifth chapter treats Apollonius' sense of the (poetic) past in his epic narrative. There are, I am well aware, many gaps both in the roll-call of authors – little mention of Hesiod, Archilochus, Sappho, tragedians, Menander, Callimachus, for example – and in the range of texts of the authors who are discussed: in no case, not even Timocreon's, is an exhaustive treatment of a writer's extant corpus attempted. In part, this is because my express focus is on *specific* questions of *poetics* (not on producing a general overview of any poet's work). In part, it is because it seems to me crucial for such discussion of poetics to be focused closely on the texts of the ancient tradition: it is only in the detailed work of reading that these problems of poetics can be adequately formulated and analysed. Therefore, I have decided to concentrate on some poems of some authors for extensive and detailed analysis, rather than allowing each chapter to grow into a monograph, and rather than offering another collection of generalizations about (all of) Greek literature. My hope in structuring the book in this way is both that the different problems treated in each chapter prove mutually enlightening (as they are mutually implicative) and that the readings offered make up for such a restriction of range by what such a closer scrutiny can reveal about the poems and the poetics under discussion.

    The second reason for my subtitle, and specifically for the phrasing 'poetics *and* Greek literature' rather than 'poetics *of* Greek literature', is to stress that this book stems in part from an involvement with contemporary work on literary theory. (Expressing my subject in the terms 'representation, intertextuality, self-reflexiveness' is – of course – already a marker of such involvement, a strategy of self-representation.) Each of my chapters makes liberal use of critical writings from areas of study other than Classics and focuses on problems central to contemporary critical debate. There is a double aim here, too. On the one hand, I turn to these contemporary critical debates for the illuminating insights that they offer into classical literature and the institutions of criticism. On the other hand, the essays in this book also regularly take a stand against what is all too often to be seen as a regrettable oversimplification of classical texts. The return to classical writing and culture is a gesture repeatedly made by contemporary critics in a remarkably wide variety of fields: I hope this book will enable that gesture to be made with a heightened awareness of the complexity and sophistication of ancient Greek texts (no one's childhood stories). *The poet's voice*, in short, is intended to contribute to a continuing dialogue between poetics and Greek literature.

I have made no attempt at the impossible task of an exhaustive bibliography over all the subjects and authors discussed. In the notes I have tried to strike a balance between user-friendly annotation and the necessary indication of my many debts to other scholars and of where further discussion may usefully be found. I have been persuaded, at the last gasp, by my publisher, to reduce the formerly comprehensive quotation of Greek to what is now a bare minimum; and, of course, all Greek is translated – in all cases with my own translations, though for Pindar based on the fine version of Nisetich – and where useful and relevant transliterated. Translations must be second best; but I understand that this is a necessary step if my aim of continuing a dialogue between Classics and other disciplines is to be achievable. Those who work on ancient Greek will be familiar with the arguments. And will probably have texts to hand anyway.

It is a pleasure to thank the many colleagues who have helped me in this project over many years. Helene Foley, Michael Silk, Paul Cartledge, Neil Hopkinson, Richard Hunter, Greg Nagy, Angus Bowie, Stephen Halliwell each read and commented on individual chapters. Parts of chapter 2 and chapter 3 were delivered to seminars in Oxford and benefited from discussion there. The readers for Cambridge University Press and the editor, Pauline Hire, offered detailed comments and general enthusiasm that have been crucial. John Henderson read, discussed, commented throughout the project: I find it pleasurably hard to imagine what working without such day to day critical and intellectual support would be like. Thanks.

Finally, my greatest pleasure is to be able to thank my wife Shoshana – with my love for her love, care, support – and to dedicate this book to our Daniel – for giving voice.

S.D.G.

1 The poet hero: language and representation in the *Odyssey*

Heavenly hurt it gives us –
We can find no scar.
But internal difference
Where the Meanings are.

Emily Dickinson

The *Odyssey* is a central text in any discussion of 'the poet's voice' in Greek poetry. Not only is Homer throughout the ancient world a figure of authority and poetic pre-eminence against whom writers establish their own authorial voice, but also the text of the *Odyssey* demonstrates a concern with the major topics that will recur throughout this book. For the *Odyssey* highlights the role and functioning of language itself, both in its focus on the hero's lying manipulations and in its marked interest in the bewitching power of poetic performance. It is in the *Odyssey*, too, that we read one of the most developed narratives of concealed identity, boasted names and claims of renown, and the earliest extended first-person narrative in Greek literature. Indeed, the *Odyssey* is centred on the representation of a man who is striving to achieve recognition in his society, a man, what's more, who is repeatedly likened to a poet.

In this opening chapter, I shall begin by looking at the fundamental issues of recognition and naming, and then discuss the interplay of the hero's lying tales with the poet's own voice as narrator. I shall be particularly concerned with the relation between representation in language (story-telling, naming, the exchanges of social discourse) and the construction of (social) identity.

RECOGNITION

First words

The proper study of mankind is . . .

῎ΑΝΔΡΑ: what is (to be) recognized in this first word of the *Odyssey*? The first question I wish to raise is how exemplary, how generalizable, a (male, adult) figure the subject of this epic is represented to be – a question focused in an English translation by the difficulty of choosing between 'a man', 'the man' or even 'man'. For the uneasy tension between

I

paradigmatic model and unique individual typical of the representation of heroes is especially marked in the case of Odysseus. On the one hand, recent critics have emphasized how Odysseus' reintegration is 'a return to humanity in the broadest sense'[1] – a paradigmatic representation of (a) man's reaffirmation of social identity. The boundaries and values of the *oikos* (household) are mapped by the transitions and transgressions of Odysseus' journey: Odysseus' travels leave behind both the extremes of civilization experienced among the Phaeacians, and also the extremes of violent transgression and distorted versions of human culture experienced in the non-human encounters leading to the Phaeacians, as the hero struggles to regain the *oikos*, disordered by his absence. Human social existence and man's place in it become defined through these different views of alternative or corrupted order. So, the normative thrust of the *Odyssey* is to be discovered not merely in the punishment of the suitors' wrongdoing but also in the projection and promotion of the norms of culture – an articulation of man's place. (And particularly since Vidal-Naquet's classic analysis of land, agriculture, food and sacrifice, many other aspects of this patterning of norm and transgression have been outlined – from the fundamental social institutions of marriage and guest-friendship to such diverse signs of the cultural system as trees, dogs, weaving, bathing . . .)[2] In *andra*, then, there is to be recognized a paradigmatic and normative representation of what it is to be a man in society, an announcement that the narrative to come will explore the terms in which an adult male's place is to be determined.

On the other hand, Odysseus is not an allegorical figure like Everyman. He is also *the* man whose special qualities allow him to survive a unique set of wanderings and sufferings and to make his return to a particular

---

[1] Segal (1962) 20. The paradigmatic qualities of Odysseus are also discussed by Taylor (1961); Segal (1967); Vidal-Naquet (1981 (1970)); Austin (1975) 81–238; Foley (1978); Niles (1978); Goldhill (1984) 183ff; Rutherford (1985).

[2] On marriage, see Hatzantonis (1974); Pomeroy (1975) 16–31; Gross (1976); Foley (1978); Forsyth (1979); Northrup (1980); Goldhill (1984) 184–95; Goldhill (1986a) 147–51; on guest-friendship, Finley (1954) 109–14; Gunn (1971); Stagakis (1975) 94–112; Stewart (1976); Edwards (1975); Bader (1976); Kearns (1982); Herman (1987) and Murnaghan (1987) 91–117, who rightly relates this institution to the problem of recognition; on trees, see Finley (1978) 78–9, who writes 168: 'Trees progressively mark his [Odysseus'] return.' On the olive, see Segal (1962) 45, 55 (with n. 31 and n.41). Vidal-Naquet (1981 (1970)) 60–1 notes that the tree under which Odysseus shelters on the beach at Scheria (as Odysseus returns from the wild travels to the civilized world of the Phaeacians) is half wild, half domestic olive! On dogs, Rose, G. (1979); Goldhill (1988c) 9–19 (both with further bibliography); on weaving, Snyder (1981); Jenkins (1985); Goldhill (1988c) 1–9; Segal (1967) 337–9; on bathing, Segal (1967) 329–34.

position. So, indeed, *andra* is immediately qualified by its (first and marked) epithet *polutropon*, 'of many turns'. Since antiquity, the ambiguity of this term has been debated.[3] As Pucci has analysed at greatest length, *polutropos* is the first of a series of distinctive *polu-* epithets indicating Odysseus' 'chief characteristic: versatility, manyness of travels, resources, tricks, stories ...'[4] (So the proem goes on to emphasize Odysseus' 'many [*polla*] wanderings' (1), to see the towns of 'many [*pollōn*] men' (2), and to suffer 'many [*poll'*] pains' (3).) *Polutropos*, 'of many turns', implies both 'of many wiles' and 'of many journeys'; and the ambiguity is significant in that it is Odysseus' wily turns of mind that allow him to survive his wanderings: the many experiences of Odysseus and his quality of being *polutropos* are linked by more than the repetition of *pol-*. What's more, Pucci adds a third meaning, 'of many turns of speech', derived from *tropos* in its sense 'figure of speech', 'trope' – although there is no secure evidence for this sense of *tropos* before the fifth century. What can be said, however, is that it is a defining aspect of Odysseus' wiliness that he is the master of tricky language (and Hermes, the only other figure called *polutropos* in the Homeric corpus, is the divinity associated particularly with deceitful communication and the problems of exchange[5]). So, too, that Odysseus is the *object* of a multiplicity of (rhetorical) descriptions in the epic is an integral element not only of the many-sided representation of the hero, but also, more specifically, of the instantiation of his *kleos*, his renown – 'to be talked of by many'. ('Tell me, Muse ...') There is, then, to be recognized in *andra*, especially as it begins its lengthy glossing with the specific and polyvalent

---

[3] For modern discussion specifically on *polutropon*, see in particular Rüter (1969) 34–9; Detienne and Vernant (1978) 27–54, especially 39–43; Pucci (1982); Clay (1983) 29ff. See also Basset (1923); van Groningen (1946). Milman Parry singles out the word as his first example of a particularized epithet (1971) 154. Bekker (1863) inaugurates a lengthy discussion among Analytic scholars, for which Rüter has extensive bibliography. For ancient discussion, see e.g. Porphyr. Schol. ad *Od.* 1.1. = Antisthenes fr. 51 Decleva Caizzi. At Plato *Hipp. Min.* 365c-d, Hippias, in discussing Homer, joins πολύτροπον, 'of many turns', and ψευδῆ, 'lying', as apparent synonyms, but Socrates says he will not discuss Homer since one cannot ask what he had in mind when he composed the lines. For the most interesting modernist treatment of *polutropos*, see Ellman (1982).

[4] Pucci (1982) 51.

[5] The only other example in the *Odyssey* is *Od.* 10.330, where Odysseus is recognized by Circe from an oracle as he tricks her. It occurs elsewhere in the Homeric corpus only in the *Hymn to Hermes* 13 and 439, applied to Hermes, for whose tricky qualities, see Kahn (1978). Hermes also helps Odysseus with Circe in particular (*Od.* 10.277ff) and supports Odysseus' grandfather, Autolycus (*Od.* 19.397ff).

polutropos, the sign of a particular figure – 'the (especial, inimitable, famous) man'.

As Odysseus struggles to reinstitute the norms of the *oikos*, and proves the only man capable of winning the struggle, this ambivalent paradigmatic status informs the narrative of *nostos* (return). And *andra* is programmatic of this.

The surprising lack of a proper name in the first line(s) of the epic, then, prompts the question not simply of *to whom* does the opening expression refer, but of *what* is (to be) recognized in such a periphrastic reference.[6] Indeed, the withholding of the name invests the proem with the structure of a *griphos*, a riddle, an enigma, where a series of expressions (of which *polutropon* is the first) successively qualifies the term *andra* as the name 'Odysseus' is approached. The rhetorical strategy of gradual revealing (that is also a continuing (re)defining) provides a programmatic model for the narrative of Odysseus' gradual re-establishment on Ithaca, where each encounter successively and cumulatively formulates the character and *kleos*, 'renown', of the hero, as his recognition is approached.

This nameless opening expression, however, does not merely set up the mapping of *andra* (as man, adult, male, husband ...) but also poses the question of what is at stake in a (proper) name, of what is the difference between saying *andra* and saying 'Odysseus': from the Cyclops' cave to standing in the hall before the suitors, speaking out the name of Odysseus is replete with significance. *Andra*, then, also announces the concealment and revealing of the name that plays a crucial role in the *kleos* of Odysseus' return. Yet, as Pucci also notes, the name is displaced by an adjective, *polutropon*, that itself expresses the very quality of deceptive wiliness that is seen most strikingly in Odysseus' constant disguises, which, precisely, withhold the proper name.[7] *Polutropon*, in other words, both marks Odysseus' capability to manipulate language's power to conceal and reveal, and, at the same time, *enacts* such a revealing and concealing. There is to be recognized here, then – another pro-

---

[6] The lack of name has often been commented on. The modern Analytic debate begins with Bekker (1863) (see n. 3). Wilamowitz in a fine example of Analytic rhetoric regards it as a 'carelessness' (*Unbedachtsamkeit*) that the poet 'forgets to name the man of many turns' (*'den ἄνηρ πολύτροπος zu nennen vergisst'*) (1884) 16. For an extensive bibliography, see Rüter (1969) 34–52, to which can be added the important works of Dimock (1956); Austin (1972); Clay (1976); Clay (1983) 10–34.

[7] Pucci (1982) 49–57.

grammatic gesture – how the *Odyssey* in a self-reflexive way highlights, first, words and their use as a concern.

There is, then, in these first words a multiform programmatic expression. The question of what is (to be) recognized in the first word(s) of the *Odyssey* is itself framed to emphasize how, in responding to this narrative which progresses through a series of defining recognitions, the reader or audience is necessarily implicated in a process of drawing out significances, connotations, relations between words (phrases, lines, scenes) – inevitably implicated, that is, in a process of defining and recognition. (And in Greek *anagignōskein* means both 'to read' and 'to recognize'.)[8] There is, then, also to be recognized in the first words of the *Odyssey* the (self-)involvement of the reader or audience in comprehending the narrative of recognition – which, as we will see, is fundamental to the normative project of the *Odyssey*.

Like its hero, the opening words of the *Odyssey* are canny in what they reveal and in what they conceal. They are programmatic not merely by the opening of a thematic concern but also by the very way that such an opening is formulated. This very brief opening discussion is intended not only to sketch the *Odyssey*'s programmatic beginning by way of introduction to the argument that follows, but also explicitly to emphasize the critical problems that – from the first – arise from the interplay between a reader's or audience's activity of recognition and the narrative of Odysseus' recognitions. So, let us turn now to the narrative of recognition by which Odysseus makes his return to Ithaca.

Seeing the pattern

That anonymity which overhangs a man until his context is complete

R. Frost

Recognition is not merely a perceptual process. It also involves authorization, power, legitimacy, as in the recognition by one country of an-

---

[8] Although *anagignōskein* is a Homeric term, there is depicted, of course, no scene of 'reading' in a narrow sense. There are, however, innumerable scenes that revolve around the difficulties of interpretation and communication. Hence my phrase 'reader or audience': it is used to avoid two chimaeras of Homeric criticism: the speculative reconstruction of necessary restrictions for the audience's comprehension of an oral performance; the presupposition that an oral performance necessarily requires clarity, transparency or ease of comprehension. For the implications of such a privileging of the spoken word, see the famous discussion of Derrida (1976), well used specifically for Homer by Lynn-George (1988).

other, the recognition of legitimate children by a father.[9] Both aspects are central to Odysseus' return. On the one hand, the need for disguise and concealment of his identity emphasizes the danger of a premature realization by the suitors of his presence in Ithaca. On the other hand, to be recognized as Odysseus is to reassert his role as head of the *oikos*, and as king. The aim of Odysseus is recognition in both senses. Each act of recognition is at one and the same time a perception of identity and an assertion of role. The *nostos* is not complete without recognition.

I wish first to consider the various moments of recognition for Odysseus in Ithaca – an interrelated series of encounters – and I will begin with a scene that has all too rarely been discussed in detail but which offers an instructive model of the process of recognition in the *Odyssey*. When Odysseus is delivered by the Phaeacians to Ithaca, he is left on the beach, the very edge of the island, asleep. Once before, blown by the winds of Aeolus, he had reached close enough to see people tending fires on the island, but then sleep had come to his eyes, exhausted as he was by nine days at the rudder (10.28ff). It is a nice irony that, as the moment of return to the fatherland is achieved, Odysseus fails to do what has been his repeated expression of desire, precisely, to *see* his country.[10] When he awakens, however, recognition is still delayed. For Athene has surrounded the island in mist, and Odysseus, alone on a shore again, fails to recognize the fatherland (13.187–94):

> But when godlike Odysseus awoke,
> from his sleep in his fatherland, he did not even recognize it,
> so long had he been away. For the goddess, Pallas Athene
> daughter of Zeus, poured a mist around, so that she might
> make him unrecognizable, and tell him everything,
> and not have his wife and citizens and folk recognize him
> before he had punished the suitors for every outrage.

After his constant desire to see the homeland, it is a further irony that even after he wakes up, it is seeing (and recognizing) that is impossible for Odysseus. The goddess' deception masks the moment of arrival. She makes the island *unrecognizable* for him (οὐδέ μιν ἔγνω 188) in order that she might make him *unrecognizable* (ἄγνωστον 191) to prevent *recogni-*

---

[9] I have found Bourdieu (1977) especially 164ff particularly stimulating on recognition, and two books which appeared after this chapter was written but which I have attempted to incorporate: Cave (1988); Murnaghan (1987).

[10] E.g. in Odysseus' mouth 5.220; 8.466; 9.28; and from others, 5.41; 5.114; 6.314; 7.76; 8.410; 9.532. On 'sleep' as a motif, see Segal (1967) 325–9.

tion (μὴ γνοίη 192) by his wife (*alokhos*), by his fellow countrymen (*astoi*) and by his own people (*philoi*).[11] The triple repetition of words of 'recognition' stress both the thematic focus of the scene, and also the different perspectives of recognition – that is, both Odysseus' recognition of the island and the recognition of Odysseus by his wife, the citizens and his *philoi*, who make up three different aspects of the *nostos*. The word for 'wife', *alokhos* (rather than *gunē*, as at 1.13), is etymologically connected with the word for (marriage-)bed, *lekhos*, and is often translated 'bed-fellow'. The full significance of this term is realized not merely in Odysseus' rejection of his previous bed-fellows, Calypso and Circe (and the offer of Nausicaa as a bride) but also in Odysseus' journey towards the bed at the centre of the house. The 'citizens' will be the figures with whom Odysseus is finally depicted as making a truce; and the varying reactions of Odysseus' *philoi* (from Eumaeus to Telemachus, Eurycleia to Laertes) form the substance of the successive encounters of the returning king. What's more, as we will see, for each of these figures the process of (mis)recognition of Odysseus is different; and for each something different depends on Odysseus' return. As Odysseus opens his eyes on Ithaca, then, both the process of recognition and what is at stake in recognition for Odysseus are immediately highlighted.

Odysseus' protecting divinity continues her manipulative trickery. She arrives in disguise, and in answer to Odysseus' question as to where he has arrived, she withholds the name of 'Ithaca' until the very last line of her speech of reply (13.236–49). She begins: νήπιός εἰς, ὦ ξεῖν', ἢ τηλόθεν εἰλήλουθας, 'You are foolish, stranger, or come from far' – if he does not recognize this island. With the same line with which the Cyclops dismisses the possibility of guest-friendship's obligations, Odysseus is introduced (as a stranger) to his homeland.[12] At the mention, finally, of the name of Ithaca, Odysseus silently rejoices at the recognition that he is in 'his own fatherland' (251); but in response defensively spins a tale about who he is – the first of the Cretan lies that I will discuss in depth later. Odysseus may know he is in Ithaca, but Ithaca is not yet to know

[11] Pucci (1987) 100, alone of modern scholars, takes ἄγνωστον as active, 'unrecognizing' (αὐτόν μιν = 'himself'). On this conversation of Odysseus and Athene, see the good comments of Clay (1983) 186–212 (whose overall theory of the role of Athene's wrath in the epic is difficult to accept, however); Maronitis (1981). Murnaghan (1987) calls this scene 'pivotal', but fails to discuss it in any detail.
[12] See 10.273. In different ways, the Cyclops and Athene both treat Odysseus as a foolish child (νήπιος, 'foolish', etymologically means 'not capable of speaking'); both bring forth, however, Odysseus' qualities of *mētis* precisely in speech.

that Odysseus is home. The (mutual) process of recognition is far from complete.

Athene reacts to Odysseus' deceit with a speech famous for its ironic banter as well as its description of Odysseus as master of deceit – I shall discuss this also further below. But for Odysseus the recognition that he is faced with (a previously disguised) Athene brings a sudden suspicion. To what extent has she been tricking him? Is this really Ithaca (13.324–8)?:

> Now I entreat you by your father – for I do not think that
> I have come to bright Ithaca, but turned off course
> to another land. I think you are teasing me,
> when you tell me this, to beguile my mind.
> Tell me if it's really true that I have reached my dear fatherland.

The recognition of the name of Ithaca that caused Odysseus' earlier joy is turned to doubt by the recognition of the goddess who spoke the name. Is he in fact home yet? Or is it some other land? He needs assurance against his suspicion of deception that he has truly reached his 'dear fatherland', the land with a history that gives him his proper place.

Athene now clears the mist sufficiently so that Odysseus can finally recognize his homeland and its topography. He rejoices again in his land and kisses the grain-giving soil (13.352–4):

> As she spoke, the goddess dispelled the mist; and the land
> was visible. Then godlike, much enduring Odysseus
> rejoiced, delighting in his land, and he kissed the grain-giving soil.

The addition of the act of kissing the soil to the expression of joy that had also been provoked by the earlier announcement of the name of Ithaca not only marks a heightening of expression after the hesitation of doubt but also qualifies the significance of this point of *nostos*: it is to the grain-giving land of Ithaca, after his journeys in the wild and uncultivated lands, that Odysseus has finally returned.[13]

The point of return to Ithaca itself – when exactly is there achieved the fulfilment of the desire for *nostos*? – is fenced with hesitations and the ironies set in play by the goddess' powers of disguise. The confusion of perception, the dangers of deceptive language, the mutual testing and the interplay of doubt and joy, all ironically defer and manipulate the regularly expressed desire 'to see the fatherland'. This complex and ironic treatment of recognition as a mutual *process*, veined with the uncertainties

---

[13] On the significance of the term 'grain-giving', see Vidal-Naquet (1981 (1970)) 45.

of (verbal) exchange, is paradigmatic of scenes of recognition in the
Odyssey.

Hesitation and deferral are integral to Odysseus' relation with Eumaeus, whose farm marks the edge of Odysseus' property – to where he
travels from the edge of the island. As Odysseus approaches the farm,
the dogs run out barking – a significantly different reception from that
offered around Circe's palace (10.216–17) where the animals 'fawn like
dogs fawn on their master when he is returning from a feast' (14.29–32):

> Suddenly, the baying dogs saw Odysseus.
> They ran at him with a great outcry. But Odysseus
> with cunning sat down. His staff dropped from his hand.
> There, by his own steading, he might have suffered an outrageous
> mauling ...

The return of the master to his own property is made dependent on his
slave's observance of the proprieties of guest-friendship, as Odysseus
is forced to hesitate – to sit down – at the moment of entrance. Yet the
hesitation is also represented as a typically Odyssean move – performed
with 'cunning', κερδοσύνῃ – and the dropped staff, *skēptron* – which
means both a beggar's stave and a king's royal sceptre – also hints at the
double role of king and beggar.[14] A return in disguise, which contains
signs of recognition (a veiled hinting that will be seen again and again,
particularly between Odysseus and Penelope).

It is in Eumaeus' hut that Odysseus first allows himself to be recognized – not by the swineherd, for whom revelation is deferred by a
long testing, but by Telemachus. That this is the first act of mutual
recognition is important not merely for the workings of revenge – Odysseus needs Telemachus' support – but also for the thematic stress on the
relations between father and son in the patriarchal and patrilineal *oikos*
(which can scarcely be overstressed). To return to the fatherland is to
return to the role of father. Here, too, however, the recognition is not
effected without its hesitations. After he has viewed Telemachus from the
vantage of his disguise – Telemachus, who calls Eumaeus ἄττα, 'daddy'
(e.g. 16.31) – Odysseus returns from outside the house in his undisguised
splendour. Telemachus is amazed and assumes the stranger is a god, and,
very properly, prays to be spared. Odysseus responds (16.186–9):

---

[14] On this scene, see Finley (1978) 168; Rose (1980); Williams (1986). Lilja (1976) 20 has
   extensive bibliography on whether it really is cunning to sit down before angry dogs.

Τὸν δ' ἠμείβετ' ἔπειτα πολύτλας δῖος Ὀδυσσεύς·
'οὔ τίς τοι θεός εἰμι· τί μ' ἀθανάτοισιν ἐΐσκεις;
ἀλλὰ πατὴρ τεός εἰμι, τοῦ εἵνεκα σὺ στεναχίζων
πάσχεις ἄλγεα πολλά, βίας ὑποδέγμενος ἀνδρῶν.'

Then much enduring, godlike Odysseus responded.
'I am not a god. Why do you liken me to the immortals?
But I am your father, for whose sake you grieve and
suffer many pains, as you entertain the violence of men.'

The echo *theos eimi*, 'I am a god', and *teos eimi*, 'I am your', at the same metrical position in the line, and the question 'Why do you liken me to the immortals?' stress the importance of the rejection of immortality with Calypso and the return to the (human) relationship with his son with all the implications of maintained generational continuity as opposed to immortality. It is as 'father' and not as 'Odysseus' that the returning hero introduces himself to his son – without using his proper name (and *ou tis* ('no one', 'not a'), the words with which he begins this assertion of identity perhaps recall Odysseus' most famous concealment of his proper name?). Moreover, the assertion that Telemachus has suffered many pains for his father further constructs a link between the two figures. Odysseus, who is so often termed 'much enduring' (as in the introductory line to this address to his son) and who so often comments on how he 'suffered many pains' (as the proem describes it (1.4)), recognizes that his son too 'suffers many pains'(189).[15] As the narrative is turned so that Telemachus and Odysseus make parallel returns from abroad and come together at the farm of Eumaeus, so the father recognizes the parallel experience of the son. 'Like father, like son ...', the essence of patrilineal generational continuity.

Telemachus, however, remains unconvinced (16.194–5):

You are not Odysseus, my father, but a divinity who is
beguiling me, so that I may mourn with still more grief.

Telemachus uses the proper name to deny that the stranger is Odysseus, his father. Both the reintroduction of the name and the use of 'my father' are relevant. For Telemachus, since his opening exchange with the disguised Athene, has shown an uncertainty about Odysseus as man and as father. Telemachus is first seen imagining the arrival of Odysseus in the hall in full military splendour (1.113–8) – an arrival quite different from

---

[15] Cf. *Od.* 13.310, where Athene says, precisely, that Odysseus will have 'to suffer many pains entertaining the violence of men', πάσχειν ἄλγεα πολλά, βίας ὑποδέγμενος ἀνδρῶν.

the insults the disguised beggar receives – and his journey to Menelaus and to Nestor is to learn about the *kleos* of Odysseus.[16] So, when Athene asks him if he is Odysseus' son, Telemachus replies that Penelope says it is so, but 'no one really knows his own father' (1.216).[17] Paternity cannot be proved, only accepted.[18] There are no recognition *tokens* between Odysseus and Telemachus. *Recognition is part of the relationship (to be) recognized.* This hesitation to accept Odysseus is not merely because he was too young to know his father who left so many years before, then, but also a part in the development of the relation of son and father, crucial to the establishment and continuity of the *oikos* for which they together fight. The son needs to accept the father as the father (as a father *recognizes* his children) – the gestures that maintain structured (patriarchal, patrilineal) authority in the *oikos*. Indeed, even as he makes his denial, Telemachus' suspicion that he is being tricked by a divinity may well remind us of his father who had suspected Athene in a similar way – as here too the mutual joy of recognition is deferred through the process of doubt, testing and acceptance.

It is only after Odysseus has explained Athene's role in his transformation that Telemachus accepts that it is his father returned. 'For no other Odysseus will come here', says Odysseus (16.204), echoing his son's use of the proper name as he asserts his identity now as both father and Odysseus (205–6):

> But here I am, that man, who has suffered evils, and wandered far.
> Now I have reached my fatherland in the twentieth year.

The suffering (παθών) and the many wanderings (πολλὰ ἀληθείς) recall and vary the proem's opening description of the man; and 'the fatherland' as the object of return takes on a particular relevance as Odysseus claims his position of father to Telemachus. Telemachus, then, recognizes his father, and the two together finally cry.[19] A significant moment in the

---

[16] See now Jones (1988) on Telemachus, *kleos* and Odysseus.

[17] I follow the standard translation here, but it is worth pointing out that γόνον, the word translated 'father', is perhaps less straightforward in the Greek than the proverbial ring of the translation might suggest. Here, it means 'descent', 'stock' or perhaps 'parentage', which is paralleled only at *Od.* 11.234 and perhaps 19.166. Most often in Homer, as in later Greek, γόνος means 'offspring', 'child' (e.g. *Il.* 5.635; 6.191). See the lengthy note in the scholia on this line, which also offers other examples of the proverb.

[18] See e.g. Barnes (1973) who writes 68: 'Fathers are not self-evident as mothers are: "genitor" is a social status.' Cf. Coward (1983) for a historical survey and bibliography of this idea.

[19] On the tears of the members of Odysseus' family, see below, p. 61.

construction of Odysseus' return is achieved, but the *nostos* is not complete for Odysseus, for Telemachus (as his *paideusis* proceeds) or for the relationship between them. There is more to come.

From the farm Odysseus travels to the palace itself, which he recognizes, in his disguise, as clearly Odysseus' house (17.264–71). That Odysseus is given a *speech* of recognition, after the narrator's many representations of the landscapes and buildings to be faced by Odysseus, marks the peculiar investment of the hero in this expression of what is to be seen in this house. At the door, the point of entrance is (once more) surrounded by deferral and hesitation. First, Eumaeus initiates a lengthy conversation at the threshold itself about who should go in first. Odysseus sends Eumaeus in ahead; he himself will wait at the margin (17.272–89). As they talk, Argus, the hunting dog, now old, flea-ridden and on the dung-heap, recognizes his master and wags his tail – and dies. Despite Odysseus' (concealed) tears at the sight, this is not merely a sentimental moment.[20] First, it is another arrival for Odysseus at an animal-guarded threshold – as at Eumaeus' house where the disguised master was threatened with (unrecognizing) violence, until he was received as a *xeinos*; and as at Circe's, where the wild animals, described as being like dogs who recognize their returning master, offered a different sort of threat to the order of things; and as at Alcinous' palace, where the doorway is guarded by gold and silver dogs, who never sleep or die, paragons of the positive qualities of guard-dogs. The boundaries of the civilized order of the *oikos* are defined in part by opposition to the outside world of the wild, the uncivilized, the uncultivated. Man's relation to the natural world is a basic factor in defining *andra*, 'a/the man', and the structure of the *oikos*. The threshold of the *oikos* is protected by an animal who articulates the boundary between the inside and the outside of the cultural sphere of the *oikos*;[21] and Odysseus' return to his own threshold must be seen within the sequence of his different approaches to animal-guarded doorways. The different depictions of animals at the threshold form a part of the system of ideas in which Odysseus' *nostos* is to be understood. At Odysseus' house, we find a hand-reared hunting[22] dog on the dung-heap – a once regal creature, his master's partner in the hunt, disregarded in

[20] The following paragraphs draw on Goldhill (1988c). It is surprising that Murnaghan does not discuss this scene of recognition.
[21] Cf. Goldhill (1988c) 9–19 (with bibliography) which builds on Redfield (1975) 192–203 in particular.
[22] On the significance of hunting here, see Goldhill (1988c) 14 with bibliography n. 66.

the disordered house without its master. The figure of Argus is used to articulate both a sense of past order and present disorder.

Second, this is a moment of mute (mutual) recognition. Odysseus is a master of deception through verbal disguise. Here, the recognition without words is in significant contrast both with Odysseus' persuasion of Telemachus and with the scenes to come both of Odysseus' manipulations of language (to effect recognition and misrecognition) and of the risks of premature recognition for Odysseus. Argus immediately recognizes Odysseus (despite his disguise) without signs (such as a scar), without the vagaries of speech.

Third, Argus acts as a model of a faithful *philos* (like Eumaeus), who contrasts with the maidservants and Melanthius.[23] But he is a *philos* (unlike all the others) who needs no testing. This recognition is without testing on both sides. Argus indeed, since antiquity, has been taken as a parallel for his returning master in his suffering: long-enduring, aged, disregarded.[24] The mutual recognition offers signs of shared experience resulting from the master's absence from the *oikos*. A recognition (for the reader) of a similarity between hound and master, that qualifies the understanding of both figures. Finally, as the scene stresses a moment of recognition and return, it also extends the hesitation at the entrance. It focuses on the act of crossing the threshold as being in itself significant. As the recognition scene with Telemachus is formulated through a system of ideas basic to the patriarchal *oikos*, so Argus' recognition articulates a complex network of significances in the return of Odysseus to the threshold of the *oikos*.

Odysseus enters the house (though he will have yet to fight for his place even at the threshold with the beggar, Irus (18.1ff)), and the slow process of (mutual) recognition within the household begins. The first person apart from Telemachus to recognize Odysseus is the old servant, Eurycleia. Unlike Telemachus' recognition (but like Argus'), Eurycleia's discovery of the scar on Odysseus' thigh is unplanned by Odysseus, who at the last attempts to deflect the nurse's perception by turning towards the shadows (19.388–9). The struggle to maintain control over revelation that so amused Athene is here critical. The moment of identification is preceded by dangerous hints of premature recognition – in particular,

---

[23] See in particular Rohdich (1980); also Rose (1979).
[24] See Richardson (1975) 80 who suggests that Antisthenes' work called περὶ τοῦ κύνος drew out the parallels between Argos and Odysseus. The obvious parallels with Laertes also seem pertinent.

the nurse's comment that the stranger looks like Odysseus (19.379–81) –
and as she discovers his identity the narrative explains at length the
circumstances of how Odysseus received the scar.[25]As Odysseus is recognized in his home for the first time, held, like a child, in the arms
of his nurse, the narrative returns to Odysseus' childhood and youth to
tell of Odysseus' birth, naming and coming of age. The piercing of his
disguise is through a sign that is layered with the memory of previous
threats, previous crises. The loss of memory – the threat of the Lotus-
Eaters – threatens *nostos*: here the re-telling of Odysseus' past marks the
re-cognition of the returned man. I will discuss below the relevance of
this passage in the narrative; here I wish to stress that not only is the
moment of recognition extended and manipulated in the narrative – and
then violently controlled by Odysseus' silencing of Eurycleia – but also,
after both the affirmation of a tie with Telemachus and Argus' different
awareness, the recognition through the scar itself realigns the question
of what is (to be seen as) a mark of identity – as the nurse through the
shadows and the disguise perceives this sign, with its tissue of past
associations, always ready to be opened into another telling of Odysseus'
story.

The manipulation of the tokens of identity is replayed (21.188ff) as
Odysseus finally brings Eumaeus and Philoetius into the plot to slaughter
the suitors, whose punishment is so important to the ethical sense of the
Odyssey. For the recognition is by the scar again – but this time it is a
planned, manipulated gesture by Odysseus as a prelude to the bloodshed
of the massacre in the hall, to enlist, as master in the *oikos*, the necessary
help of his *philoi*. For the herdsmen, the scar brings different associations
from the personal involvement of Eurycleia in the naming and childhood
of Odysseus. The scar for the herdsmen is a different sign, a different
recognition; different issues.

The trial of the bow which leads to the massacre is explicitly established as a contest to compare those present with Odysseus: to fail to
string the bow is to be seen to be a lesser man than its owner (21.85–95).
Telemachus, however, is the only one present even to come close to passing the test – the son like the father.[26] Odysseus' (re)appearance before
the suitors is, then, significantly at a contest that proves his superiority,
that he has no equal. Even when Odysseus begins the slaughter with

[25] On this scene, see Auerbach (1953) ch. 1 and for an opposing view Köhnken (1976) with
bibliography; Clay (1983) 56–68. Auerbach is brilliantly criticized by Lynn-George
(1988) 1ff and by Cave (1988) 10–24.

[26] On Telemachus' role here, see Goldhill (1984) 189–90; Goldhill (1986a) 149–50.

the apparently accidental shooting of Antinous – from the threshold –
the suitors fail to recognize the disguised king, as they have failed to
recognize all the portents of his imminent return.[27] *Xeine*, 'stranger', they
begin their outraged address to the man who could string Odysseus' bow
(22.27). Odysseus responds (35–41) not by revealing his name but by
claiming that, contrary to their predictions, he has returned (the *polutropos* announces he is *hupotropos*, 'returned'), and that they are faced
with destruction for their outrages against the *oikos* (36), maidservants
(37) and the wife of a still living man (38), outrages which show fear
neither of gods (39) nor men (40). Even after Odysseus thus reveals the
significance of his return as the fulfilment of the promise of just revenge
for transgression, Eurymachus not only responds with a conditional
recognition, 'If indeed you are ...' (45), but also attempts to divert the
logic of his necessary punishment by placing the blame for the suitors'
behaviour on the dead Antinous (48ff). What is revealed in this scene is
not merely Odysseus' return, but also the suitors' misrecognition of
Odysseus and of their own (responsible) position, a misrecognition that
continues to the moment of death.

After the purging of the house of the suitors and their corrupt associ-
ates, the *nostos* continues with Odysseus' reunion with Penelope. The
recognition of husband and wife is one of the most discussed elements
in the *Odyssey*, and it shows all the signs of deferral, refusal and irony
that have marked the earlier points of return. Even after the death of the
suitors, Penelope will not accept Odysseus until she has tested him – to
Telemachus' confusion (23.97–103) – and each meeting with Odysseus as
beggar before the death of the suitors 'leads the couple to the brink of
recognition only to leave our expectations unfulfilled as he [Homer]
makes them veer away at the last moment'.[28] I will discuss the complex
verbal exchanges of husband and wife below: first I want to look at how
these scenes, like the other junctures of the narrative of return, produce
their various delays of recognition by the interplay of disguise, appearance and the faculty of sight.

For their first face to face meeting, Odysseus demands that Penelope
wait until night – deferral, again – with the express aims that she might
not be forced to deal with the hubristic suitors and that she might not
see his pitiful clothes (17.564–73), but with the result also that the en-

---

[27] In particular, Theoclymenus' prophecy, on which see Erbse (1972) 42–54; Fenik (1974)
233–44. On the suitors' failure or refusal to recognize, see Murnaghan (1987) 56–90.
[28] Fenik (1974) 42.

counter will take place in the uncertain light of the fire at night. When Eurycleia sees the scar, despite the shadows, and turns to see if Penelope has spotted that this is her husband, at the key moment Penelope is looking away (19.476–8):

> She looked at Penelope with her eyes,
> wanting to indicate that her dear husband was here.
> But Penelope was not able to look that way, nor perceive [*noēse*];
> for Athene had turned her perception [*noon*] aside.

The repetition of words of perception emphasizes the visual barriers to recognition (as the servant but not the mistress sees through the disguise). The scene indeed goes on to play with the idea of 'vision' and recognition: Penelope tells the disguised Odysseus a dream in which a metamorphosed Odysseus appears in order to prophesy his return (19.535–53) – a dream which the disguised Odysseus then interprets to indicate his imminent return. (I will discuss this interplay of disguises and interpretation later.) Penelope, however, turns from the implications of this her vision by pointing out that some dreams are true, but others are deceptive, and the scene ends with the queen returned to her bedroom, crying for her absent husband, until sleep closes her eyes.

Similarly, after the slaughter of the suitors, Eurycleia rushes to tell Penelope to come and 'see with her eyes what she has desired all her days', the return of Odysseus (23.5–7); but Penelope refuses to believe that this can be a μῦθος ἐτήτυμος, a 'true tale', and at first calls the nurse 'mad' (23.11) and then merely 'old' (23.24), but finally is persuaded to go and see what has been done by her . . . son.[29] The meeting takes place in the firelight (23.89), like their first exchange. Husband and wife sit in silence on opposite sides of the room (23.89–95):

> Then she sat opposite Odysseus, in the firelight,
> by the other wall. He sat by the tall pillar, looking down,
> waiting to see if his majestic wife would say anything
> to him, when she saw him with her eyes.
> She sat in silence a long while; wonder held her heart.
> With her gaze, now she stared at him full in the face,
> now she failed to recognize him with the foul clothes on his body.

Again, the recognition is marked by the repeated words of perception – ὁρόων, ἴδεν, ὀφθαλμοῖσι, ὄψει, ἐσίδεσκεν, 'looking', 'saw', 'eyes',

---

[29] Besslich (1966) 88 notes how ἠδ' ὃς ἔπεφνεν, 'and who has killed them' (*Od.* 23.84), is separated far enough from παῖδ' ἐμόν, 'my son', to allow a suggestion of Odysseus.

'gaze', 'stared' – and by misrecognition (blindness?). Odysseus' appearance – he had worried about his 'pitiful clothes' for their first meeting – deceives Penelope. The antithesis that describes her reaction is hard to appreciate. As printed in the Oxford text and translated here,[30] it seems to imply that the opposition is between at the one time staring into the face of Odysseus, at another time failing to recognize him. If this opposition is right, there is perhaps some irony in the assumption, after all the misrecognitions, that a steady gaze could reveal Odysseus in his disguise. Perhaps it indicates a contrast between a willingness to see and believe and an inability to recognize.

It is, however, only after his bath and the beautifying change from Athene that Penelope, to the background of the marriage music which Odysseus has arranged to deceive and delay the dead suitors' relatives, is prepared to accept her husband's return at least to the point of testing him with her trick about the marriage bed. She has misread the disguised words and appearance of her husband, and now looks of testing 'signs' (*sēmata* 23.110) between them. After the physical, external mark of the scar, the sign that leads to recognition here is the private and secret knowledge of the bed at the centre of the *oikos* – and Odysseus' reaction to its violation. To Nausicaa, Odysseus can describe nothing finer than the state where husband and wife, like-minded in attitude, maintain the *oikos*, (and critics have recognized this ideal of like-mindedness in the mutual testing, mutual steadfastness of Penelope and Odysseus[31]). Their like-mindedness, however, like the private signs of recognition, also excludes others: Telemachus fails to understand his mother's reaction to Odysseus, though Odysseus rejoices (23.97–111); Odysseus' testing of Penelope is seen as restrained beyond any normal human reaction;[32] Penelope's appearance before the suitors gives joy to Odysseus, though

---

30 ὄψει δ' ἄλλοτε μέν μιν ἐνωπαδίως ἐσίδεσκεν,
   ἄλλοτε δ' ἀγνώσασκε κακὰ χροῒ εἵματ' ἔχοντα.
   On this passage, see the discussion of Fernandez-Galliano and Heubeck (1986) ad 94–5.

31 See e.g. Harsh (1950); Whitman (1958) 303; Amory (1963); Beye (1968) 178; Erbse (1972) 55ff; Austin (1975) 181ff, especially 231; Finley (1978) 3ff; Van Nortwick (1979); Russo (1982); O'Sullivan (1984); Emlyn-Jones (1984); Thalmann (1984) 160–3, 170; Murnaghan (1987) 118–47; and for a different view to this tradition, see Henderson (1986) 27, 37–40.

32 Cf. *Od.* 13.332ff, where Athene says another man would have gone home immediately to see his wife and child (cf. *Od.* 11.440ff). Amphimedon (24.167) says that Odysseus ordered Penelope to set up the bow-contest. This mistake has been read as arising from the suitor's mistaken assumptions about Odysseus' likely behaviour; for discussion and bibliography, see Goldhill (1988c) 1–9.

the suitors fail to understand that they are being beguiled.[33] Yet Penelope's testing of Odysseus provokes from him the sort of angry outburst that he has been restraining throughout his adventures. It is the knowledge admitted in a moment of uncharacteristic lack of control, as Odysseus of the many wiles becomes the victim of an (Odyssean) deception, that confirms for Penelope Odysseus' identity. The symmetry of the mutual testing results in a paradoxical recognition of Odysseus as untypically revealing of his identity and knowledge. Once again, the narrative realigns the dynamics of control and revelation.

The moment at which Penelope and Odysseus retire to the bedroom – another threshold to be crossed, protected by a delaying trick – and to their marriage bed has seemed to critics since Hellenistic times to be a fitting conclusion to the *Odyssey*.[34] Odysseus has built up stage by stage the series of relationships by which 'a/the man' is defined within the *oikos*, and Penelope seems the point towards which so much of Odysseus' travelling has been tending. But this is (first) to repress the connotations of the terms *oikos* and 'fatherland'. For the household and the fatherland have a history, form a continuity, and hence the need to refound the relationship with Laertes, his own father. So for Odysseus, 'the Ithacan', the relations between his own *oikos* and the island also need to be re-established.

The scene of recognition with Laertes is also fenced with ironies and a deferral which have seemed to many readers positively cruel, as Odysseus reduces his father to abject misery with yet another deceptive story.[35] (Odysseus also sits by dry-eyed while Penelope cries, and is himself mocked by Athene in disguise: recognition again and again involves a reciprocal testing.) Odysseus' story to Laertes is of how he once entertained the travelling Odysseus: ἄνδρα ποτ' ἐξείνισσα, he begins: 'a/the man I once played host to . . .' (24.266). Odysseus' language punningly

---

[33] The critics also fail to understand the *homophrosunē* of Odysseus and Penelope here; Odysseus' reaction is called 'not . . . natural' by Kirk (1962) 246. Many other critics agree with this judgement. For discussion, see Goldhill (1988c) 6–9. See also, most recently, Byre (1988).

[34] See Page (1955) 101–36 (with bibliography on the analytical tradition on which he draws); Kirk (1962) 244–52. For a critique of Page, see Wender (1978), with further bibliography, and Moulton (1974). On the Hellenistic ending, see Apthorp (1969) 64ff; Erbse (1972) 166–77; and for most recent discussions, Fernandez-Galliano and Heubeck (1986) ad xxiii 297–xxiv 348 and Goldhill (1988c) 26 n. 2.

[35] See Wender (1978) 57–60 (with bibliography); Thornton (1976) 115–6; Finley (1978) 224–33, and most recently the sensible comments of Fernandez-Galliano and Heubeck (1986) ad xxiv 205–412.

recalls the epic's opening concealment of his name, as here he hides himself from his father. In this scene, Odysseus uses the word 'Odysseus' once, to say that he has not seen Odysseus for five years (24.309), and Laertes uses it once in a conditional clause 'If you are in fact Odysseus, then give me a sign . . .' (24.328–9). Father and son, like Eumaeus, both hesitate to proclaim the name of Odysseus in recognition.

The recognition tokens which Odysseus uses give some indication of the importance of the meeting with his father. First the scar is used again, though with a further specific point, since it was to Laertes, his father, that Odysseus is described as returning from Autolycus after the initial hunt and expedition abroad. Each use of the scar is different, as the sign is differently manipulated, tells a different story, and constructs a different relation between the partners in recognition. The return of Odysseus explores the varying possibilities of the tokens of identity, the *difference within* the tokens of identity. As Cave writes: 'The scar is the mark of the treacherously concealed narrative, waiting to break the surface and create a scandal; it is a sign that the story, like the wound, may always be reopened'.[36] Second – and the addition of a further token to what was previously sufficient is itself significant and puts a strong focus on the addition – Odysseus reminds Laertes of the fruit-trees he planted for his son. This is both relevant to the particular context – Laertes is found by Odysseus working in the garden – and also indicative of a further element at stake in the *nostos*, namely, the patrimony that a father passes to his son, which we have seen Telemachus and Odysseus together fight for in the hall, but which is now placed in a wider generational context of the three generations of each man and his one son. Odysseus is placed now as the son, the inheritor, and he is to inherit the trees (which produce food, which are rooted in the soil of the *oikos*, which need human care across the generations). Odysseus tells how 'when he was a boy' (24.338) his father had taken him through the orchard and named all the trees for him. Particularly in a patriarchal, patrilineal culture, the father's power to name is crucial to the role of the father: the scene of paternal naming and recognition is a foundation of a child's social identity (although, of course, Odysseus is named by his maternal grandfather, Autolycus, as the first proof of the scar recalls). In another sense, however, Laertes does give Odysseus his name. For Odysseus is identified by his patronymic, *Laertiadēs*, 'son of Laertes' (as Laertes is called by his disguised son, *Arkesiadēs*, 'son of Arkesias' 24.270). Odysseus recalls being a child, and

---

[36] Cave (1988) 24.

his father's naming[37] (of the trees) as signs of recognition between son and father. It is not merely the fruit-trees that form Odysseus' patrimony. The father of Telemachus is recognized by reminding his father of what he has passed on.

Indeed, in the fight against the suitors' families, all three generations of men stand together, a visible incarnation of maintenance of the patrilineal, patriarchal family. As Laertes says, rejoicing (24.514–15):

> What is this day for me, dear Gods? I am overjoyed.
> My son and grandson are vying in courage.

Athene responds by encouraging him to throw the first spear at the onrushing Ithacans. She too calls him *Arkesiadēs*, 'son of Arkesias', adding in the patronymic a further generational tie. The possible problems of transition between the generations – the sort of conflict so often depicted in Greek texts, and assumed to be a major factor in early social history – are avoided in the *Odyssey* by the reciprocal recognition of son and father, both Telemachus and Odysseus, and Odysseus and Laertes, and by each father having only one son.[38] In Telemachus' attempt in the bow contest or in Odysseus' near killing of his father with his false tale, there are perhaps indications of the very repression of such conflicts.[39] The *Odyssey* constructs for Odysseus' *oikos* a model of passing on which avoids the death of the father. The well-known problems about the status of Laertes in the hierarchy of the household may be thought to result from this (idealized) model of inheritance without any disastrous conflict or tension.

Odysseus' meeting with Laertes, then, prompts a question not merely about why Odysseus tricks his father but also about what it means for the adult male to return to his father, and for recognition to take place between such figures. As such, this scene must be placed within the

---

[37] Page (1955) 107 stretches a point when he finds the use of ὀνομαίνω here 'unhomeric' (cf. Shipp (1972) 362). Fernandez-Galliano and Heubeck (1986) ad loc. are rightly less worried, as is Wender (1978) 49; Erbse (1972) 214–15 argues the case in most detail. On naming and the recognition, see also Whitman (1958) 304–5; Wender (1978) 60–2.

[38] Generational conflict is, of course, a staple of tragic drama. Discussion of an agrarian crisis in early Greece, focused on problems of land tenure and the transition of property between generations, remains vexed, especially on particular texts (e.g. on Hesiod, see Millett (1984) against Will (1957); Detienne (1963); Will (1965)). I mean here merely to suggest that each father having one son avoids the obvious difficulties of splitting the property (κλῆρος), and that the willing support of all three men for a common aim avoids the possible tensions of the son of mature age not having his own *oikos*/authority.

[39] On the ambiguousness of Telemachus' bow attempt, see Goldhill (1984) 189–91; Goldhill (1986a) 149–50.

sequence of recognition scenes, not merely to confirm that deception is typical or characteristic of Odysseus, but rather to continue the exploration of what is at stake in the process of recognition. Odysseus and Telemachus recognize each other without tokens but through Odysseus' explanatory words: as Telemachus had said, 'no one *knows* his own father'. Odysseus takes his place through Telemachus' acceptance and recognition (as the father recognizes the son). The word of the father suffices. In a different way, Argus and Odysseus effect a mutual process of acknowledgement. Without language, without the possibility of disguise, but with a memory of past glories in present disorder and with the significance of a past relationship. Eurycleia's perception of the scar pierces Odysseus' disguise, a scar layered with the recollection not merely of an earlier relationship but also with the naming and maturation of Odysseus. Odysseus' nurse again holds Odysseus, but is prevented from the expression of recognition by Odysseus. She, too, must practise a strategic concealment of knowledge. For Eumaeus and Philoetius, recognition comes through the controlled exposure of the scar now as a guaranteed token of identity for Odysseus' *philoi*, but without the close associations of the nurse and her role in the naming of Odysseus. All too late, the suitors recognize Odysseus at the end of an arrow (to end their reckless eating of the house). A recognition in death, as the second episode in the Underworld makes plain.[40] But their failure to recognize the pervasive logic of transgression and revenge continues even into Hades. Penelope, even when Odysseus appears rejuvenated from the bath, tests him with a trick which leads to an uncharacteristic outburst from Odysseus that confirms his identity for his wife. And following that recognition we find Odysseus without any disguise, but using (characteristically) deceptive words, fooling his unrecognizing father almost to death, before Laertes recovers to rejoice in the day that brings his son and grandson together to compete in valour. Each of these recognition scenes is, then, a mutual process, each recognition forms and takes place as an interrelation between figures linked in the *oikos*' system of power, property and authority. As a series, the scenes of recognition constitute an exploration not only of the tokens of recognition – the signs of identity – but also of the possibilities of mutual authorization, that is, an exploration of what it is to recognize.[41] Each of the deferrals, hesitations and

---

[40] On this episode, the so-called Second Nekuia, see Wender (1978) 19–44; Moulton (1974) 161–4 (with bibliography); Finley (1978) 221–3. Agamemnon authorizes the *kleos* of Odysseus and Penelope in reaction to Amphimedon's tale 24.192–202.

[41] Cf. Whitman (1958) 301–5.

manipulations that dog the process of recognition not only emphatically extends recognition beyond a moment into a process, but also invests that process with a set of ironies and misrecognitions that are not the obverse of the act of recognition but part of the (unending) movement towards *establishing* recognition. The *Odyssey* sets in juxtaposition different and developing models of recognition in the formulation of differing and developing interrelations of *philoi*.

An understanding of Odysseus' identity is being constantly formulated in the series of these scenes of mutually constitutive recognitions, but not merely in *contrast* with the figures Odysseus encounters. Rather, Odysseus and each of his *philoi* are linked in a network of similarities *and* differences in the search for his proper place in the property and proprieties of the *oikos*. So, for example, Telemachus is the son who is to look like, act like and suffer like his father; Argus too suffers in his age and disregard like his master and Laertes; Eurycleia enacts a policy of concealment, as Eumaeus struggles to maintain the order of the *oikos* against the suitors; Penelope's 'like-mindedness' is seen not only in her faith and forbearance but also in her weaving wiles; Laertes is described in terms all too suited to Odysseus' earlier disguise of ancient beggar. The defining relations between *philoi* in the *oikos* are dis-covered, then, through an interplay of similarities and differences that the narrative of disguise, recognition and return sets in motion.

Laertes, however, is not the final act of recognition or of *nostos*. Together with Dolius and his sons – further recognizers of Odysseus[42] – the men are ready to fight to regain Odysseus' place in Ithaca. It is, however, rather with a god-ordered truce between the noble families of Ithaca that the *Odyssey* reaches its conclusion. A thunderbolt from Zeus and the ministrations of Athene stop the work of returning from continuing into a further bloody battle. Odysseus' travelling, however, is projected beyond this formal closure. In the Underworld, Teiresias tells Odysseus that his search for *nostos* will not be finally fulfilled until he can appease Poseidon, which can only be achieved by travelling to a place which does not know the sea and there to make certain ritual sacrifices. He will know when this place is reached by carrying an oar – a man will eventually

---

[42] Dolios and his sons join the meal of Odysseus and his other *philoi*. Dolios asks if Penelope yet knows of his return or should he send a messenger to announce it (24.404–5) – a question which neatly points both to the complexity of Odysseus' reunion with Penelope as portrayed in the *Odyssey*, and to the possibility of other narratives of recognition. On Dolios, see Wender (1978) 54–6, who agrees with the Analytic strictures on this scene, although not with their conclusions.

ask what is the 'winnowing fan' that he is carrying; and then Odysseus will recognize through this misrecognition that the sea is not known (11.119ff). This story is repeated to Penelope by Odysseus before they even go to bed; indeed, his first words after her acceptance are (23.248–51):

> My wife, not yet have we come to the end of all
> our trials. There is yet to come an immense toil,
> long, and difficult, which I must complete.
> For so the soul of Teiresias prophesied for me . . .

Odysseus and Penelope have not yet reached an end of their travail. There is more to come. Odysseus goes on to repeat at length Teiresias' instructions (23.264–84) and his remarks about old age. Odysseus must make another journey to effect his *nostos*, a journey away from Ithaca, to ... where? A place which does not know the sea (but knows about winnowing, and therefore crops?) Somewhere which does not know the *Odyssey*, or Greek or the fame of Odysseus; somewhere different even from all the places Odysseus has yet visited (by sea). For Odysseus there is more to come for (or before) his *nostos*.[43]

In my opening discussion, I mentioned how critics have often seen the *Odyssey* as a journey of definition for 'a/the man of many turns'; *nostos* as the return into the nexus of relationships by which his place in society is formed. Certainly in the *Odyssey* we see the nexus of Odysseus' relationships of authority, power, place being slowly developed – from the edge of the island, to his own property, to the town, to the house itself and its bedroom, re-forming ties, obligations, understandings with his son, his faithful servants, his wife, his father and the townspeople. Odysseus' reintegration is formed through the scenes of mutual recognition that construct these interrelations. Each act of recognition – the perception and authorization of these interrelations – is surrounded, however, with suspicion, doubt, irony and hesitation. Crossing the threshold of recognition is marked by deferral. Moreover, the narrative projects still more journeying for Odysseus. The formation of interrelations through the travelling of *nostos* is not to be completed yet. But deferred to a further journey. Another threshold. Recognition is to remain a continuing process. The social identity of the man formulated by his *nostos*, by the relations constructed in this *nostos*, is, then, not yet completed.

The series of recognition scenes, then, does not constitute merely a

---

[43] See in particular Bergren (1983) 50ff.

'map' of a man's or the man's role in society. Rather, throughout the narrative we see a process of continuing exploration of the possibilities of recognition through the different models of recognition. As Aristotle says, 'It is recognition throughout.' The audience/reader's role is crucial here.[44] For it is the audience/reader's recognition which formulates differences and interconnections between the various scenes and their constitutive elements. In other words, the audience/reader is also involved in a process of exploring recognition. The audience/reader becomes implicated in recognizing the differences between a man and the man, that is, between recognizing a cultural norm and a specific identity (that which stands out from a cultural norm). This is not merely a point about an audience/reader's active construction or authorization of sense (although it is the case, as I have noted, that *anagignōskein* means in Greek both 'to read' and 'to recognize'). Rather, it demonstrates an important aspect of the ethical, normative thrust of the *Odyssey*. The *Odyssey* does not offer simply a didactic message about norm, transgression and punishment, but turns back on the reader the work of moving through the different models of recognition towards a recognized model of social identity and social behaviour. What is (to be) recognized in *andra*. The complex interplay between the narrative of recognition and the audience/reader's activity (*anagignōskein*) is, then, of fundamental importance to the functioning of the *Odyssey* as a normative text. The discourse of recognition is finally an ethical disourse. As I began by saying, recognition is not merely a perceptual process. It also involves authorization, power, legitimacy ...

NAMING AND DISGUISE

When one names oneself, one always names another.

Brecht (in *Mann ist Mann*)

Odysseus' disguises – crucial to the narrative of return – are most often verbal: the concealment of identity by concealing the name. While language is used to veil, mislead and test, recognition (as the articulation of social identity) involves the power of words to define, determine, predicate – the scene of nomination. The act of naming is the gesture of legitimation and ordering without which it is hard to imagine a relation to language and in language. The thematic focus on naming in the

---

[44] For an extended discussion of the ideas in the following paragraph from one particular and stimulating perspective, see Brooks (1984).

Odyssey therefore forms a fundamental link between recognition and the telling of tales – and thus between the first and third sections of this chapter.

The use of names in the *Odyssey* has received considerable attention from critics.[45] Many names, particularly of minor characters, seem to have a special significance – the bard in Ithaca, for example, is called, in Stanford's translation, 'Fame-man, son of Joy-maker' – but it is particularly the name of Odysseus on which discussion has focused. The choice and sense of the name 'Odysseus' are especially brought to the fore in the tale of how Odysseus received his scar. The recognition of the scar leads to the tale of Odysseus' first blood, first kill, when he was scarred – his initiation into the male world of hunting. This in turn leads to an explanation of how he came to Autolycus, his grandfather, to receive gifts – the fulfilment of Autolycus' request made at Odysseus' birth and naming in Ithaca. The story of the scar takes Odysseus back through the transitions by which he became, in all senses, the object of recognition. Eurycleia, who holds Odysseus now, held out the first son to his grandfather (19.403–4):

> Autolycus, now you yourself find the name to give
> to the dear child of your child. He is much prayed for.

Autolycus is asked to choose Odysseus' name – with the broad hint that he is πολυάρητος, 'Much-prayed-for': an invitation at least to choose a typically well-omened name. Autolycus himself has already been described (19.395–8), however, as pre-eminent for his thievery and use of oaths, the manipulations of deceitful action and language associated with his patron god Hermes.[46] Now this man chooses a name for his grandson (19.406–9):

> My son-in-law and daughter, give him the name
> I tell you. For *I* come here hateful to many
> men and women on the fruitful earth.
> Wherefore let his name be Odysseus, a sign of such hate.

The name is *epōnumon*, a name to declare the essence of its bearer. Because Autolycus up and down the land has been hated (*odussamenos*) by men and women, the name Odysseus (*Odysseus*) is chosen. The pre-

---

[45] See e.g. Dimock (1956); Podlecki (1961); Brown (1966); Austin (1972), on whom I draw in the following paragraphs; Bergren (1983) 65–7; Clay (1983) 54ff; and, in more general terms, Sulzberger (1962). On the *Iliad*, see e.g. Nagy (1979) 69ff (with bibliography).
[46] See Kahn (1978) *passim*.

cise sense of this etymological play has been much discussed. Does it imply simply 'one who is hated', or rather 'one who causes hate'? Both Dimock and Austin in order to preserve what is perceived as a significant ambiguity, suggest the translation 'trouble',[47] a term which is 'pregnant with active and passive meanings' and which indeed captures much of the reciprocal nature of Odysseus' violent and deceptive interactions with the world. Odysseus' given name is a sign of his experiences to come.

The narrative of Odysseus' *nostos* can certainly be seen to fulfil the implications of this inaugural act of naming. Indeed, at four points in the *Odyssey* the narrative is expressed precisely in terms of Odysseus' relation of ὀδυσσέσθαι, 'hate', with the gods. First (1.62), Athene, when she begs Zeus to free Odysseus, asks why the king of the gods so hates (*ōdusao*) the hero. Second (5.339–40), Ino, the goddess who saves Odysseus as he attempts to land in Scheria, asks why Poseidon so hates (*ōdusat'*) him. Third, Odysseus himself, in the breakers off Scheria, recognizes the source of his troubles as Poseidon's continuing hatred (*odōdustai*) (5.423). Finally (19.275–6), when the disguised Odysseus tells Penelope that her husband will return, he explains that the fleet was lost because Zeus and Helios hated (*odusanto*) him.

At four turning points of the narrative, then, Odysseus' relation to the divine is expressed in language which seems to assert through the predictive and prescriptive etymology of his naming the identity of man and name. As Autolycus implied in calling the name *epōnumon*, 'rightly named', the *nomen* proves to be an omen. Eurycleia's recognition turns back to the past to validate itself, as the name turns out to have been always already indicative for the future.

Birth, naming, first blood, a return home laden with gifts to his *oikos* – the scene of recognition turns back to the series of events through which Odysseus became the man he is, turns back to the transitions, the passages of his 'journey to manhood'. The scar is not merely a token of identity but a sign which indicates the story of how Odysseus became that which is, in its full sense, the object of recognition. As with Odysseus' stories among the Phaeacians, the narrative of return itself turns back to express the present as a function of the past. The recognition turns back to the past to validate itself.

There is more, however, to the interplay of the scene of naming and the scene of recognition. For naming and recognition are necessarily interrelated in their parallel structures of delineation and authority. For like

---

[47] Austin (1972) 3; cf. Dimock (1956) 53.

recognition, naming always involves an act of classification. To name is to assert a relation in the exchange of language (a relation of power as well as definition). One never names, one classes.[48] Different namings assert different relations – *philos*, *xeinos*, father, lord, king, child etc. The proper name in particular is invested with a classificatory force that is inherently concerned with what is, in all its senses, the property of an individual. On the one hand, the proper name, like all names (signs) can be seen in its uses and combinations as part of a system of differences – open to dissemination.[49] To say 'Odysseus', or 'Odysseus, son of Laertes', or 'Odysseus the Ithacan', or 'Odysseus of the many wiles', or 'Odysseus, my father', etc. is to assert a different relation to the subject. On the other hand, the proper name, as a mark of identity, as that which stands for the sum characteristics or connotations of a subject, can be seen as having a special connection with the individual and a special power for and over the individual. Indeed, in each culture – and specifically in ancient Greek cultures – the use of the proper name is invested with cares, controls and restrictions and implies a particular positioning within the exchanges of language.[50] To use the name 'Odysseus' makes a difference. (A difference the significance of which is raised by the opening words of the epic.)

It is not by chance, then, that the scene of recognition returns to the scene of nomination. It is not only the significance of the given name that is focused on in the episode of the scar but also the importance of the name as a sign of identity and authority for the act of recognition.

Both Odysseus and other members of the *oikos* demonstrate the need for caution with regard to the name. Eumaeus, for example, when Odysseus tries to find out the name of the swineherd's absent master, prevaricates for some twenty lines, finally utters the word 'Odysseus', but immediately adds (14.145–7):

> Stranger, I am ashamed to name him even when he is not here.
> For he is particularly kind to me, and cares for me in his heart.
> I call him honoured lord, even when he is absent.

---

[48] See e.g. Lévi-Strauss (1966) 161ff, especially 185; Leach (1964); Tanner (1979). This is, of course, now a standard object of anthropological research.

[49] 'Dissemination' is a term developed by Derrida for the slippage between signs in language perceived as a system of differences. See e.g. Derrida (1981) *passim*.

[50] For the specifics of Greek cultural taboos, see e.g. on women's names, Schaps (1977); on names in funeral speeches, Loraux (1981a) (index, 'anonymat' and 'éloge'); on law and insults, Clay (1982). This topic has been much discussed with regard to Athenian tragedy: see e.g. Jouan (1978); Zeitlin (1982b), especially 23ff; Goldhill (1984) (index, 'naming').

Aidōs, roughly translated 'shame' – the force whose observance prevents transgression of the orderings of the structures of society – restrains Eumaeus from the free utterance of the name of the absent master. He is happy to call him ἠθεῖον, 'honoured lord', 'lord and brother', 'kind master', but the specificity of the name is held back.[51] The 'hatred', 'trouble ' of 'Odysseus' is to be turned to a more auspicious naming. So Penelope in her half-asleep conversation with the disguised Athene uses an elaborate periphrasis for Odysseus, without mentioning his name (4.814–6):

> Since first I lost a noble, lion-hearted husband,
> who surpasses the Danaans in all sorts of virtue,
> a noble man, whose fame is broad in Greece and midmost Argos.

The man whose *kleos* reaches heaven is not named. She even asks Athene directly about her husband without mentioning the name and receives an equally circumspect answer (4.832–7):

> 'Please tell me about that pitiful man too,
> whether he is alive somewhere still and sees daylight,
> or whether he has already died and is in Hades' halls.'
> The dark shape replied and said:
> 'As for that man, I will not tell you the whole story,
> whether he lives or is dead. It is bad to babble vainly.'

Kai keinon, says Penelope, 'that man too ...'; *keinon ge*, replies Athene, 'As for that man'. The refusal to utter the name seems to be connected both with the need for the caution of *euphēmia* – the silence that prevents an ill-omened expression[52] – and with the absence of the master of the *oikos*. So *nostos* involves the recognition – predication – that the *xeinos* is 'Odysseus'; the master returned.

It is in particular Odysseus, however, who refrains from the utterance of his own name. This is not merely in the lying tales he tells for strategic reasons to conceal his identity. In Scheria, Arete, the queen, asks him directly who he is – and receives no answer. Alcinous, too, makes more than one attempt to discover who the stranger is. Odysseus' unwillingness to name himself raises the question not only of what it means to use the name 'Odysseus', but also and more precisely what it means to say

---

[51] 'Odysseus' name is a tangible reality which Eumaeus goes to remarkable lengths to circumvent', Austin (1972) 6.

[52] Greek religious ceremonies usually begin with a command to maintain silence, εὐφημεῖτε, precisely to avoid the possibility of an ill-omened utterance. See Burkert (1985) 73, 199, 248, 273.

'I am Odysseus'. The *xeinos* is properly not asked who he is until he has eaten and drunk, but Odysseus extends the delay over several days and in the face of some prompting from his hosts. What difference does it make to delay offering his name so long?

The most extensive discussion of this question is to be found in the important study of Bernard Fenik. He places his interpretation carefully in the major traditions of Homeric scholarship. First, he argues tellingly against the position that Odysseus' failure to answer Arete's question indicates an earlier version of the text, where the question was immediately answered, which has been awkwardly grafted into the present text. He then notes certain psychological approaches which see the delay as 'a certain natural reluctance' on Odysseus' part 'after the enormous trials of the last days and under the physical and mental exhaustion that wears him down' – or even as an awareness on Odysseus' part of his 'loss of self-awareness and heroic identity'.[53] Fenik is willing to accept that an element of 'believability' is inherent in the scene: 'the poet has provided the raw material for each of us to complete the picture for himself'.[54] But he questions the principle of searching for a rigid, precise and absolutely clear psychological picture behind the silence, as if there were 'no middle ground between haphazard, fortuitous behaviour on the one hand and absolutely defined motivation on the other'.[55] More importantly, Fenik asks whether the '*thematic* significance' of Odysseus' silence may 'compromise' an 'inward personal motivation'. It is through the recognition of this thematic significance that Fenik proceeds in his analysis, by considering Odysseus' silence as part of 'the dynamics of a typical Odyssean situation'. 'There is ... the fact that all important identifications in the *Odyssey* are subjected to considerable delay.'[56] There delays are regularly used 'to produce an elaborate range of emotions and ironies, especially through the favourite technique of allowing persons to speak of things to an unrecognized stranger that touch him deeply'[57] – Eumaeus' talk of Odysseus' property, Penelope's description of her dream are two examples. Delaying the pronouncement of a stranger's name is typical of the *Odyssey*'s search for 'drama, suspense, irony', and the growth of curiosity among the Phaeacians is an essential foundation of the Scheria interlude. Thus, concludes Fenik, 'it would ... contradict an unchanging bent of the *Odyssey* if the hero *did* answer Arete and name himself directly'.[58]

---

[53] Fenik (1974) 16.   [54] Fenik (1974) 16.   [55] Fenik (1974) 16.   [56] Fenik (1974) 53.
[57] Fenik (1974) 53 (extending the thesis of Hölscher in particular).
[58] Fenik (1974) 53.

It is indeed important to emphasize how this scene is constituted within 'the dynamics of a typical Odyssean situation', and also – as we have seen in the first section of this chapter – how the manipulation of such dynamics is used in the different recognition and disguise scenes to such different effect. (Being 'typical' is never a sufficient critical conclusion.) But it is also important not to occlude the linear progression of the narrative. What difference does it make that this extended scene of withholding the announcement of identity should occur at this point in the text?

When Odysseus reaches Scheria, he has been depicted through the stories told at the palaces of Menelaus and Nestor to Telemachus (who has been travelling precisely to find out about his father); through the reflections and memories of Penelope, Telemachus and his other *philoi*; through the debate of the gods, and through the description of his time on Calypso's island and his escape from it. After his arrival on Scheria, we have seen his tactful supplication of Nausicaa, and his acceptance at the palace. Between Arete's question and its answer, however, Demodocus sings two songs directly related to Odysseus' past (as hero at Troy), and one song indirectly related to Odysseus' position – the story of Aphrodite and Ares with its tale of adultery and punishment.[59] Odysseus has demonstrated his athletic prowess, and deflected all moments of danger with care. Certainly the deferral of the answer to Arete's question helps build up Odysseus through these scenes and the announcement of name becomes a finely prepared dramatic climax. But since Odysseus has already been offered his trip home, elaborate gifts and Nausicaa's hand in marriage and an *oikos*, even if he receives further gifts after his story, it is not merely in order to raise Odysseus' status among the Phaeacians that his name is deferred.

Odysseus announces his name at the beginning of the four book (9–12) first-person narrative of his travels from Troy to Ogygia. The announcement of name is not only a conclusion of the doubt as to Odysseus' identity but also the opening of the story which explains the process by which Odysseus came to Scheria and which is indeed an essential factor in understanding Odysseus, not least in the terms by which he announces himself (9.19–21):

> I am Odysseus, son of Laertes, who in all tricks
> surpasses men, and my fame reaches heaven.
> I live in bright Ithaca . . .

[59] On this song's relation to the epic, see Burkert (1960); Braswell (1982).

The narrative has been turned so that the announcement of Odysseus' name and his self-description as pre-eminent in trickery, famed to heaven and an inhabitant of Ithaca open the extended self-representing narrative. To say 'I am Odysseus' is to begin the story that tells what it is to be Odysseus.

The episode of this narrative of Odysseus which further revolves crucially around the use of the proper name is, of course, the first extended scene, set in the Cyclops' cave,[60] and this will offer further insight into what it means to say 'I am Odysseus'. The Cyclops immediately asks the strangers who they are (9.252–5). As much as his question seems to violate the expected norms of guest-friendship, so Odysseus' reply is perhaps surprising in its apparent willingness immediately to identify himself (9.259–64):

> We are Achaeans wandering from Troy,
> driven by all manner of winds over the vast expanse of the sea.
> We desire to get home, but we have come now one way,
> now others. So, I suppose, Zeus wished to plan for us.
> We profess to be the men of Agamemnon, son of Atreus,
> whose fame is now the greatest under heaven.

The name 'Odysseus' is, however, notably absent from the marks of identity. It is Agamemnon's *kleos* which he mentions.

The question of the name returns when the drunken Cyclops requires more wine (9.355–6):

> Be kind, and give me more; and tell me your name
> right now, so I may give you a guest-gift to make you rejoice.

The giving of the name will lead to the giving of a guest-gift. After the Cyclops has drunk still more, Odysseus offers a name (9.364–7):

> Cyclops, you ask my famous name? I will tell you.
> You give me the guest-gift as you promised.
> No One is my name; my mother and father and all other
> companions call me No One.

After the corrupting gift of wine, the deceptive name – which leads to the famous trick by which the Cyclops prevents the other Cyclopes from helping him – is responded to with an equally improper guest-gift,

---

[60] On the much-discussed Cyclops scene, I have found the following most useful: Page (1955) 1–20; Schein (1970); Kirk (1970) 162–71; Glenn (1971); Calame (1976); Newton (1983); Mondi (1983); Clay (1983) 112–32; Bergren (1983) 45–50; and the works on guest-friendship cited in n. 2.

namely, to be eaten last. The reciprocities of guest-friendship are perverted to a reciprocity of transgression. With Odysseus, guest-friendship always involves *taking in*.

There is a double pun[61] in the famous trick by which the Cyclops is outwitted. For as the syntax changes when the other Cyclopes ask Polyphemus if he is being hurt, *outis* appears in the form *mē tis* (which has the same sense) (9.405–6; 9.410). The pun is articulated by Odysseus as narrator, who comments on the success of his game with the name (9.413–4):

> So they spoke and left. My heart laughed within me,
> that my name and my brilliant wile had deceived them.

It is Odysseus' 'wile', 'deceit', *mētis*, that has triumphed. His name *outis* and its synonym *mē tis* in the exchange between the Cyclopes and Polyphemus is itself a *mētis*. *Mētis* is both the description of and an essential sign in the game of words.

When Odysseus finally escapes, he cannot resist the opportunity to taunt the blind monster (9.502–5):

> Cyclops, if ever any mortal man asks you who it was
> that inflicted the shameful blinding of your eye,
> say Odysseus, sacker of cities, blinded you,
> the son of Laertes, who has his home in Ithaca.

The boast is the statement also that he is 'Odysseus', with his father's name and place of inhabitation – the normal markers of identity, which contrast precisely with his earlier general description of themselves as Greeks of Agamemnon's force. For the Cyclops this is – he recognizes – the fulfilment of an oracle he learnt long ago,[62] that he would be blinded by 'Odysseus' (9.513–6):

---

61 At least a double pun. Photios writes that Ptolemaeus Chennos says that *outis* was a nickname of Odysseus because of his big ears (*ous* = 'ear', *otis* = 'bustard with long ears') (Ptolemaeus Chennos fr. 11 Chatzis = Photios *Biblio.* (190) 147a11). This etymology is accepted at face value and developed by Carpenter (1946) 140–1. Ptolemaeus also writes that the name 'Odysseus' was given because his mother, when pregnant, fell down in a heavy rain storm by the road (ὁδός/ὗσεν), a story repeated in the scholia to *Od.* 1.75 and attributed to Silenus the Chian; cf. Eust. 1871.20. Like the scar, the name, a token of identity, can tell different stories.

62 Action is seen here as a fulfilment of that which is already declared. Therefore Todorov writes (1977) 64 'Every non-discursive event is merely the incarnation of a discourse, reality is only a realization.' So too Detienne (1967) 56 writes of oracular pronouncement 'La parole oraculaire n'est pas le reflet d'un événement préforme, elle est un des éléments de surréalization.' Cyclops' failure to recognize the truth of the oracle is part of its verification.

> But I always expected some big and noble mortal
> would come here, clothed in great strength.
> Now someone meagre, a nobody, a weakling
> has blinded my eye, when he had tamed me with wine.

The contrast of predicates contains yet another pun. Cyclops expected a 'big' and 'noble' man to come, instead he was blinded by a 'weak' (*oligos*), 'powerless' (*outidanos*), 'worthless fellow' (*akikus*), or, to keep the echo of *outis* in *outidanos*, a 'nobody'. Cyclops' failure to recognize πολύμητις 'Οδυσσεύς, 'Odysseus of the many wiles', 'of much *mētis*', is heard once more in the irony of his description of the man who tricked him by the word *outis* as *outidanos*. The polysemy of the name continues to sound in Polyphemus' language.

The Cyclops, however, has the last word. He offers Odysseus a guest-gift if he will come back and get it, and when Odysseus taunts him further, he curses Odysseus by praying to his father, Poseidon (9.528–35):

> Hear me, Poseidon, earth circling, dark haired.
> If I am truly yours, and you profess to be my father,
> grant that Odysseus, sacker of cities, son of Laertes,
> who has his home in Ithaca, does not reach home.
> But if it is fate for him to see his own people and reach
> his well-built home and his own fatherland,
> let him come late and badly, having lost all his crew,
> in a foreign ship, and let him find troubles at home.

The curse echoes precisely Odysseus' self-description, and its content indeed predicts the course of the narrative in terms we have already seen to be significant. To reach home is described as to see his *philoi*, *oikos* and fatherland; and when Odysseus does return it will be in a foreign ship without his crew, to find troubles at home. Odysseus' declaration of his name is the stimulus and perhaps even the condition of possibility of the curse which lays the terms of Odysseus' odyssey. It is the manipulation of the power of language and in particular the power of the proper name which is narrated here by Odysseus. The name is invested with a (dangerous) power which not only declares the fame, authority, position of the subject but can also be turned against the subject in curse, oath, defamation, and utilized in beguilement. Odysseus' manipulation of naming to deceive the monster is followed by the monster's manipulation of the name against Odysseus – and now by Odysseus reciting this story of names. The first extended episode related by Odysseus in Scheria demonstrates to the full what is at stake in naming oneself, what is at stake in withholding the name.

The focus on the name of Odysseus in this scene, then, looks back to Odysseus' unwillingness to answer Arete and forward to the scenes on Ithaca where Odysseus again and again adopts a fictitious persona, a false name. The delay of Odysseus' *nostos* through the anger of Poseidon (his 'hatred' of Odysseus, 'man of hate'), which is co-extensive with Odysseus' deferrals of self-identification, stems from Odysseus' declaration of his (significant) name to the Cyclops and from the Cyclops' turning of Odysseus' boast against the utterer (realizing the significance of the name). Naming and withholding the name indeed form an essential dynamic of the narrative of the *Odyssey*.

The pun on *mētis/mē tis/outis* has a further significance, however. For one of the commonest epithets applied to Odysseus is πολύμητις, 'of many wiles' (*polumētis*). As Austin has shown, this epithet is used almost invariably in the *Odyssey* to introduce a speech by Odysseus, or to describe Odysseus as speaker, and Austin has claimed that far from being merely ornamental, the epithet *polumētis* emphasizes that 'when Odysseus speaks he is usually pleading a case, marshalling his most persuasive arguments'.[63] Austin's excellent study perhaps underestimates in this conclusion the deceptive manipulation of the situation implied by *mētis*.[64] Athene, whose description of Odysseus stands at the head of the Ithacan episodes, stresses precisely this deceptive element in Odysseus' characterization (13.291–9):

> The man who could beat you in all tricks
> would be wily and a rogue, even if it were a god up against you.
> Outrageous man, subtle in *mētis*, insatiate of tricks, so it is not your way
> to cease, even in your own land, from deceits
> and roguish tales, which are dear to you through and through.
> But come, let's talk no more of this; we both know
> sharp practices, since you are by far the best of all men
> in planning and tales, and I am famous among all the gods
> for *mētis* and sharp practice.

Only a consummate rogue could outdo Odysseus in every trick. *Skhetlie*, 'outrageous', which is how Odysseus addressed the Cyclops is scarcely polite and colours the force of ποικιλομῆτα, 'subtle in *mētis*', and δόλων ἆτ', 'insatiate of tricks'. This bantering, ironic address also draws Odysseus and Athene together: they are similar, he in his pre-eminence among mortals for counsel (*boulē*) and for speaking (*muthoi*), she among the gods

---

[63] Austin (1975) 11–80.
[64] See Detienne and Vernant (1978) *passim* and Pucci (1986).

for her *mētis* and resourcefulness. (It is in order to weave together a *mētis* (13.303) that Athene has come to her hero.) As with Athene, so for Odysseus tricks and deceptions are part of his very nature: 'they are dear (*philoi*) to you through and through'. Odysseus may desire to return to his *philoi*, but elements of what is *philos* travel with him. Indeed, when Odysseus announces his name to the Phaeacians, it is qualified by ὃς πᾶσι δόλοισι ἀνθρώποισι μέλω, καί μευ κλέος οὐρανὸν ἵκει: Odysseus' 'fame reaches heaven' and he is 'pre-eminent for all tricks among mortals'.[65] Indeed, his fame is precisely that of the arch-trickster, arch-manipulator of words and plans. The puns which form the essence of Odysseus' tricky escape from the Cyclops, then, manipulate the very term by which Odysseus is most often represented as a speaking character. The way in which *polumētis Odusseus* uses or withholds a name is a defining aspect of his *mētis*, of what it is to be (*polumētis*) Odysseus. To say 'I am *outis* and that is my name' is to veil the name 'Odysseus', but also to reveal something important about the man for whom lies and deceit are *philoi*. To hide the name in Odysseus' case is telling.

To name oneself 'no one' is not to be without a name, then. (It is not to return to some pre-cultural, pre-linguistic state as seems sometimes to be suggested. From whatever outside Odysseus makes his return, it is not outside language.) As Alcinous says, a human cannot be without a name: *Ou . . . tis*, he says, is anonymous (8.550–4):

> Tell me the name that your mother and father and
> the others who live around your city call you there.
> For no one of men is absolutely anonymous,
> neither bad man nor good, when he is first born.
> But parents name everyone, when they give birth.

The parents (or in Odysseus' case, a grandparent) name a child and in society a person has a name (which, of course, are not necessarily the same – as in the case of Irus, the beggar whose parents named him Arnaius (18.5–7). A person on the margins of society – a begger, a king – may find his name/identity affected by such social positioning. It is as a wandering man that Odysseus shifts the name he uses.) A name comes with a history, with connotations. To use the name 'Odysseus' (with its etymon of 'trouble', with the fame that attaches to it) or *polumētis Odusseus* or *outis* (which with *mētis* points towards Odysseus' description as a speaking subject) is not simply to point to some 'essential idea', not

---

[65] Suerbaum (1968) translates this as 'famous for tricks among all mortals'; but see *Od.* 13.292. Segal (1983) calls it 'ambiguous'.

simply and absolutely to *refer* to a subject. Rather, in the exchanges of language, there can be no absolutely neutral, 'degree zero', reference. The name is always already inscribed in the network of differences which make up social discourse. So, too, to refer to oneself is to enter oneself (as speaking subject) into this social discourse. To say 'I am Odysseus' is not simply self-*reference* but also self-*representation* – it begins to tell the story of Odysseus.

Naming, then, may now be seen as an essential factor in the process of *nostos* and recognition, and an essential aspect in any discussion of self-representation – it is the unachieved aim of saying in his own hall 'I am Odysseus' that founds the return. There is, first, a continuous defining of Odysseus through the predications by which Odysseus refers to himself and is referred to by others. The various namings of Odysseus provide a basic element in the process of defining 'a/the man', from the first mention of *andra ... polutropon*, 'a/the man of many turns', to the proclamation εἴμ' Ὀδυσσεὺς Λαερτιάδης ὅς ..., 'I am Odysseus, son of Laertes, who ...' Naming disseminates recognition throughout the narrative of return. There is also an express indication of the significance of Odysseus' name for the narrative of his odyssey, and, moreover, an awareness of the dangers and powers involved in using or withholding a name. Odysseus is both master of and mastered by his name. Indeed, the *Odyssey* articulates how naming is both referential and at the same time descriptive, authorizing, classifying (much as recognition is both a perceptual and a legitimating process). When the narrative reverts again and again to the concealment or deferral of the name, this recognition of a gap between a subject and his proper name (a name could only ever be a *sign* of identity) raises the question of what's in a name.

The use and manipulation of the name in the *Odyssey* indicates, then, a further key aspect of the narrative of *nostos* – a concern for the complex relations between man and his language, particularly in self-representation. The arguments presented here are designed to demonstrate that this is no casual feature of the narrative of return, but rather a constitutive dimension of narrative itself, and in particular of narration – the stories that are told of the self. To which I now (re)turn.

TELLING A TALE

To speak is to assume a responsibility, which is why it is to incur a danger.
Todorov

Telling is both a responsible and a commercial act.   Barthes

The *Odyssey* is, as 'Longinus' puts it, 'mostly story telling'.[66] There are two particular sets of stories that I wish to consider in this section, the tales Odysseus tells in Ithaca where he conceals his identity – the so-called Cretan lies[67] – and the narrative of his journeys to Scheria that he tells to the Phaeacians. In both cases, I shall be dealing with types of self-representation. How do the tales which Odysseus tells inform our understanding of 'the man of many turns'? How do the stories which Odysseus tells about himself bear on what I have been discussing in the previous two sections, namely, the relations between man and his language and the construction of social identity through recognition?

The first Cretan story is told by Odysseus to Athene (13.256–310). He is a Cretan, he claims, on the run after killing the son of Idomeneus, and he has been left behind by Phoenician sailors. There is no mention of Odysseus in this story, although the Cretan fought in Troy and 'suffered pains' (*pathen algea* 13.263; cf. 1.4); and his ship has been brought here by an 'unwilling deception' (13.277). (As I will discuss below, several of Odysseus' deceptive stories contain episodes of deception.) This story is delivered in reply to Athene's deception, her disguise. The deceptive first-person narrative is an exchange (of language) and, indeed, Athene in her recognition – a speech I discussed in the previous section – not only describes Odysseus as an arch-deceiver but also links herself and the hero together in their shared powers of trickery and misrepresentation. As the disguised *xeinos*, it is within the reciprocities of guest-friendship that Odysseus' lies are offered. The deceptive exchange of language both enables Odysseus' extended reintegration into the exchanges of social intercourse and marks him as a sign and source of 'trouble' within such social exchanges.

It is also as a Cretan that Odysseus answers Eumaeus' quite properly delayed enquiry to a *xeinos* (14.187), 'Who are you, and from where? What is your city and who are your parents?' This enquiry and the story Odysseus tells in response have been prepared for, however, not merely in the preceding rituals of guest-friendship. For the previous exchange of Eumaeus and Odysseus also focuses on beggars' false tales in relation to the homecoming of Odysseus. Odysseus first asks Eumaeus who his master is, and in a speech I have already looked at, Eumaeus hesitates to name the man he is prepared to praise. He begins this speech as follows (14.122–7):

---

[66] 'Longinus' *De Sublim.* 9.13.
[67] On the Cretan lies, see Trahman (1952); Marg (1957) 12ff; Todorov (1977) 59ff; Walcot (1977); Maronitis (1981); Haft (1984).

'ὦ γέρον, οὔ τις κεῖνον ἀνὴρ ἀλαλήμενος ἐλθὼν
ἀγγέλλων πείσειε γυναῖκά τε καὶ φίλον υἱόν,
ἀλλ' ἄλλως κομιδῆς κεχρημένοι ἄνδρες ἀλῆται
ψεύδοντ', οὐδ' ἐθέλουσιν ἀληθέα μυθήσασθαι.
ὃς δέ κ' ἀλητεύων Ἰθάκης ἐς δῆμον ἵκηται,
ἐλθὼν ἐς δέσποιναν ἐμὴν ἀπατήλια βάζει.'

Old man, no one who has wandered could come here with a report
of that man and persuade his wife and dear son;
but vainly, wandering men in need of sustenance
tell lies, nor do they want to tell the truth.
Any vagrant who comes to the people of Ithaca
goes to my mistress and babbles deceitful tales.

The opening phrases of the speech (which will hesitate to name Odysseus) seem to hint at the varying possibilities of reference for the king. 'Old man ' addresses Odysseus in his disguise; 'no one' [*outis*] perhaps recalls Odysseus' own concealment of his name in the Cyclops' cave; 'that man', *keinon*, is Eumaeus' reference to Odysseus, which like Penelope's and Athene's use of *keinon*, refuses to name the master; and 'who has wandered' may recall the opening of the epic, 'the man who wandered many ways ...' Eumaeus seems to assume that Odysseus, like others before him, will wish to go to Penelope with a story about her absent husband in order to obtain a recompense of food or clothing. The lying of wandering men is taken for granted. Indeed, the language seems to set up a punning interplay between 'wandering' and 'truth': *alēthēn* 120, 'I have wandered'; *alalēmenos* 122, 'wandering'; *alētai* 124, 'wanderers'; *alēteuon* 126, 'vagrant'; *alēthea* 125, 'truth' – note also *allōs* 124, 'in vain'. The tale of a wanderer deviates from the path of truth?[68] Eumaeus himself, to follow his suggestion that Penelope and Telemachus will not be taken in by such story-telling, proceeds to express his deep pessimism about the possibility of Odysseus' return (14.133ff). Odysseus responds (14.149–52):

Dear host, since you completely deny it, and say still
that man will not return, then your heart is ever untrusting.
But I will not speak in the same way, but say on oath that
Odysseus is coming. May I get a reward for good news
immediately, whenever that man reaches his home.

---

[68] Cf. Strabo 1.2.23: ἀλαζὼν δὴ πᾶς ὁ πλάνην αὑτοῦ διηγούμενος, 'everyone who tells the story of his own wandering is an *alazōn* (wanderer/braggart)'.

Odysseus is prepared to say under oath that Odysseus is coming home (which will provide him with a reward for good news on the spot, that is, as a beggar he will receive the cloak that he desires). The present tense of what is a prophecy for the future also reveals what is the case: Odysseus is in the process of effecting his return. Odysseus swears to what we already know to be the truth, and the repetition of words of speaking (*anaineai*, 'you deny'; *phēistha*, 'you say'; *muthēsomai*, 'I will say'; *euangelion*, 'good *news*') emphasizes the irony of the exchange here as a series of misplaced speech-acts: the oath conceals a truth as it reveals another (has Autolycus passed on his prowess 'in oaths' to his grandson?); Eumaeus denies that what has happened will happen; and the reward for good tidings which will not be claimed until the very moment of Odysseus' arrival only ironically represents Odysseus' return to the *oikos*. Odysseus goes on to make his oath, calling to witness Zeus, the guest-friend table and the hearth of Odysseus; but first, with continuing irony, he expresses his hatred of beggars' lies (14.156–7):

> Hateful to me like the gates of Hades is the man
> who, yielding to poverty, babbles deceitful tales.

Odysseus, who looks like (*eoikōs*) a beggar, hates the person who yields (*eikōn*) to poverty and tells deceitful tales. Deceitful tales are 'dear' (*philoi*) to Odysseus (as the deceptive man is 'hateful' (*ekhthros*)), and this expression of distaste for deceptive wanderers' tales stands as a prelude to his own Cretan lie.[69] For it is in response to this speech of Odysseus that Eumaeus finally asks the stranger who he is.

This second Cretan story, then, is significantly preceded by an exchange which focuses on the possibilities and motivations of deceptive speech, particularly in such stories with regard to Odysseus' homecoming. And the tale itself depicts Odysseus as a Cretan who, amongst other adventures, is the sad victim of deception: a Phoenician's lies lead him into slavery (*apatēlia* 258, 'deceitful tales', echoes *apatēlia* 157, 127; and *pseudea* 296, 'lies', echoes *pseudont'* 125, 'they lie'). This tale is lengthy (193–359), and introduced with a claim of its absolute veracity:

---

[69] The only other time that the expression 'Hated to me as the gates of Hades is that man who ...' occurs in the Homeric poems is the famous passage where Achilles dismisses Odysseus' persuasion as deception (*Il.* 9.312). The rejection of the beguiling Odysseus in the mouth of the best of the Achaeans becomes here a mark of beguilement in Odysseus' disguise as a lowly beggar. For an extended analysis of textual interrelations of the *Odyssey* and the *Iliad*, see Pucci (1987).

ταῦτα μάλ’ ἀτρεκέως ἀγορεύσω 192, ‘I will say these things quite truly’.[70] It constructs a story of a life full of journeying and suffering, a picture of a Cretan who willingly and unwillingly has wandered from place to place. It is not only this general similarity to Odysseus’ own story that has been noted. Also, like Odysseus’ earlier narrative of his attack on the Cicones (9.39ff), the Cretan sails to a foreign city which his men attack to their own cost. In this case, it is only by supplicating the Egyptian king that the Cretan makes an escape from the soldiers who wish to kill him – a supplication which succeeds because of the Egyptian king’s respect for Zeus Xenios.[71] So the Cretan goes to Troy, is involved in the sack of the city, and experiences a storm on leaving. So, the Cretan collects guest-gifts from all the inhabitants of the land which takes him in. Both the similarities and the differences from Odysseus’ own experience are evident. The explicit connection of the story with the home-coming of Odysseus, however, is made towards the end of the telling. The stranger claims to have met and been entertained by Pheidon, the Thesprotian king, who had entertained Odysseus (14.321–2), and who shows the Cretan the absent Odysseus’ accumulated guest-gifts. Odysseus, swore Pheidon (331), is at present in Dodona consulting the oracle whether he should return home openly or in secret. The Cretan, then, claims to have met a man who swears to have seen and helped Odysseus recently. Only the existence of Odysseus, the choice between an open or secret return and the collection of guest-gifts correspond to the narrative of Odysseus’ return so far, and the Cretan claims no direct contact with the absent king.

Eumaeus is moved by the story, and convinced by it all, except that part which pertains to Odysseus (14.361–5):

> Ah! wretched stranger, you have greatly moved my heart,
> telling in detail how much you suffered and wandered;
> but I think part at least is not in order; nor will you
> persuade me in your story about Odysseus. Why must
> a man such as you lie pointlessly?

An echo of the pun between ‘truth’ and ‘wandering’ may be heard in *alēthēs* (362), ‘you have wandered’, (*alēthēs* = ‘true’), and the assumption that the wanderer is lying (*pseudesthai* 365). The stranger has spoken οὐ κατὰ κόσμον, ‘not according to order’, ‘not what is fit’, with regard to

---

[70] A remark which leads Todorov (1977) 61 to comment ‘Invocation of the truth is a sign of lying.’

[71] See in particular Herman (1987) 54–8.

the absent king. 'The only part of the narrative Eumaeus treats as false is the only part which is true.'[72] Eumaeus remains convinced of his master's destruction, and, he says, he has even lost interest in asking about him since the time when an Aetolian man deceived him with a *muthos* (14.379–85):

> Since an Aetolian man deceived me with a tale;
> he came to my home after he had killed a man and
> wandered over many a land. But I treated him well.
> He said he had seen him with Idomeneus in Crete,
> repairing his ships which storms had shattered.
> He said he would come either in summer or autumn,
> bringing many possessions, with his godlike crew.

The Aetolian liar was also a wanderer (*alētheis* 380, 'wandered') and also told a tale of Crete and Idomeneus. He said Odysseus would return in summer or autumn, laden with gifts and with his companions. As with Odysseus' own Cretan lies, the Aetolian told a tale which hints at elements of the truth, even as it fabricates and misrepresents. Eumaeus' disappointment in the Aetolian is set in an ironic parallel with Odysseus' deception. The men exchange tales of Cretans, Odysseus to deceive and yet test Eumaeus' fidelity, Eumaeus to express his fidelity, and yet to be deceived as to the stranger's identity, although not to be taken in by this Cretan tale about his absent/present master. The exchange of stories turns not merely on Odysseus' misrepresentations, but on an interplay of deceptive tales.

It also leads to a further proposed exchange of words, a ῥήτρη (393), 'a verbal covenant', or 'wager'. Odysseus remarks on Eumaeus' lack of belief even in his oath (391–2), and suggests a deal: if the master returns, Eumaeus will give him a cloak; if he does not return as promised, Eumaeus may have his servants throw him off a cliff to teach all lying beggars a lesson. The irony of the already returned master's manipulation of the servant is clear, but Eumaeus avoids the wager with an appeal to the propriety of guest-friendship – How could he kill a man whom he had invited into his home? – and the exchange turns finally to the sacrifice and the consumption of the evening meal, the 'guest table' by which Odysseus had sworn his oath. The deceptive exchange of language reverts finally to the ordered exchange of guest-friendship (a marked contrast with the Cyclops episode).

That night, the stranger tells Eumaeus a further story, this time of a

---

[72] Todorov (1977) 61.

direct, if long passed, encounter with Odysseus, in which the hero takes an active and key role. This is an anecdote with strongly marked object, to persuade Eumaeus to give him a cloak in the inclement night.[73] A story for a cloak. Hence it begins with an elaborate and periphrastic apology for speaking what perhaps should not be said (14.462–7) (a *politesse* which demonstrates that desire – which gives rise to narrative – must be veiled in language).[74] The story is an episode from the siege of Troy, an ambush led by Odysseus, Menelaus and the Cretan, in which the Cretan finds himself without a cloak and freezing to death. (A god 'deceived' him (488) – again the deceiving tale expressly mentions deception.) Odysseus, typically of his character as counsellor and fighter (he claims 490–1), comes up with a scheme. The Cretan is told to be quiet, and Odysseus calls for a volunteer to run back to Agamemnon with a message, and the volunteer naturally leaves his cloak as he runs off. So the Cretan passes the night comfortably. The story has its desired effect on Eumaeus, who regards this tale as told most suitably, to the point (οὐδέ τί πω παρὰ μοῖραν ἔπος νηκερδὲς ἔειπες 509, 'Nor have you said anything contrary to what is right or unprofitably'); and he provides the stranger with a comfortable and warm bed for the night. It is noticeable, however, that the Cretan's tale is predicated on Odysseus' manipulative skill with words, his prowess in counsel (491) and *muthoi* (492). Once more, *mētis* is both the subject and the nature of the narrative (as the Cretan retells Odysseus' *muthos* to gain himself again a warm covering). The lying story also reveals a truth of *polumētis* Odysseus, the speaker.

In Eumaeus' house, then, we see not merely Odysseus telling a false tale to protect his disguise and to test Eumaeus' fidelity, but a series of exchanges that revolve around wandering, deception, misplaced faith; a series of conversations, set in the context of the reciprocal rituals of guest-friendship, that both veil and reveal the two speakers in a complex network of truths and fictions, fidelity and belief.

The next time that Odysseus tells a Cretan tale is in his own palace to Antinous, the leader of the suitors. This shorter story (17.415–44) also mentions a voyage to Egypt and the Cretan's escape from death. The escape, however, is not through a direct supplication of the king of Egypt that results in being treated as a *xeinos*. Rather, Odysseus merely states (17.442–5):

[73] On the second Cretan lie, see Redfield (1973) 38; Svenbro (1976) 23–4; Walcot (1977) 15–16; Detienne and Vernant (1978) 30–1; Nagy (1979) 235–8; Edwards (1985) 33–4.

[74] See e.g. Barthes (1975); Barthes (1978); Tanner (1979). On classical material, see e.g. Carson (1986) who draws heavily on Barthes (1978); Goldhill (1987b).

> But they gave me away, into Cyprus, to a *xeinos*,
> who arrived, Dmetor Iasides, who ruled strongly in Cyprus.
> From there, I have now come here suffering woes.

He is given to a *xeinos* to take to Cyprus. The word *xeinos* recalls the previous magnanimous display of guest-friendship by the Egyptian king, as it changes the story. Why does Odysseus change his version? The scholiast notes rightly that in this version all mention of the returning king is repressed – there is no talk of the Thesprotians. As much as his previous tale of Odysseus was construed by Eumaeus as a deliberate attempt to please the listener, so it is easy to appreciate here the beggar's unwillingness to recall Odysseus before the aggressive suitors. But there is a further reason. For the Cretan's tale is put into a particular context. The speech opens (17.415–21):

> Give, friend. You do not seem to be the worst of the
> Achaeans, but the best,[75] since you look like a king.
> So you must give alms more generously than the others.
> I would spread your fame through the endless earth.
> For I once lived in my own house among people,
> prospering in wealth, and often I gave to a wanderer,
> according to what he was and what he wanted when he came to me.

The story of the Cretan's reversals of fortune is told to demonstrate the propriety of giving generously to a *xeinos*. The first words, *dos*, *philos*, 'give, friend', are an appeal for alms, and in the address *philos* a claim to be treated as a *xeinos*.[76] Antinous, the addressee, is described as 'not seeming to be the worst', since he 'looks like a king'. The vocabulary of 'seeming' and 'being', of 'looking like' (as the disguised king speaks to the pretender) points precisely to the gap between appearance and reality in this exchange. Antinous dismisses the beggar sarcastically as a 'ruiner of the feast' – the previous telling of the tale had led to the guest table of Eumaeus – and sends him away from his table (17.447). Odysseus immediately stresses the disjunction between Antinous' appearance and his behaviour (17.454):

> For shame! There is not, then, in you a mind to match your looks.

The Cretan's tale is thus constructed as a testing of Antinous, as host and king. It stands in significant contrast with Eumaeus' reaction to a

---

[75] On the importance of ἄριστος in Homeric epic, see in particular Nagy (1979), with bibliography.
[76] The link between *philos* and *xeinos* is shown by Benveniste (1973) 275ff.

similar situation, the previous telling of the tale. The omission of the story of the Egyptian king's beneficence and the Thesprotian king's guest-friendship serves to stress the absence of such behaviour here in the man who would be king. 'The change in emphasis between versions ... demonstrates that the story *can* be used by the teller to convey subtly facts about himself and different aspects of his personality, as well as convey warnings and suggest paradigms for behaviour.'[77] The story is a fiction to reveal the truth.

It is Penelope who next asks Odysseus directly who he is. She has indicated her desire to question the stranger about her husband. Odysseus, however, begins by talking of Penelope (19.107–9):

> My lady, no mortal on the endless earth could fault you.
> For your fame reaches to broad heaven,
> like some blameless king ...[78]

This flattery of Penelope also recalls the expression by which Odysseus had announced himself to the Phaeacians ('And my fame reaches to heaven' (9.20)) and also the periphrasis by which Penelope had referred to her husband ('His *kleos* is broad through Greece and midmost Argos' (4.726, 816)). Odysseus' language, as it deflects a direct reply, hints towards the truth and towards a parallelism between Penelope and himself, which will be further expressed in the series of 'reverse similes'[79] (where Penelope, for example, is likened to a sailor returning to land). Here, Penelope with her *kleos* is 'like a king'.

Odysseus requests that he is not asked about his name: μάλα δ' εἰμὶ πολύστονος, he says, 'I am much grieving'. (Odysseus *polumētis, polutlas, polutropos* etc. again hides and hints at his identity in the assertion 'I am *polustonos*'[80] – as recognition is diffused through the language of self-representation.) But the queen will not accept such brooking. She replies with a lengthy speech (19.124–63) about her troubles with the suitors, how she longs for Odysseus' return, and how she has tricked the suitors with her weaving. Her story of grief concludes with the restatement of her question about the stranger's identity. If his is a tale of woe, let it be in exchange for her tale of misery. Odysseus' response is the next tale of

---

[77] Emlyn-Jones (1986) 8.

[78] There is a difficulty in construing the remainder of this sentence; see e.g. Stanford (1959) ad xix 109ff and Russo (1985) who follows Monro's emendation of ἦ to ἤ.

[79] Cf. Foley (1978) *passim* and on these lines especially 11ff. *Kleos* will be discussed in the next chapter. On *kleos* in the *Odyssey*, see Segal (1983).

[80] On πολυ- compounds, see n. 3 above.

Crete, which begins, as his narrative to the Phaeacians opened with a description of Ithaca, with a general picture of the island (19.172ff). Again, his picture of the Cretan recalls earlier descriptions of Odysseus, particularly in the line (170) 'wandering through many towns of men, suffering pains', which echoes many terms of the *Odyssey*'s proem in particular. This tale, however, turns on a relation of guest-friendship between the Cretan and Odysseus. The Cretan now claims to have entertained Odysseus in his home and given him guest-gifts. In the first tale, there was no mention of Odysseus; in the second, the Cretan claimed to have met a man who entertained Odysseus as a *xeinos*; in the next, to have been on a military expedition once with the king; now he claims to be a *xeinos* of the king. The fictions and the truth of the speaker are approaching one another, at least in the stories told.

The comment that follows the story is different from previous remarks on Odysseus' tale-telling (19.203):

ἴσκε ψεύδεα πολλὰ λέγων ἐτύμοισιν ὁμοῖα·

In his speech, he made his many lies seem like the truth.[81]

'Lies like the truth', 'lies similar to reality', expresses not only the plausibility of Odysseus' narration but also the manner in which his tales can hint at a truth while resisting any direct expression of it. Indeed, the proof Odysseus offers of the truth of his tale – his final convincing of the doubting if moved queen – is the description of his own clothing and jewelry[82] of twenty years earlier (19.221ff) and the effect of Odysseus and his companions on those who saw them. The representation of the actual past is woven into Odysseus' misrepresentation.

Penelope is deeply moved, but Odysseus tells her a further story to stop her weeping. This is (again) an anecdote about the Thesprotian king and Odysseus' trip to Dodona. But there is a marked difference in the re-telling of the tale. For now the Cretan has the Thesprotian king say that Odysseus reached Thesprotia after the loss of his companions sailing from Thrinacia (the island of the Sun); the crew's fault in eating the cattle of the Sun is placed as the cause of their destruction. Odysseus'

---

[81] On the translation of this line, see Stanford ad loc. and Russo (1985) ad loc. This line is significantly echoed in Hesiod *Theog.* 26–8 and forms a basis of Pucci's subtle analysis of Hesiod's self-reflexive writing (Pucci (1977)), now interestingly criticized by Ferrari (1988). West comments (1966 ad 27) that the Homeric line is 'less satisfactory of the two as Greek, and the less firmly integrated in its context'. This bizarre judgement, however, stems from West's polemic that Hesiod predates Homer.

[82] On the dog brooch, see Rose (1979) 223ff.

survival by hanging onto the keel of his ship and his rescue and transport by the Phaeacians finds a place in the narrative. The Thesprotian king's story in the story of the Cretan brings the misrepresentation once more closer to the actuality of (the narrative of) Odysseus' journey. Again, Odysseus' deceit *manipulates* the difference between truth and fiction in his 'lies like reality'.

This exchange between Penelope and Odysseus leads to the queen's offer of a bathing which results in Eurycleia's recognition of her master – where Odysseus' physical and verbal disguise is penetrated (to reveal the truth that the man who looks like her master is the master). Penelope, however, remains unaware of the interchange between nurse and stranger, and after the bathing again questions Odysseus. After outlining her grief, and her doubt as to what she can, or should, do, she asks the guest to interpret a dream for her. She dreamt that an eagle killed her geese which she was feeding; she grieved, but the eagle claimed to be Odysseus, returning to kill the suitors (19.535–53). The metamorphosed king reads the dream in which he appears (metamorphosed) in the same way as the eagle (Odysseus) in the dream indicates: 'Odysseus himself', says Odysseus himself, 'has indicated how the dream is fulfilled' (19.556–7). The ironic interplay of self-representation and disguise reaches a brilliant climax. As each Cretan lie has brought the Cretan into closer and closer contact with Odysseus, here the disguise of Odysseus and Penelope's dream overlap, to the extent that Odysseus can both maintain his fictive persona and at the same time express what is the case without falsehood. The different levels of fiction in the text are so manipulated that the same statements signify with equal point, even as they signify different things, on each different level. Lies like the truth.

The tales Odysseus tells, then, do more than chart 'a progressive rise in Odysseus' fictitious status throughout the lies',[83] as he approaches the adoption of the status he once held in his *oikos* and Ithaca. Nor can it be said simply that 'His lies are blatant misstatements of fact'.[84] Rather, in his falsehoods which are like the truth, there can be seen an awareness and manipulation of language's subtle possibilities of veiling and revealing elements of truth in fiction. The fictive personae that Odysseus creates through his tales cannot but in different ways reveal both himself and others in their reactions to him. Indeed, it would be difficult to maintain a simple and absolute opposition between the 'true representation' of Odysseus and his fictive personae, but rather the tales construct a series

[83] Haft (1984) 301–2.   [84] Wilkerson (1982) 112.

of different shifting levels of representation (in the exchanges of language between *polumētis* Odysseus and those with whom he converses). Telling tales not only may conceal identity and test the listener, but also are telling about the speaker. Homer, the teller of tales, makes his hero a tale-teller who manipulates different levels of fictional (self-)representation.

The first-person narratives in which Odysseus represents himself as a Cretan who has wandered far, are preceded in the *Odyssey* by the extensive first-person narrative in which Odysseus represents his wanderings to the Phaeacians.[85] The relations between this long tale and Odysseus' Cretan stories have all too rarely been adequately discussed, despite the fact that in ancient writing the discussion of truth and falsehood with regard to the *Odyssey* is focused in particular on the Phaeacian narrative.[86] (Certainly since Eratosthenes, Odysseus' wanderings were regarded by at least some critics as merely a fantastic and untrue tale.) This critical tradition of Odysseus as fabricator and braggart, however, leads to important insights into the narrative technique of the poem, even if the question 'Does Odysseus lie through books 9–12?' may not receive a single-word answer. Although I certainly will not make any attempt to prove that Odysseus' Phaeacian tales are lies, I will be investigating what in the narrative techniques of the *Odyssey* makes possible such an evaluation. Now Alcinous, in the break in Odysseus' tale in Book 11, may seem to raise precisely the problem of the status of Odysseus' stories (11.363–8):

> Odysseus, we do not think, to look at you, that you are
> a braggart and rogue, like many men the black earth
> feeds, far-scattered fellows, fabricators of lies, lies that
> no one could ever see to test. In your case, there is a shape
> to your words, and you show sound sense;
> you have spoken a tale knowingly like a poet.

As so often in the *Odyssey*, the narration of a tale prompts a comment on its telling. Athene declares that it would take an *epiklopos*, 'rogue', to

---

[85] On the first-person narrative, see in particular Marg (1957); Maehler (1963) 9–34; Suerbaum (1968); Voigt (1972). Suerbaum has extensive further bibliography to which can be added Frontisi-Ducroux (1976); Stewart (1976) 146–95; Moulton (1977) 145ff; Thalmann (1984) 157ff; Walsh (1984) 19ff.

[86] See in particular Strabo's discussion of Homer 1.2.1ff, usefully discussed with bibliography by Schenkeveld (1976). Pindar's remark in *Nem.* 7.20–3 is particularly important: 'For the critical picture of an Odysseus who is all λόγος and no ἔργον, whose celebrity far exceeds any martial accomplishments he can claim, begins here in Pindar, and continues through Gorgias, Antisthenes, and the tragedians to become one of the clichés of Western literature' (Most (1985) 149 (with references and useful discussion of the Pindaric lines)).

outstrip Odysseus in tale-telling (13.291) and here Alcinous says that Odysseus does not resemble a 'rogue', *epiklopos* (or a 'braggart', 'charlatan', ἠπεροπῆα) to those watching. He is not like typical wandering men who construct lies of which there can be no seeing and testing (although it is not clear how this is different from Odysseus' tales). Rather, Odysseus' words have 'shape', 'form', μορφή, and there is good sense in them; his story is like a tale of a bard who is skilful and knows (ἐπισταμένως has both senses). It is the 'form' of Odysseus' speech which brings conviction (like a poet?) – though it is difficult securely to comprehend what is meant by the term *morphē*[87] here. Indeed, Odysseus opens his long narration with a question about the ordering of his story (9.14–16):

> What, then, first, what last shall I say?
> For the heavenly gods have given me many cares.
> Now, then, first I will tell my name ...

This retrospective narration within the narrative of the *Odyssey* marks its own deliberate ordering. So, indeed, the narration ends with a comment on the technique of story-telling (12.450–3):

> Why should I tell the rest of this story?
> For already yesterday I began telling you and your
> noble wife in the house. It is distasteful for me
> to tell a story again, once it has been well told.

The oral poet's Odysseus finds repetition distasteful (*ekhthron*) when it comes to telling stories (*muthologeuein*)!

The complex structuring of the *Odyssey*'s narrative, furthermore, is stressed by another retrospective. In Book 23, Odysseus after making love with Penelope exchanges stories (23.300–1):

> When they had taken their pleasure in delightful love,
> the pair took pleasure in tales, speaking to one another.

The pleasures of love lead to the pleasures of *muthoi*, as once again Penelope and Odysseus exchange versions of the past. Penelope is briefly described as telling of her suffering in watching the suitors and their feasting (302–5). Odysseus, however, narrates all the sufferings he both had caused and experienced – the active and passive sense of his name, 'trouble' – and Penelope listens with pleasure wide-awake (23.310–3):

> He began how first he had destroyed the Cicones, then
> had come to the fertile land of the Lotus-Eaters;

---

[87] See e.g. Walsh (1984) 6ff. Cf. for the use of μορφή *Od.* 8.170.

and all the things the Cyclops had done, and how he had
taken revenge for his strong companions, who had been eaten and
not pitied.

He begins his story with the Cicones, and the narrative reports a brief account of each of the tales he tells. Unlike the *Odyssey*, these proceed in chronological order, and each is told in similar restricted detail, so that what has extended over eight books is now narrated in some thirty-one lines[88] (and in the space of a single night). The retelling of the tale cannot but emphasize the difference in repetition: the reordering of events into a linear pattern of chronological order, the removal of the thematic repetitions (guest-friendship etc.), the repression of so much detail, stress the *Odyssey*'s manipulation of the narrative order as well as its narrative techniques of expansion, repetition and choice of material. The narrative within the narrative, then, marks the text of the *Odyssey* as a composed, a constructed artifice. (That is, re-telling raises the question of re-presentation.) The (self-)awareness of a narrative as composed, as ordered in a particular way, as using particular material, stands against Auerbach's famous description of Homeric narrative as presenting the surface of the world without the depth provided by silences and gaps, as it stands against the assumption of a simple, paratactic linearity of narrative, which seems to be supposed by certain exponents of oral theory.[89] Rather, the different modes and structures of narration in the *Odyssey* demonstrate that far from an unmediated presentation of material there is always already in story-telling the manipulation of representation.

The differing levels of poetic narration, moreover, are importantly at play in the lines leading up to Odysseus' first-person narrative of his wanderings. This extensive scene in the court of Alcinous offers a further, highly relevant insight into the nature of tale-telling, as viewed in the *Odyssey*, and provides a particular context for the first-person narration.

Three times the bard of the Phaeacian court, Demodocus, is brought forward to entertain and Odysseus' reactions to the bard's performance – he is twice reduced to tears – are essential to the narrative's development towards his recognition and the announcement of his name. Two of the

---

[88] Aristotle (*Rhet.* 3.16, 1417a14) notoriously says this passage has sixty lines. It is usually assumed either that Aristotle's text is corrupt, or that Aristotle misremembered the Homeric text, or that this is further evidence for the unreliable state of our text of Homer.

[89] Auerbach (1953) ch. 1. Kirk, for example, calls paratacticism 'unsophisticated' (1962) 169; see also Notopoulos (1949); Notopoulos (1951). I have argued against this view of Homeric narrative in Goldhill (1988c). See Lynn-George's critique of Auerbach (1988) 1ff.

songs are directly related to Odysseus' past as hero at Troy and provide an essential background on the one hand to the picture of Odysseus in the *Odyssey* (which has often been seen as constructing an extended commentary on or against certain of the values and indeed the world-picture of the *Iliad*[90]) and on the other hand to the esteem in which Odysseus is held by the Phaeacians – he arrives to them already a subject for epic song. These two songs provide an importantly different perspective on Odysseus and his fame. The first song (8.73ff) is of a quarrel between Odysseus and Achilles,[91] and the pleasure of Agamemnon at such a dispute, since it fulfilled an oracle that predicted the fall of Troy (does this allude to the *Iliad*, where the quarrel of the best men, Achilles and Agamemnon, leads to the death of Hector, which heralds the fall of Troy? The festival that turns to violence is a pattern, however, suggestive of many other narratives from the Centaurs and Lapiths or Zeus and Prometheus – a violation of the celebration of the immortals themselves – to Odysseus' final slaughter of the suitors at a feast day of Apollo. The allusiveness of myth is always to a network, a system of tales . . .) (8.73–83):

> The Muse stirred the bard to sing of the famous deeds
> of men, a song whose fame then reached broad heaven,
> the quarrel of Odysseus and Achilles, son of Peleus,
> how they once fought at a luxurious festival of gods
> with terrible words, and Agamemnon, lord of men,
> rejoiced in his mind, that the best of the Achaeans were fighting.
> For so had Phoebus Apollo spoken in an oracle to him
> at sacred Pytho, when he entered the stone doorway
> to consult him. For that time was the beginning of trouble rolling on
> for the Trojans and the Greeks, through the plan of great Zeus.
> These things the famous bard sang.

The performance of the bard is represented only as reported speech, framed by the inspiration of the Muse and the concluding expression, 'these things the famous bard sang'. The violence of the language of the quarrel is represented merely in the summing up phrase ἐκπάγλοις ἐπέεσσι, 'terrible words'. So, too, the pronouncement of Apollo – a speech within a song within the epic – is not in direct speech. The famous singer's famous song of the famous deeds of men is merely outlined in these seven lines of description, as the focus shifts to Odysseus' tearful reaction as he listens to this version of his past (8.83–95).

---

[90] In particular, see Nagy (1979) 15ff; Clay (1983) 96ff; Edwards (1985); Pucci (1987).
[91] On this, see in particular Marg (1956); Diano (1963); Nagy (1979) 15ff; Edwards (1985) 38ff.

The second song Demodocus sings is the tale of Ares and Aphrodite and their discovered adultery.[92] Again, the description of the performance marks what follows as a reported summary of the song (8.266–9):

> He struck up on the lyre, and began finely to sing
> about the love of Ares and sweet-garlanded Aphrodite,
> how first they slept together in Hephaestus' house
> in secret.

The subject (ἀμφ', 'about') and the particular focus (ὥς, 'how') are expressed in as general an expression as that which introduced the quarrel between Odysseus and Achilles. The narrative, however, immediately seems to shift to a more direct form of expression as details of the plot and Hephaestus' machinations are described, and as the characters interact with direct speech (8.290–5):

> He rushed into the house,
> and grabbed her hand, and spoke to her using her name:
> 'Let's go, dear, to bed here and make love.
> For Hephaestus is no longer about, but, I suppose, has
> already gone to Lemnos to see the wild-voiced Sintians.'
> So he spoke, and it seemed pleasing to her to make love.

The brusque proposal of Ares, like the interchanges that follow once he has been trapped, are marked off as direct speech. Unlike the 'terrible words' which summed up the violent language in a phrase, the violent language itself is represented.

This far longer story also ends with 'These things the famous bard sang' (367). The contrast between this song of Demodocus and his previous performance is not merely in the relation of the subject material to Odysseus, its tone, or the reaction of the listening hero.[93] It is also in the nature of its mode of representation.

The third song is requested by Odysseus himself – a gesture which has worried many commentators and which certainly seems pregnant with possible meanings. For it once again reduces the hero to tears, and leads to Alcinous' final demand to know the identity of this *xeinos*, who is so moved by songs of the fall of Troy. Why does the hero returning from Troy ask for the song which narrates the final acts of the siege, and, moreover, his role in it? Odysseus' request has been seen as an attempt to increase his reputation before the announcement of his identity; as a

---

[92] See Burkert (1960); Braswell (1982).
[93] The relation between the song – divine adultery, with no lasting consequences – and Odysseus' own situation is discussed by Braswell (1982) and Burkert (1960).

typically roundabout way to effect a recognition; as a statement of how far Odysseus has travelled – in spiritual terms, or in terms of 'heroic identity' – from Troy and the world of the *Iliad*.[94] It certainly looks forward to the ironies and dramas of the future scenes where as a disguised *xeinos* Odysseus is faced with and prompts talk about himself (scenes which will also test Odysseus' emotional reactions and the behaviour of his hosts[95]). It also has a role to play as a prelude to the extended self-representing narration of Odysseus. Not only does it take Odysseus back to the point from which his narrative journey begins Ἰλιόθεν (9.39), 'From Troy . . .', so that Odysseus' story can be seen as a continuation of Demodocus' epic tale; but also it provides a further narrative viewpoint, as it were, in the picture of Odysseus. Further to the tales of Helen and Menelaus, who tell Telemachus the story of the Trojan horse from the inside (4.266–89, discussed below); further to the narrative description of Odysseus' escape from Calypso, there is now also a different bardic voice in the epic, constructing the story of Odysseus. Odysseus requests and receives a tale which represents himself as hero, and then proceeds to tell the next episode of the story himself (self-representing himself as hero). The story of Odysseus is made up of these different strains in the exchange of narratives.

This third song of Demodocus is also represented in a different way from the first two performances. Like the other two songs, it is introduced with language that indicates the reported nature of the song to follow (8.499–501):

> He began, stirred by the goddess, and showed forth his song,
> starting from when the Argives boarded their well-benched ships,
> and sailed away, after setting fire to their shelters.

So, like the previous two songs, it is concluded with the phrase 'These things the famous bard sang'. This short and condensed song, however, seems to be divided into four sections, the Trojan council (the Trojan horse from the Trojan side after Menelaus' version from the Greek side), the sack of Troy, Odysseus' and the other Greeks' dispersal through the town, and finally Odysseus' most terrible fight in Deiphobus' house. These sections are punctuated by the repetition of words of speech: 'he sang', 'he said' (the subject is Demodocus), ἤειδεν (8.514), ἄειδε (8.516), φάτο (8.519), markers which do not occur in the other two songs. Each

---

[94] See in particular Mattes (1958).
[95] See in particular Fenik (1974) 8–60.

section has strong elements of the summarizing seen in the first song (8.514–15):

> He sang how the Achaeans' sons destroyed the town,
> pouring out of the horse, leaving their hollow ambush.

There is, however, also what appears to be direct authorial commentary in the song. The description of the Trojan council's division of opinion concludes (8.509–11):

> For the city was destined to be destroyed when it took in
> the vast wooden horse, where all the best Argives sat
> bringing death and doom to the Trojans.

It is unclear whether this comment is to be taken as part of the reported song, a perhaps more vivid representation of the performance of Demodocus, or whether it is a comment like 'he sang', 'he sang', 'he said', which should not be attributed to Demodocus. Not only does this represented song, like the versions of his travels that Odysseus tells to Penelope, give a differently constructed narrative of events already told in the *Odyssey*, but also it helps develop the complex variety of modes of narration.

This song also reduces Odysseus to tears and his weeping is described in a remarkable simile (8.523–30):

> As a woman weeps, fallen over the body of her dear husband,
> who has fallen before the city and his people, trying
> to ward off a pitiless day from the city and his children.
> She sees him dying and gasping for breath, and winding
> her body around him, she shrieks piercingly, while men
> behind her hit her back and shoulders with their spears,
> as they drive her into slavery, to toil and misery.
> Her cheeks are washed with the most pitiful weeping.

After the description of Penelope in the first four books of the *Odyssey*, this certainly constitutes what Helene Foley has aptly called a 'reverse simile', a simile in which one spouse is described in terms applicable to the other (Penelope's weeping for a supposedly lost husband is a refrain of the Ithacan books[96]). But it also draws in an extraordinary way on the song which has just been described. It is in the context of a sacked city that the wife cries: like a victim indeed of Odysseus' rush 'like Ares' through Troy. The song of Demodocus is not a discrete unit, but is

---

[96] Foley (1978); although she does not discuss this simile in depth, see her suggestive comments 20. Cf. Diano (1963) 419f; Pucci (1979) 125–6.

echoed immediately in the framing narrative (as it echoes Menelaus' story). In this way, the possible significance of Demodocus' song for the narrative is opened. It is precisely such a juxtaposition of the simile and the song of Demodocus, like the juxtaposition of Odysseus' request and his reaction to it, which poses the question – but makes any certain answer hard to find – why this song should have been requested by Odysseus or why Odysseus' tears should be the means or the prelude of his recognition. It is in such juxtapositions – such gaps – that the work of reading the *Odyssey* takes place (and why 'reading' cannot usefully mean 'discovering that which can be said with certainty'). The varied critical responses to this text – like Alcinous' and Odysseus' very different responses to Demodocus' song – can only continue to testify to the active work of the reader in the construction of meaning.

There is, then an elaborate preparation for the first-person narrative of Books 9–12, not merely in the lengthy delay of Odysseus' name in answer to Arete's question but also in the significant interplay of subtly different modes of narration, different songs within the epic narrative, different voices telling the story of Odysseus. Now we are to hear another voice – the self-representing story of the hero.

The general point that a first-person narrative has a different authority, a different relation to actuality from a third-person narrative has often been made in narratological criticism.[97] In particular, the different structuring of an authoritative viewpoint in these differing narrative modes has been extensively investigated and contested. Although the Phaeacian story is like the Cretan stories (and many other speeches in Homer) in that it is a first-person narrative within the framework of a third-person narrative, it seems to raise in a heightened manner particular questions with regard to its status or authority as a story. The Cretan tales are explicitly marked as lies in the framing lines; the signification of the stories, their elements of fiction, falsehood and suggestion may be analysed, as I attempted above, in contrast with the authoritative framing narrative – as with Odysseus' working of the Phaeacian episode into his lies to Penelope. Even as such signification may be considered or questioned, it is always in the context of Odysseus' conning. Even such markers of truth and falsehood, however, are occluded in the Phaeacian

---

[97] Most modern studies take their start from Genette's work (1966, 1969, 1972), some of which are available in English in Genette (1980) and Genette (1982b). For one view of a more extensive history, see Culler (1975) especially 189ff.

narrative. There are no explicit comments on the nature of the story in the framing narrative, expect for the ambiguousness of the Phaeacians' enchanted reaction and Alcinous' remark that Odysseus speaks like a knowing poet – which may seem to point towards a question about the status or authority of Odysseus' utterances. Moreover, the framing narrative does not exclude the possibility of falsehood (as the various ancient and modern critics' questioning of the (absolute) veracity of the tales could suggest). Odysseus' encounter with Calypso and on Thrinacia are certainly described elsewhere in the *Odyssey*'s narrative, but all the other stories, as well as Odysseus' reactions to and involvement in them are part only of the self-representing narrative. How, then, is the first-person narrative to be authorized?

This change in the narrative voice as Odysseus takes over the telling, then, affects a listener's or reader's role in what might be called the narrative exchange. In the Ithacan episode, like Telemachus after the recognition, the listener or reader observes the art of Odysseus' testing and deceptive language, evaluates or questions its 'lies like the truth'. In Scheria, with the lack of even such markers of truth and falsehood for the first-person narrative, the readers or listeners find themselves placed in a similar position rather to Alcinous and Arete. The hearing or reading of this tale of Odysseus is not to observe a scene of deception, or simply observe a scene of enchanting story telling; but rather, like Alcinous, to listen to tales told (as if) by a (the) poet.

The first-person narrative of Odysseus in Alcinous' palace, then, can be seen to perform several functions in the text of the *Odyssey*. First, by telling Odysseus' travels in retrospect it sets Calypso's island as the starting point for Odysseus' return – and thereby forms a series of particular juxtapositions, which are of fundamental importance in the dynamics of *nostos*. Second, it develops a different view of Odysseus: the representation of Odysseus as he represents himself. The multiplicity of voices in the description and understanding of 'a/the man' is essential to the complex poetic texture of the *Odyssey*. What critical gestures have to be made if the episode in the Phaeacian palace is to give rise to descriptions of Homer's poetic voice as simple, direct and unsophisticated? Third, the narrative within the narrative may be thought to raise for the reader or listener a series of questions about (self-)representation and authority in story-telling. Not least the often posed doubt about the veracity of Odysseus' tale. To recognize a possibility of uncertainty about the boundaries between truth and fiction in Odysseus' narrative (especially with regard to the importance of this narrative for understanding *nostos* and 'a/the man') is to recognize in Odyssean (*polumētis*) language an essential duplicitousness. It is a language which both veils and reveals not only in the exchanges of social discourse with its disguises, testings and emotions, but also in the very narratives of self-representation, the narratives by which the self is formulated.

Tale-telling, then, is the means by which Odysseus conceals himself and describes himself: always telling. What is (to be) recognized in *andra* is formulated by this repertoire of songs within songs, and narratives within narratives – the network of differing narrative modes that also highlights the self-reflexive awareness of the ordering of the artistic work. What is told, how it is told and to whom it is told is a thematic concern of the tale of the *Odyssey*. As naming, that crucial gesture of recognition, raises the question of self-representation – of how saying 'I am Odysseus' is to begin to tell the story of Odysseus – so the first-person narratives of Odysseus are of particular importance in the multiplicity of views of the (much-troped) hero. For how Odysseus is represented as representing himself is a key aspect of the *Odyssey*'s deployment of deceitful language – the manipulations, disguises, fictions that language can effect. 'A/the man' is *made up* by the language in which he represents himself and is represented. And for 'a/the man', duplicitous fictions are a necessary part of the representation and formulation of the self. Man's place is (to be) found only in and through the displacements of language.

It is, however, the poet, the professional manipulator of words, the creator and preserver of reputations and representations, who must remain a key figure in any such discussion of the relations between man and language in the *Odyssey*, and it is to the poet to which I must now turn to complete this discussion.

THE VOICE OF THE BARD

And they said, 'But play, you must.
A tune beyond us, yet ourselves.

A tune upon the blue guitar
Of things exactly as they are'.
                              Wallace Stevens

The word 'bard', 'singer', ἀοιδός, occurs only once in the *Iliad* (*Il.* 24.720), but representations of bards appear again and again through the

Odyssey, inaugurating the history of the poet in the text.[98] The importance of Demodocus, the bard in Alcinous' court, and his three songs has already been discussed. It is also significant that it is in Scheria that there is such an emphasis on poetry and music. Scheria, as a 'transitional' world between the savagery of Odysseus' travels and the human world of Ithaca, is a society where civilized behaviour reaches its heights (8.246–9):

> For we are not excellent boxers or wrestlers,
> but we run lightly on our feet and are best in ships,
> and always the feast, harp and dances are dear to us,
> and changes of clothing and warm baths and beds.

Music and dance are part of the self-proclaimed prowess of the Phaeacians. Alcinous boasts how the Phaeacians excel all others 'in seafaring and speed of feet and dance and song' (8.253) – a speech which introduces the dance of the Phaeacian youths and the song of Ares and Aphrodite. The song of Demodocus is to demonstrate the excellence of the Phaeacians in singing, and Odysseus, like the Phaeacians, reacts with pleasure. Song is a defining aspect of the Phaeacian world.

When Odysseus requests Demodocus to sing of the Trojan horse, he precedes his request with a present of meat, and with the explanation that bards are of all human beings worthy of honour and respect because the Muse has taught them songs and holds them in particular esteem (8.479–81). The request itself specifies the song that Odysseus wants to hear (8.492–5) and is framed by two comments on Demodocus' singing. First, Odysseus praises the bard – either the Muse or Apollo must have taught him (8.489–91):

> For all too in order do you sing the fate of the Achaeans,
> all the Achaeans did and suffered and toiled,
> as if you were there yourself or heard it from one who was.

The bard sings 'all too according to the order of things', *liēn kata kosmon*. It is as if he were at Troy or heard it from an eye-witness (to the man who was there). An accurate representation of reality 'in order', *kata kosmon*, is the object of the poet's voice. The qualification *liēn*, 'all too'

---

[98] A much discussed topic: see Kraus (1955); Marg (1957); Lanata (1963); Maehler (1963); Treu (1965); Koller (1965); Vernant (1965) 51–94; Detienne (1967) especially 9–27; Harriott (1969); Stewart (1976) 146–95; Svenbro (1976) especially 1–73; Murray (1981); Scully (1981b); Murray (1983); Bergren (1983) 38ff; Thalman (1984) especially 157ff; Gentili (1983); (1984); Thornton (1984) 23–45.

in order, leads Walsh to suggest that Odysseus in these lines questions
the traditional assumption that a song should be composed *kata kosmon*,
and evaluated (at least in part) according to that criterion. He argues that
there is for Homer's Odysseus 'a second "order" external to song, the
human context of performance into which the song must fit. The song
that suits a social order will be "appropriate" because it is what the
audience wants, or perhaps because it is morally proper.'[99] So, he continues, Odysseus' tears represent an engaged audience, whereas the Phaeacians' enchantment indicates a contrasting, less involved reaction. The
combination of the Phaeacian pleasure in listening and the assumption
of the truth of the poetic voice seems, to Walsh, 'more closely aligned
with the assumptions that each Homeric poet inherits from generations
of poets before him'.[100] It is difficult, however, to take *liēn* as a negative
term here,[101] as Walsh requires, nor is there any reason to assume that
the song of Demodocus is in some way 'inappropriate' to audience or
morals, despite Odysseus' tears – he will, after all, go on to request a
further song about the Trojan war and cry then too, before lavishly
praising the singer. Nor can a rigid opposition between the 'traditional'
audience of the Phaeacians and Odysseus with his 'critical idiosyncracy'
be maintained.[102] Certainly, there is little suggestion of a norm of impas-
sive or disengaged listening to tales elsewhere in the *Odyssey*. None the
less, Walsh does point towards an important sense of differing paradigms for the poetic exchange: Odysseus, as an audience engaged to the
point of a powerful overflow of emotion and as a tale-teller who is always
personally involved in the (first-person) story he tells, offers a different
model from his hosts. It is also in the contrasting responses of audiences

[99] Walsh (1984) 8–9.   [100] Walsh (1984) 5.
[101] λίην may have the negative sense of 'too much' in Homeric Greek (the lexica agree),
but only, it appears, where there is already a negative evaluation expressed or strongly
implied in the sentence – which makes it hard to distinguish between the senses 'extremely', 'very' and 'too much', 'to an excess' (e.g. between 'Do not be extremely
troubled'/'Do not be excessively troubled', *Il.* 6.486). Most commonly λίην is an
intensive (especially in the phrase καὶ λίην which starts a sentence 'Aye, certainly...').
The phrase οὐ κατὰ κόσμον is common (e.g. 3.138; 14.363; 20.181) which may help
stress λίην but cannot determine its tone. Ameis-Hentze (1900) gloss λίην κατὰ κόσμον
with εὖ κατὰ κόσμον. καὶ λίην in a negative statement, as at *Il.* 1.533, is, as Dawe (1988)
70 comments, surprising.
[102] Walsh also says (1984) 5 that 'Clearly ... the Phaeacians are exceptional. Perhaps
Odysseus' tears more accurately figure the norm for Homer's audience.' I do not see
how this can be reconciled with Walsh's other statements on the Phaeacians as audience.
On the difference in audience response, see also Harriott (1969) 121–2.

and performers, differing paradigms of poetic truth, that the *Odyssey* develops (its representation of) the exchange of poetic performance.

It is to sing according to how things are, that is the criterion of judging the performance to come also – and Odysseus promises that he will spread the fame of the bard in return for the requested song (which will sing of the *kleos* of the hero) (8.496–8):

> If you could tell me this according to how it happened [*kata moiran*],
> I will speak of you before all mankind, and say
> that the kind goddess has given you a remarkable song.

Odysseus' tears follow Demodocus' performance and his further extensive praise for the singer (9.2–11). To listen to a bard sing is a pleasure that crowns a feast (even as it reduces Odysseus to tears). It is with this description of feasters listening to the fine poet that Odysseus begins his tale to the Phaeacians at the feast.

In the Phaeacian court, then, it is not merely the different songs of the bard which form a frame for Odysseus' song, but also the explicit discussion of the role and performance of the singer.

The bard Phemius plays an important role in Odysseus' palace in Ithaca. He claims – to save his life – that he was forced to sing for the suitors (22.330–60) and Odysseus spares him from the final massacre.[103] But his first appeal is as a poet (22.345–9):

> You will be sorry in time to come if you kill a poet;
> I, who sing both for gods and for men.
> I am self-taught, and the goddess has implanted all sorts
> of songs-paths in my mind. I seem to sing before you
> as to a god. So do not long to behead me.

It is because of the power of the poet's voice (for the future) – the power to make known and preserve the name of men – and because he is a self-taught, god-inspired poet that Phemius claims his life. There would be grief (*akhos*) hereafter (rather than *kleos*?) were Odysseus to kill a bard. The poet defends himself on the grounds of his privileged role in the presentation and construction of the reputation of men through song. Odysseus, as he completes the revenge which founds his *kleos*, is faced by – and spares – the bard, preserver and constructor of fame.

---

[103] His fate can be contrasted with the bard left behind by Agamemnon to protect Clytemnestra, who is abandoned on a desert island by Aegisthus; see Moulton (1977) 145 n. 15; Scully (1981b); Pucci (1987) 228ff.

Phemius is first described as singing – by compulsion – as Telemachus and the disguised Athene talk privately (1.154–5). The bard's song is further described after Athene has made her disappearance. The theme is briefly stated (1.326–7):

> He sang the return of the Achaeans, the bitter
> return which Pallas Athene inflicted on them from Troy.

Like the *Odyssey*, Phemius' song is a song of *nostos*. And after Athene has just left, the song is also of Athene's role as the force behind the bitter return of the Achaeans. The song has evident parallels with the framing narrative. Indeed, it disturbs Penelope precisely because of its relevance to her case; like her husband, she cannot hear such a tale without becoming emotionally involved (1.337–44):

> Phemius, you know many other enchantments for mortals,
> deeds of gods and men, which bards make famous in song.
> Sit beside them and sing one of those, and let them drink
> their wine in silence. Stop this song, so bitter,
> which always gnaws into the heart in my breast,
> since unforgettable grief bears down on me in particular.
> For I long for so dear a person, when I remember that
> man, whose fame is broad in Greece and midmost Argos.

The remembrance of her (unnamed) husband makes this song of the 'bitter' (λυγρόν 327) return of the Achaeans so 'bitter' (λυγρῆς 341) to her. The context of the singing is the feast (as in Scheria), but the queen's language adds a further insight into the description of the functioning of poetry. For, the poet knows *thelktēria*, 'enchanting things'. *Thelgein*, 'to enchant', is used in a variety of contexts but in particular to describe verbal and sexual seduction (which are often intertwined in Odysseus' case and in much later literature[104]). It is the term used for Circe's bewitching (10.291, 318, 326), and for Calypso's control over Odysseus (1.56–7); when the suitors are overcome by desire for Penelope (18.212), and then when she beguiles them into giving her presents (18.282). It is such enchantment that Telemachus fears when Odysseus appears for the first time undisguised before him, as if he were a divinity (like Hermes who 'enchants' the eyesight of men (5.47; 24.3)). The songs of the bard, then, are, in Penelope's eyes, a beguiling enchantment for mortals: a possibly deceitful or dangerous allure, which, for her, wastes her spirit.

---

[104] See e.g. Barrett (1964) ad 1274; Kahn (1978) 139ff; Buxton (1982) (index, *thelgein*); Easterling (1982) ad 335; Goldhill (1984) 164–5.

Her tearful reaction to a song in which Odysseus is implied, looks forward to Telemachus' tearful reaction to Menelaus' mention of Odysseus (4.113–16) – a scene which also parallels Odysseus' convering of his head when he hears his own name in Demodocus' songs. The tearful reactions to stories relevant to the wandering Odysseus link together the family in a shared emotional response. Songs 'enchant' – a possibly dangerous power – but also affect Odysseus, Telemachus and Penelope with grief; and each of these expressions of grief affect and move the plot in different ways.

Telemachus' reaction to his mother's request shows the immediate effect of Athene's advice. He justifies the bard's performance (1.346–52) and concludes that she should return to her room and her weaving, if she cannot bear to listen (352–7). He finishes (358–9):

> Tale-telling is man's business,
> all of us and particularly me. For mine is the authority in the house.

Tale-telling (*muthos*) is the men's concern and particularly Telemachus'. For his is the *kratos* in the house. Telemachus's rebuke to his mother is an assertion of his (incipient) male, adult role. Song has become the focus not merely for an emotional reaction or involvement, but for the disorder in the house, its uncertain structures of power. As Alcinous halts the singing of Demodocus in response to his guest's concealed tears, so Telemachus sends his mother upstairs to cry in private, as he attempts to take control of the *muthoi* in the house.[105]

The control and evaluation of *muthoi* play a major role in Telemachus' visit to Menelaus' palace. There is a bard at the wedding celebrations (4.17–18), but it is in the exchanges between Menelaus, Helen and Telemachus themselves that the reaction to and manipulation of *muthoi* are stressed.[106] Menelaus' grieving reminiscence of Odysseus prompts Telemachus to cry. Helen arrives at this moment and she immediately recognizes Telemachus by the resemblance to his father (4.138–46, *eoikota* 'like father, like son'). This recognition leads to Menelaus' amazement that the son of his friend Odysseus should be in his house, and this speech brings them all to tears. It is within this emotional context that Helen mixes a drug into the wine (4.220–1):

> She threw a drug into the wine they were drinking,
> pain-removing, anger-removing, inducing forgetfulness of all evils.

---

[105] It is worth noting that Phemius does not continue the song, since Telemachus sends the suitors away, so that Penelope gets her way after all.

[106] The following section is taken in part from Goldhill (1988c).

This drug, *pharmakon*, which could conquer even the grief felt over a dead parent or child (4.224–5) was given to Helen in Egypt, the home of *pharmaka*, good and evil (4.230):

> Drugs, many good ones mixed, many bitter.[107]

With her *pharmakon* mixed into the wine, Helen starts the *muthoi*. And as so often in the *Odyssey*, a tale contains a comment on its telling (4.238–42):

> Now sit and feast in the hall,
> and enjoy tale-telling. For I will say fitting things.
> I will not tell everything nor name
> all the trials of Odysseus, strong in mind.
> But here is one thing the stalwart man did and endured.

To delight the audience (like a bard?) Helen will tell a tale which is *eoikota*, which is translated 'fitting', 'like a truth', 'easily believable'. *Eoikota*, however, is also one of the key terms in the discourse of disguise and (false) appearances ('like', 'to be like', as Telemachus 'looks like', *eoikota*, Odysseus). Indeed, her tale will be of appearances and disguise. Her story, she goes on, is selective and partial – but one example of the many possible *muthoi* of Odysseus' sufferings; and it is a fitting example for Telemachus not only in that it sings of the *kleos* of Odysseus, but also in that it may hint of what is to come when Odysseus returns in disguise.

Helen's story depicts herself as keen to help the disguised Odysseus, keen to return to her husband (like a good wife) and rejoicing in the Trojan men's destruction. In this self-representing story, 'her aim, it appears, is not only the *kleos* of Odysseus, but also her own "fame" among the assembled men'.[108] Odysseus' powers of deceit are matched by Helen's, whose inward feelings have changed (4.259ff). Helen's story places the teller firmly to the fore: she is the only one to recognize the master of disguise; she aids and abets the Greek cause; she ends her story with flattery of her husband and blame of Aphrodite.

Menelaus, however, replies with a further *muthos*, the tale of the Trojan horse. He first praises his wife's tale, spoken *kata moiran*, 'according to due', 'as it happened', 'as is fit';[109] and he himself will also offer a single example to show the excellence of Odysseus. This is the story of how Odysseus managed to prevent any sound coming from the Trojan

---

[107] On the sense and implication of this line see Bergren (1981) 213–14.
[108] Bergren (1981) 208.
[109] Bergren does not discuss this line. See Goldhill (1988c) 22–3.

horse, as Helen attempts to deceive those inside by imitating their wives' voices. The story is again of concealment and trickery. Odysseus and the Greeks are in the horse trying to enter rather than escape from the city, but now threatened by the possibility of discovery through the deceitful language of Helen. The woman who was the saviour is now the danger; the woman who concealed threatens to uncover. The paradigmatic figure of an adultress imitates each man's wife to tempt an error (she behaves like each man's good wife?). Both stories tell of Odysseus' cunning exchanges with Helen (both include the same summing up phrase 242/ 271), but there is considerable contrast in the depiction of Helen. If she appeared as a true ally in the first *muthos*, Menelaus' story constructs a different view of the double-agent.[110] (The two, agreeable stories may seem difficult to reconcile. *eoikota*?) The *pharmakon* (which can be 'good mixed and bitter') leads to double tales of double-agents behaving duplicitously.

The juxtaposition of these two stories, then, with their different re-presentations of Helen has indeed raised for critics a problem: what is to be made of such a difference? Does the contrast indicate the contrasting nature of (personal) recollections of the past – the inevitable differences of retelling?[111] Or are the stories to be reconciled to produce a single composite picture? There is no further reaction from the story-tellers – say, of 'pain' or 'anger' or 'memory of evils' – to guide a response. Is this the effect to the drug – to allow the juxtaposition of such stories without apparent conflict or emotional response from the participants?

Menelaus' story, moreover, does not correct Helen's story but praises it. The two stories are juxtaposed as *supplements* to each other. Yet each introduces a subverting doubt into the truth value of the other. Neither can be securely used to establish a level of truth from which the other deviates (and, as we have seen, a further account of the Trojan horse is offered in the Phaeacian episode). The two stories, then, cannot be reformulated as a secure opposition as if they were absolutely contradictory with mutually exclusive claims on truth. Nor can the supple-

---

[110] 'La texte épique s'y emploie ... en projetant ... la pluralité des lectures sur les deux pans du diptyque' (Dupont-Roc and Le Boulluec (1976) 35).

[111] Often expressed in psychological terms; e.g. 'The subtle, tense interplay shows in perfect clarity the weakness of Menelaus, the isolation and helplessness of Helen, their animosity and the reconciliatory attempts which they quietly employ to ease it.' Beye (1968) 174. Kakridis (1971) 40–9 rehearses the predictable Analytic response that the two stories represent two imperfectly combined traditions of Helen in Troy. See now Collins (1988) 46–67.

ment be reformulated as merely adding more of the same – as if there were no significant difference between the stories. In this exchange, there remains an *irresolvable* uncertainty in the relation between the representations and also in the relation between the representations and any supposed 'master-version' of the Trojan war.

Helen and Menelaus may swap a pair of tales over wine to create pleasure, but the result is pain (4.291–3):

> Great Menelaus, son of Atreus, leader of people,
> This is more painful; for none of all this kept bitter
>   destruction from him,
> Not even if his heart within were made of iron.

The stories, which were of pain endured for a greater good, lead for Telemachus to more pain, in that not even such an iron spirit as Odysseus', not even such deeds, saved him from bitter destruction. If Menelaus' song seems in uneasy juxtaposition with Helen's, Telemachus' reaction seems to indicate no influence of the drug to remove pain. Telemachus seems scarcely seduced by the enchanting words of his hosts. Indeed, he proposes immediately that all should retire to bed (the opposite reaction to Odysseus' stories for which the audience would and do stay up all night). The interchange of Telemachus, Helen and Menelaus, apparently designed to relieve pain and to educate Telemachus about his father, seems to lead to Telemachus' increased grief. There is no straightforward *paideusis*, no painless lesson, for Telemachus in this initiation into social exchange.

The model of the telling and reception of a tale is difficult, then, in this scene. Menelaus praises Helen for speaking *kata moiran*, 'as it happened' (as she had promised *eoikota*, a 'fitting' tale); but then tells a tale himself which may be thought at least to contrast with the self-representation of his wife in the previous *muthos*. To both, and despite Helen's drug, Telemachus reacts with an expression of increased misery. The *pharmakon* introduces not unmixed pleasure, but an uncertain duplicitousness in the exchange of language. The problematic relation between *muthoi*, the listener and (self-)representation projects a complex model for the enchanting truth of the poet's voice.

Odysseus' story of the Sirens, too, offers an image of the power and reception of song.[112] The danger of the Sirens is the enchantment of their singing (12.44–5):

---

[112] On the Sirens see Pucci (1979) and Segal (1983) 38–43.

> But the Sirens enchant with their shrill song,
> sitting in their meadow ...

Like Penelope's description of the bard's songs, like Calypso's and Circe's spells, the Sirens song 'enchants', *thelgein*. This song threatens death and not merely delay, however. Around the Sirens lie the rotting flesh and bones of those who have heard. Odysseus, as Circe suggested, alone of his crew may listen to the song, provided he is tied to the mast, and so he can repeat it to the enchanted Phaeacians (12.184–91):

> Come here, Odysseus of many tales, great glory of the Achaeans;
> pull up your ship, to listen to our voice.
> For no one yet has sailed past here in his black ship,
> until he has heard our mouths' sweet-sounding voice,
> and takes pleasure in it, and learns more, and goes on.
> For we know all that the Argives and the Trojans
> suffered in broad Troy because of the gods.
> We know everything that happens on the teeming earth.

The dangerous allurement is to hear the voice and learn. Not merely pleasure but knowledge is offered. Indeed, the Sirens know everything that happened in Troy, everything in the world. The Sirens, like a bard, claim a privileged – even absolute – access to truth and knowledge;[113] but their voice leads the listener to disaster. Odysseus is, indeed, overcome by the enchantment of the Sirens' song and begs his men to set him free. They tie him more tightly to the mast and row on. The power of the Sirens' song of knowledge enchants even the man who knows of its enchanting danger.

The reaction of the Phaeacians to the performance of which the Sirens' song is a part, is silence (13.1–2):

> So he spoke; but they all remained quiet, in silence;
> they were held in a spell through the dark hall.

The listeners are held in a spell, κηληθμῷ, enraptured. Their reaction to the earlier break in the narration is the same (11.333–4). At that pause, Alcinous breaks the silence with the lines I have already quoted which liken Odysseus to a knowing poet (11.367–8). This reaction to Odysseus' tale-telling is seen also in Ithaca. Eumaeus describes the stranger to Penelope in the following way (17.514, 518–21):

---

[113] Schadewaldt (1965) 85 notes that in this universal knowledge the Sirens function as 'dämonische Gegenbilder der Musen'. See also Pucci (1979) 126–7.

> Such things he tells, he would enchant [*thelgein*] your very heart . . .

> As when a man looks at a bard, who has learnt from
> the god to sing words pleasing to mortals;
> and they violently desire to hear him, when he sings.
> So that man sitting in the hall kept enchanting [*thelgein*] me.

The repetition of *thelgein*, 'to enchant', draws together Odysseus'
power of language not only with the poet's power to enrapture and
enthral but also with the dangerous spells and bewitchings which have
threatened his *nostos*. His *muthos* makes him seem like a man who knows
– again, the connection of the poet with the voice of truth. Odysseus'
lying tales are also spoken like the bard's authoritative narrative.

So, as Odysseus starts to string his bow – as he is about to adopt his
true identity before the suitors – the hero is again likened to a poet, but
this time it is not by one of the listeners to his tale-telling (21.405–9):

> But Odysseus of the many wiles
> Once he had taken up the great bow and looked it all over,
> as when a man who knows the lyre and the song,
> easily stretches the string on a new peg,
> holding the well-turned sheep-gut from both sides,
> so, without ado, Odysseus strung the great bow.

The poet who has had Odysseus tell his tales like a poet, now has the hero
prepare his bow for battle . . . like a poet string a lyre. Using this bow to
rid his home of the suitors will be like playing a (heroic) song. The lyre
and the poet, lauded so often as accompaniments to the feast, are ironically likened to the bow and its user who are to destroy the present
(corrupt) feasting of the suitors. Odysseus is again likened to a singer
who knows – ἐπιστάμενος – and the point of the comparison is strength-
ened by his close inspection of the bow, by which he is to make himself
known to the suitors. As Odysseus prepares to complete the act which
will gain him the *kleos* of a revenge successfully obtained (the justice
announced in the opening debate of the gods), he is likened to the figure
who may construct and preserve such *kleos*, the singer. The hero is not
merely the subject of the poet's song, but likened by the poet to the poet
himself.[114]

The way in which Odysseus and the figure of the poet are drawn
together can be seen in a different way in two further similes. When

---

[114] A commonly made assertion; see e.g. Moulton (1977) 145–53; Walsh (1984) 19–21; and
the works quoted in n. 115.

Nausicaa comes to the beach to wash clothes and play ball, she is likened to Artemis in a lengthy simile (6.102–9). When Odysseus wakes and approaches the young girl, his first words of supplication are (6.149–152):

> I supplicate you, mistress. Are you divine or mortal?
> If you are a divinity, who holds broad heaven,
> I liken you most closely to Artemis, daughter
> of great Zeus, in beauty, figure and stature.

The interplay between the voice of Odysseus and the framing voice of the poet is again complex. Moulton comments 'The echo is lightly ironic in a sophisticated way: Odysseus apparently so wild and desperate, possesses the resilience and tact to describe Nausicaa to her face exactly as she is independently described by the singer. It is not for nothing that Alkinous and Eumaeus call him ἀοιδός ('bard').[115] Odysseus' 'tact' is also the poet's 'description'. Does the juxtaposition authorize Odysseus' 'tact' as the voice of truth? Or does it mark a difference in signification when the same words occur in Odysseus' speech and in the framing narrative? Does such an ironic and sophisticated echo bear testimony to a self-consciousness and manipulation of the poetic voice by the poet? Are we to recognize self-recognition here?

The conjunction of hero and poet affects both figures. It marks the hero not merely as a man of action but also as a man of words. Or rather it constructs words as a particular sphere of action in which Odysseus excels. The various elements of the self-awareness of language and of Odysseus' manipulation of the medium come together in the description of the hero as 'like a poet'. So, especially but not solely in Alcinous' palace, Odysseus is both the gainer and commemorator of glory – even the gainer of glory through the act of commemoration. Although the figure of the poet is associated with the voice of truth and knowledge, that is, with the power to describe, preserve and make pleasurable the truth of things (the authoritative narrative), he is also associated through the similes likening Odysseus to a bard with the power of language to deceive, to create a narrative which is like the truth (but a falsehood). 'Homer does not explicitly suggest that singers may therefore sometimes deceive their audiences', writes Walsh cautiously, 'but he has certainly made the inference inevitable for the later tradition.'[116] Throughout the *Odyssey*, we see different models of the functioning of songs both in their affect on listeners and in their relation to truthful (self-)representation.

---

[115] Moulton (1977) 121.   [116] Walsh (1984) 20.

In numerous *muthoi* we see selective and partial as well as feigned versions of events. We see a claim of absolute knowledge that threatens destruction to the listener. There is an ambiguousness in the 'enchantment' that words can have over a listener. In the narrative of the *Odyssey*, the fictive is always part of the voice of truth.

What I hope to have shown in this chapter is the *Odyssey*'s fundamental interest in the relations between man and language – language as the medium of recognition and representation in social exchange. In particular, the multiplicity of Odysseus' self-representations – from naming to the tales he weaves of himself and his guises – demonstrate the fictive power of the word: how language may conceal, reveal, manipulate, but is always telling. This interest in the mastery of words is also seen in the repeated self-descriptions and (self-reflexive) discussions of the bard's voice of authority – the voice that tells it how it is (*kata kosmon, kata moiran*). Yet the depiction of the deceptive hero as 'enchanting like a bard' also seems to point to a more complex (self-)awareness of the seduction and fictiveness of *muthoi*. Above all, I hope to have demonstrated how a discussion of the representation of the poet and his role cannot be adequately isolated from such questions of tale-telling, of naming, of the bard's *muthoi* in relation to other *muthoi*. As we will see in different ways in the following chapters, to analyse the poet's voice is necessarily to become involved in the whole range of questions of what it means to use language in society.

2 Intimations of immortality: fame and tradition from Homer to Pindar

Fame, Fame, Fame, Fame

D. Bowie

In ancient Greek culture of all periods,[1] the notion of *kleos* is linked in a fundamental way to the poet's voice, and no adequate discussion of the poet's voice could ignore this topic. I will translate *kleos* by 'fame', 'glory' or 'renown', but some further glossing of this complex term is immediately necessary. *Kleos* is etymologically and semantically related to the verb *kluo* 'I hear' – *kleos* is 'that which is heard', 'a report', even 'rumour'. So Telemachus, when he returns to Ithaca, asks Eumaeus for the *kleos* from town (16.461).[2] *Kleos* is applied to what people talk (of), and an object like Nestor's shield has a '*kleos* which reaches heaven' (*Il.* 8.192), and heroes' armour is often described as *kluta*, 'with *kleos*', 'talked of'. 'Things, places and persons acquire *kleos* as they acquire an identity in the human world, as stories are told about them.'[3] A good example of this sense of *kleos* in the context of (the representation of) poetic performance – an example which also shows how the connotations of the term move inevitably towards an idea of 'glory', 'reputation' – can be seen in the invocation of the Muses before the catalogue of the ships in the *Iliad* (*Il.* 2.485–6):

> ὑμεῖς γὰρ θεαί ἐστε, πάρεστέ τε, ἴστε τε πάντα,
> ἡμεῖς δὲ κλέος οἶον ἀκούομεν οὐδέ τι ἴδμεν ...

---

[1] 'Heroic glory' is also an important topic in the Indo-European tradition. See in particular Schmitt (1967) 61–102; Nagy (1974) 231–55.

[2] Edwards (1985) 71 n. 2 argues that (86) 'even where the sense of "rumor/report" seems dominate [sic] for κλέος, the meaning "fame/renown" is as a rule also present'. If indeed *kleos* always refers to a narrative (to be repeated), then it will be hard to distinguish the two senses with any rigour. Pucci (1980) and Pucci (1988) – stimulating articles – see the distinction between the two senses as a crucial problem of Homeric poetics – the attempt to keep separate '*kleos* (rumour – ignorance) and *kleos* (voice – mnēme)' (1980) 186. It is not clear to me, however, that *kleos* is absolutely 'a source of ignorance' or that, in Homer, *kleos* ever means something *false*, as is required for Pucci's arguments to hold.

[3] Redfield (1975) 32.

69

> For you are goddesses; you are present and know everything.
> But we only hear the *kleos* and know nothing . . .

The assumption, common throughout early Greek writing, that presence is a prerequisite of accurate knowledge, constitutes the poet as the *instrument* of the Muses, whose message is heard (ἀκούομεν) and passed on through the poem. Yet what is passed on is the stories of the great achievements of mortals, striving to perpetuate their name through their deeds. '"That which is heard", *kleos*, comes to mean "glory" because it is the poet himself who uses the word to designate what he hears from the Muses and what he tells the audience. Poetry confers glory.'[4] *Kleos*, then, is that which is sung in two, overlapping senses, both the words to be heard (from the Muses/poet) and the fame or glory that such a song confers on the subjects of the song.

Kleos is that for which the heroes of the *Iliad* and *Odyssey* fight. Both Hector and Achilles, as we will see, in different ways express their motivation in part at least by an appeal to *kleos*. So, too, in the *Odyssey*, when the ghosts of the defeated suitors enter the Underworld, it devolves on Agamemnon to deliver a speech extolling the *kleos* of the victory. *Kleos*, however – and not merely in military contexts – necessarily implies a form of glory that is won by others' defeat and loss of position. *Kleos* may be 'a measure of one's value to others and oneself',[5] and even 'a specific type of social identity',[6] but it is important that it is a measure, an identity, formed by *competitive* action in a *hierarchical* society.[7] So, when Hector challenges a Greek champion to a duel, he concludes (*Il.* 7.84–91) that he will kill that man and let the Greeks raise for him a tomb (*sēma*) which will be a sign for future generations, who will say that Hector killed him as he sought to excel (*aristeuonta*). And these comments of future generations will preserve Hector's *kleos* (*Il.* 7.91):

> So someone in the future will say. And my *kleos* will never perish.

Hector's *kleos* as victor – the proclamation of which significantly concludes his speech of challenge – depends on his triumph, on its visible sign in the *sēma* of his dead opponent, and on the recognition offered by

---

[4] Nagy (1979) 16.
[5] Segal (1983) 22.
[6] Redfield (1975) 34.
[7] Redfield's formulation (1975) 33–4 '*kudos* and *kleos* . . . are more nearly free goods, and the total amount of each within the social system will vary from time to time' is too vague with regard to the *competitive* nature of *kleos*.

(nameless) others in the future. And Hector announces it as his aim and promise.[8]

Yet mortality provides a necessary limit to such competitive striving for fame, and the preservation of *kleos* requires a memorial at the end. As well as the *kleos* of notable achievement, there is also 'a *kleos* associated with death',[9] and 'specially associated with the gravestone'[10] as such a final memorial. So, a noble death in battle, where a tomb is raised by one's *philoi*, is opposed to Odysseus' present obscurity by Telemachus (1.237–41; 14.367–71; cf. 5.306–12); and in the *Iliad* the possibility of *kleos* for the victim of war is brought to the fore by the cases of Hector and Achilles. Not only does the great *kleos* of the victim redound to the great *kleos* of the victor, but also the performance of funeral rites and the establishment of a *sēma* – as opposed to desecration of a corpse by animals or humans – provides the visible memorial of the dead figure, a memorial significantly described in Homer's language as 'for future generations to enquire about' (ἐσσομένοισι πύθεσθαι e.g. *Od.* 11.76). Both the *Iliad* and the *Odyssey*, as we will see, develop the concerns of *kleos* through an investigation of the relations between a striving for *kleos* through competitive achievement and the establishment of *kleos* in death.

Kleos, then, is a fundamental element of the intricate competitive value system presented in the Homeric poems, a fundamental aim of both military and other action, a fundamental function of the poetic enterprise. *Kleos* is the perpetuation of the name in and through the social exchange of poetry; it is the name of that exchange – and in Homer *kleos* is to be gained *in exchange* for the stake of the hero's life and suffering. This chapter will end with a discussion of Pindar, a fifth-century writer whose *epinikia*, poems to honour victors in the games, mark the extension of the tradition of poetic immortalization. Pindar's lyrics also take an individual man in the moment of success, a success achieved at the expense of others, his defeated competitors, in order to perpetuate the moment as and in *kleos*. For Pindar, *kleos* is the aim of the toil of athletic activity, and it is his poetry which forms and preserves that fame. It might be tempting, then, to see the construction and perpetuation of *kleos* as a constant function of the poet's voice through the range of different periods and writers I am discussing, and there is little doubt that in the extremely

---

[8] King (1987), following Scholes and Kellogg (1966) 210, notes the irony that the tomb at the end of the *Iliad* will be Hector's own

[9] Edwards (1985) 73. See in particular the discussions of Loraux (1982); Vernant (1982); Schnapp-Gourbeillon (1982).

[10] Redfield (1975) 34.

general model offered so far there are certain common denominators that recur in many of the texts considered in this chapter: 'the Hellenic poet is the master of *kleos* '.[11] But any proposed continuity of competitive values in ancient Greek culture also conceals a history of differences, and the paradigm of the poet conferring *kleos* through his poetry on heroic action must be analysed in more detail. That is the aim of this chapter. In each of the works under scrutiny, the specific configurations and deformations of the search for and construction of *kleos* will be investigated in as much depth as space permits, in order to trace some of the differences within the tradition. I shall begin with a discussion of the *Iliad* and the *Odyssey*, where the terms to be transformed through the tradition are articulated in a privileged way (and where the topic of *kleos* has been investigated by recent critics with considerable sophistication[12]). In my second section, I shall be looking briefly at various developments of *kleos* particularly in lyric poetry through the sixth and fifth centuries, and finally I shall be looking at Pindar.

CRITICAL EXCHANGES

Trailing clouds of glory ...   Wordsworth

The *Iliad* is a poem much concerned with the limits and transgressions of power. The epic not only explores the possibilities of human success and destruction in the context of a war (involving humans and divinities) caused by an act of adultery and seizure, but also focuses for its motivation on a conflict in the Achaean collectivity between 'the best' and 'the most kingly' of the Achaeans. The title ἄριστος ᾽Αχαίων, 'best of the Achaeans', is claimed for himself by Achilles, but it is also the case that Achilles is the warrior in the *Iliad* with the greatest military *aretē*, whose *aristeia* is the last, longest and most climactic in the narrative: as Nagy has argued, 'it is overall an Iliadic theme, that Achilles is "the best of the Achaeans"', and deserves that title as a title.[13] Agamemnon calls himself βασιλεύτατος, 'most kingly', as Achilles calls himself 'best', and despite

---

[11] Nagy (1979) 16.
[12] See e.g. Marg (1957); Maehler (1963) 10–14; Detienne (1967) 61–102; Schmitt (1967) 61–102; Nagy (1974); 231–61; Nagy (1979) *passim*; Redfield (1975) 1–41; Pucci (1980); Floyd (1980); Griffin (1980) 95–102; Nagy (1981); Vernant (1982); Loraux (1982); Schnapp-Gourbeillon (1982); Segal (1983); Edwards (1985) 71–93; Frontisi-Ducroux (1986); Edwards (1987) 149–58; King (1987) 28–47 and now Lynn-George (1988). Also scattered comments in Schein (1984) 17, 68, 71, 178; Thalmann (1984) index *sub kleos*.
[13] Nagy (1979) *passim*. The citation is from page 26. See also Edwards (1984).

the influence and authority of other rulers over their own contingents and the army overall, Agamemnon remains a figure of supreme authority.[14] The conflict between Agamemnon and Achilles sets in tension claims of status based on position and on achievement; and the specific cause of the quarrel is Agamemnon's decision from his position of power to take from Achilles the mark of his status, namely the *timē*, 'honour', that his captured concubine Briseis represents. Indeed, throughout the epic, from the interplay of the gods to the beating of Thersites, from Diomedes' assaults on Aphrodite and Ares to Hector's upbraiding of Paris, power, its exercise, misuse and effect in social and military exchange, remains a thematic focus of *Iliad*.

In the course of the narrative, the limits of Agamemnon's authority and the extremes of Achilles' commitment are explored in particular depth. This investigation is developed with exemplary force and complexity in the repeated scenes of supplication in *Iliad*.[15] Supplication is a social ritual which articulates the boundaries of power. A suppliant by the act of supplication acknowledges the power of the supplicated figure and attempts from a position of weakness to prevent the figure of power from using his power or to direct it in a particular way. On the battlefield, supplication is a matter of life and death where the defeated attempts to control the absolute power of the victor to kill. As well as the physical performance of the ritual,[16] where contact opens the possibility of contract, supplication may proceed by an appeal to the values of pity and reverence (*aidōs*);[17] by an offer of ransom money – exchange of goods for life; by an appeal to the higher power of the gods as protectors of social values.[18] Supplication is an appeal for limitations to the use of power, for a relation of exchange to bound the relation of dominance.

[14] For bibliography and discussion of the figure of Agamemnon, see Taplin (1990) and now also Collins (1988) 69–103. For a catalogue of terms of power in the *Iliad* and bibliography, see Descat (1979).

[15] Supplication has been the subject of much recent discussion. Gould (1973) remains a crucial study; Griffin (1980) 24–6, 54–6; Macleod (1982) 16–35; Pedrick (1982); Thornton (1984); Mueller (1984) 28–76. A particularly important critique of Gould is to be found in Lynn-George (1983) to which I am indebted.

[16] For descriptions of the varying physical actions of supplication, see Gould (1973) 74–8. Lynn-George (1983) discusses both the assumptions behind such an 'ethnographic' treatment and the fact that the traits outlined by Gould never appear all together in any one supplication. Lynn-George (1988) 200–9 comments well on the too rigid distinction enforced by critics between verbal and physical supplication.

[17] On the link between *aidōs* and supplication, see Gould (1973) 85ff, following the seminal analysis of Benveniste (1969) I 92–101, 335–53; II 245–54. Also Claus (1975).

[18] For a fascinating discussion of this sort of plea, see Serres (1979).

Like all such cultural rituals to control power, the claims of the weaker
(or the stronger) for the authority of the institution need to be set against
the manipulations and trangressions of practice. By 'manipulation and
transgression' I do not mean simply an example such as the Cyclops'
rejection of any such rules or divine authority for them (*Od.* 9.269–80).
Rather, the practice of the institution reveals its complexity in exchanges
such as Diomedes' and Odysseus' killing of Dolon, just as he is about to
make the physical and verbal contact of supplication, after they have led
him into providing the information they require.[19] In such a case, the
man in power frustrates (the contract of) the institution not by rejection
but by avoidance. Power manipulates the boundaries of the institution
whose function and fiction it is to impose boundaries on power. It is
because of the dynamics of power *in* the performance of the ritual that
one cannot hope simply to draw up a fixed pattern of rules for 'proper',
'full' supplication (as Gould, for example, attempts with his distinction
between (full) 'supplication' and (mere) 'figurative supplication').[20] For
the definition – the acceptance and utilization of (the boundaries of)
supplication – is a *part* of the power relation that it delimits. The interplay
between the claims of the institution and the acceptance of the institution
by the figure of power constitutes supplication as an uneasy instantiation
of the control and contestation of power.

Supplication, then, is an exchange that inherently involves the limits
and transgressions of power, and repeated scenes of supplication structure the narrative of the *Iliad*, as many recent critics have emphasized.
The structure of scenes of supplication has been extensively analysed,
but what is less often commented on is that the only two figures to
recognize and then reject a supplication are Achilles and Agamemnon.
There are five scenes of supplication in battle. In the first two incidents,
Agamemnon refuses to let his brother send a prisoner to the ships to be
ransomed although his supplication appears to have been accepted by

[19] *Il.* 10.454ff. Gould (1973) 81 rightly notes that Dolon's supplication is never completed.
Griffin (1980) 54, less carefully, treats it merely as an example in his catalogue of slain
suppliants (although he does call it 'the most deceitful of these scenes' of supplication).
[20] Gould here follows Kopperschmidt. Gould recognizes that 'the rules of the game ...
can be played to, or by' (81), but when he argues (77) that 'the distinction between
"complete" and "figurative" supplication is crucial if we are to understand the response
of the person supplicated', he places the *recognition* of supplication and its obligations
outside the manipulative power-play of the institution. See Lynn-George (1983) 36–
113.

Menelaus;[21] he then rejects a pair of suppliants – brothers – whose limbs he lops off.[22] When Achilles returns to the battle, he rejects suppliants three times culminating in the slaughter of Lycaon. This acts as a prelude to his outrageous treatment of Hector's corpse. The 'most kingly' and the 'best' of the Achaeans are placed by their very positions at the limits of power relations, and both Agamemnon's behaviour as a leader of men and Achilles' behaviour as a heroic warrior pose difficulties about the limits of acceptability. It is not by chance, then, that it should be these two warriors in battle who are seen to reject a role in the institution which depends on the articulation of limits of acceptability precisely with regard to the exercise of power and dominance. The fact that it is only Agamemnon and Achilles who reject suppliants in battle raises a question about the similarities and differences of these two warriors and their commitment to and use of power.[23]

The opposition of Agamemnon and Achilles, then, is used to explore in different ways the role of (supreme) power,[24] and the utilization of power, as we will see, proves a crucial element in the *Iliad*'s depiction of a hero's commitment to *kleos*. Achilles, however, after the death of Patroclus, turns his wrath against Hector, and the opposition of Hector and Achilles is also fundamental to the thematic structure of the epic. For Hector, although he occupies a similarly crucial role in the Trojan war effort, is depicted in a quite different way from Achilles. In particular, as Redfield has discussed at length in his already classic study, Hector is represented in a full range of social relations within Troy.[25] In the famous scenes of book 6, Hector is depicted in exchanges with the women of the city, with his mother and sister, Laodice, with his sister-in-law, Helen, and brother, Paris, and with his wife, Andromache, and son,

---

[21] *Il.* 6.45ff. Gould (1973) 80 calls this 'the most direct affront to the rite of supplication'. I have discussed it in Goldhill (1990).

[22] Peisandrus and Hippolochus, *Il.* 11.130ff. The ferocity of this scene is often commented on, e.g. Griffin (1980) 53–4; King (1987) 14ff; Mueller (1984) 84; Schadewaldt (1938) 50; Fenik (1968) 85; Edwards (1987) 200–1.

[23] Griffin (1980) 53–6 is typical when he treats rejection of supplication in battle as a norm, as if it makes no difference that it is Achilles and Agamemnon alone who behave in such a way, and as if a different reaction to the dictates of social exchange in battle was not expressed by a scene like that of Glaucus and Sarpedon in Book 6 (on which see below).

[24] See e.g. Redfield (1975) 13–17, 92ff; Nagy (1979) index *sub* Agamemnon; Donlan (1979); King (1987) 14ff; Edwards (1987) 164–6; Taplin (1990). See also Collins (1988) 69–103.

[25] Redfield (1975).

before returning to war. Hector is fighting to preserve this life of Troy in which he is depicted. Hector does not merely open a view of 'a rich, functioning society of the Homeric world'[26] that would otherwise be lacking in this military poem; rather, 'it is Hector's story that gives Achilles' story meaning: Hector affirms all that Achilles denies'.[27] Achilles can only carry into battle on his shield a representation of a social world he cannot take part in.[28] Hector fights under a series of ties and obligations that contrast significantly with Achilles' commitment. Both great warriors are committed to *kleos*, but their opposition dramatizes the different potential allegiances involved in such an ethic.

This brief and general sketch of the oppositions between Achilles and Hector and Agamemnon develops a framework which is crucial to the discussion of *kleos* in the *Iliad*. For although the model of noble action leading to *kleos* to be preserved in song is seen time and again in the *Iliad*, Achilles, Hector and Agamemnon demonstrate through their varying allegiances and through their varying involvements in power the potential for difference and conflict within such a model – a potential which leads to the specific complexity, even tragedy, of the *Iliad*'s view of human endeavour.

It is the commitment of Achilles to the logic of *kleos* that I wish to investigate further here. Now Achilles is in a privileged position with regard to his fate. He has a specific choice. The terms of his decision oppose a long life without distinction and a short life with immortal *kleos*.[29] Achilles poses in the starkest terms the logic of 'loss' and 'recompense' that informs the pursuit of *kleos*: life for song.[30] Achilles' withdrawal and then return to battle invest the *Iliad*'s narrative with a pattern of deferral and reaffirmation of this choice in such a way as to open the basis of his choice to differing understandings, to question the wagers of mortality. Achilles' death, the fulfilment of his decision, is

---

[26] Redfield (1975) 28.

[27] Ib.

[28] On Achilles' shield, see for discussion and bibliography Taplin (1980), to which may be added Schein (1984) 140–2; and in particular DuBois (1982).

[29] For discussion and recent bibliography on Achilles' choice, see Schein (1980) 91–6 and in particular Schadewaldt (1965) 234–67.

[30] I purloin the terms 'loss' and 'recompense' from Michael Lynn-George's brilliant and extensive study of the *Iliad*, which appeared after this chapter was substantially completed. I have been able only to add some references and to raid some quotations where his more detailed and complex argument bears on mine. In particular, his arguments linking the ideas of *kleos* to the construction of identity in language bridge the concerns of my first two chapters.

constantly projected but never finally narrated – there remains anticipation at the heart of the construction of *kleos*: 'the work of immortal glory was already accomplished and is never yet fully completed'.[31]

That Achilles chooses to pursue *kleos* at such an expense needs first to be explored with regard to the ideals articulated by the other heroes in the *Iliad*. That a hero risks his life in the pursuit of *kleos* on the battlefield is evident; that many heroes die young is a recurring element of the pathos of the *Iliad*; that the pursuit of *kleos* is seen within a wider reflection on mortality has been the subject of much recent criticism.[32] Two speeches have been analysed in particular detail. The first of these is Glaucus' response to Diomedes (*Il.* 6.145–51):[33]

> Great-hearted Diomedes, why do you ask my ancestry?
> Like the generation of leaves, so too is men's.
> The wind pours some leaves on the ground, the flourishing wood
> puts forth others and the season of spring follows.
> So one generation of men grows and another ceases.
> If you want, learn this too so that you may know well
> my ancestry; many men know it.

Glaucus asks why Diomedes demands his ancestry (γενεή),[34] but goes on to give an extensive account (152–211) of his forebears. It is the famous lines that link his opening question and his answer to Diomedes that give Glaucus' speech its importance in the present discussion. For the image of the endless repetition of nature's generation and destruction of leaves significantly introduces the narrative of genealogy. These lines do not merely express the common contrast between the cyclical pattern of the natural world and man's linear passage from birth to death, (though the simile draws on such a contrast to make its point). Yet there is also something more than Schein's assertion that 'Glaucus puts his emphasis as much on the stock that survives to put out new leaves as on the leaves that bloom and are poured on the ground like dead warriors'.[35] For Glaucus formulates a juxtaposition of the undifferentiated pattern of the

---

[31] Lynn-George (1988) 272.

[32] E.g. Marg (1976); Nagy (1979) 118ff; Griffin (1980); Schein (1984) *passim*; Edwards (1984) and especially Vernant (1979); Vernant (1982); Loraux (1982).

[33] Diomedes in general is set against Achilles, as a great warrior who does not achieve the excess of Achilles. See Anderson (1978); Rutherford (1982) 146 n. 9.

[34] The word translated 'ancestry' and 'generation' is the same (γενεή). On this translation problem, see Marg (1976) 18; Griffin (1980) 72. On Glaucus' speech, see also Gaisser (1969) (with bibliography) and Vernant (1982) 51ff; Letoublon (1983).

[35] Schein (1980) 70. Cf. Mueller (1978); Edwards (1987) 204–6.

leaves' coming to be and passing away with the narrative of his ancestors' search for success, which leads to Glaucus' own presence on the battle-field with the obligation to seek the glory of success that such an ancestry requires (*Il.* 6.207–10):

> He sent me to Troy and enjoined me greatly
> always to excel and be greater than others,
> and not to shame the race of my fathers, who became by far
> the best men in Ephyre and broad Lycia.

Humans' individual efforts 'to be the best'[36] (*aristeuein*) and their preservation in *kleos* – to record themselves in and as a narrative, a genealogy – are set against (the *lēthē* of) the continuity of the trees.[37] Apollo (*Il.* 21.463–6) echoes these lines when he refuses to fight Poseidon over mere mortals 'who like the leaves at one moment flourish, full of fire, eating the fruit of the earth, at another waste away lifeless'. Apollo from his immortal perspective expresses only similarity between the leaves' brief existence and men's coming to be and passing away. He does not even mention the regeneration of spring. For the immortal Apollo, men's inevitable mortality makes them not worth fighting about. For Glaucus men's mortality makes fighting for *kleos* a requirement that offers the possibility of something to set against a continuity of oblivion.

Mortality, then, is the condition, in all its senses, of man's search for *kleos*. After their exchange of words, however, Glaucus and Diomedes, because they discover their inherited tie of *xeinosunē*, do not swap blows, but exchange armour as a sign of the ties and obligations of guest-friendship. The search for *kleos* through military victory is subordinated to the maintenance of social exchange, the gift substituted for violence. This scene and its values will be echoed particularly in Achilles' later battlefield encounters.

A second speech offers further insight into a link between mortality and *kleos*, namely, Sarpedon's speech to Glaucus (*Il.* 12.310–28), and it has also been extensively discussed by critics.[38] Sarpedon's speech contains a double movement. On the one hand, Sarpedon seems to praise 'the warrior's role: in it, a man becomes godlike'.[39] Sarpedon's need to fight

---

[36] This line is repeated in the report of Peleus' advice to Achilles (*Il.* 11. 784), which further draws together and contrasts Achilles' reaction to the need to best and Glaucus' and Diomedes' reactions. See Letoublon (1983).

[37] Cf. *Il.* 20.200ff with Pucci's analysis (1980) 173–5.

[38] In particular, Pucci (1988); Redfield (1975) 99–102. Also Mueller (1978); Griffin (1980) 72–3; Schein (1980) 70–2; Vernant (1982) 51ff.

[39] Redfield (1975) 101.

is linked to the honour with which he is treated (310–14), but also to the expectations of his people (318–21). Sarpedon is fighting to 'substantiate or validate the truth of his royal portrait by giving evidence through his action'.[40] The recognition of the Lycians depends on his enactment of the expectations of his role in the front line of the battle. On the other hand, Sarpedon continues (322–8):

> My friend! If we could but escape this war
> and if we could be fated to live ageless, immortal,
> for ever, I would not fight in the front rank myself,
> nor would I send you to the fight for glory.
> But as things are – for still the countless ends of death
> wait upon us, which a mortal cannot escape or avoid –
> let us go; either we will give the boast to someone, or someone to us.

If immortality were a possibility, then Sarpedon would not fight in the fore. But as death in one of its many guises is a necessity, then on to battle and the chance of *eukhos* – the boast that comes of victory. Sarpedon may be treated like a god in the honour he receives in his society, but he must risk and finally lose his life like a man. 'For Sarpedon, all the difference lies in the transition from "as if" to the impossible condition "if", a passage which marks the break between a sense of immortality ("as if we were immortals") and the reality of mortality.'[41] For Sarpedon, too, the condition of mortality informs heroic endeavour.

The force of Sarpedon' speech comes from this double movement and the recognitions it gives rise to. The system of competitive honour, which forms the hero's social status, leads him to risk his life, in the hope and expectation also of a memorial beyond death. Yet there is the constant regret of mortality, the recognition that 'it is the pressure of mortality which imposes on men the compulsion to have virtues'.[42] This is not merely *'noblesse oblige'*[43] or 'death for glory', but a commitment marked at the same time with risk and even fear. It is these tensions in the hero's action and motivation which the figure of Achilles brings into sharpest focus. For Achilles' decision not to return home to Phthia but to die young in battle in return for an 'immortal *kleos*' is not so much a contradiction of these other heroes' commitment to *kleos*, as an extreme

---

[40] Pucci (1988) 140.
[41] Lynn-George (1988) 156.
[42] Griffin (1980) 93.
[43] Griffin (1980) 73. For a more sensitive view of the problematic position of the hero in *Iliad*, see Redfield (1975); Vernant (1982); and in particular Lynn-George (1983), (1988).

version of it. Other heroes risk their lives in the search and hope for *kleos*; Achilles willingly proceeds to a certain early death for a surety of immortal *kleos*. If Glaucus' and particularly Sarpedon's speech develops an awareness of the terms and tensions in which heroic action is conceived, Achilles' choice expresses in the starkest formulation the limit case of that logic.[44]

Achilles' return to battle, however, although it is marked in many ways as a gesture that will fulfil the terms of his choice,[45] is also motivated by his *mēnis*, the 'wrath', which the first word of the epic sets up as its problem and focus. If Achilles' choice dramatizes in an extreme form the logic of a commitment to *kleos*, it is Achilles' *mēnis* that qualifies in a crucial way the nature of that commitment. For it is Achilles' particular involvement in the ethos of competitive honour that brings the tensions and paradoxes of such an ethos to a head.

The tensions set in motion by Achilles' particular commitment are demonstrated most clearly in one of the most complex and discussed scenes in Greek epic, namely, the great embassy scene of book 9.[46] It would take many pages to attempt an adequate analysis of this encounter, but there are two points that are especially important for the argument of this chapter. The first is to mark immediately that the episode dramatizes a clash of values, that is, a conflict *within* a value system. There are many detailed aspects of conflict in the three speeches of the members of the embassy and Achilles' different replies, and these elements of conflict in the scene have led to one of the most intense critical debates in Greek epic. I intend to concentrate here only on the differing appeals to, and rejections of, *philotēs* in this encounter,[47] and how such concerns relate to Achilles' commitment to *kleos*. For it is in this area that

---

[44] 'Si Achille semble pousser jusqu' à ces dernières conséquences – jusqu' à l'absurde – la logique d' honneur c'est qu' il se situe en quelque façon au-delà des règles ordinaires de ce jeu' (Vernant (1982) 46). The transgression of the 'rules of the game' will form the basis of the following discussion.

[45] Both Thetis (e.g. *Il.* 18.95–6) and Achilles' divine horses (*Il.* 19.404–25) remind him of the significance of his return to battle. See Wilson (1974).

[46] The literature on this topic is immense. See in particular Eichholz (1953) 137–48; Parry (1956); Whitman (1958) 181–200; Lohmann (1970) 213–82; Lloyd-Jones (1971) 8–24; Reeve (1973); Claus (1975); Friedrich and Redfield (1978); Schein (1980) 104–16; Adkins (1982) 302–12; Lynn-George (1983) especially 127ff; Mueller (1984) 44–9.

[47] Schein (1984) 99–120 discusses *philotēs* from this aspect. On Achilles and Patroclus as *philoi*, see Sinos (1980). Hooker (1987) in the most recent lexical discussion of *philos* in Homer, like many before him, fails to take account of the rhetorical manipulation and contestation of the term in the texts.

the crucial question of obligation and allegiance is posed with most insistence and manipulated with the most rhetorical force.

The embassy is greeted by Achilles as φίλτατοι ἄνδρες (*Il.* 9.204), 'most *philoi* men', 'nearest and dearest companions in arms'. They share food and wine, the norm of social reciprocity between *philoi*, and then Odysseus begins the task of persuasion. He outlines the Argive sufferings – which is what Achilles through Thetis begged Zeus to bring about, in order that the Greeks might feel the need of him the more: Achilles' wrath is *oulomenēn* (*Il.* 1.2), 'destructive', for both Greek and Trojan forces. Odysseus begs Achilles to return now rather than later: later, even help will be an *akhos*, 'grief', rather than a *kleos* for him, since no cure can be found for the evil that has already burst forth. This leads Odysseus to recall Achilles' father's advice to his son, an admonishment to restrain his proud and violent nature (254–6):

> My child, Athene and Hera will grant you
> strength, if they wish; but you must restrain in your heart
> your great-spirited temper. For friendliness is better.

Philophrosunē, which I have translated 'friendliness', is a rare word in Greek of all periods and occurs in Homer only here.[48] It indicates a general disposition towards *philotēs*, the normative relation between *philoi*. The recollection of Peleus' advice is placed between the description of the Argive suffering and the (carefully edited) description of Agamemnon's offer of gifts. It acts as a bridge between the two aspects of Odysseus' rhetorical exegesis, constructing Achilles' attitude and the need to change it as the crucial element of the embassy's request. So Odysseus concludes with an appeal for Achilles to pity all the Greeks even if Agamemnon is all the more hated (300–3). *Philophrosunē* means here to ignore his personal relation of hatred for Agamemnon on behalf of the desperate Greeks, his *philoi*.

Achilles' response is one of the most dramatic and forceful speeches in Greek literature. He rejects Odysseus' speech and Agamemnon's offer in the most violent language; and he turns in a series of aggressive statements and rhetorical questions[49] to interrogate the need to fight. Agamemnon's appropriation of his *timē* challenges the logic of martial achievement

---

[48] It is particularly rare in poetry. It occurs once in Pindar *Ol.* 6.165 and otherwise in no other poet. It occurs in Herodotus (5.92.3) and in Plato (*Laws* 628c11; 640b8; 740e4) and with some regularity in Plutarch.

[49] Reeve's criticism (1973) 194 of Parry (1956) (who regards these questions as 'unanswerable') is rightly questioned (on this score at least) by Schein (1984) 108 and (1980) 129.

within the collective enterprise of the Achaeans, and significantly it is
here that Achilles talks of his choice of fates most explicitly, as he raises
the possibility of rejecting the search for *kleos* and returning to Phthia.
Yet he also manipulates the language of *philotēs* in this sustained outburst
(337–43):

> Why must the Argives war with the Trojans?
> Why did Agamemnon collect the people and lead them here?
> Was it not for the sake of beautiful-haired Helen?
> Or do the Atreids alone of speech-endowed humans
> care for [*phileousi*] their wives? For whoever is a good and sensible man
> cares for [*phileei*] and cherishes his woman, as I too
> cared for [*phileon*] her from my heart, although she was a spear-prize.

The answer to Odysseus' use of the appeal to *philophrosunē* is to turn
the language of *philotēs* against its user. His rhetorical questions set
Agamemnon's snatching of Briseis parallel to the rape of Helen, the very
cause of the war, as an outrage against *philotēs*. The ties and duties
assumed by Odysseus are signs of transgression for Achilles. The obligations of reciprocity and the reciprocity of obligation are broken for
Achilles by Agamemnon's misuse of authority and power.

The reaction to Achilles' lengthy tirade on the failure of exchange and
his unwillingness to accept the offer of recompense is silence.[50] The
aporia is crossed finally by Phoenix.[51] His is a speech from a position of
close association as Achilles' tutor. He, too, adopts and manipulates the
obligations of *philotēs* in his arguments. He calls Achilles φίλον τέκος,
'dear child' (437, 444), and *philos*, 'dear' (601), and he tells two stories that
revolve around the claims of *philotēs*. After Odysseus' appeal through
Achilles' father, Phoenix from Phthia calls him 'child' as he offers him
advice (and will be called 'papa', ἄττα, in return 9.607).[52] The first tale,
the story of Phoenix's own early life, which establishes his link with
Achilles, finds its motivation in a quarrel between Phoenix and his father
over a concubine.[53] The father's relation with the girl (*phileeske* (450))

---

[50] On the importance of silence in this exchange, silence as a bar and requirement of
exchange, see Lynn-George (1988) 50–152.

[51] Phoenix has often been regarded as an interpolation: see e.g. Page (1959) 287–315.
Contra Motzkus (1964) 84–115 (with bibliography). See also Reinhardt (1961) 212–42;
Willcock (1964); Rosner (1976); Schein (1984) 110–13; Scodel (1982); Thornton (1984)
108–10; Edwards (1987) 224–9; Lynn-George (1988) 135ff.

[52] 'The decisive process in Phoenix's discourse will be the transformation of that central
term "father"' (Lynn-George (1988) 136).

[53] On the parallels between Phoenix's story and Achilles' position, see in particular Rosner
(1976); Scodel (1982).

leads to his wife's hatred (ἐχθήρειε (452)), and she persuades Phoenix to sleep with the girl. Phoenix's resultant exile and curse leads him eventually to Phthia where Peleus' loving reception (μ' ἐφίλησ' ὥς εἴ τε πατὴρ ὃν παῖδα φιλήσῃ, 'who cared for me like a father cares for his own child' (481)) is returned by Phoenix's loving care of Achilles (ἐκ θυμοῦ φιλέων, 'caring for you from my heart' (486)). Phoenix's narrative formulates his story and specifically his intimate relation with Achilles in terms of the mutual ties and obligations of *philotēs*.

Phoenix's autobiographical tale is followed by the description of the divine Λῖται, 'the Supplications'[54] – figures whose appeals to Zeus result in the punishment of those who ignore pleas made to them. This leads to a specific injunction which draws together the strands of Phoenix's rhetoric (520–8):

> But as things are, he is giving much now, and has promised more for
> the future.
> He has chosen the best men from the Achaean army
> and sent them to supplicate you, the Argive men who are
> most dear to you yourself. Do not despise these men's words
> and journey. Before, your wrath caused no resentment.
> So we learnt of the famous deeds of men of old too, the heroes,
> whenever violent rage came upon one of them.
> They were approached with gifts and beseeched with words.

The men who have come in supplication are singled out as *philtatoi*, 'most dear', as well as 'best' – a claim of authority linked to a claim of obligation. It is the approach of such men that Achilles is rejecting, as well as the gifts of Agamemnon. Previously, Achilles' wrath caused no angry resentment, because it is a trait also told of the heroes of old; it is part of the κλέα ἀνδρῶν, 'the famous deeds of men'. Achilles' behaviour is to be judged by the criteria of what men have done for *kleos*. As the embassy first approaches, Achilles is described as singing the κλέα ἀνδρῶν, 'the famous deeds of men', to the listening Patroclus (189): in a scene which revolves around Achilles' commitment to competitive honour, he is discovered singing the achievements and renown of the heroes.[55] Not

---

[54] I translate Λῖται as 'Supplications' because the most common translation 'Prayers' may make it seem that the Λῖται are addressed primarily to the gods (as Thornton (1984) 114 n. 7 points out). It also links this passage to the regular use of the verb λίσσομαι in the various supplication scenes. On this description, see in particular Rosner (1976) 319–24 and Thornton (1984) 114–24 (with further bibliography); Aubriot (1984).

[55] 'Artifice littéraire, procédé "en abŷme", bien sûr!' (Vernant (1982) 55). This is well explored in Frontisi-Ducroux (1986). In a similar self-reflexive way, Helen is depicted weaving with a double cloth a tapestry which represents the events of the Trojan war. On this, see Bergren (1979); Snyder (1981); Jenkins (1985); Kennedy (1986).

only does Phoenix's remark here seek to place Achilles in the context of the heroic *kleos* he seeks – and Phoenix is about to turn to a lengthy tale of Meleager as a persuasive parallel – but also his recollection of the self-reflexive moment of composition stresses that the *kleos* at stake is (made up in and by) the *Iliad*.

Phoenix speaks in and for *philoi* (ἐν δ' ὑμῖν ἐρέω πάντεσσι φίλοισι, 'I speak before you, all *philoi*' (528)) and his exemplum is of a hero who should have yielded to his φίλτατοι ἑταῖροι, 'nearest and dearest companions' (585–6), but lost his offered gifts by turning too late to fulfil his obligations of protection.[56] Achilles, however, not only rejects this story – he claims to have no need of such *timē* (607) – but also once again turns the language of *philotēs* around (612–5):

> Do not confound your spirit with grieving and mourning,
> as a favour to the hero Agamemnon. You ought not to care for [*phileein*]
> that man, lest you become hated by me who cares for [*phileonti*] you.
> It is good for you, with me, to cherish whoever cherishes me.

Phoenix, if he claims a tie of *philotēs* with Achilles, ought, Achilles claims, to share his friends and enemies – the normal protocol of the reciprocal duties of *philotēs*. Phoenix should come over to Achilles, not come in supplication. Indeed, he asks Phoenix alone to stay with him, a mark and recognition of his tie (and a challenge to the collective *philotēs* assumed by the embassy?). Achilles turns the reciprocity assumed in the relation of *philotēs* to his own advantage to deflect the claim made upon him. As fifth-century writing discovers again and again, the logic of *philotēs* cannot subsume a conflict of interest.

Ajax speaks third and briefly. But to the point. He stresses Achilles' savage nature, which is evidenced by his failure to take account of 'the *philotēs* of his companions' (630). It is the norm of society to accept financial recompense even for a dead child – to control wrath at an outrage by an institution of exchange – and yet Achilles refuses massive offerings for a mere girl. Ajax appeals to the *aidōs* of the shared house; picking up Achilles' and Phoenix's terms, he appeals as Achilles' κήδιστοι and φίλτατοι, 'most cherished' and 'most dear' friends – again a claim based precisely on the mutual obligations of a social relationship. Achilles'

---

[56] On the Meleager story, see in particular Willcock (1964), especially 147–54 (bibliography 147 n. 4) who develops Kakridis (1949) 21–5, who shows how the tale is turned precisely to emphasize the *philotēs* of Meleager's companions – a 'scale of affection' leading up to *philoi hetairoi*. See also Braswell (1971) and for a good survey of earlier views Heubeck (1984) 128–36 (with bibliography).

response to this third speech is particularly telling. For he appears to agree with Ajax's argument (645–8):

> You seem to have said everything much as I would like.
> But my heart swells with anger when I remember
> those deeds . . .

Achilles seems to agree with Ajax's interpretation of things, while rejecting his conclusion because of the force of his anger. For Achilles, there is a (self-)recognition of the extremism of his position, but it is an extremism required by his wrath. Achilles recognizes the claim on his obligation by his *philoi*, but cannot act upon it.

The embassy scene, then, sets different obligations in conflict with one another. Achilles' commitment to his personal honour, his pursuit of his *kleos*, leads to the ignoring, even transgression, of values and duties highly important to the norms of human social exchange, particularly *philotēs*, with its sense of *aidōs* and mutual affiliation and obligation. In the *Iliad*'s depiction of Achilles, *kleos* cannot be pursued without coming into conflict with other claims. Indeed, Achilles pursues his commitment even after the recognition of the propriety and claim of Ajax's opposed position. (*Kleos* is the site of transgression.) Such commitment is motivated explicitly by Achilles' wrath. Achilles' wrath, then, as it fuels his pursuit of *kleos*, also leads him to the very limits of acceptability within the normative claims of social exchange.

This leads to my second brief point which follows on closely from the first. Achilles, by this living on the margins of acceptability, poses the question of the bounding of a commitment to individual achievement within a social system that depends on reciprocity, as well as competition. The best of the Achaeans, in his search to be best, becomes a problematic figure to incorporate. The search for *kleos* that is set as a norm for heroic endeavour becomes a problematic value under the distorting force of Achilles' wrath.

This is turn emphasizes that the value of the *Iliad*'s opening term, *mēnis*, remains a *question* to be explored through the text. To what degree is Achilles' *mēnis* that which makes possible his *kleos* or his single-minded pursuit of it? To what degree does this anger set Achilles apart from social norms, to what degree is *kleos transgressive*? Is *mēnis* inherent in Achilles as *aristos*, as a hero? Can *mēnis* indeed be made part of social norms, of heroic exchange? Or is it an emotion that overtakes this hero only on occasions, that irrupts into society as a disruptive force, that destroys the possibility of secure social exchange? Achilles' recognition that his wrath prevents him acting on his agreement with Ajax and the embassy's different attempts to reinscribe Achilles into the collective enterprise articulate differing responses to the problem of the hero's wrath. When Phoenix indicates that he found no fault previously with the anger which he now reproves, his partial response dramatizes the difficulty of a secure and consistent evaluation of the place of *mēnis* in the pursuit of *kleos* – and how the rhetorical use of *mēnis* is always already an evaluation. *Mēnin*, like *andra*, the first word of the *Odyssey*, opens a field of investigation, a site of questioning.

The embassy scene, then, with its violent exchanges of language – violence of and to language – turns on violence to and in institutions of exchange; that this scene has led to one of most intense critical exchanges among the *Iliad*'s readers (as readers repeat the process of evaluation of Achilles and the embassy dramatized in the scene) shows how the poem of *kleos* inevitably involves its audience in the exchange that is narrative, the crisis – decisions – of criticism. Reading the *Iliad* is not merely to recite the *kleos* of Achilles, but to be an active part of the process of its recovering.

If *philotēs* is a term of conflict between Achilles and the embassy, it also remains a crucial factor in Achilles' story. For it is Patroclus who has the strongest claim to be Achilles' φίλτατος ἑταῖρος, 'dearest companion', and it is Patroclus' appeal and then death and avenging which structure Achilles' return to battle. Patroclus' first words in the epic are a question addressed to Achilles 'What need do you have of me?' (11.606). As Lynn-George comments, 'Silent until this point late in the eleventh book, his words ... adumbrate a need not yet foreseen by Achilles'[57] – a need which will return Achilles to battle and to death. Patroclus' tears at the Greeks' suffering (unlike the grief of Phoenix) immediately arouse pity in Achilles: like the embassy Patroclus beseeches Achilles (λισσόμενος 45) to aid the Greeks. Achilles' angry response (49–100), as once more he recounts his outrage, seems about to repeat his rejection of *philtatoi*. Yet Achilles does agree to send Patroclus in his armour to the battle, according to Patroclus' request – the sufferings he asked Zeus to cause have reached such a point – and it is the acceptance of this plea of this *philos* that sets in motion Achilles' fateful return to battle – a return specifically to take revenge for his lost *philos*. In his withdrawal from battle, Achilles' *mēnis* sets his commitment to *timē* over and above the

---

[57] Lynn-George (1988) 128.

claims of his *philoi*, now Achilles' *mēnis* drives him to fight to fulfil an obligation of *philotēs*. At each point in the narrative, Achilles' wrath informs his expressions of reciprocal affiliation and duty.

Indeed, not only does Achilles find no 'pleasure' (18.80) in Zeus' fulfilment of his early prayers for honour, since his φίλος ἑταῖρος, 'dear companion', has died[58] (*Il.* 18.79–81), but also he seems to define his willingness to die as a function of his failure of *philotēs* as much as his pursuit of *kleos* (*Il.* 18.98–104):

> Let me die straightaway, since I was not there to protect
> my companion as he was killed. Very far from his fatherland
> he died, and he lacked me to be his protector in the battle.
> But now, since I am not going to my dear fatherland,
> nor was I any light of salvation for Patroclus, nor for my other
> companions, the many who were crushed by godlike Hector,
> but I am sat by the ships a useless weight on the earth ...

His failure to support the other Greeks also now after the death of Patroclus becomes a source of grief and self-reproach. So, when Achilles affirms his return to battle with the wish (121) νῦν δὲ κλέος ἐσθλὸν ἀροίμην, 'now may I win a noble *kleos*', the pursuit of fame is framed in the context of his complex relations to the affiliations and responsibilities of *philotēs*. Indeed, Thetis comments on Achilles' desire to return to battle (128–9):

> Yes, indeed, child, it is in truth not a bad thing
> to ward off desperate destruction from friends in danger.

Does Thetis' assertion that it is 'in truth not a bad thing' to protect companions threatened with death, after Achilles' rejection of the embassy and loss of Patroclus, offer a corrective or a bitterly ironic commentary on Achilles' desire to fight now? The motivation of the death of a *philos* and his recognition of his failure in the duties of a *philos* colour significantly Achilles' willingness to die (in exchange) for glory.

The embassy scene, then, and Achilles' return to battle dramatize and set in opposition different claims on a hero. It is within this problematic framework that Achilles pursues *kleos*, and the evaluation of Achilles

---

[58] He even reproaches himself with having destroyed Patroclus himself (*Il.* 18.82 τὸν ἀπώλεσα) on which Rutherford (1982) 155 comments, 'Nevertheless, for all his hatred for Hector, the supreme horror of the situation of Achilles lies in his recognition that he himself has destroyed his beloved friend.'

and of the effect of his *mēnis* on such pursuit remains a critical question in reading the *Iliad*. This is nowhere more clear than in Achilles' treatment of his enemies, and in particular Lycaon and Hector, as he pursues revenge for Patroclus and *kleos*.

Lycaon supplicates Achilles (*Il.* 21.74–5):

γουνοῦμαι σ᾽, Ἀχιλεῦ· σὺ δέ μ᾽ αἴδεο καί μ᾽ ἐλέησον·
ἀντί τοί εἰμ᾽ ἱκέταο, διοτρεφές, αἰδοίοιο.

I supplicate you, Achilles. Respect me; show me pity.
I am, O cherished of Zeus, as a suppliant who should be respected by you.

This appeal is replete with moral claims. Lycaon appeals to the institution of supplication (γουνοῦμαι, ἱκέταο); to *aidōs*; to pity. He is before Achilles as a suppliant who ought to be treated with *aidōs*. Indeed, he has not only been ransomed by Achilles before, but also has eaten with him (76ff). Yet Achilles rejects this appeal: now that Patroclus has died (100), no Trojan, least of all a son of Priam, will survive Achilles' wrath (101–2). He continues (106–10):

ἀλλά, φίλος, θάνε καὶ σύ· τίη ὀλυφύρεαι οὕτως;
κάτθανε καὶ Πάτροκλος, ὅ περ σέο πολλὸν ἀμείνων.
οὐχ ὁράᾳς οἷος καὶ ἐγὼ καλός τε μέγας τε;
πατρὸς δ᾽ εἴμ᾽ ἀγαθοῖο, θεὰ δέ με γείνατο μήτηρ.
ἀλλ᾽ ἔπι τοι καὶ ἐμοὶ θάνατος καὶ μοῖρα κραταιή·

But, dear one, die, you too. Why do you grieve so?
Patroclus died also, a far better man than you.
And do you not see how fine and large I too am?
I am of a good father; a goddess, my mother, gave birth to me.
But death and powerful fate await me also.

In the bitterly ironic address *philos*, Achilles appears to accept the claim of reciprocal obligation to which Lycaon appealed. *Aidoios* and *philos* are inherently linked in Homeric language, and the recollection of a shared meal is also an assertion of a mutual tie. The word *philos* recognizes and accepts this tie – a duty to protect – as the following imperative 'Die, you too' ignores any such obligation. It is as if Achilles in this distortion of language grimly echoes his self-reproach that he has destroyed his *philos* Patroclus by sending him to die in battle. If the embassy scene sets the value of *philotēs* against Achilles' search for *kleos* and his motivation of *mēnis*, in this supplication the force of *mēnis* leads Achilles to subvert and transgress in bitter violence the language and obligation of social reciprocity. Where Glaucus and Diomedes in their observance of *xeinosunē* stress the ties and duties of social exchange over and above the conflict of battle, Achilles rejects any such claim, any such control or limit, to the logic of killing those who oppose him in his wrath.

Many recent critics have seen in Achilles' words here a recognition of 'his fundamental kinship with those he kills'.[59] 'He invites the Trojan youth to join him in the only solidarity and shared humanity that mean anything to him, the solidarity of their shared mortality, the solidarity of death.'[60] 'There is ... only an engrossing vision of death, which sweeps aside what are now mere trivialities – mercy, ransom and hope.'[61] Yet if Achilles is recognizing humans' shared bond of mortality – a bond that is recognized by many of the heroes and the gods in different ways – it is at the expense of the bonds which constitute human society and language.[62] If the scenes of supplication 'bring out ... important things about heroic life and death',[63] then one of these 'important things' is Achilles' transgression of the norms and limits of the exchanges of 'heroic life'. The conjunction of the address *philos* with the injunction to die subverts the very associations of solidarity and collectivity in the Homeric poem, the very imperatives of social discourse.

Achilles' *mēnis*-dominated pursuit of *kleos* in society sets him at odds with his society and its behavioural norms, then. The *Iliad* is the poem of Achilles' *kleos* as the best of the Achaeans, but it is not merely as supreme in the qualities valued in and by society that Achilles is represented. Rather, Achilles' *mēnis* and particular commitment to his *timē* and *kleos* lead him even in his triumphs to go beyond the norms and limits of a hero's involvement in violent power and the pursuit of individual success.

In a similar way, the savagery of Achilles' treatment of Hector threatens to turn the best of the Achaeans into a bestial figure. At the moment of victory, Achilles rejects Hector's request to have his body ransomed with a shocking expression of the desire to mutilate – to eat raw – Hector's

---

[59] Griffin (1980) 55.

[60] Schein (1984) 148.

[61] Whitman (1958) 207.

[62] Nagler writes (1974) 149: 'One sees Achilles rejecting every compact of human intercourse: sympathy for one's age mate ... , *aidōs* for the guest, for the suppliant, for him with whom one has broken bread, all these are flung into the river with the body of Lykaon.'

[63] Griffin (1980) 56.

corpse.[64] The imagistic association of heroes' violence with the savagery of the world of wild beasts reaches a culmination in Achilles' *aristeia*.[65] Achilles proceeds to maltreat Hector's corpse even after Patroclus' last rites (with their savage human sacrifices).[66] The violent exchanges of the battlefield are distorted by Achilles' *mēnis* to a display of violence against a corpse: the chase of Hector around the city walls becomes the dragging of Hector's body around the tomb. The *Iliad*'s dominant question of the limits of power in the relations of exchange between humans is raised in starkest form by the unchecked expression of violence towards a bare body, which even – especially – when a dead body, is covered by the restraints of social discourse.

Indeed, the assault on Hector's body is termed an 'outrage' (ἀεικείη/ ἀεικίζω[67]) by the narrative voice (24.19; 24.22) and by Apollo (24.54).[68]

[64] On the significance of the raw meat-eating/cannibalism, see Redfield (1975) 197–9; Detienne (1977) 135–60; Sourvinou-Inwood (1986) 40–7. On the mutilation of corpses in general see Segal (1971) *passim*; Vernant (1982) 63ff. Combellack (1981), following Leaf, claims that Achilles has no desire for cannibalism, but rather expresses the certainty of Hector's body being eaten through the Homeric idiom of an *adunaton* 117: 'He mentions cannibalism as the most impossible thing he can think of in order to emphasize the certainty of Hector's body being eaten.' What Combellack ignores is that in all his other examples, both Homeric and his own, the *adunaton* is something highly desired (such as immortality, becoming the President of the United States). It is Achilles' expression of cannibalism as an impossible *desire*, not an *impossible* desire, that is relevant (see Nagy (1984)). On cannibalism as a sign of barbarian/barbaric behaviour, see now Hall (1989) ch. 1. On Hector's death in general, see also Schadewaldt (1965) 268–351.

[65] See e.g. Segal (1971) 38ff; Redfield (1975) especially 160ff; Moulton (1977) 99–116; Mueller (1984) 116–20; King (1987) 1–45.

[66] Even if this is a recollection of some older ritual practice, as is suggested by e.g. Rohde (1925) 14–16, the difference from Greek sacrificial practice at all historical times is sufficient to make it seem at least abnormal; see Henrichs (1980) for bibliography and case studies. The sacrifices are put in context well by Schnapp-Gourbeillon (1982) who writes 82 'Les funérailles de Patrocle sont tout entières à placer sous le signe de l' excès, de la démesure . . . Ce rituel est . . . à la fois détournement et transgression.'

[67] On ἀεικείη, see Long (1970) especially 135–9 *contra* Adkins (1960). See also Segal (1971) 18ff, who sees such 'outrage' as a theme in the treatment of bodies in the *Iliad*. Vernant (1982) 69 analyses superbly the relation between the treatment of the body and *kleos*: where desecration and lack of memorial is the inverse of 'la belle mort' of the glorious warrior. See too Schnapp-Gourbeillon (1982) who compares the treatment of Hector and Patroclus 83: 'L'un est indissociable de l'autre: à excès d'honneur, excès d'indignité'.

[68] The rhetoric of Apollo's argument here must not be forgotten, though Hera, who argues with him, does not deny that Achilles is behaving outrageously, but asserts merely that Achilles as the child of a god and Hector as the child of a mortal cannot receive the same *timē*.

Apollo significantly describes Achilles' behaviour as a complete lack of pity and respect (ἔλεος/αἰδώς 44), the qualities to which Lycaon unsuccessfully appeals. When Hector realizes the gods have (mis)led him to meet Achilles and his death on his own (22.297), he resolves to die nobly (304–5):

> May I not perish without effort at any rate, without fame,
> but after some great deed for future generations too to learn.

In death, Hector hopes to achieve some greatness, some *kleos*. Achilles in his triumph, which is also an expression of *akhos* and *mēnis*, is the object of a narrative of blame. In this narrative of victor and victim, the attribution and claim of *kleos* remain a question.[69]

The gods, aware of the outrage to Hector, require Achilles to return the body to Priam for burial. The supplication from the old man to the killer of his child reduces both participants to tears, tears which interrupt the ritual of supplication with uncontrolled grief.[70] Achilles, who has eschewed not only pity and respect but also food, sleep and sex, in the last book of the *Iliad* participates in each of these practices of exchange (though his anger is not completely repressed[71]). Yet the end of the epic is not with this supplication, but with a funeral conducted under a truce – a ritual of loss taking place under the certainty of continuing violence and destruction.[72] Macleod expresses a sense of this reintegration and loss:[73]

> *Iliad* 24 is not a happy ending. The conclusion of the poem is overshadowed by the coming death of Achilles and fall of Troy; and it constitutes only a slight break in the war. But the *Iliad* is great not least because it can speak authentically for pity or kindness or civilization without showing them victorious in life. Its humanity does not float on

[69] Rutherford (1982) 154 n. 49 goes so far as to suggest that for Achilles *kleos* itself has no value in the context of revenge: 'The κλέος gained from his victory does not seem to alter this picture [of Achilles' lack of rejoicing at Hector's defeat], for even glory no longer means anything to Achilles.' See, however, *Il.* 22.207.

[70] Cf. Monsacré (1984) 188–96, who does not take sufficient account, however, of the disruptive force of grief (as opposed to the reintegrative effect of mourning – which Achilles also distorts in his refusal to end mourning for Patroclus with a feast and sleep).

[71] See e.g. *Il.* 24.560; 24.567–70.

[72] 'There is a recurrent anticipation in the retelling such that the narrative of the *Iliad* makes of much of its retelling of the story of the past a foretelling never entirely fulfilled' (Lynn-George (1988) 270). The funeral of Hector, whose death guarantees the death of Achilles, as the closing scene of the work is a fine example of how this narrative technique works against closure. See also Frontisi-Ducroux (1986).

[73] Macleod (1982) 16. See also Taplin (1980) 15–17.

shallow optimism; it is firmly rooted in a awareness of human reality and suffering.

What does such a reading mean for the *Iliad* as a poem of *kleos*?[74] Achilles cannot be seen simply as a hero of martial prowess, as if the final acceptance of supplication in no way qualifies and colours his earlier behaviour in battle. Nor, however, can he be seen simply as a hero of 'transcendent personal sympathy'[75] as if his wrath, the war, the violent transgressions of social interaction, are merely stages of a journey towards what is already always known, namely, what it is to be 'wholly and definitively a man'.[76] Achilles remains inevitably and problematically αἰναρέτη, as Patroclus calls him, 'terrible in goodness'. In the case of Achilles in particular, the ending of the *Iliad* leaves a question about the definitions of and the connections between *aretē/aristos* and *kleos*.

The sense in which Hector is an essential foil to Achilles with respect to *kleos* can now be articulated more precisely. Hector too seeks *kleos* for his father and himself in military action, yet this is qualified by precisely the quality that Achilles so lacks with regard to Hector and Lycaon, namely, *aidōs*. Where Achilles subverts the language and institutions of *aidōs*, Hector places *aidōs* as a fundamental element in his motivation to fight (*Il.* 6.441–6):

> But especially strongly
> I feel *aidōs* for the Trojan men and long-dressed women,
> if I were to withdraw from war like a coward.
> Nor does my spirit so direct me, since I have learnt to be
> always noble and to fight in the front rank of Trojans,
> winning great glory for my father and for me myself.

The obligations of Hector's position in the society of Troy lead him to fight to defend Troy in the front rank. 'Hector has placed his life at the service of others.'[77] And it is Hector, with his moments of indecision and illusions,[78] who is to be destroyed by the figure of Achilles, and it is

---

[74] It is noticeable that Macleod, like many critics, refers to the *Iliad*'s greatness. The *kleos*, of the *Iliad* is ... whose?

[75] King (1987) 45 – a view typical of many critics on the ending. *Contra* e.g. Mueller (1984) 75: 'The final wisdom of the *Iliad* is not the attainment of a new and more human order born out of the destruction of the warrior code, but the temporary and ordered vision of the sufferings and contradictions of human life.'

[76] King (1987) 45.

[77] Redfield (1975) 28.

[78] Discussed most stimulatingly still by Redfield (1975) especially 128–59. See also the brief comments of Rutherford (1982) 157–8 and Mueller (1984) 36–44, 60–76.

Hector on whom the pathos of the *Iliad* focuses. Hector's *kleos* as a victim, then, and Achilles' *kleos* as victor, destined to die for his victory, set in contrast differing constructions of the aim of *kleos* within the value system projected in the *Iliad*, and dramatize the differing effects of *mēnis* and *aidōs* on the pursuit of *kleos*. The conflict between Hector and Achilles itself (dialectically) expresses a key element in the role and functioning of *kleos* in and as heroic narrative.

The *Iliad*, then, places *kleos* as an aim of the heroic endeavour. And the *Iliad* is the *kleos* of Achilles (and Hector and ...). Yet the *Iliad* also poses a series of questions about *kleos* and Achilles' involvement in it. To what degree is *kleos* simply and only a matter of individual commitment? What limits and controls does society, its institutions and values, have on such an individual pursuit? What happens to these institutions and values in a situation of conflict of interest? What is the expense to an individual and a community of a commitment to the pursuit of *kleos*? Does the loss of life find adequate recompense in the perpetuation of *kleos* in the discourse of others? Does Achilles' *mēnis* form a unique case that offers a specifically distorted view of an individual commitment to *kleos* or does it constitute an extreme example which points to the inherent contradictions of the value system?

Kleos is a process and an object (in all its senses) of exchange, and its thematic exploration in the *Iliad* takes place in and through an exploration of relations of exchange – the institutions and values of reciprocal duty and affiliation, such as *philotēs*, *aidōs*, supplication, that make up social discourse. Achilles' *kleos* cannot be viewed – read – apart from his uneasy standing with regard to (the boundaries of) such relations of power, and, as we have seen with the interrelations of the claims of *kleos* and the claims of *philotēs*, the *Iliad*'s tragic picture of Achilles is formed in the tensions between such claims. *Exchange is always a critical process.* The *Iliad*, then, is a founding narrative of heroic *kleos*, but it is a narrative which contests the value it projects and instantiates.

THE REVISIONARY GLEAM

Where is it now ... ?   Wordsworth

The *Odyssey* appropriates, redefines and sets itself against the *Iliad*, particularly with regard to the value of *kleos*. The *Odyssey* is, as 'Longinus' writes, an 'epilogue to the *Iliad*' and it is an epilogue that is self-consciously an *epigonos*.[79] The *Odyssey* offers a different view of the action leading to *kleos*, a different view of the constitution and construction of *kleos*, and perhaps most importantly it dramatizes a meeting between the hero of the *Iliad* and its own hero in the underworld where the discussion revolves precisely around the relations between *kleos*, achievement and mortality. The *Iliad* links its *kleos* as epic and the *kleos* of its hero; the *Odyssey* and its hero construct *kleos* in contest with the *Iliad* and Achilles.

It is first with regard to his use of language and disguise that the complex relation between the figure of Odysseus and the value of *kleos* can be seen. *Kleos* is inherently linked to the promotion and preservation of the name in the language of others. Yet not only is Odysseus distinguished for his concealment of his name and his false tales about himself, but also his very name signals his ambiguous position in social exchange, the 'trouble' that his deceptions cause. Odysseus, as we have seen, by proclaiming his name in victory brings down Polyphemus' curse; and far from openly pursuing the achievements and success that ensure heroic *kleos* in the *Iliad*, in the narrative of recognition and return he tests his *philoi* and pursues his revenge by a strategy of manipulating a series of rumours and tales about himself (falsehoods like the truth). The *Odyssey*'s narratives of disguise and trickery deflect a simple and direct association of action and praise.

The ironies for the construction of *kleos* that the narrative of concealment sets in play are seen at the very moment of the completed victory. Odysseus has the bard strike up a marriage-song over the bodies of the suitors (23.135–7):

> So that someone listening outside, a traveller on the road
> or one of the neighbours, might say it is a wedding,
> lest the fame [*kleos*] of the slaughter becomes broad in the town ...

This passage[80] captures well Odysseus' paradoxical involvement with 'fame' and how the interrelations of disguise, recognition and naming, that I discussed in the last chapter, affect the project of *kleos* in a crucial

---

[79] 'Longinus' De Sublim. 9.12.9. Redfield (1975) 39 writes 'The poet of the *Odyssey* is the first great critic of the *Iliad*'. See Heubeck (1954); Redfield (1973); Rüter (1969) 247–54. See also Segal (1983); Edwards (1984). Nagy (1979) argues for the conflict of an *Iliad* tradition and an *Odyssey* tradition (thereby circumventing the thorny problem of respective dating). Pucci (1987) 29 sees the relation between the two epics primarily as one of literary interaction, so that his notion of 'intertextuality' explicitly ignores the historical basis of the term as first defined by Kristeva.

[80] This passage is also discussed by Armstrong (1958a); Segal (1983); Edwards (1984).

way. On the one hand, he has killed the suitors – the marriage-song is apt both as an ironic comment on the failure of the suitors' wooing and as an accompaniment to the reunion of husband and wife. Telemachus, who claims after his travels to know his father's *kleos* for planning and strength, none the less expresses disbelief that such a revenge could be completed, 'so few against so many' (16.241–4). In this fulfilment, Odysseus achieves a *kleos* that is heightened in force by the very structure of doubt and affirmation: 'to delay truth is to constitute it'.[81] On the other hand, Odysseus has the bard fabricate a false song to prevent any *kleos* of the slaughter being spread. This *kleos* is a tale of woe for the suitors' relatives – against whom Odysseus is protecting himself – as it is Odysseus' victory song. Odysseus uses a bard's song not to promote *kleos* but to conceal and restrain its direct declaration. Yet even this concealment adds to the *Odyssey*'s praise of Odysseus as *polumētis*, as the man canny enough to achieve this particular, remarkable victory. The hiding of the immediate fame of the deed broadcasts the canniness of Odysseus (especially in the witty suitability of the marriage-song as disguise). The *Odyssey* is a narrative of *kleos* for the man who manipulates narratives of *kleos*.

The difficult relations between the figure of Odysseus and a narrative of *kleos* are further articulated in the episode in the Phaeacian court. The blind bard Demodocus is led forward and his first song commences (8.73–5):

> The Muse led the bard to sing of the famous deeds [*klea*] of men,
> a lay whose fame [*kleos*] at that time reached to broad heaven,
> the quarrel of Odysseus and Achilles, the son of Peleus.

The deeds of men lead to their perpetuation in song (*klea andrōn*), but the achievements of song also have their own glory (*kleos*). The Muses' inspirations, it would seem, are not all equal.[82] (This transference of *kleos* from the song to (the subject of the song to) the singer is a dynamic that will be fundamental to Pindar's poetry in particular.) This famous story of Achilles and Odysseus is scarcely known – even to ancient scholars – apart from this reference,[83] but the sense of a conflict between Achilles

[81] Barthes (1975) 262.
[82] Cf. *Od.* 1.351–2, where Telemachus says men ἐπικλείουσι, 'honour', 'give *kleos* to', the most recent song.
[83] It was a *zetema* of Hellenistic criticism. A fragment of Sophocles (fr. 566 Pearson) has been taken as a reference to this story. For a balanced view of earlier scholarship, especially the views of Von der Mühll, see Clay (1983) 98–100.

and Odysseus has been seen as an explicit indication of a more general opposition between the two heroes and the two epics.[84] Indeed, Demodocus' final song, which Odysseus himself requests, is about the fall of Troy; Odysseus' trick of the Trojan horse brings down the city after ten years unsuccessful military effort. Demodocus' song not only provides a bridge between the narrative of *nostos* and the *Iliad*'s narrative (where the fall of Troy is regularly foretold though not depicted), but also makes Odysseus and his qualities of guile the crucial instrument of Troy's capture. In Demodocus' first song, Odysseus is audience to his own *kleos* in the story of his quarrel with Achilles; in Demodocus' final song, Odysseus is both patron and audience to a song which establishes his *kleos* (as opposed to Achilles'?) in the field of war. As with the ordering of the wedding-song in his own house, Odysseus manipulates the relation between the voice of the bard and his own *kleos*.

Demodocus' songs are a prelude to Odysseus' own performance before the Phaeacians. After being audience and patron of his *kleos*, Odysseus is to be his own bard. He announces his identity thus (9.19–20):

> I am Odysseus, son of Laertes, who through all my tricks
> am a concern to men, and my fame reaches heaven.

In no other place in the *Iliad* or *Odyssey*, despite the repeated exchanges of names and boasts, does a hero arrogate *kleos* to himself in this way.[85] *Kleos* is set as the stake of conflict, a term of evaluation of others in the future or past, a memorial to be competed for. Iliadic figures are scarcely reticent of their achievements, but a man's *kleos* as a marker of social identity is conceived as necessarily formed by the recognition of others. Here, Odysseus extends the rhetoric of an appeal to *kleos* to an affirmation of the already fulfilled promise of (self-proclaimed) achievement. The poet has Odysseus reveal his identity by singing his own praise.

Odysseus' story-telling, however, which this announcement introduces, also instantiates the ideal of μύθων τε ῥητῆρ' ἔμεναι πρηκτῆρά τε ἔργων, 'to be a speaker of words and a doer of deeds'.[86] His *muthoi* are

---

[84] Marg (1957) 22 writes 'Odysseus gegenüber Achilleus: die Besten gegen die Besten, Gestalt gegen Gestalt – fast Gedicht gegen Gedicht.' See also Hölscher (1967) 5–9; Rüter (1969) 252–5; Finley (1978) 86–7, 124–6; Clay (1983) 96–112; and especially Nagy (1979) 15ff.

[85] Segal (1983) 24–6 considers other possible cases, none of which provides an adequate parallel. At 19.127–8 (discussed below), Penelope refers to her *kleos*, but it is only to say that it would be greater if Odysseus were to come home – an expression of future *kleos* – but now she has grief, *akhos*.

[86] *Il.* 9.443 – it is what Phoenix is to teach Achilles. See e.g. Thalmann (1984) 179–82 on the ideal.

about himself as a 'doer of deeds', and also the manipulation of *muthoi* is the Odyssean deed *par excellence*. The *Odyssey*, by turning to the self-representing narrative, has its hero enact his *kleos* as he narrates it.

Odysseus' control of language and story-telling, then, introduces a complex and ironic dynamic into the relation between the poet's voice and *kleos*. The hero of *mētis* is not merely the subject but also the audience, patron, singer – the manipulator – of (his) *kleos*.

It is also with regard to heroic action, however, that the *Odyssey*'s view of *kleos* demonstrates its difference from the *Iliad*. In the *Iliad*, the *kleos* of Achilles is dependent on his own behaviour, and he is fiercely committed to his personal status; even Hector, who is set in a complex web of social commitments, relies on his own personal achievements for his success or failure. But in the narrative of *nostos*, Odysseus and Penelope require each other's achievements: Odysseus not merely has to return to Penelope but also has to find (in) her the proper end to his quest; Penelope needs the return of Odysseus to give 'her story ... a fitting conclusion and dramatic meaning'.[87] 'The *kleos* of each is dependent on the action of the other.'[88]

This interdependence and its effect on the discourse of *kleos* is introduced in the first exchange between Penelope and the disguised Odysseus. Penelope asks the stranger his name and Odysseus characteristically deflects the question[89] (19.107–9):

> My lady, no mortal on the limitless earth
> could reproach you. For your fame [*kleos*] reaches broad heaven,
> like some blameless king ...

The 'reverse simile'[90] attributes to a woman the kingly quality of *kleos* (which in itself may mark a deviation from the association of *kleos* predominantly with male activity in the *Iliad*). Odysseus here confers *kleos* on his wife (as she recalls her husband's *kleos* on more than one occasion). This praise, however, is also part of Odysseus' testing of his wife's fidelity, that is crucial to the *kleos* of both of them. Indeed, she replies (19.124–9):

> Stranger, the gods destroyed my excellence [*aretē*], my beauty
> and figure, when the Argives embarked for Troy,

---

[87] Redfield (1975) 34.   [88] Edwards (1984) 81. Cf. Nagy (1979) 36–41.

[89] Odysseus asks not to be asked about his lineage (19.116–8). Segal (1983) 30 writes 'The situation utterly reverses heroic practise.' Odysseus' unwillingness to reveal himself may run counter to the norms of exchange developed in the *Iliad* (e.g. between Glaucus and Diomedes), but it is scarcely atypical for the hero Odysseus.

[90] See for this term Foley (1978).

and with them went my husband Odysseus.
If that man were to come and to take care of my life,
then my fame would be greater and finer.
But as things are, I grieve.

The absence of her husband means the destruction of her excellence
(ἀρετή) as well as her looks. She uses the same expression to put off
Eurylochus' suit (18.251–5): what is before the suitors a defence becomes
before her husband a highly charged and ironic claim of fidelity. As
Odysseus tests Penelope, she confirms that his return is a necessary end
to her struggles: νῦν δ᾽ ἄχομαι, 'But as things are, I grieve', she asserts.
She deflects Odysseus' attribution of *kleos* with the claim that Odysseus'
absence provides her rather with *akhos* – the inverse of *kleos*.[91] As husband and wife proceed towards a recognition which is a prerequisite of
their *kleos*, it is through the offering and qualifying of *kleos* that Penelope
reveals her story of fidelity to the disguised Odysseus and the king tests
his queen.

The complementarity of Odysseus and Penelope is also evident in the
form of their action – both their long-suffering endurance and in particular the *mētis* which distinguishes their like-mindedness. Indeed, if Odysseus' announcement of his own *kleos* before the Phaeacians is surprising,
so too the boast of his *doloi*, his tricks, as a self-introduction indicates his
paradoxical position with regard to what might be supposed to be the
norms of narratives of *kleos*.[92] For although, as Rüter notes, this claim
may refer back to Demodocus' song of Odysseus' role in the Trojan horse
episode – he announces himself as the hero of Demodocus' *epos* – none
the less the association of the hero with *doloi* remains profoundly ambiguous.[93] For *doloi* are the antithesis of heroic deeds in competition, the
opposite of the forthright, upright, face to face striving for *kleos* in the
fore of the battle. *Dolos* might be thought to 'lead to the exact opposite of
kleos, namely "shame" and "disgrace"'.[94] Indeed, Odysseus announces
that in his *doloi* he is a concern for men – both a concern in song (the
subject of *kleos*), and also a 'worry', 'a problem' – an ambiguity which
indicates once more Odysseus' ambivalent status in his tricky exchanges

---

[91] See Nagy (1979) *passim*, especially 94–102, for the relation between *akhos* and *kleos*.

[92] Penelope (4.815) glosses Odysseus' *kleos* by calling him 'distinguished for all sorts of
virtues', παντοίῃς ἀρετῇσιν, whereas here Odysseus boasts of πᾶσι δόλοισι, 'all my
tricks'.

[93] Rüter (1969) 254. He sees this as self-praise by the *Odyssey*-poet for himself and his
epic – a further twist to the dynamics of *kleos* in this scene.

[94] Segal (1983) 31.

in human society.[95] The association of Penelope, a female, with such *doloi* parallels and further emphasizes the ambivalence at the heart of Odysseus' heroic behaviour. For the linking of deceptiveness and the female in particular is a recurring feature of the hierarchical opposition of the sexes in early Greek writing.[96] Penelope, in order to preserve the order of the house, must draw on qualities especially dangerous in the female figure at the centre of the *oikos*. The association of Odysseus with Penelope and with her (female) trickery further marks 'the paradoxes and contradictions in Odysseus' "heroism"'.[97] A hero of deception is necessarily an anomalous figure.

It is not merely the strategies of *mētis*, however, that distinguish the representation of Odysseus in the *Odyssey* from the heroic action of the *Iliad*. For both Odysseus' desire for home and the activities that the fulfilment of this desire requires set Odysseus in opposition to the paradigm of Achilles, Hector and Agamemnon. Achilles in the *Iliad* chooses to lose his *nostos* to win immortal *kleos*; Hector, who is set in a system of social relations in Troy that Odysseus strives to re-establish in Ithaca, is led by his sense of *aidōs* and his own *hamartia* to reject appeals from each member of his *oikos*, a series of rejections which shows both what is at stake in Hector's fight and what he loses in his defeat. In the *Iliad*, Hector's *kleos* (as victim) seals the destruction of his *oikos*. His *nostos* is as a corpse. The exemplum of Agamemnon in the *Odyssey* is returned to again and again. It is the paradigm of a failed *nostos*, an unfaithful wife, and a *kleos* as victim that undermines his *kleos* as victor over Troy. Odysseus, however, not only has the *kleos* of his feats in Troy – that are recalled by Helen, Menelaus and Demodocus in particular – but also achieves the *kleos* of a successful return and a completed revenge. Odysseus' triumph is a trumping of the achievements of other heroes.

The contrast between Agamemnon's and Odysseus' *kleos* is brought to the fore in the two reactions of Agamemnon in the Underworld to news of Odysseus. In the first episode in the Underworld, Agamemnon relates his own 'most pitiful death' (11.412) at the hands of Aegisthus. He singles out also the horror of a woman's deceptiveness and capability for transgression ('know that there is nothing more awful and more terrible [*kunteron*] than a woman who conceives such deeds' (11.427–8)). Odys-

---

[95] See Segal (1983) 28 who also notes that μέλω in this sense occurs only here in the first person.

[96] See in particular Arthur (1973); Detienne and Vernant (1978); Bergren (1983).

[97] Segal (1983) 31.

seus sees this story of Clytemnestra as a parallel to Helen (11.436–9) – both women leading to men's deaths – but Agamemnon responds with a more general point (11.441–3):

> Therefore now you too do not ever be kindly to a woman.
> Do not tell her the whole story, which you know well,
> but tell her part, and let part be hidden.

He immediately qualifies this advice, however, with a recognition of Penelope's good sense, and a promise that Odysseus will not die by a woman/his wife (ἔκ γε γυναικός 11.444). None the less he concludes with an admonition to Odysseus to return in secret: ἐπεὶ οὐκέτι πιστὰ γυναιξίν, 'for no longer are women/wives to be trusted' (11.456). His praise of Penelope is framed by his assertion of the untrustworthiness of women as a race, and his advice to return in secret is certainly followed by Odysseus, and Penelope's trustworthiness as a wife is markedly put to the test.[98]

In the second episode, Agamemnon hears of Odysseus' return and revenge from Amphimedon. He reacts to the suitor's tale of woe with an expression of Odysseus' fortune[99] (24.192–8):

> Fortunate son of Laertes, Odysseus of the many devices,
> you have indeed obtained a wife with great excellence.
> What excellent sense there is in blameless Penelope,
> daughter of Icarius! How well she remembered Odysseus,
> her wedded husband! Wherefore fame of this goodness
> will not perish, but the gods will provide for mortals
> a pleasing song for Penelope the sensible.

Agamemnon praises Odysseus' fortune because he has obtained a wife with great virtue (*aretē*).[100] He praises Penelope's mind – her sense and her attitudes (φρένες) – and the fact that she remembered her husband. The *kleos* of this virtue (*aretē*) will never perish.[101] Penelope will become

---

[98] On these lines, see now Collins (1988) 60–7.

[99] On a tale of woe being for another a tale of joy, see Nagy (1979) 94–103; Rutherford (1982) 158 n. 61; Edwards (1984) 86; and, from a different perspective, Svenbro (1976) 18–36.

[100] The phrase σὺν μεγάλῃ ἀρετῇ, 'with great excellence/virtue', has been taken to qualify both the verb – Odysseus' behaviour – and the noun ἄκοιτιν – Penelope's qualities – despite Chantraine's assertion (1948–53) II 136 that σύν phrases are always adverbial in Homer.

[101] Edwards (1984) 88 n. 36 tentatively suggests that this remark, usually taken to refer to the *kleos* of Penelope, refers to the *kleos* of Odysseus – which is, then, preserved by Penelope's action. See also Nagy (1979) 196 and Thalmann (1984) 169 n. 20, who refer it respectively to Odysseus and Penelope. Where *kleos* is mutually implicative, any ambiguity may be significant.

the subject of song for future generations, as now Agamemnon outlines
a direct link between action and the poet's voice whereby noble deeds
lead to *kleos*, which leads to preservation in song (a model to be set against
the complexities of Odysseus' performances that have led to his success).
What is more, Agamemnon goes on to contrast Penelope with Clytemnestra, who is destined to be the subject of a 'hateful song' (στυγερὴ ἀοιδή
200) and to provide a 'bad report' (χαλεπὴν φῆμιν 201) for the race of
female women (θηλυτέρῃσι γυναιξίν 202). In the first episode in the
Underworld, women's general untrustworthiness and the exemplum of
Clytemnestra lead to a warning to return in secret; here Clytemnestra's
generalizable case is in opposition to the fame of Penelope.[102] Any doubts
raised in Agamemnon's first speech are triumphed over here in the *kleos*
of husband and wife, as Telemachus' doubts about the possibility of
revenge prefigure a final, heightened fulfilment. In such an exchange,
however, Agamemnon also implicitly contrasts his fate – his *kleos* – with
Odysseus', as he had explicitly compared the two in the first episode
in the Underworld. Amphimedon is to tell the story of Odysseus to
Agamemnon in order to set the two figures, the two stories of return,
once more here at the conclusion, against each other.

Agamemnon, then, sacker of Troy, whom Odysseus describes to the
Cyclops as having the greatest *kleos* of contemporary humans (9.264) – a
remark which is part of the rhetoric of Odysseus' concealing *mētis* – is
the figure to confer and confirm the *kleos* of the narrative of Odysseus'
nostos and revenge precisely because of his own failure to effect a return,
and the need for revenge (rather than *kleos*) that he bequeathed to his
son, Orestes. Agamemnon's speech is important not only because it
responds to Amphimedon's tale by praising Odysseus' and Penelope's
kleos – 'a final opinion upon the magnitude and moral character of the
events'[103] – but also because it is Agamemnon who declares such *kleos*.

The actions that make up Odysseus' *nostos*, however, are also in marked
contrast to the actions that lead to *kleos* in the *Iliad*, and this is not merely
because of the shift from the battlefield to a different setting of the
uncertain world in which Odysseus moves. Odysseus not only returns in
disguise but also his disguise is the lowest rank in the social hierarchy.[104]

---

[102] 'The house-destroying *dolos* of Clytemnestra ... contrasts with the house-preserving
dolos of Penelope, as *aischos* ['shame'] contrasts with *kleos*' (Segal (1983) 32).

[103] Edwards (1984) 89.

[104] There are no episodes of disguise in the *Iliad* (though on the λόχος, 'ambush', see
Edwards (1984) 15–42). Perhaps part of the function of Helen's story about Odysseus
in Book 4 is to set a scene of (Odyssean) disguise as part of the Trojan war, as the Trojan
horse places (Odyssean) *mētis* at the forefront of military virtues.

This disguise leads to a series of humiliating experiences. Indeed, while heroic evaluation is based on the performance of great deeds, it is being long-suffering that is a hallmark of Odysseus' struggles in the *Odyssey*.[105] Furthermore, the very fight in the hall by which Odysseus conquers his enemies relates somewhat uneasily to the battle scenes in the *Iliad*.[106] Odysseus throws off his rags (22.1) – a divesting of disguise for the dénouement, which also leaves Odysseus without the normal armour and arming scene of an Iliadic *aristeia*.[107] The bow itself is a weapon associated with inferiority.[108] He proceeds to kill the unarmed suitors as they feast in his own house (purification will be required after such a slaughter[109]). Rather than the exchange of names and boasts leading to a contest of strength, Odysseus announces himself without any genealogy (22.3ff) and the immediate response of Eurylochus (22.45ff) is to try to avoid any fighting by putting all the blame for the suitors' transgressions on to the dead Antinous.

As the fight progresses, Telemachus brings armour for the avengers, and Melanthius finds weapons for the suitors. The battle becomes described in language more closely approaching the *Iliad*'s battle narratives, with speeches of encouragement, descriptions of blows, and the intervention of Athene on the direction and effect of the fight.[110] There is one particularly striking similarity. In the *Iliad*, as I have mentioned, the repeated scenes of supplication help articulate the epic's interest in the limits and transgressions of power. Odysseus is approached in supplication by Leodes, in terms that recall in particular the supplication of Achilles by Lycaon.[111] Odysseus has been in the position of a stranger at the mercy of others: now he is in the position of power, indeed the arbiter

---

[105] Clay (1983) 111 writes 'The traditional *kleos* of Achilles demands spectacular martial accomplishments, unflinching courage, and a splendid death on the field of battle. The *kleos* of Odysseus on the other hand resides in endurance and survival and the accomplishment of the Return through the aid of *mētis*.' See also Crane (1988) 147–9.

[106] On this fight as a λόχος, see Edwards (1984) 15–42, especially 35–8. For a useful overview of battles in the *Iliad*, see Fenik (1968); Mueller (1984) 77–107.

[107] See in particular Armstrong (1958b); also Shannon (1975) 20–30.

[108] The bowman is a figure secondary to the warrior with a spear: see e.g. Bond (1981) ad 161. In its associations with the ordered life of Odysseus as master of the *oikos*, the bow here plays a similar role to Achilles' spear which only he can properly use. See Shannon (1975) 31–86.

[109] *Od.* 22.481–4. See Parker (1983): on purification in Homer generally 130–43; on this passage 114 n. 39, where he notes that the purification is of the house and not of Odysseus; on purification by sulphur 57f, 227f, with bibliography 227 n. 114.

[110] The similarities are discussed by Pucci (1987) 128–37.

[111] For the parallels in detail, see Pucci (1987) 128–37.

of life and death over the man who led the suitors' religious rites. Odysseus rejects Leodes' plea that he had found the suitors' transgressions intolerable – a defence supported by the narrative's first description of him when he has his attempt in the bow contest[112] – and he kills him on the grounds that Leodes must have participated in prayers to prevent Odysseus' 'sweet *nostos*' (321–3). Achilles rejects Lycaon's plea – a plea, like Leodes', that he is not responsible for the cause of, in his case, Achilles' wrath – with an assertion of the necessity of death for all men. Odysseus' response denies mercy to Leodes because his performance of prayers and his desire for Penelope constitute a specific transgression, and even a contributory threat to Odysseus' return. Like Achilles, Odysseus uses his power to reject a supplication in battle: unlike Achilles, Odysseus' rejection is placed within the search for *nostos* and the re-establishment of the hierarchy of the *oikos*. As Pucci comments, 'The contrast between Achilles' answer to Lycaon and Odysseus' to Leodes orchestrates, above the formal similarities of the scene, their difference as a central theme.'[113]

This scene is followed immediately by a second supplication of Odysseus, this time by the bard, Phemius. He overcomes his uncertainty whether to approach the king, and clasps his knees and speaks (344):

> I supplicate you, Odysseus. Respect me; show me pity.

This remark is identical to Leodes' opening plea, and the phrase σύ μ' αἴδεο καί μ' ἐλέησον, 'Respect me; show me pity', occurs in Homer only in these two speeches and as the opening remark of Lycaon's supplication of Achilles in the *Iliad*. It may seem an inauspicious citation by the bard, but Phemius' plea (with the assistance of Telemachus) is accepted by Odysseus, and the bard's life is spared. Now Odysseus shows that unlike Achilles and unlike Agamemnon in battle he can spare suppliants (under certain circumstances). In the two scenes of supplications, Odysseus not only adopts and adapts the role of the best and most powerful heroes in the *Iliad*, but also enacts the evaluation of *philoi* essential to the re-establishment of order in the *oikos*. And it is precisely in the evaluation and treatment of *philoi* that the dangerous extremes of Achilles' search for *kleos* are found.

It is a bard who is spared by Odysseus. Phemius' desperate plea, as I discussed in chapter 1, is based on the bard's power to immortalize in

---

[112] 21.144–8. He is the first suitor to try to win Penelope in the contest.
[113] (1987) 138.

song. The bard who preserves in song speaks here (in the voice of the suppliant) to preserve his own life. As Odysseus is depicted in the *Odyssey* fighting for *kleos*, to establish his *nostos* which is his *kleos*, so the bard he encounters promises him a song of renown rather than its antithesis, grief (*akhos* 345). Odysseus and the bard forge an exchange where the poet's life and song depend upon his master's deeds and pleasure, and where the poet boasts his own worth to justify his survival. Indeed, Phemius says that he sings for gods and men (θεοῖσι καὶ ἀνθρώποισιν ἀείδω 346), claims that a god inspires him (θεός ... ἐνέφυσεν 347–8) and claims to sing before Odysseus 'as before a god' (ὥς τε θεῷ 349) (which may emphasize 'the worthiness of Phemius or the god-like portrait of Odysseus'[114] or both). In the exchange of Odysseus and Phemius which takes the form of an accepted act of supplication, the complex dynamics of *power* in the relation between heroic deeds, the poet's voice and *kleos* are themselves represented in the epic narrative of *kleos*.

It is in the two scenes in the Underworld, however, where the *Odyssey* constructs in starkest form the conflicting paradigms of Odysseus and Achilles.[115] In the first episode in the Underworld, Odysseus sees Achilles approach (11.467–70) with Patroclus, Antilochus and Ajax (who is called (469–70) 'the best of the Greeks after Achilles' as in the *Iliad* – but as Nagy comments wryly, 'Odysseus can afford to be generous in spirit to the two most heroic Achaeans of the *Iliad* tradition; the *Odyssey* will make him the most heroic Achaean in the *Odyssey*',[116] and this encounter will prove crucial to that redefinition of the title of *aristos*). Achilles' opening remark is characteristically forceful[117] (473–4):

> Outrageous man! What even greater deed will you plot in your mind?
> How could you dare to come down to Hades, where the corpses
> live, senseless, the shades of dead men?

Skhetlie, 'outrageous', is the term that Odysseus uses, for example, to the Cyclops (and that Athene uses of Odysseus). It expresses, perhaps, some aggression towards Odysseus' daring rather than the sympathy and shared tears that Agamemnon shows. Odysseus responds not only by

---

[114] Pucci (1987) 229. He discusses this scene 228–35.

[115] Cf. Hölscher (1967) 5–9; Rüter (1969) 252–5; Finley (1978) 178; Nagy (1979) 35; Edwards (1984) 43ff.

[116] Nagy (1979) 36. Cf. Edwards (1984) 47–8.

[117] On this speech, see Edwards (1984) 49–50. On character through speech, see Parry (1956); Reeve (1973); Friedrich and Redfield (1978); and, most recently, the stimulating study of Martin (1990).

telling Achilles the reason for this descent into Hades, but also by lavishly praising Achilles as most blessed (μακάρτατος 483) of mortals in the past and future. The Greeks honoured (ἐτίομεν 484) Achilles like a god in his own life, and among the dead he has great power (μέγα κρατέεις 485). All this should banish grief (*akhos* – ἀκαχίζευ 486) from his death. Achilles' reply is famous (488–91):

> Do not try to talk round *death*, bright Odysseus.
> I would rather be a hired hand working the land for another,
> a man without a portion, to whom there is no great livelihood,
> than to be the lord of all the wasted corpses.

Odysseus' praise is offered to be denied. Achilles orders Odysseus not to try to 'talk round' (*paraudan*)[118] the misery of death. (Odysseus' way with words, as in the *Iliad*, cuts little ice with Achilles.) Achilles would rather have the lowest social position among the living than rule among the dead. From the time of the scholia at least, these lines have been seen to relate to Achilles' choice in the *Iliad* for a short life and *kleos* rather than a long and undistinguished existence.[119] Rüter, like Nagy, Hölscher, Clay and others, argues that Achilles here in the *Odyssey* reverses his position of the *Iliad* on the desirability of *kleos*. The hero who willingly chooses to end his life for *kleos* and who brings about great destruction because of a slight to his *timē*, his social status and honour, now regrets death to such degree that he would prefer life without any *timē*.[120] Odysseus is to make his return to the living to effect his *nostos* precisely in the disguise of a man without *timē*. Odysseus' humiliating experiences

---

[118] 'Jemandem durch Zuspruch etwas annehmbar zu machen suchen.' Ameis – Hentze ad loc.

[119] Clay comments well (1983) 111 on the relation between Agamemnon's and Achilles' speeches in the first episode in the Underworld that Achilles' choice, like Agamemnon's description of his fate, seems to offer 'harsh uncompromising polarities ...: *nostos*, homecoming, and *kleos* are regarded as mutually exclusive'. It is such polarities that Odysseus transcends.

[120] Rüter (1969) 251ff; Clay (1983) 108ff (with further bibliography). Edwards (1984) 51 argues that 'the opinion Achilles expresses in the *Odyssey* ought to be seen more as a continuation of his position in the *Iliad* rather than a reversal of it, since nowhere in the poem does he state a preference for κλέος over a νόστος'. At *Il.* 9.414f, Achilles makes it plain that going home would mean the destruction of his *kleos*; he threatens to go home; but follows through his desire for *kleos* to the end. Achilles actively chooses *kleos* and death over *nostos*. Edwards does not consider Achilles' reversal of his previous concern for social status. So, too, Finley (1978) 124 writes 'No rejection of heroism but the incompleteness of young death speaks in Achilles' wish for even the humblest life on earth.' Achilles' speech is not a rejection of heroism *tout court* but it does represent a redefinition of the terms in which heroism is conceived for Achilles in the *Iliad*.

must be seen within the light of the greatest hero's new-found willingness to endure the lowest forms of life in preference to death.

Achilles goes on to ask about his father and son, and Odysseus tells him of Neoptolemus' achievements at Troy.[121] In the *Iliad*, Achilles in his search for personal glory and concomitant rejection of a continuity of life in the *oikos* mentions his son but once only to say that he does not know if he is alive even (19.326–7). From the perspective of the Underworld and the *Odyssey*, he now shows considerable concern (as Odysseus will reforge his paternal links with Telemachus); and Achilles' reaction to Odysseus' story of Neoptolemus' triumph is joy. Achilles' early death, as both he himself and Priam in the *Iliad* remark, means that his father Peleus has no son to guard him.[122] When Odysseus, Telemachus and Laertes stand together against the suitors' relatives, it offers a paradigm of generational reciprocal support and continuity that reverses the result of Achilles' choice in the *Iliad*.

In its estimation of *nostos*, then, and the relation of *nostos* to the requirements of *timē* and *kleos* (even to the point of death), the first episode in the Underworld resituates the Achilles of the *Iliad* in such a way as to set Odysseus and his values – by extension, the *Odyssey* itself[123] – over and against the paradigms of the *Iliad*. As Edwards comments on this manipulation, 'The *Odyssey*'s strategy here is one of μῆτις [*mētis*]. It lays a verbal, poetic ambush for Achilles and the tradition which promotes him as an ethical and spiritual model.'[124] Odysseus goes to the Underworld to rewrite the epic tradition.

The second episode in the Underworld begins with a conversation between Agamemnon and Achilles, the heroes whose quarrel sets the *Iliad* in motion (24.15ff). Achilles contrasts Agamemnon's glorious life in Troy, beloved of Zeus (24–7), with his inescapable fate (29) and its results (30–4):

[121] This is discussed in detail by Edwards (1984) 59–67. He notes 67 that Neoptolemus, unlike Achilles, leaves Troy unscathed and 'The substitution of a νόστος [*nostos*] for the hero's death in Neoptolemus' case is credited to a λόχος [*lokhos*] and the patronage of Odysseus.'

[122] There is a tradition that Peleus was exiled while Achilles was away (see e.g. Eur. *Tro.* 1126ff), which story may have been included in the *Nostoi* (a theory proposed most recently by Edwards (1984) 54 n. 26 against Severyns and Lesky). The loss of a son as a danger for a father is often recalled in *Iliad* (e.g. 4.477–9; 5.22–4; 5.153–8; 22.59–71; 23.222–5).

[123] 'In setting up his hero as an equal – if not superior – to Achilles, the poet of the *Odyssey* stakes the highest claim to the excellence of his own poem.' Clay (1983) 106. Cf. Segal (1983).

[124] Edwards (1984) 69.

> Would that you had met death and fate among the people of Troy
> in possession of the honour which you used to rule!
> Then the Achaean force would have made you a tomb,
> and you would have won fame for your son also in the future.
> As it is, it was fated for you to be taken by a most pitiful death.

Telemachus uses similar terms to regret his father's disappearance. No tomb, no *kleos* for descendants,[125] and a lack of honour. Agamemnon responds by blessing Achilles precisely for his death in Troy. Indeed, he goes on (37–97) to describe at length Achilles' glorious funeral rites, the fine tomb, which will be a landmark for future generations (80–4) and the games that the heroes held.[126] Agamemnon concludes (93–7):

> Thus you have not lost your name even in death, but always
> and among all men will your fame be fine, Achilles.
> But for me, what pleasure is it to have toiled through the war?
> For in my homecoming Zeus plotted my bitter destruction
> at the hands of Aegisthus and my destructive wife.

The hero's end narrated here is a guarantee of the preservation of his name and the continuation of his *kleos*. Achilles is set explicitly against Agamemnon, the value of whose military exploits is lost because of his death on coming home. Agamemnon's failed *nostos* is recalled as a prelude to Amphimedon's talk of Odysseus' success, and set in contrast with Achilles' *kleos*. It is the figure of Odysseus, however, who transcends the opposition of death for glory and the disaster of a failed *nostos* (without even a glorious death). The exchange of the two leading figures of the *Iliad*, then, significantly stands before Amphimedon's tale and the final acts of the epic where three generations of males fight for the *oikos*. When the *Odyssey* looks back to the *Iliad*, it is to appropriate its heroes, its actions, its *kleos*, in a strategy of redefinition, incorporation and contestation. In all its senses, the *kleos* of the *Odyssey* sets itself against the *kleos* of the *Iliad*.

If the *Iliad* explores the relation between immortal *kleos* and the hero's mortality, the *Odyssey* further challenges a simple relation between heroic action and renown. While the model of great achievement leading to *kleos* which is preserved in song (and its analogue of bad deeds leading to poetry of blame) is represented in the *Odyssey*, both in itself as the epic of Odysseus' *kleos* and in the claims of, say, Demodocus, Phemius or

---

[125] Nagy (1979) 36 writes that here 'Achilles himself considers that Agamemnon too has left behind a *kleos* for the future.' Unaccountably, this seems to ignore the potential construction.

[126] See Whitehead (1984).

Agamemnon, such a model is also subject to considerable complication and indeed investigation in the epic. Odysseus' actions are set against those of the warriors of the *Iliad* both explicitly and implicitly: competition in *kleos* becomes also a contest as to the constitution of *kleos*. The *Odyssey*'s estimation of *nostos, timē, dolos,* as well as *kleos* must be seen in the light of the *Iliad*'s exploration of the hero's commitment to personal achievement. Despite the *Odyssey*'s gestures of re-evaluation, however, Odysseus' constant strategies of *mētis* and *dolos* also inevitably invest his achievements with a certain ambivalence, the doubleness proclaimed in his name, the 'concern' he is for men. The *Odyssey*'s *kleos* is also of a hero of ambiguous stature. What is more, Odysseus' self-representing narratives and manipulations of narratives of *kleos* introduce a complex dynamic of revealing and concealing that place the veils of *mētis* between achievement and its recognition in *kleos*. In short, the *Odyssey* by focusing on Odysseus as producer and product of narratives of *kleos*, explores the involved dynamics of power at work in the poet's voice (as preserver and constructor of *kleos*).

Both the *Iliad* and the *Odyssey*, then, raise questions in different manners and from different perspectives about the *kleos* that they instantiate and promote. Critics have emphasized that *kleos* is established as the aim of heroic endeavour; and that a noble burial after a noble death seals a noble life with – and as – a memorial for future generations; and that heroic poetry preserves the *kleos* of outstanding men, and that the *Iliad* is the *kleos* of Achilles as the *Odyssey* is the *kleos* of Odysseus. Such generalizations, however, cannot do justice to the complex way in which the term functions and is investigated in each poem and as part of the relation between the poems. (Textuality cannot be replaced with anthropology.) It is, moreover, in reaction to and in comparison with these two great Homeric poems' construction and contestation of *kleos* that later writers of *kleos* must be read. And it is to the developing tradition of poetry as *kleos* that I wish now to turn.

POETICS AND POLITICS

Historians of Greek literature have read in the fragmentary remains of sixth- and fifth-century Greek lyric poetry[127] signs of crucial develop-

---

[127] By 'lyric poetry' I mean to include the disparate genres of choral lyric, sympotic lyric, elegy and iambus – much along the lines of Campbell's *Greek Lyric Poetry*.

ments in the poet's voice. In comparison with Homer, the lyric corpus has seemed to offer both a sense of committed, individual voices (touched by helplessness, racked by desire), and also a sense of specific, contemporary political involvement, that has made it easy to attempt to link such poetic differences to changes in social and cultural conditions. In this section of the chapter, I wish to look at two particular trends in lyric poetry that provide an essential background to Pindar's writing and its relation to Homer especially with regard to *kleos*: first, the shifting relation between the poet and the figure of renown; and second, the influence of the ideology of the developing *polis* on the narratives of *kleos*. For unlike Homer, when Pindar writes his *epinikia*, he celebrates (in the main) a contemporary victor who has hired him to sing his praises; a victor, what's more, whose (involvement in a) *polis* is a fundamental element in the possibilities of praise and success. It is the development of these conditions for the production of *kleos* that I wish to investigate here. This precise focus means that – with regret – I will not be discussing many aspects of lyric poetry that are relevant to the poet's voice in general – most noticeably, the self-representation of Archilochus, the public, religious poetry of, say, Alcman, the female voice of Sappho. This multiplication of modes of poetic production, the multiplication of places from which to speak, is indeed a fundamental element in the development of the possibilities of praise poetry. My selective treatment of the poetry that deals most explicitly with *kleos*, must also be seen in and against the *range* of lyric poetry's (public) voices, and I will try to indicate some of these alignments in the course of the more detailed discussion of the poetry of *kleos* itself.

The shifting relation between poet and the figure of *kleos* can be paradigmatically seen in these famous lines of Theognis (237–54)[128] – lines that indeed are to be placed against the public, authoritative ritual voice of an Alcman, the manipulation of persona in Archilochus, and the anatomy of desire in Sappho or Anacreon, as Theognis, in his constructed role as normative poet of the symposium, adopts the language of memorialization to discuss deception in an erotic affair (a voice set against and drawing on the possibilities of utterance in the *polis*). I quote them in full:

---

[128] The authenticity of these lines and their role in the collection of verses under the name of Theognis has been one of the most extensively discussed problems in the criticism of Theognis. See e.g. Kroll (1936) 151–73, 285–95; Carrière (1948a) 102–4 (with useful bibliography); Carrière (1948b) 106, 189–90, 194–5; Hudson-Williams (1910) ad loc.; Harrison (1902) 124; van Groningen (1966) ad loc.; Gerber (1970) ad loc.

σοὶ μὲν ἐγὼ πτέρ᾽ ἔδωκα, σὺν οἷς ἐπ᾽ ἀπείρονα πόντον
    πωτήσῃ, κατὰ γῆν πᾶσαν ἀειρόμενος
ῥηιδίως· θοίνῃς δὲ καὶ εἰλαπίνῃσι παρέσσῃ
    ἐν πάσαις πολλῶν κείμενος ἐν στόμασιν,
καί σε σὺν αὐλίσκοισι λιγυφθόγγοις νέοι ἄνδρες
    εὐκόσμως ἐρατοὶ καλά τε καὶ λιγέα
ᾄσονται. καὶ ὅταν δνοφερῆς ὑπὸ κεύθεσι γαίης
    βῇς πολυκωκύτους εἰς Ἀίδαο δόμους,
οὐδέποτ᾽ οὐδὲ θανὼν ἀπολεῖς κλέος, ἀλλὰ μελήσεις
    ἄφθιτον ἀνθρώποις αἰὲν ἔχων ὄνομα,
Κύρνε, καθ᾽ Ἑλλάδα γῆν στρωφώμενος, ἠδ᾽ ἀνὰ νήσους
    ἰχθυόεντα περῶν πόντον ἐπ᾽ ἀτρύγετον,
οὐχ ἵππων νώτοισι ἐφήμενος· ἀλλά σε πέμψει
    ἀγλαὰ Μουσάων δῶρα ἰοστεφάνων.
πᾶσι δ᾽, ὅσοισι μέμηλε, καὶ ἐσσομένοισιν ἀοιδὴ
    ἔσσῃ ὁμῶς, ὄφρ᾽ ἂν γῆ τε καὶ ἠέλιος.
αὐτὰρ ἐγὼν ὀλίγης παρὰ σεῦ οὐ τυγχάνω αἰδοῦς,
    ἀλλ᾽ ὥσπερ μικρὸν παῖδα λόγοις μ᾽ ἀπατᾷς.

I have given you wings, with which you will fly
over the boundless sea and all the land, aloft,
with ease. You will be present at feasts and banquets,
every one, resting on the lips of many;
and the desired young men with sharp-voiced flutes
will sing, decorously, beautifully and high,
of you. When you go beneath the hiding places of dark earth
to the tearful halls of Hades, never –
not even in death – will you lose fame; rather, you will be
a care for mortals and have always an immortal name,
Cyrnus. You will travel through the Greek land and through the islands,
crossing the fish-filled, unharvested ocean,
not seated on the back of horses; but the shining gifts
of the Muses will transport you.
To all alike who care for such things, future generations too,
you will be a song, while earth and sun are.
But I receive scant respect from you.
You deceive me with words as if I were a small boy.

The 'winged words' of Homeric *epos* become wings to transport the
subject of Theognis' verse far and wide. The emphatic σοί, 'you', however, first word of the first couplet, juxtaposed to ἐγώ, 'I', immediately
signals the different relations of poet and subject from that in Homeric
epic. Here, the figure addressed in the poem is conceived as the projected
audience – the recipient – of the poem in a manner quite different from

the *Odyssey*'s and the *Iliad*'s restricted use of apostrophe and restricted projection of a contemporary audience[129]. In part, this results in a fore-grounding of the individual poetic persona[130] as dominant force in the exchange (ἐγώ ... ἔδωκα, '*I* have given ...' – a further rhetorical gesture of 'sealing' (*sphrēgis*)[131] and a boast which is (self-)fulfilled in every reading of the poem. In part, this shift of emphasis is the closing of distance between poet and subject that the fiction of contemporaneous-ness inevitably creates, the vivid risk of the exchange of poetic utterance. There is more, however, here also: for the shifters ἐγώ, 'I', and σοί, 'you' – markers of the difference and rhetoric of *dialogue* – also stand without the framing of a narrator's voice. There is no position outside the poem's dialogic exchange from which the lines can securely be read. The poet enters his poem in (the fabrication of) an exchange. This opening of dialogue will further find its point when the μέν ('on the one hand'), which separates the σοί ('you') and ἐγώ ('I'), finds its response in the final couplet.

This sense of a more explicit involvement of the poet in dialogue with a projected audience is a dominant aspect of the Theognidean corpus, not merely in the poems addressed to Cyrnus. The didactic *gnōmai* again and again instruct, cajole and stricture the reader/audience; the poet talks of rejection by and involvement with his audience; his exile; impoverishment; and moral certainty. This audience is described by Nagy in an important article as an 'ostensibly integral community of *philoi* that is the *polis* of Megara'.[132] 'Ostensibly integral' may be taken to imply the active and uneasy formulation of an audience (and a *polis*). For on the one hand Theognis' poetry declares itself to – *and thus is part of the fabrication of* – a group of *philoi*. The poetic performance creates and marks a group (which may be seen as a microcosm of the *polis*[133]). On the other hand, the *philoi* are always opposed not merely to *ekhthroi* ('enemies' as opposed to 'friends'), but also to the πόνηροι/κακοί/μῶροι

---

[129] On Homeric apostrophe and the relation to an audience, see Block (1982); Frontisi-Ducroux (1986) 27–9, 47–78; de Jong (1987) 13, 18 and especially 53ff. Grillo (1988) 9–67 is less useful.

[130] So Theognis is treated as a highly individual person(a), e.g. 'Just a casual perusal of the corpus reveals a poet who is virtually Achillean in temperament and outlook, and one who is as deeply committed to the notion of revenge as are the greatest of the Greek aristocratic figures ... Theognis is subject to abrupt outbursts of begrudging bitterness and revengeful pique' (Tarkow (1977) 112).

[131] Theognis' 'seal' has been most extensively discussed; see e.g. Woodbury (1952) and Ford (1985) both with good further bibliographies.

[132] Nagy (1985) 27.   [133] See Levine (1985).

('evil'/'bad'/'foolish'): the *philoi* are the ἀγαθοί/ἐσθλοί/καλοί/σοφοί ('good', 'noble', 'fine', 'wise').[134] They are a group apart from, distinct from, the collective of the *polis*. Moreover, it is an audience addressed as 'good', 'noble', 'fine', 'wise', as it is instructed by the poet in the values of what it means to be 'good', 'noble', 'fine', 'wise'. It is an audience challenged by the poetry to see the tensions (of the *polis*) within itself – as, indeed, in the lines under discussion Cyrnus is singled out for his deception of and as a *philos*. Indeed, 'a very large number of verses in the collection are concerned with friendship [*philotēs*] – political, personal, erotic'.[135] The poet's disquisitions to the community of *philoi* turn on the problematic values of *philotēs*, as the integration of the community is shown to be open to the violent political and social tensions that lead towards disintegration. If the vocabulary of *philotēs* is instrumental in the *Iliad*'s articulation of the conflict of heroes, so too the normative terminology of *philotēs* is a key structuring principle of Theognis' involvement with the limits and transgressions of social order. The role Theognis plays, however, is not Homer, but Phoenix – ἐν δ' ὑμῖν ἐρέω ... φίλοισι, 'I speak before you my *philoi*' (*Il.* 9.528). Or rather, Theognis on the one hand authorizes his utterance from the Muses and as the inherited wisdom of the good and noble (ἀγαθοί) of previous generations (which will make him also famous).[136] But on the other hand, far from being the voice simply through which such wisdom about *philotēs* pours, the poet is crucially involved in the reciprocity of *philotēs* – in which his poetry also has a *performative* value. It is within the context of a relation of *philotēs* that Theognis offers Cyrnus wings, and, as in Homer, the dynamics of this relation affect significantly the connections between the poet's voice and *kleos*.

To return to Homer to gloss the lines of Theognis under discussion is far from gratuitous. Not only does Theognis elsewhere liken himself explicitly to Odysseus,[137] but also these lines frequently echo the Homeric epics in a striking way. Commentators have collected the majority of the parallels, but there have been few attempts to investigate the significance of what is a remarkable density of allusion, beyond such general remarks as 'Theognis' wish [is] to remind his audience of Homer who above all confers immortality on his heroes'.[138] Theognis' adaptation of

---

[134] On these oppositions, see for the most recent discussion and bibliography Cobb-Stevens (1985).

[135] Donlan (1985) 224; and on these lines Gentili (1977).   [136] See Theognis 23–8.

[137] Theognis 1123ff, as discussed by Nagy (1985) 74–81; van Groningen (1966) ad loc.

[138] Campbell (1967) 362. The density of allusion has now been explored at great length by Sacks (1987).

Homeric discourse is, however, complex – not only is it a rewriting of Homer's language of praise, but also it necessarily involves a strategy of rereading which is instigated by the last couplet's surprising conclusion. This complexity can be seen clearly in the opening phrase. If the wings of praise echo Homer's 'winged words', what is the effect of the recipient of *kleos* being said to have wings and fly over land and sea? Is it merely a heightened turn of rhetoric (destined to become a perennial trope via Ennius) – 'enthusiastic praise',[139] which uses the Homeric past to add grandeur to the present? Or is it, as Carrière, with an eye on the final lines, believes, closer to sarcastic parody – not so much heightened as overblown?[140] The phrase ἐπ' ἀπείρονα πόντον, 'over the boundless sea', occurs only once in the *Iliad* and *Odyssey*, as Achilles looks out 'over the boundless sea' after the loss of his *timē*.[141] Is the precise context of Achilles' sense of outrage to be activated at least when the final couplet is reached? Is the twist of the final couplet more effective if there is no hint of the reversal in the preceding lines? How can the final couplet *not* invest the earlier lines with some extra, ironic significance?

The expressions of praise set the promise of Cyrnus' renown first in the context of the symposium – the collectivity of *philoi*. He will be sung at banquets and feasts by the young men whose decorous behaviour (εὐκόσμως) and desirability (ἔρατοι) are the subject par excellence of poets of the symposium such as Theognis. Both θοίνη, 'banquet', and εἰλαπίνη, 'feast', are rare words touched with the grandeur of Homeric feasting. Indeed, the reward offered for anyone who will undertake the expedition of the Doloneia is to be allowed 'always to attend feasts and banquets' (*Il.* 10.217). It is, presumably, as song (*kleos*) that Cyrnus' presence is promised. Theognis has turned the Homeric prize to an expression of praise. The songs that will be sung will be 'beautiful and high'. The symposium at which Cyrnus is imagined 'lying in the mouths of many',[142] is a paragon of parties, as the praise amongst all men across all land and the sea is the height of glorification.

Even in death, Cyrnus will not lose his *kleos*. Both the phrase ὑπὸ κεύθεσι γαίης, 'beneath the recesses of the earth', and the phrase Ἀΐδαο δόμους, 'halls of Hades', occur only once in Homer, in the same line

---

[139] See e.g. Hudson-Williams (1910) ad loc. Carrière (1948a) ad loc. corrects 'enthusiastic' into 'sarcastic'.

[140] Carrière (1948a) 102–4 ('c'est une pure et simple parodie'); Carrière (1948b) 106; 189–90; 194–5.

[141] *Il.* 1.350. But cf. *Od.* 4.510.

[142] The verb 'lying' (κεῖσθαι) is used both of symposia (particularly κατακεῖσθαι) and of the dead, particularly in epitaphs. It is also used of 'storing up' treasures: κειμήλια κεῖται.

(*Il.* 22.482), where Andromache describes the loss of Hector: is the bitter pathos of that scene to be recalled here in the supposed death of Cyrnus? The Homeric line is broken here into two expressions, and the adjectives δνοφερῆς, 'dusky', and πολυκωκύτους, 'much bewailed', further stress Theognis' rewriting. δνοφερά, 'dusky', occurs only very infrequently in Homer, twice applied to night (*Od.* 13.269, *Od.* 15.50.) and twice to a stream of water compared to tears (*Il.* 9.15; *Il.* 16.4.). Here, Theognis calls 'the land' dusky (cf. Hesiod *Theog.* 736 – γῆς δνοφερῆς). πολυκώκυτος, 'much bewailed', is a *hapax legomenon*. Theognis breaks the Homeric expression of grief and mourning with the signature of his individual (re)usage. So, where Homer's Agamemnon says of Achilles (*Od.* 24.93–4):

> So, not even in death have you lost your name, but always
> among all men will there be your noble fame, Achilles

Theognis makes *kleos* the object of future loss, and *onoma*, 'name', the object of permanent possession. *Aphthiton*, 'immortal', the crucial qualifier of *fame* for Achilles, is here transferred to *name* for Cyrnus – and the vocative 'Cyrnus' is delayed in the poem precisely to be juxtaposed to the word 'name'. (It is the only occasion in the collection where the vocative is left so late.) The poem frames the name of Cyrnus – the performance of *kleos*. ἀνθρώποις μελήσεις, 'you will be a concern/care for men', however, adds a different note. It recalls in particular Odysseus' announcement of *kleos* – ἀνθρώποισι μέλω, 'I am a concern for men ...' (*Od.* 9.20), where the ambiguity of μέλω, 'be a care, concern', was noted. Is the ambivalence of Odysseus' self-proclaimed fame as the archdeceiver to be recalled here as Theognis approaches the final couplet's accusation of treachery? So at 251 Theognis repeats the verb (μέμηλε), juxtaposed to the promise that Cyrnus will be a song for future generations. Agamemnon sets in opposition the fates of 'pleasant song' and 'hateful song' (*Od.* 24.197–200). Both the verb μέμηλε, 'to be a care', and the *unqualified* use of 'song' may seem double edged when the poem is reread in the light of the final couplet. As Tarkow asks, 'when, in short, does the *aprosdokēton* [sting in the tail] begin'.[143]

'But I on the other hand', αὐτὰρ ἐγὼν (253), answers 'To you on the one hand', σοὶ μέν, of the opening line. Theognis follows the boasted claim of poetry's power to immortalize with a statement of the failure of

---

[143] Tarkow (1977) 114.

reciprocity. His *philos* has failed in the obligation of *aidōs*.[144] The beloved Cyrnus deceives the poet with words as if he were a παῖς, a 'boy'. (Gentili's observation[145] that the verb ἀπατάω, 'deceive', is used regularly in erotic contexts and that this couplet refers specifically to a failure of erotic exchange – 'amore efebico' – adds a particular point to the word παῖς, which even here qualified by μικρός, 'small', recalls the normal address to the object of Theognis' poetry and desire, ὦ παῖ.)[146] The poem may frame the name Cyrnus, but it also frames Cyrnus as a figure of deceit: the *kleos* which is perpetuated in and as this poem, is of Cyrnus' failure to match the obligation of reciprocal exchange lauded – apparently – in the opening lines of the poem. Cyrnus will be on the lips of many, but as what sort of an exemplum? The echoes and rewriting of the Homeric discourse of praise do not merely 'remind [the] audience of Homer' as a paradigmatic model of immortalizing fame, but also serve to mark the parodic turn of praise, as renown becomes an everlasting reputation for deceit. Both the dense allusions and the reworking of Homeric language stress the particular involvement of the figure of the poet in the fabrication of *kleos*, the exchanges of poetic performance.

These lines, then, finally take revenge on Cyrnus for his transgression, and they do so in a manner which fits the crime. For if Cyrnus has deceived Theognis with words, Theognis offers the promise of immortalization in his words – the 'loyalty' of *philos* to *philos* – only to stain such a promise with the reversal of the final lines: 'after an enthusiastic and optimistic description of this demonstration of loyalty, Theognis brutally deceives his young friend's expectation of where the poem is heading'.[147] Theognis, who likens himself to Odysseus, uses the deceptive powers of language to effect a revenge on an outrage to *philotēs*. The language of praise becomes an ironic reminder of failed *aidōs*, and a demonstration of the reversals of revenge. Within the exchanges and transgressions of *philotēs* that structure the relation of poet and addressee, the language of *kleos* itself is informed by an ironic doubleness and deceit.

These lines draw on the poet's claim to immortalize a person's deeds in *kleos*, but both the poet's position with regard to that exchange and

---

[144] 'The poetry of Theognis is based on an ideology that awards the highest priority to the quality of being *philos*' (Nagy (1985) 29); see also Donlan (1985).

[145] (1977) 115.

[146] Gentili also notes the similarity between these lines and 1263–6, which also address a boy (ὦ παῖ) and accuse him of not showing *aidōs*. But this echo, first noted by Couat (1883) 257–90, has recently been denied by Vetta (1980) ad 1266.

[147] Tarkow (1977) 114.

the effect of the final reversal on the whole poem, make it quite insufficient to regard these lines merely as demonstrating a continuity in poetic function or as proving that a lyric poet's concern or aim is to perpetuate his addressee in *kleos*. Once again, the language of praise refers to the simple model of great deeds immortalized in poetry, as it works through, manipulates and distorts such a model in the specificity of poetic production.

The shifting relation of poet and addressee in lyric poetry and the interest in the construction of *kleos* can be seen from a different angle in Ibycus fr. 263 (Page). Many lines of this extensive poem in praise of the tyrant Polycrates[148] are lost or fragmentary; clearly enough, however, the final stanza's praise of Polycrates is approached in the opening verses which survive[149] by a version of the Trojan war (1–22), with a catalogue of heroes involved in the siege of the city. Ibycus offers, however, a catalogue of heroes whom he will *not* celebrate (10ff): 'Now [it is] not for me to sing of lusting Paris who deceived his host, nor long-ankled Cassandra, nor . . .' – where to name is to record as it is to pass over, and where – paradigmatically – the day of the capture of Troy is announced as *anōnumon*, 'nameless', 'not to be named'.[150] This rhetoric of *praeteritio*[151] adds a specific twist to the contrast Ibycus makes between the Muses' *sophiē*,[152] 'wisdom' 'skill', and a mere mortal's incapacity to record the ships and men of the expedition – an opposition that echoes Homer's introduction to the catalogue of ships *Il.* 2.484–93 (23–7): 'The

---

[148] Critics, worried about the apparent praise of youthful beauty, have doubted at length whether this is the famous tyrant Polycrates: White (1954); Barron (1964) and (1969) 136–8; Sisti (1966); West (1970) 206–9; Péron (1982) 36–8; Woodbury (1985) 207–20 (with extensive further bibliography).

[149] Some lines before the first verse of our fragment are certainly lost, though there is no way of telling how many verses or what they contained. Fraenkel (1975) 288–91 attempts a reconstruction.

[150] Cf. *Od.* 19.260 where Troy is called Κακοίλιον οὐκ ὀνομαστήν, 'Evil Troy, not to be named', by Penelope because it has taken Odysseus from her. In Ibycus, Troy's capture is not to be named as the heroes are not to be recounted – a pointed reworking of Homeric usage. Lavagnini (1947) 207 glosses ἀνώνυμον with ἄδοξον, 'in quanto la città perisce senza gloria per l'inganno del cavallo'. The lack of reference to the horse or the trick makes this difficult to accept. Maehler (1963) 75 n. 3, who denies that there is a relevant echo of *Odyssey* 19 here, glosses the phrase with 'der Troja namenlos gemacht, seinen Namen ausgelöscht hat'.

[151] On the rhetorical structure of the fragment, see Snell (1944); Nannini (1982) 75–6; Rissman (1983) 47–8.

[152] On σοφίη and the Muses, see West (1978) ad 649 and Nagy (1985) 23–6 and, on its surprising use here, Woodbury (1985) 200–1.

Helikonian[153] Muses with their skill and knowledge could well embark on [an account]. But a living mortal man could not say in each detail how great a number of ships came from Aulis . . . '[154] Ibycus refuses to re-count the heroes at Troy and their ships (as he sets up the roster of heroes as a priamel to Polycrates' fame): his expression of human, poetic limitation is also a subordinating, appropriating gesture towards the heroic narratives of the past.[155]

The final lines of the poem make explicit a connection between the poet and his patron in terms of *kleos*, but there are problems of translation (46–8):

> τοῖς μὲν πέδα κάλλεος αἰὲν
> καὶ σύ, Πολύκρατες, κλέος ἄφθιτον ἑξεῖς
> ὡς κατ᾽ ἀοιδὰν καὶ ἐμὸν κλέος.

If the first line is printed as it is here (in Page's text), then πέδα is taken as a preposition and the lines can be translated 'Among them [the heroes], Polycrates, you will have an immortal fame for beauty, as too is my fame for song.'[156] (It may be assumed, despite μορφάν 49, 'shape', that 'beauty' is not merely a physical attribute – the definition of what is *kalos* plays a crucial role in lyric poetry's distance from epic, as Sappho's fr. 16 shows

---

[153] In calling the Muses Helikonian, Ibycus is also echoing Hesiod (*Works and Days* 646–62). On the possible significance of this, see Barron (1969) 134, who writes 'By recalling these lines, Ibycus sets his own reputation as a poet more tactfully before his audience'. See also Treu (1955) 283ff and Gianotti (1973) 404–6 for Ibycus' relation to Hesiod.

[154] For the problems of the text here – I have translated Barron's text – and for the many suggestions made on these lines, see Woodbury (1985) 197–200, especially 197 n. 10, 199.

[155] Which is not to say that Bowra (1961) 252–7, who follows Schneidewin, is right to see this poem as indicating a self-conscious change in direction of poetic career for Ibycus – an argument developed in most depth by Sisti (1967). For a more sensitive approach along these lines, see Woodbury (1985) 193–206. Page (1951), who calls this poem 'spiritless and trivial', focuses his criticisms on the poem's use of the past (165): the heroes' 'splendid virtues are reduced to form a background for the mention of a pretty face'. So, too, Sisti (1967) 74 calls the use of Homeric language 'superficiale e limitata alle espressioni piu convenzionali dello stile epico'. For a more sensitive approach to Ibycus' attitude to Homer see in particular Péron (1982) 50–6.

[156] This reading of πέδα is followed by the first editors, who remove the stop at the end of 46 in the manuscripts, and by others including Wilamowitz (1922) 511; Fränkel (1975) 289 (who also says he does not understand the grammar of the last two lines); van Groningen (1958) 187; Sisti (1967) 74; Gentili (1978) 396, 400 n. 13; Woodbury (1985) 203–4.

in a privileged way.)[157] Campbell, however, puts a comma after αἰέν, and construes πέδα as a verb (= μέτεστι): 'they share in beauty for ever, as you too, Polycrates, will have undying fame, as song and my fame can give it.'[158] In either case, Polycrates is promised 'immortal fame', *aphthiton kleos*, Achilles' object of desire, though in the first case the fame is specifically for 'beauty'. In either case, the final line also puts the *kleos* of the tyrant in relation to the poet's *kleos* (as Polycrates' fame is also the culmination of the *kleos* of the (Homeric) heroes). Yet the ὡς clause, too, has a certain ambiguity of construction. In my translation of Page's text, καὶ ἐμὸν κλέος, 'as too is my fame', is made parallel to Polycrates' 'immortal fame', and κατ' ἀοιδάν, 'for song', qualifies this fame of the poet. The fame of the poet for his song is unfading as, too, is the fame of his patron: ὡς, 'as', indicates an analogy between the poet's *kleos* and his patron's.[159] In Campbell's translation, however, καὶ ἐμὸν κλέος is dependent on κατά. The *kleos* of Polycrates is made crucially *dependent* on the song and the *kleos* of the poet: the two are not analogous but coextensive; Polycrates' fame is 'according to the song and fame' of the poet.[160]

If πέδα is a syntactic obscurity that leaves a complex choice for editors, the reasons offered by editors for their choices are based not merely on linguistic usage but inevitably also on their assumptions about what is suitable praise for a poet to offer a tyrant/patron. So Gerber writes[161] in favour of the verb: 'The former seems preferable ... since the fame which Polycrates will have probably includes more than simply fame for beauty.' So Woodbury[162] on behalf of the preposition: 'What poets do promise is what the first construction offers ... It seems clear that the

---

[157] On Sappho's fr. 16 see DuBois (1978); Thorsen (1978); Most (1981); Rissman (1983) 30–65; Barkhuizen and Els (1983) and Winkler (1990) (ch. 6). On the similar problem of the sense of *agathos* and its distance from epic in Simonides' Scopas fragment, see Woodbury (1953); Donlan (1969); Gentili (1984) 88ff; and in particular Svenbro (1976) 141ff.

[158] Barron (1969) especially 135–6, West (1970) 206–9, Gianotti (1973) 407–10 defend the manuscript's stop; Bowra and Gerber prefer a comma. Péron (1982) 35–6 translates and prints a stop, though is uncertain in his discussion.

[159] This is the more common view; it includes e.g. Page, Wilamowitz, van Groningen, Bowra, Sisti, Gerber, Gentili.

[160] So e.g. Barron (1969) 135; Gianotti (1973) 407–10; Snell (1961) 54–6; 'he says, playfully but clearly, that he is the equal of the tyrant' (56); so, too, Wellein (1959–60) 40f writes 'Ibycus has made it clear that he alone, the poet, is responsible for the immortality of Polycrates.'

[161] (1970) ad 46.   [162] (1985) 203–4.

preposition serves their purpose better than the verb.' These two critics demonstrate how an element of presupposition about what is suitable praise affects their readings of the poem. A recognition of this active involvement of the reader in the poetic exchange is crucial for appreciating the force of the ambiguity of the ὡς clause. For the final phrase raises the fundamental *question* of the interdependence of poet and subject in the production of *kleos*. Is the fame of a powerful tyrant *dependent on* the *kleos* of the poet? Or is the fame of the tyrant simply like the fame of the poet? Is the poet dependent on the tyrant for his subject and livelihood? Such ambiguities may or may not lead to a gesture of resolution based on criteria such as what is suitable praise; it depends, of course, on the reader or audience – and the patron is the audience *par excellence*. The patron as audience is also implicated in demarcating the praise he is offered by the poet. The ambiguous language of *kleos* manipulates and veils the lines of power in the poetic exchange.

In short, in the final lines of this poem there can be read the complex interplay of rhetoric and power enacted in the poetry of patronage. The rhetoric of *dependence* marks the inevitable *dialectic* of power involved – performed – in such poetry: the repetition of the term *kleos* suggests a close interrelation between the poet's and the patron's fame, but the final phrase veils the precise nature of the interrelation in a certain ambiguity. While there is a recognition in Homer of the bard's need to satisfy his audience by his performance, and some elements of the text of Homer have been claimed since antiquity to be the result of a political patronage,[163] it is only here in lyric poetry that the poet and the subject of his poetry become directly linked (as subjects) and discussed as linked within the poetry. Immortalization in song as a rhetoric of poetic production inevitably changes when the figure of *kleos* is living and in a position of power – and this is a fundamental difference between Homer's poetry of praise and the lyric poetry which echoes it. 'To what degree is the *kleos* of the subject of the poem subject to the *kleos* of the poet/poem?' is a question raised by the final lines of Ibycus' poem and replayed again and again in the encomiastic literature of Greece and Rome.

My final examples of the developing relation between the poet and the figure of *kleos* start from two epigrams said to be by Simonides, the

---

[163] See in particular, Arist. *Rhet*. A 15, 1375b30, who recounts the accusation of the Megarans that the Athenians had added lines to the text of the catalogue of ships in order to justify their military expansionism.

most famous ancient writer of epitaphs.[164] The first is a couplet whose authenticity and provenance has been questioned by scholars (fr. 14 West).[165] It is quoted by Aristides as an example of 'self-praise in passing', which is the subject of his speech from which it comes, Περὶ τοῦ παραφθέγματος:[166]

> μνήμην δ' οὔτινά φημι Σιμωνίδη ἰσοφαρίζειν
> ὀγδωκονταέτει, παιδὶ Λεωπρέπεος.

> I say no memory is the equal of Simonides',
> The eighty-year old son of Leoprepes.

Aristides, with fine rhetoric, says that the second line is added so that no one could mistake the first as the arrogance or stupidity of youth. The couplet clearly utilizes the clichés of dedicatory epigrams and epitaphs. φημί, as with other first-person verbs of speech, inscribes what Austin and Searle[167] call 'the illocutionary' in the dedication: 'I declare', 'I announce' ... The first person is also often used in epitaphs for a personification of the dead person, particularly with the verb κεῖμαι, 'here I lie'. Here, the two functions overlap as the poet declares his own identity, his own praise. So, too, the identification of a person with age and father's name is typical of epitaphs in particular (and this line occurs also in another dedicatory epigram that comes down under the name of Simonides).[168] In his (self-)praise of his memory, Simonides' identification as an eighty-year old child takes on a further particular point (though not necessarily, as Aristides suggests, merely that he is old enough to know what he is talking about). Memory, however, may seem a surprising faculty to immortalize in the memorial of verse (even in passing). (There are many stories, which may begin from this epigram, that Simonides invented a mnemonic system which enabled him to perform feats of memory.)[169] The word μνήμην, 'memory', however, echoes another par-

---

[164] The authenticity of most of the epigrams ascribed to Simonides is questionable. Hauvette (1896) and Kaibel (1873) offer stringent criteria for accepting an epigram as genuine. Boas (1905) criticizes both, before developing his own system. West (1974) 1–21 has some sensible general remarks on the problems of transmission of this material.

[165] I have discussed the history of the discussion of this epigram in detail in Goldhill (1988b).

[166] Aristides Or. 28.59ff.

[167] Austin (1962); Searle (1969).

[168] Fr. 28 Page; 147 Bergk. This repetition is the sole reason offered by most scholars for the fragment's inauthenticity.

[169] See e.g. Marmor Par. FGrH 239 A 54; Call. fr. 64 Pfeiffer; Cic. de or. 2.86.351–4; Cic. Tusc. 1.24.59; Quint. XI.2.11; Pliny NH 7.24.89; Aelian Hist. Anim. 6.10; Amm.

ticular common feature of epitaphs, the use of the word μνῆμα, 'memorial', to refer to the monument to which the dedication is fixed. It is particularly common as the first word of the dedication, as with Simonides fr. 6 (Page), 26b (Page), 39 (Page), and many epigrams by other composers.[170] Simonides immortalizes his memory in an epigram which puns on the clichés of funerary dedications, his own expertise. The poem is not merely self-praise, but self-praise which proceeds through the self-mocking of parodic citation. To praise a patron requires a complex rhetorical awareness of the limitations and distinctions of flattery and glorification; so, too, self-praise is fenced here with a (defensive) rhetoric of self-deprecation.

A second epigram of Simonides also stands at an oblique angle to the norms of funerary verse (fr. 37 Page):[171]

> A great drinker, a great eater, a great slanderer
> Of men, here I lie Timocreon of Rhodes.

The verb *keimai*, 'here I lie', as well as the structure of the couplet, signal the *topoi* of an epitaph. What begins in the first line as an abusive epigram in the tradition of poetic invective – Archilochus' paradigmatic persona – turns in the second not only to an apparent self-promotion of abuse but also a self-promotion in the form of a permanent memorial (with its implications of pride and praise). Simonides wittily manipulates the conventions of funerary verse to speak ill of Timocreon (for speaking ill of men).

Timocreon's own poetic fragments construct a verbal assault on Themistocles, the great Athenian politician, in particular. Fr. 410 (Page) opens with a priamel of praise: 'If you praise Pausanias, or you Xanthippos, or you Leutuchides'. This leads to the 'name-cap' of Aristeides: 'but I praise Aristeides'. This, however, turns out to be a false announcement of subject as this *topos* of praise itself becomes a priamel for the insults to Themistocles: 'since Leto hated Themistocles, the liar, the unjust, the traitor who ...' The structuring of the poetry of praise acts as a foil for the poetry of blame.[172] So in fr. 411 (Page), Timocreon begins another

---

Marcell. 16.5.8. See Blum (1969) 41–6; Slater (1972). Slater in particular is criticized in Goldhill (1988b).

[170] The evidence is collected in Peek (1955) especially nos. 52–285. For a full study of the evidence, see Goldhill (1988b).

[171] The authenticity of this epigram also cannot be certain.

[172] Scodel (1983) 107 writes 'The piece thus depends on the matching and opposed topics of encomium and invective, because it is one pretending to be the other'. She discusses the reasons for Timocreon's hatred 104–7.

poem of even 'ruder defamation of Themistocles'[173] thus:

> Muse, set the fame [*kleos*] of this song
> throughout Greece,
> as is fit and just.

Timocreon appeals to the Muse to spread the *kleos* of this song through-out Greece (as is right and just) – a song which is to announce and perpetuate the defamation of its subject, Themistocles, whose name means 'Famed for Rightness'. Again, the poetry of blame manipulates the language of *kleos* as the immortalization of heroic deeds.

Timocreon's self-defence against the accusation of medizing in the Persian war is self-deprecating to good effect – a further twist to Archi-lochus' (in)famous self-representation as a coward who fled in battle (fr. 412 Page):

> It was not Timocreon alone, then,
> who dealt with the Medes;
> there are other crooks too,
> I am not the only one to lose my tail.
> There are other foxes too.

Even in the competitive, self-promoting culture of ancient Athens, effec-tive self-praise requires a certain rhetorical reticence, even, as here, to the point of a humorous, apparent undercutting. Plutarch's comment after quoting these lines is apposite (*Them.* 21):

When the citizens of Athens began to listen willingly to those who traduced and reproached him, Themistocles was forced, with somewhat obnoxious frequency, to put them in mind of the great services he had performed, and ask those who were offended with him whether they were weary of receiving benefits often from the same person – so rendering himself more odious.

The rhetorical manipulation of the memory of fine deeds, that is *kleos*, becomes the thematic focus of a work of memorializing history, as Plutarch recognizes in his tale the complexities of the fabrication of *kleos*, especially in praise of oneself.

Simonides and Timocreon, then, show well not only the variety of enunciative positions adopted by the poet of praise but also the complex interrelations of the language of praise and the language of blame (which are never simply opposed) in lyric poetry.

---

[173] The description is Plutarch's, who quotes the lines *Them.* 21.

While these brief examples show the complexity of different poets' manipulations of the language of praise, it would be quite wrong to conclude from these fragments that sixth- and fifth-century lyric poetry withdraws from the process of constructing *kleos* as a memorial of achievement. Especially in the funerary epigrams of writers such as Simonides (but in much other poetry too), a connection between *aretē*, 'excellence', 'virtue', and *kleos*, is repeatedly asserted. So, Simonides writes (fr. 9 Page):[174]

> Unquenchable fame these men made for their dear fatherland,
>   when they embraced the dark cloud of death.
> Nor by this death have they died, since their virtue glorifies
>   them and leads them upwards out of the house of Hades.

Asbeston kleos, 'unquenchable fame', may recall in particular the *Odyssey's* phraseology – Odysseus promises Alcinous 'unquenchable fame' if the king helps Odysseus reach his fatherland (*Od.* 7.333); Menelaus raises a tomb for Agamemnon to be his 'unquenchable fame' (*Od.* 4.584). The *aretē* which glorifies (κυδαίνουσ᾽) the dead warriors means that their death is no death, and it raises them up from Hades (which may perhaps hint towards Odysseus and the praise his *aretē* wins from the Underworld). Yet two further interrelated aspects of this epigram distinguish its discourse of praise from the Homeric epic in a way that points to a crucial development of poetry in the sixth and fifth centuries. First, the dead here are said to have wreathed their *fatherland* with *kleos*. *Kleos* does not apply directly to the fallen in battle, nor to their *aretē*, but to the country for which they fought. Second, these lines do not name the warriors either as individuals or as a collective body. This is not merely because a monument may have made the identification clear, nor merely because the memorial achieves an importance as (a genre of) poetry precisely through its general and generalizable qualities. Rather, the commitment to the state in the formulation of praise is a corollary to a realignment of the terms of individual success. It is to the increasing involvement of the state and in particular the *polis* in the language of praise that I wish to turn to conclude this section of the chapter.

---

[174] The authenticity of this epigram has often been doubted. It is quoted from *Anth. Pal.* 7.251, where it is ascribed to Simonides and said to be about 'those who died with Leonidas'. Bergk, followed by Bowra and Edmonds, suggested that this was an epitaph for the dead of Plataea. Campbell thinks that the rhetoric 'though undoubtedly impressive, suggests the fourth century rather than the early fifth'. The evidence is, however, far too piecemeal to make such a general observation.

It is precisely in the area of memorializing the dead that the *polis* can be seen to dominate the discourse of praise. Nicole Loraux in her ground-breaking study of the funeral oration in Athens has shown how the state introduces a ritual and instaurates a body of texts that are fundamental to understanding the development of the self-projection of the state and the individual's role in it.[175] The public funeral oration over those who have fallen in war for the *polis* – in a shared public tomb – replaces the glorification of an individual with the praise of the city as a collectivity. The state-appointed orator praises the city in front of the citizens, as the warriors are buried together in a single δημόσιον σῆμα, 'state monument', which is also a sign of the democratic state's claim on and over the individual. This ritual is perhaps an extreme example óf the way in which the fifth-century democratic city in particular is formed in an ideology of the subsumption of the individual in the collectivity of the *polis*. That a person fights and dies for the *polis*, however, is a commonplace of sixth- and fifth-century writing that fundamentally alters the lineaments of praise in all areas of Greek discourse. A 'noble death' alters in constitution and rhetorical implication, as the glory of the dead moves 'from aristocratic celebration to collective praise'.[176] The extent of this change can be seen for example in the terminology of this famous epigram, which mentions neither fatherland nor *polis*, and may even at first sight seem highly 'traditional' in its memorialization of Leonidas for his *aretē* (fr. 362 Page):

> For those who died at Thermopylae
> a famous fate, a noble destiny;
> their tomb, an altar; a memorial instead of tears; their pity, praise.
> Such a shroud neither decay
> nor all-conquering time will waste.
> This shrine of heroic men holds the fine reputation
> of Greece in attendance.[177] Leonidas too bears witness,
> the king of the Spartans, who has left a great adornment
> of virtue, and an everlasting fame.

---

[175] Loraux (1981a), now translated as Loraux (1986). See also Loraux (1982). Since Loraux, there has also appeared Clairmont (1983).

[176] Loraux (1981a) 42; elsewhere ((1982) 32) she writes '*la belle mort est toujours en elle-même déjà discours*: un *topos* rhétorique, le lieu privilégié de l'enracinement d'une idéologie, du monde d'Achille à celui de la cité démocratique'.

[177] West (1970) 210 rightly points out that οἰκέτης should not be translated as 'inhabitant' as it most often is here. But it does not have quite the same connotations as δοῦλος: hence 'in attendance' rather than 'as a slave'.

The fate/fortune (*tukhē*) of the Spartans is εὐκλεής, 'glorious', 'of good fame', their death/destiny is noble (*kalos*). This is not a tautology[178] but, in the opening terms of what will be a catalogue, sets in juxtaposition the crucially interdependent terms of the proper death and the possibilities of *kleos*. In calling the tomb an altar, Simonides treats the dead warriors as heroes[179] – a gesture that is not merely rhetorical but is also reflected, for example, in the rites surrounding the collective tomb of the war dead in Athens.[180] Heroic status is achieved by those who die in battle for the city. It is a tomb at which mourning is replaced by memorialization, pity with praise. The reaction of an Achilles, say, to the death of the warrior Patroclus is replaced by an *encomium*[181] and a glorification – recognition not remorse. This tomb is a shrine specifically of *agathoi andres*. Loraux discusses at length this formula for the citizen soldier fallen in combat.[182] *Agathos anēr*, 'the good man', and *agathos genesthai*, 'to prove oneself a good man', take on through the sixth and fifth centuries the specific connotations of proving one's *aretē* in the context of fighting for the (collectivity of the) city. (The Homeric hero *is agathos*, the fifth-century citizen must become *agathos* – ἀγαθός γίγνεσθαι.) 'S'il chante les *agathoi* des Thermopyles, Simonide connaît le prix d'une *arétè* plus positive, qui trouve dans la cité son terrain d'action.'[183] Leonidas, the king of the Spartans, is singled out, but as an example of their shared bravery ('Leonidas also bears witness . . .'). The result is an inheritance of great credit for *aretē*, and everlasting *kleos* (significantly last word, picking up εὐκλεής, 'of good *kleos*'). This epitaph, then, demonstrates clearly the poet's function in the construction and preservation of *kleos* for mighty martial deeds. What has changed in the context of the *polis* is the conditions of possibility of fame. Now a 'noble death', which makes possible the destiny of a 'fine fame' and even heroic status, depends on fighting in and for the collectivity of the state.

---

[178] Here I differ from Loraux (1981a) 37ln. 185 who writes 'εὐκλεής μὲν ἡ τύχα, καλὸς δ' ὁ πότμος, n'est il pas lui même pléonastique, redoublant la formulation de la belle mort'. Rather, it significantly separates the differing constituent factors of 'la belle mort'.

[179] On the cult of the dead at Thermopylae, see Wilamowitz (1913) 176; Bowra (1961) 349; and, against these writers, Podlecki (1968).

[180] Loraux (1981a) 37–42.

[181] An encomium is Diodorus' term for this poem (xi.11.6) (which has been contested); see Podlecki (1968) 257–62.

[182] Loraux (1981a) index *sub Agathoi*, and *anēr agathos*.

[183] Loraux (1981a) 100 – as several recent writers have emphasized in their analysis of the Scopas ode in particular. See e.g. Woodbury (1953); Donlan (1969); Gentili (1984) 88ff; and in particular Svenbro (1976) 141ff.

The poet becomes the spokesman, the interpreter, the questioner, the advocate of the *polis* – the *sophos* who, like Solon, plays a (leading) role in the *polis*. In this light, it is worth returning to Theognis. For the poetry of Theognis transcends its parochial commitment to a sector of sixth-century Megaran society precisely in that it is 'political poetry in the truest sense, an explication of how life is to be led in the *polis*.'[184] So, Nagy has argued, 'the attitude of Theognis towards his community is ... parallel to that of the generic lawgiver';[185] he represents a 'moral authority'[186] who is also a 'response'[187] to Megaran society and to Theognis' position in it – the 'dispossessed pilot' seeking to straighten the veering ship of state.[188] It is within the tensions of the *polis* that Theognis is necessarily set. Edmunds specifies this relation further: Theognis' poetry, he writes, 'creates its audience anew wherever it is recited. This poetry even includes instructions for some particular means of its diffusion, namely, the symposium and the pederastic relationship. In this way, the poetry of *sophiē* establishes its reciprocity with the city'.[189] As the city provides the arena for poetry, so the poetry seeks to create 'the true city in that city'.[190]

This 'primacy of the state as the recipient of an individual's energies and affections ... is a demonstrable concern'[191] of Tyrtaeus' poetry also. Here, too, as the sense of *agathos/aretē* is sited within the context of the *polis*, the role of the poet develops.[192] Tarkow writes of the tension in Tyrtaeus' writing between the 'obsessive concern with non-individuality'[193] that the developing ideology of the Spartan state incorporates, and the self-consciousness of the poet as he seeks to establish a new *aretē* against the poetry of the past. Ibycus, Theognis and Simonides link the fame of the poet and the fame of the subject of poetry; but in the case of Tyrtaeus' exhortatory elegiacs, addressed to anonymous warriors, where no single fighter is identified or instructed by name, 'the recipient is the *polis*, or the *pas dēmos* ['the whole people'] of the Spartans, and thus his own individual fame is bound up with a group in much the same way as will be the individual fighter's'.[194] This connection be-

---

[184] Figuera and Nagy (1985) 2.   [185] Nagy (1985) 31.   [186] Id. 36.   [187] Id. 41.
[188] Id. 81.   [189] Edmunds (1985) 110.   [190] Ib.   [191] Tarkow (1983) 55.
[192] See e.g. Shey (1976); Jaeger (1966); Bowra (1938) 39–70 and the excellent edition of Prato (1968). A similar change of focus has been noted in Xenophanes' verse, where Jaeger (1966) 130, for example, writes that in Xenophanes 'the welfare of the polis is the standard measure for the value of ἀρετή'. See also the important discussion of Svenbro (1976) 77–107.
[193] Tarkow (1983) 61.   [194] Tarkow (1983) 63.

tween fighter and poet is further extended by Tarkow, who argues that Tyrtaeus' verse is 'practising what he is preaching' as his poetry dedicates itself to the 'selfless furtherance of the military and political destinies of the state'.[195] The poems' rhetoric of assertive statement (rather than questioning, proof or clarification) is not merely 'exhortatory propaganda of what should be; it is also an enthusiastic statement of what is'[196] – the commitment to the *aretē* of involvement in the collectivity of the state and its military obligations. So, Tarkow concludes, 'his self-consciousness, while on the one hand according well with so much of what poetry in the Archaic Age reveals, accords on the other hand with the new Spartan system itself, for it is camouflaged self-consciousness and self-assertion, submerged in the very discourse of the group which it affirms'.[197]

This tension is particularly evident in the discourse of *kleos*. In poem 9, Tyrtaeus lists the benefits first of dying for the state (27–34) and second of surviving the battle on behalf of the state (35–42). The living warrior receives *timē* from all, as the dead warrior is mourned by all (27–8).[198] The *timē* that is crucial to Achilles' and, say, to Sarpedon's rationale for risking life in war becomes the reward for a struggle which is 'this common good for the city and all the people', ξυνὸν δ᾽ ἐσθλὸν τοῦτο πολήί τε πάντι τε δήμῳ (15).[199] *Timē* becomes not merely an expression and justification of the hierarchies of Homeric society, but a reward and sign of commitment to the collectivity of the *polis*. So when the promise of a 'good *kleos*' is announced and the continuity of the dead warrior's name is declared, it is placed in the context of fighting and dying for one's fatherland (31–4):

> Nor ever does his good fame perish, nor his name;
>   although he is below the land, he is immortal,
> the man whom wild Ares destroys as he excels in steadfastness
>   and in the struggle for his land and children.

A good *kleos* and a *kleos* for being good, as well as the name of the (unnnamed) warrior, will be preserved, as the dead become immortal under the land (ὑπὸ γῆς) because of their death for the land (γῆς πέρι) and for the continuity of the race (παίδων). Yet this memorial is here dependent on the memory – the mourning – of the entire *polis*, present

---

[195] Tarkow (1983) 66–7.   [196] Tarkow (1983) 67.   [197] Tarkow (1983) 69.
[198] On these lines, see also Shey (1976) 16–19.
[199] Jaeger (1966) 120ff notes this line in particular as marking a radical change in ethos in its ideology of collectivity and commitment of the individual to the common weal.

and future generations (27–30).[200] The poet promises *kleos* from the citizens as part of the exhortation to fight for the city rather than as a claim of his own poetic role and power. There is in Tyrtaeus also a *rewriting* of the terms of praise in the context of the developing ideology of the collectivity of the *polis*.

In this section, then, I have been tracing briefly through various poetic responses two integral developments in the Greek poetic tradition, which despite certain elements of continuity, fundamentally reconstitute the discourse of praise. Both the shifting relations between the poet and the subject of the poetry of praise – particularly in the poetry of patronage for a live and powerful figure – and the involvement of the individual in the *polis* will prove to be highly relevant to Pindar and the discourse of praise in the *epinikia*, and it is to Pindar that I wish to turn to conclude this chapter.

THE LIMITS OF PRAISE AND THE PRAISE OF LIMITS

The history of modern criticism of Pindar – a history which has been repeatedly reconstructed (as a genealogy) by critics[201] – turns on the notion of praise. It has become a *topos* of Pindaric criticism to name Bundy's development of Schadewaldt's formalist model of the *epinikion* ('victory ode') as a praiseworthy strategic move which opens new possibilities of understanding the Pindaric ode.[202] Although the dangers of reductionism inherent in the application of such a formalist model have been regularly asserted,[203] the articulation of the conventions of Pindaric composition around a central aim of glorifying and praising the victor has become a productive principle of analysis both for circumventing the critical impasses of previous generations and for investigating the literary

---

[200] 'Unlike what happens in the epic, the keeping alive of his memory is now made to depend on the continuity of life in a polis'. (Jaeger (1966) 122).

[201] See in particular Thummer (1968) 1–16; Young (1970a); Köhnken (1971) 1–18; Lloyd-Jones (1973); Hamilton (1974) 3–13; Carey (1981) 1–13; Most (1985) 11–41.

[202] Schadewaldt (1928); Bundy (1986) (first published 1962). Bundy describes and catalogues the rhetorical conventions and repeated formal devices of what he calls (35) 'oral, public, epideictic literature dedicated to the single purpose of eulogizing men and communities'. Bundy is followed most closely by Thummer (1968) and his formal model qualified in particular by Köhnken (1971); Hamilton (1974); Greengard (1980), but few of the critics mentioned below fail to mark their affiliations to and/or distance from Bundy's work.

[203] Most recently by Most (1985) 11–41. See also Young (1970b); Lloyd-Jones (1973); Rose (1974) 145–55; Lefkowitz (1975) 71–93; Lee (1978); Crotty (1980); Carey (1981) 1–13; Bernardini (1983) 22ff.

and social conditions of production for Pindar's odes. Finding the proper place for praise motivates both the criticism and the poetry of Pindar.

The importance of the construction of praise and the permanence of glory in the *epinikion*, then, make Pindar's work fundamental to this chapter. There is, moreover, in the Pindaric corpus a self-reflexive concern with the construction, aims and function of poetry which has been long recognized: Schadewaldt ('Sieglied-Motiv'), Bundy ('subjective foil'), Thummer ('Lob für den Dichter und seine Kunst') and Hamilton ('Poet's task'), all analyse the many references to poetic process within Pindar's poetry as a conventional element of the *epinikion*. The utilization and manipulation of such conventions, however, play an integral role both in the representation of a relation between poet and patron, and in the poet's articulation of the limits and possibilities of praise (a process which cannot be reduced to a mere convention). Self-awareness is a constitutive element of Pindar's rhetoric of praise. In attempting to evaluate the interplay of convention and manipulation, genre and individuality in such self-reflexive remarks about poetry in Pindar's poems, critical attention has focused on the general issue of the use of the first person in Pindar.[204] To what degree is Pindar's use of ἐγώ, 'I', to be taken as a marker of a personal statement? Or as a sign of a general (choric) statement? Can Pindar's poetic voice be distinguished from Pindar as (auto)biographical subjectivity? In these three interrelated problems, then – the construction of *kleos*, the self-reflexive concerns of poetry and the status of the first-person utterance – Pindar's *epinikia* offer a corpus of texts germane to the discussion of the poet's voice.

My approach to what could clearly be discussed at far greater length and in far greater detail than I have allowed myself here is the following. First, utilizing recent scholarly discussions, I shall outline briefly in general terms some general aspects of Pindar's *epinikia* (as poetic productions) which develop some of the concerns of the earlier sections of this chapter. Second, I shall look at one ode in more detail – a poem that has been surprisingly rarely discussed, *Olympian* 6.[205] My design here is first

---

[204] Particularly Lefkowitz (1963), (1980), (1984), (1988). Also Fraenkel (1975) index *sub* (2.2.5) The self in lyric poetry; Young (1968) 58f; Young (1971) 3–14 (with useful bibliography of earlier scholars 10); Fogelmark (1972) 98; Hamilton (1974) 113–15; Kirkwood (1981); Carey (1981) in general 16–17 and useful discussion of individual passages 51–3, 56–7, 116–17, 159–64, 173; Rösler (1985). Des Places (1947) 5–11 and Kranz (1961) are less useful.

[205] There are, of course, articles on some points of interest in this ode, but the only full-length study is the highly idiosyncratic Carne-Ross (1976).

to view Pindar's corpus as a series of poems composed in and against the literary tradition of *kleos* that I have been sketching; second, to take a single poem as a paradigm for discussion (rather than merely supporting my general points with a series of decontextualized quotations or references, as is so common in Pindaric scholarship). In this way, I hope to take account of both some general features of the logic of praise in the *epinikia* and the specificity of at least one poem.

The sympotic poetry of Theognis is sung ἐν φίλοισι, 'to and among *philoi*', a performance which marks and constitutes the (aristocratic) group within the city and the group as a city; Pindar's poetry, a performance hired to mark the place of an individual within his city, sets out to construct a network of *philia*.[206] First, the *epinikion* aims at a relation of *philia* between poet and patron, where the financial relation of patronage is formulated as a relation of social obligation and debt. Apart from the direct address of the victor as a *philos* (e.g. χαῖρε, φίλος· ἐγὼ τοὶ τόδε πέμπω, 'Greetings, *philos*; I send this to you . . .' *Nem.* 3.76–7), there are two interrelated rhetorical strategies that are most commonly utilized to express the poet's position as a *philos*. First, Pindar makes 'repeated appeals to his patron's *xenia* or hospitality'.[207] This language need not be recuperated in a biographical narrative of the poet's wanderings (which is not to deny that the historical Pindar may have travelled in the practice of his art). Rather, the rhetoric of *xenia* combines the Homeric representation of the wandering bard with an instantiation of the language of 'the paths' of song to praise and expect the patron's maintenance of a privileged model of reception and reciprocal exchange – the relation that founds patronage. In the *Odyssey*, the bard receives his livelihood by singing; the (self-)representation of the lyric poet in sympotic literature replaces such recompense with an image of poetry as an object of exchange between *philoi*, while 'court poetry', such as that of Ibycus, with its (heroic) praise of contemporary figures also makes plain the interplays of power involved in the literature of patronage. Pindar, whose songs are requested and paid for by an individual in search of immortal *kleos*, substitutes for the (subordinating) gesture of praising on (financial) demand a series of different models of exchange between *philoi*. Where

---

[206] See Crotty (1982) 76–103. See also Schadewaldt (1928) 314f; Gundert (1935) 32–9; Bowra (1964) 387–8; Bell (1984) 22–31. The traditional ethics associated with *philia* are valorized at *Pyth.* 2.83ff, on which see Lefkowitz (1976) 29–30, 168–9; Carey (1981) 59; Most (1985) 111–18.

[207] Steiner (1986) 77. Passages are collected by Gianotti (1975) 14 from almost all the triumphal odes.

seventeenth- and eighteenth-century poets, to frame a perhaps misleading contrast, speak from the position of 'humble servant', Pindar's
texts seek to create an (aristocratic) ideal of *philia*, for which the affiliations and obligations of *xenia* provide a crucial and recurrent rhetoric:
'Pindaro, insomma, sente ancora il suo rapporto con un vincitori e i
commitenti sotto la protezione di Zeus Xenios, secondo il modello della
società aristocratica classica.'[208]

So, in *Pyth.* 10, his earliest extant poem, for the Thessalian boy,
Hippocles, Pindar writes (64–6):

> I put my trust
> in the warm *xenia* of Thorax –
> it is he who has yoked this four-horsed chariot
> of the Muses, eagerly tending my song,
> loving one who loves him back,
> leading one who leads in a kindly way.

Pindar declares his trust in the 'warm *xenia*' of Thorax, his patron, who
has 'yoked this chariot of the Muses' – which appears to be an indication
of patronage[209] and of inspiration for the poet. Patronage as *xenia* and
as stimulus for the poet may also be implied in the phrase (applied to
Thorax) ἐμὰν ποιπνύων χάριν, 'bustling on my behalf' or 'tending my
song'.[210] So, Thorax is said to be in a relation of reciprocal *philia* with the
poet – 'loving one who loves him back', φιλέων φιλέοντ' – and to lead
the poet who leads him in a kindly fashion – ἄγων ἄγοντα[211] – where the

---

[208] Gianotti (1975) 14. His discussion (3–16) of the role of money in Pindar is especially
relevant here. See also (from the perspective of Sahlins' sociological model) Campagner
(1988). On patronage and the fee, see Gzella (1971); Bremer (forthcoming); Woodbury
(1968).

[209] We have no way of knowing why Thorax was a patron of Pindar on behalf of Hippocles.

[210] Nisetich, following the scholia, takes ποιπνύω as transitive and ἐμὰν χάριν to refer to
the gratitude and grace of song (for which see below). Most commentators, however,
take ποιπνύω intransitively (as it always appears in Homer) and translate ἐμὰν χάριν
'for my sake'.

[211] ἄγων ἄγοντα is a more difficult expression than φιλέων φίλοντ' ('The strained phraseology seems due to a juvenile over-eagerness for effect' Fennell (1879) ad loc.; Silk (1974)
190 n. 5 notes this as one of the 'manifestations of hyperformality in this, Pindar's first
ode'). Such doubling, however, is also common in tragedy, for example. On the complex
use of the similar phrase φέρει φέροντα in the *Oresteia*, see Neitzel (1979). I take it to
imply not merely a shared journey – 'each taking the other's arm' – but more specifically
the patron's 'lead' for Pindar's song (cf. also *Pyth.* 7.13, *Pyth.* 2.17 for ἄγω as stimulus to
song) and further Pindar's leading not merely of the patron but also of the athlete home
in the comastic and encomiastic chariot of song: ἄγω is used by Pindar of the presentation of songs and glory at *Nem.* 7.62 and *Pyth.* 3.70–3 (cf. also *Ol.* 2.10; *Ol.* 8.87–8).

pair of doublets stress the reciprocity of the relationship.[212] These claims of the *xenia* and *philia* of poet and patron, however, are framed here in *Pyth.* 10 by a gnomic expression of man's inability to know the future – 63 'There is no telling what will be a year from now' – and of the need to test man's attitudes like precious metal: 67 'Gold and a straight mind show what they are on the touchstone.' That the patron's performance of *xenia* is surrounded by such recollections of uncertainty frames the language of *xenia* as an exhortation as well as an encomium. The poem does not merely mark the *xenia* of poet and patron but is an element in its construction.

The uncertainty of the translation of the phrase ἐμὰν ποιπνύων χάριν points to the second particular rhetorical construction *philia* between poet and patron – the poem as *charis*.[213] Indeed, the two translations suggested above – 'bustling on my behalf' and 'eagerly tending my song' – bring to the fore two aspects of *charis* that help make it such an important part of the language of praise. On the one hand, it expresses a relation between the individual and the group: the gratefulness of the city and family towards the victor's moment of triumph. The poet expresses this *charis* for the group and in return receives the gratefulness of the victor and his group for the song: *charis* unites the group, the victor and the poet in a community of gratitude. Hence, 'bustling on my behalf (*charis*)' can be taken to indicate the reciprocal *charis* of poet and patron. So, in *Ol.* 10, Pindar sings 11–12 that he will pay his debt with a song to be shared (κοινὸν λόγον), a mark of 'dear gratitude' (φίλαν χάριν): the *logos* he offers is shared – it is of and for the group, as it is for posterity and for the athlete[214] – and it is aimed at (ἐς) *charis* which is called *philan*, a token of *philia* (rather than merely 'dear'). *Charis* links the performers and recipients of song in a bond of *philia*.

On the other hand, *charis* is also a common expression for the 'grace' of song, both its beauty or suitability of form and its effects. It is a quality which endears the song to its recipients. *Charis*, then, expresses both the gratefulness of the social production of the *epinikion* and the gracefulness of its artistic achievement.

---

[212] Gildersleeve (1979) ad loc., alone of the commentators, suggests that φιλέοντ' and ἄγοντα might refer to the athlete, Hippocles. After πέποιθα and ἐμὰν χάριν this strains the Greek somewhat, but would link all three in relations of *philia*.

[213] This phrase is the title – das Lied als Charis – of the standard chapter on the topic: Gundert (1935) 30–76. See also Verdenius (1979) 12–15; Mullen (1982) 100–10; Most (1985) 68–98.

[214] Cf. *Ol.* 7.21; *Isth.* 6.69, for further expressions of the *common* basis of praise, on which see Bernardini (1983) 35–6.

Gianotti distinguishes two further senses of *charis*:[215] first 'splendour and glory', the splendour, for example, of the Olympic games or the glory of the Olympic champion. (His examples are *Ol.* 1.18; *Ol.* 8.79–80.). This sense is close to 'beauty' (of song). Secondly, 'favour' or 'gift', particularly from gods towards humans. *Charis* 'can be used to designate the athlete's victory and the joy that attends upon it, but it can also be used to designate the favour of the god that blazes into appearance for the hero, sometimes a gift given in return for his deserts, sometimes an inexplicable grace that descends upon him'.[216] The divine influence that is in Pindar's poetry crucial to human achievement also expresses itself in and through *charis*.

These different senses of *charis*, however, are particularly difficult to separate clearly and rigorously, especially when *Charis*, 'Grace', and *Charites*, 'Graces', are represented as divine figures by Pindar. Indeed, the 'Graces' (*Charites*) are invested not merely with the power to inspire and create song – a function associated also with the Muses – but also, in *Olympian* 14, for example, a hymn to the Graces, with a controlling influence over the successful achievement of all pleasant aspects of mortal and divine existence (*Ol.* 14.3–9):

> O ladies, whose tuneful voices
> haunt the lanes of glittering Orchomenos
> and who guard the Minyans born of old,
> hear me, Graces, for I pray:
> if anything sweet or delightful
> warms the heart of any mortal man,
> whether he has beauty, or skill,
> or the light of victory shining upon him,
> it is your gift.
> Even the gods depend on you
> and would renounce
> ordering the dance and feast
> without your favour . . .

Even the gods could not turn to feasts and dances without the Graces, and the splendour, nobility and wisdom of man depend on the Graces' creative inspiration. The divine aspect of *charis* informs the (expression of) gratitude of men. The close interrelations of divine support, human success, the gratitude of the group and the success and power of poetry

---

[215] (1975) 75–6.
[216] Mullen (1982) 100. Mullen makes *charis* the central term of his analysis of the *epinikion*, in which he includes any sign of success or divine favour (see especially 100–10). In this, he underplays the sense of (social) gratitude and of poetic grace.

in recording that support, success and gratitude – a fundamental nexus of ideas throughout Pindar's poetry – are formed in a significant way through the language of *charis*. The ties of *philia* between poet and patron, athlete and group, that *charis* encapsulates, cannot, then, be viewed separately from the widest concerns of divine and human interaction in individual success that provides an essential framework in Pindar's poetry for the construction of praise.[217]

Charis, then, formulates more than a relation of *philia* between poet and patron: it also sets that relation within the context of the social group and the *divina commedia* that is human achievement. This way in which the poetry of praise is to be seen as part of a wider, group celebration and a celebration of the wider ideals of the group, is further developed in Pindar's striking use of the language of the symposium and the *kōmos*. Indeed, the social context for the production of the lyric poetry of, say, Theognis, becomes for Pindar a key metaphor for the production of the *epinikion*: (*Isth.* 6.1–4):

> As at the flourishing symposium of men
>   we mix the second bowl, so now
>   here is the second song
>   poured by the Muses
>   for Lampon's family of fine athletes.

The simile of the 'flourishing symposium of men' runs into and overlaps with the expression of the production of song as the mixing of a second bowl of the Muses' songs. Song is (like) the wine of the symposium, and so the stanza ends with a prayer to be able in the future to pour a further libation with or in 'honey-voiced songs' (*Isth.* 6.7–9):

> and may it be ours,
>   to fill a third bowl, pouring it out
>   to Zeus Olympian the Saviour,
>   libations of honey-voiced songs streaming over Aegina.

A third libation to Zeus the Saviour concludes the ritual libations of the symposium: as the prayer for a third victory for Phylacides is poured forth, it draws on the (teleological) model of a religious performance to imply an inevitable logic of future success.

The symposium, an institution of *philoi*, a place for the formation and maintenance of shared ideas of behaviour and attitude, a performance

---

[217] The interplay of divine and human are discussed particularly stimulatingly by Köhnken (1971); Young (1971); Lloyd-Jones (1973); Lefkowitz (1976); Crotty (1982); Bell (1984); Most (1985); Segal (1986b), each with relevant bibliography.

with its own notion and practice of limits and controls, does not provide
a frame for Pindar's *epinikia* only because it also offers a tradition of praise
and blame poetry to which Pindar's poetry of *kleos* may be affiliated.
Rather, the return of the victor and the praise of his individual, outstanding success are assimilated to the stable and stabilizing social activity of men as a group of *philoi*. The return of the successful athlete and
the glorification of achievements which separate him from other men
have been discussed by critics as dramas of social reintegration.[218] (Indeed, this crisis of reintegration links the athletes to the heroes to whom
Pindar turns for his exempla, and specifically to the question of the hero
and social integration that I have considered above with regard to the
Iliad and *Odyssey*.) The language of the symposium, in which the performance of the poem becomes itself part of a celebration, 'an expression of
the ties that bind together members of the community',[219] aims to dramatize – and to control – the return and praise of the individual victor
as the collective celebration of *philoi*. And much as the poetry of the
symposium turns repeatedly to the expected limits and deprecated transgressions of behaviour between *philoi*, so, too, as we will see, the *epinikion*
returns to the limits and transgressions of individual achievement. The
epinikion sites the victor within the context of a collective, normative enterprise for which the symposium provides a privileged ritual
model.[220]

The language of the *kōmos* further develops this aspect of the performance of the *epinikion*. For the *kōmos*, a celebrating procession of re-
vellers, or, say, Dionysiac worshippers, adds an element of travel, of
transition, to the collective principles of the symposium. The *kōmos* is
part of the religious life of the city and is part of the symposium, and
Pindar utilizes these connotations of such a procession to express both
the presentation of the *epinikion* to the victor and the return of the victor.
So, *Nem.* 9 opens (1–4):

> We will process from Sikyon
> – come, Muses, leave Apollo's side –
> to the newly built town of Aitna,
> the rich house of Chromios,
> whose doors are flung wide, though not wide
> enough for all the guests streaming in!

---

[218] Especially Crotty (1982) 104–38. See also Segal (1986b).

[219] Crotty (1982) 81. See also Slater (1977) 200–2.

[220] Further ritual models for the poetic performance – weddings, funerals, libations – are
discussed by Rubin (1980b); Segal (1981); Rusten (1983); Bernardini (1983) 157ff;
Brown (1984); Steiner (1986) 131–4.

The first word of the poem (κωμάσομεν, 'we will process, celebrate') establishes a context for performance other than that of financial patronage.[221] A revelling procession from the site of the Nemean games to the victor's house in Aetna – where the gates of the rich house can scarcely contain the patron's hospitality – turns the *choreia*[222] of the *epinikion* to the rejoicing of *philoi*, the praise of individual achievement to the (ritual) celebration of a group.

So *Pyth*. 4, Pindar's longest poem, begins with a capturing of the moment of celebration (1–5):[223]

> Today, Muse, you must stand beside
> a man beloved,
> Arkesilas,
>   king of Cyrene,
> and join him as he celebrates ...

Pyth. 4 is much concerned with *nostos*. The ode tells at great length the story of the *nostos* of Jason and the Argonauts (within the context of a foundation myth, a return to the past for the origin of the fatherland that depicts foundation both as 'the bringing home (ἀγκόμισαι 9) of Medea's prophecy'[224] and the return of the clod of Libyan soil to its home in Africa); furthermore, thè ode makes an explicit request (270ff) for the return from exile for a citizen of Cyrene, Damophilos. (It is the only poem of Pindar to make such a direct political intervention.) In its opening lines, the poet appeals to the Muse to stand by king Arkesilas (a *philos*) to pay him the song he is due, as he takes part in a *kōmos*, παρ' ἀνδρὶ φίλῳ ... κωμάζοντι. The victor and king himself – a man apart – is depicted as a part of the *kōmos*, so the 'crisis of *nostos*' becomes a celebratory procession. So, in the final stanza of the poem, Damophilos' desire to return is represented as a wish to see his *oikos* and to join the symposium. The ring composition – opening and closing with the depic-

---

[221] On these lines and the motif of the *kōmos*, see Bundy (1986) 22–4, and, with further bibliography, Slater (1984); Heath (1988).

[222] *Choreia*, 'song and dance in a chorus' – the performative aspect of the *epinikion* – is discussed by Mullen (1982); Calame (1977); and, with further bibliography, Goldhill (1986a) 267–74.

[223] So Segal (1986b) 180. Steiner (1986) 51 also neatly links the *kōmos* and the *charites*: 'Though the actual song and dance are but a momentary act, delivered by a band of mortal celebrants, the eternally revelling Muses and Graces stand as guarantors of the possibility of repetition and renewed performance' – a possibility crucial, of course, to *kleos* as lasting glory.

[224] Burton (1962) 168. See also on *nostos* Segal (1986b) 89–105; Robbins (1975) 206–13.

tion of a group celebration – shows both how the circle of *philoi* is formed as an ideal, and how the *epinikion* maps a dynamic of separation and reintegration which cannot be reduced to merely a representation of that ideal.

Pindar's poetry, then, aims to establish a context of praise which (re)constitutes a relation of patronage in the institutions of *philia* that mark the normative affinities of the household and city. As in the Homeric epics and the lyric poetry discussed in this chapter, Pindar's poetry of *kleos* is closely intertwined with the formation, maintenance and transgressions of *philia*: the place of the outstanding individual is found through the norms that *philia* promotes. Indeed, the praise of an individual victor is hard to separate in the *epinikia* from praise of the *genos* ('race') and praise of the city.[225] Where, for example, the dedicatory epigrams discussed in the second section of this chapter make the city the very condition and beneficiary of praise, Pindar's victors both adorn and draw stength from the city, which has its own genealogy of *aretē*, its own history of achievement. A similar dynamic of reciprocal strengthening and glorification obtains between the individual and his *genos*, where ancestry and the education of a life among the *agathoi*, 'good/noble', are together an enabling factor in individual success, as much as such success establishes for itself a place in the history of the *genos* as a paradigm and potential force for future generations' achievements.

So, in *Nem.* 3, for Aristocleides of Aegina, Pindar turns to sing of 'Aeacus and his race' (28) – from Aegina; and in instantiation of the maxim 'praise the noble' celebrates first Peleus, who rejoiced 'in ancient virtue' (32), and then Telamon. The story of Peleus leads to the story of his son, Achilles, through the *gnōmē* συγγενεῖ δέ τις εὐδοξίᾳ μέγα βρίθει (40), 'There is a great weight in inherited glory', 'in the glory that is in the *genos*.' Indeed, these stories of the past heroes of Aegina are framed by praise of Aristocleides – praise, because 'he has not shamed the assembly of ancient warriors' (12–18) and because indeed 'he has added to its glorious renown' (67–70). So, the victor is written into place in and against the exemplary world of the heroic past.[226] The poet's expression of the general significance of the individual's victory is shaped as a

---

[225] Praise of the *genos* and praise of the *polis* are regarded as *topoi* by Bundy (1986); Thummer (1968); Hamilton (1974).

[226] On the use of mythic exempla, see in general Köhnken (1971); Young (1971); Rose (1974); Carey (1981) 7–13; Bernardini (1983). There are also, of course, many studies of individual poems' use of myth. I have learnt in particular from Bresson (1982); Most (1985); Segal (1986b).

continuation of the logic of exemplification that the retelling of the (normative) *muthoi* of earlier times involves. Through such *muthoi*, then, 'immortal praise' finds its formation and significance in the temporal framework of the continuing history of *genos* and *polis*.[227] The ideal *oikos* of the *Odyssey* – with its struggle to maintain itself in glory through the generations; the poetry of patronage of later lyric – with the development of contemporary praise against an epic tradition; the framework of the *polis* for individual action and renown – integral to the voice of the poet in the fifth and fourth century – are combined by Pindar's texts through the articulation of this complex context of praise in the aristocratic group within the city and its history. As much as in the *Iliad* the figure of Achilles through his search for immortal *kleos* explores the boundaries of man's existence within a social group and in contradistinction to the divine world, so for Pindar the poetry of *kleos* strives to articulate the place of the outstanding individual within the norms of social discourse, and with regard to the limits of mortality that the divine frame ensures, and also within the history of achievement and transgression that myth expresses.

Yet if the city and its (aristocratic) citizens – set in the frame of divine power and in the historical narrative of past glories, future renown – provide the scene and source of praise, the city also provides a more problematic framework, as phrases such as 'the crisis of integration' may suggest. For the city and the family constitute both the context of praise and renown, and the site of envy, slander, ignominy. The conflicts surrounding the heroic individual, the successful athlete, are focused in Pindar's writing on the dangers of *phthonos* and *mōmos*. 'envy' and 'blame'. *Phthonos*, 'envy', is the negative but perhaps expected response to another's success: 'the great man is bound to provoke the φθόνος [*phthonos*] of men'.[228] There is the further danger, however, of divine *phthonos* – the commonly expressed fear through all periods of ancient Greek writing, that the gods resent and punish a human's surpassing of

---

[227] On time in Pindar, see Vivante (1972); Segal (1974); (1985); (1986b) 180–93; and in particular Hurst (1984) with useful bibliography of earlier discussions 156 n. 1.

[228] Lloyd-Jones (1973) 126 n. 102a (though his use of *Agamemnon* 939 as evidence is contentious, to say the least, in its ignoring of the context of the line). Kirkwood (1984) 173 writes '*Phthonos* is both neighbourly and natural.' This takes Aristotle perhaps too readily as an example of general Greek attitudes. On *phthonos*, a much discussed Pindaric topic, see Lloyd-Jones (1973) 122–7, 135–7; Bowra (1964) 186–7; Thummer (1968) 80–1; Eitrem (1953); Gouldner (1965) 45–60, especially 55–8; Crotty (1980) 2–12; Köhnken (1971) index *sub* Neid; Bundy (1986) index *sub* φθόνος; Lefkowitz (1976) index *sub* envy.

the limitations of human life either in the boast or in the achievement of outstanding success. On the one hand, the envy of other human beings leads to the blame, detraction and slander of the successful. This constitutes the defining other for the truth of Pindar's praise: so Most writes of *Pyth.* 2 'Two modes of discourse, Pindar's truthful praise and others' futile slander, are contrasted with one another ... others may slander [the victor], but to no avail: only Pindar's truthful praise receives public recognition.'[229] *Phthonos* bounds praise. Pindar's poetic voice is constituted against the possibility of others' envious slander, and the discourse of gratitude, friendship, hospitality and requirement that I have been discussing, forms a context of praise where the positive construction of a community and necessity of praise is in constant tension with the exclusion and deprecation of this *phthonos* of others. The truth and memorial of *kleos* is won not only in the recording of the successful competition of the athlete, but also against the negation and slander of other accounts.

On the other hand, the dangers of incurring *phthonos*, and particularly divine *phthonos*, set a limit to and control for the expression of praise, even to the poet's defence against the blame of others. Again and again in Pindar, direct praise and mythological exempla are broken off with gnomic remarks about the need to stay within limits:[230] 'Pindar's practice is ... to draw attention to and even comment on the process of juncture.'[231] But this rhetoric of limits is not merely a formal device that (self-reflexively) marks the development of the poem. Rather, as Pindar 'explores ... the boundaries of the concepts of praise and language',[232] there is a constant awareness of the precariousness of praise, where excess leads not merely to a lack of credibility but also to the threat of divine *phthonos*. It is here that the widest concerns of Pindar's poetry – the place of man in the order of things, the relation between gods and individual success – are deeply interwoven with what are often regarded merely as formal generic markers of the *epinikion* – the interrelated gnomic expressions of human limits and poetic limits (*Pyth.* 2.49–53):

> God achieves his every aim exactly as he wills –
> god, who overtakes the eagle flying

---

[229] Most (1985) 109–10.
[230] Bundy (1986) 73f discusses 'the countless appeals to propriety in introductions and conclusions' and lists key terms for this *topos*.
[231] Greengard (1980) 5.
[232] Young (1979) 143.

> and passes by the dolphin
> skimming through the sea.
> And he curbs the man
> whose thoughts soar on high
> and gives to others ageless glory.
> But I must shun the loud monster
> of bitter speech ...

The narrative (21–48) of Ixion's attempted rape of the goddess Hera – a narrative of transgression of limits and of the relations between men and the gods – is broken off with a set of *gnōmai* that oppose divine fulfilment and human insufficiency – an insufficiency expressed by god's 'curbing', 'bending' (ἔκαμψε) of any human who aims high in his thoughts (who aims, that is, to surpass his human limitations). This opposition, however, finds a place also for human success through divine aid, even as it records human defeat – the logic of the competitive ethos: god 'gives to others ageless glory'.[233] This comment on the possibilities of human glory leads into a remark by the encomiastic poet on his own role: 'I must shun the loud monster of bitter speech:'[234] 'the theological grounding of human success which has been achieved by the myth and its subsequent interpretation must have consequences for this poetic self-definition as well: because success is bestowed by the gods, to praise it is to confirm the divine order, just as to criticize it is to blame not only the successful man, but also the gods themselves who have made him successful'.[235] The role of the divine in human success not merely grounds the necessity of praise and the rejection of slander, but also marks in the threat of ὑψιφρονῶν τιν' ἔκαμψε βροτῶν, 'he curbs the man whose thoughts soar on high', a precarious boundary between suitable praise and an encomium that leads to *phthonos*. It is this boundary that

---

[233] 'The description of god's superiority to man in his bending down one mortal whose thoughts are directed upwards but giving others an ageless κῦδος [glory] (51–2) draws the consequence from this opposition between divine fulfilment and human deficiency by concluding that any attainment within the human domain, just like any failure, is the result not of human capacities but of the intercession of a god' (Most (1985) 87). On these lines, see also Lloyd-Jones (1973) 121–2; Lefkowitz (1976) 21–3; Crotty (1980) 3–4, 9–11; Burton (1962) 118–20; Carey (1981) 40–3, especially ad 52.

[234] 'Crowding', Nisetich's translation of ἄδινον is preferred by Most (1985) 88 n. 69 to Slater's 'strong, violent'. But see Silk (1983) 322–4 with n. 68 for discussion of the difficulties of this word.

[235] Most (1985) 88. He is extending the views of Lloyd-Jones (1973) 122 and Crotty (1980) 2, who writes 'Slander is presented as a refusal to accept the yoke of mortality placed on us by the gods.'

Pindar constantly negotiates in his self-reflexive awareness of the limits of praise and his praise of limits.

The poet and the victor are linked, then, by a shared need to avoid falsely constituted praise. The structuring proprieties of Pindar's *epinikia* – not merely the explicit remarks on excess and control but also the implicit restraints of, say, the limiting of an exemplary story with a concluding *gnōmē* – represent the shared aim of the avoidance of *phthonos* and slander in the (precarious) construction of (due) praise. Yet, while Pindar's praise and instantiation of καιρός ('measure') mark a tension between (self-)restraint and (self-)glorification, Pindar's poetry also claims the voice of true praise in competitive opposition to the other voices of *phthonos* and even other poets.[236] So, *Pyth.* 2 continues by juxtaposing Pindar's avoidance of slander with Archilochus' reproachful poetry of hate (54–6):

> for in the distance I have seen
> bilious Archilochus often in distress,
> swollen with harsh words of wrath.
>   To prosper
> in accord with heaven's will,
>   is wisdom's noblest part.

Archilochus is a paradigm of slander – as Pindar is of praise – not only in his hateful, heavy words (*barulogois ekhthesin*), his distress (*amēkhaniē*), his biliousness (*psogeros*), but also in the implication that Archilochus fails to appreciate or to instantiate the truth that wisdom's finest part is 'to prosper in accord with heaven's will' (or 'one's own proper fate', σὺν τυχᾳ πότμου) – a *gnōmē* which further extends the defining limit of divine power in the necessity of praise and the possibility of success. Like the athlete's activity, Pindar's rhetoric is agonistic in its pursuit of true – measured – *kleos*. Indeed, not only is the poet likened in his poetry to the athlete,[237] but also the author becomes himself an exemplum for others: 'the poet's attitude [is an] example of correct behaviour',[238] of a 'courageous, ameliorative and moral'[239] position. Where Homer's *Odyssey* suggests the hero as bard of his own song, where Theognis sings his advice as a *philos* in a group of *philoi*, Pindar, the encomiastic poet, can offer himself as a paradigm in the shared striving for *kleos* within the proper

---

[236] Cf. e.g. Lefkowitz (1980) 42 'The poet in speaking the truth portrays himself as a *combatant*.'

[237] Lefkowitz (1980) especially 33; Steiner (1986) 111–21; Bernardini (1983).

[238] Lefkowitz (1980) 34.   [239] Lefkowitz (1980) 38.

limits: poetry is the *mirror* of noble deeds (ἔργοις καλοῖς ἔσοπτρον *Nem.* 7.14) in all senses.

This use of a first-person utterance to construct an exemplum both of true praise and of properly limited behaviour raises the question of the status of the 'ego' in Pindar's poetry. This has been the subject of much recent debate. In reaction against a highly influential group of mainly German scholars who have treated the corpus of Pindar's poetry as an opportunity for biographical exegesis of the poet's life and political struggles (a critical approach that goes back to the scholia), many modern scholars, following Bundy's lead, state that in ancient epinician poetry 'what poets said about themselves followed defined conventions'.[240] Not only do utterances about the poet's role have a place in the formal construction of the ode – as transitional devices, rhetorical 'foils' to highlight praise or as 'pronominal namecaps' to bring a priamel's climax[241] – but also the first-person utterances constitute 'a virtual mythology of poetic behaviour',[242] where the poet's description of his own toil to make poetry, his own dangers from *phthonos*, his own success represent a complementary model for the athlete: ' "personal" references express the poet's understanding of the meaning of victory', as 'the victor's achievement' is portrayed 'in terms of his [Pindar's] understanding of his own art'.[243] In this way the poet makes himself a paradigmatic figure in his poetry (*Nem.* 8.35–9):

> May I never have such a character, father Zeus!
>> May I tread the simple paths of life,
>>> leaving behind in death
>>>> no infamy to taint my children.
>>> Some men pray for gold,
>>> others for limitless land.
>> but I would wish
>>>> to lay my limbs in earth
>>> beloved by my fellow citizens,
>>> because I praised the praiseworthy
>> and scattered blame
>>>> on those who deserved it.

---

[240] Lefkowitz (1980) 29 – redefining the terms of her study of 1963.

[241] These technical terms and analysis are taken from Bundy (1986) 3 n. 11, 6, 21, 41, 45, 85. See also Hamilton (1974) 16–17; Thummer (1968).

[242] Lefkowitz (1980) 29.

[243] Lefkowitz (1980) 49. This last remark is hard to reconcile with her earlier comment (29) that first-person utterances 'will not tell us about Pindar's own individual view of the poet's profession.'

A narrative (23–34b) of how Odysseus tricked the Greeks into giving him Achilles' armour as a prize exemplifies how 'words are a morsel to the envious [*phthoneroi*] who always attack the noble but not the base' (22–3). It concludes with the dangerous possibility that slander might 'lift into view the spurious glory of the obscure' (34b).[244] Against such a possibility, Pindar prays that his own nature be never of such a sort, but that his choice[245] of a simple life might leave to his children a *kleos* that does not speak (of) evil (μή ... δύσφαμον). So, where others may have other material desires for gold or for land, the *ego* of the poem seeks the success of the approval of the group by his performance of praising the praiseworthy and blaming the wrongdoers: the poetic exchange of the ode's memorialization stands as a model of proper and just attribution of value and reputation as opposed to the corrupt glory of the slanderous and base. So, as the poem records the *kleos* of the victory, the proper performance of that praise (in its widest social, as well as poetic, context) also promises the *kleos* of the poet. In the paths of life, like the paths of song, the *ego* of the poem composes himself as an example and guarantor in the precarious pursuit of a *kleos* that is not *dusphamon*, 'speaking ill'. Thus when he concludes these remarks with the promise that *aretā*, 'excellence', 'virtue', will flourish in this way (40ff), Pindar 'does not specify whose *aretā* because the general truth applies to the poet, victor and hero'.[246] Pindar's 'I' is also part of the normative logic of exemplification that implicates the *muthoi* of the figures of the past in the formation of lasting praise.

Yet, if the *ego* of the poem often seems to be part of a generalizing rhetoric – 'if I were you' – it is the case that first person in Pindar's *epinikia* also appears as 'a contingent historic individual',[247] as the figure who is paid to sing,[248] and as an individual who is linked in a series

---

[244] The rejection of Odysseus is explicitly a rejection of Homer (Pindar's poetic competitor) in *Nem.* 7, on which see for discussion and bibliography Most (1985) 148–56, 180–2.

[245] ἐφαπτοίμην, 'embrace', 'fasten on', is a term from wrestling that also echoes the action of the envious against the noble – ἅπτεται (22): in a poem for a wrestling victory, the action of detractors and the poet are significantly expressed in the language of wrestling. See Lefkowitz (1980) 36–7; Steiner (1986) 111–21.

[246] Lefkowitz (1980) 36. Cf. Carey (1976) 34–5 who adds performers and audience to his sense of the collective.

[247] Most (1985) 117.

[248] What Svenbro (1976) 185 calls 'auteur contractuel', which he distinguishes from 'auteur fictif' – who 'dans sa sincérité prétendue doit garantir la véracité de la louange commandée.' I have tried to show how the complex dialectic between contractual, fictional and social imperatives cannot be adequately expressed in this way as an opposition between (sincere) financial contract and a fiction of praise – an opposition which seems to depend to a worrying degree on Romantic notions of artistic integrity, sincerity, originality.

of social relations with the victor and other citizens,[249] and, say, as a Theban citizen. Yet the poet as exemplary figure is not simply opposed to the poet as historic individual. For, as much as the specifics of an individual victor's achievement and family are inevitably framed in the language of general significance, so, too, the poet's different rhetorics of self-representation provide different positions from which to speak, which are also always different expressions of the general possibilities and imperatives of praise.

This sense of the variety of positions from which praise comes may help throw new light on the old question of the choral 'I' in Pindar's poetry. Since the scholia, scholars have debated whether the use of the first person refers to the poet, Pindar, or to the chorus who sings the ode. Lefkowitz, who considers the topic at greatest length, notes that in the *Paeans* there are clear examples of the chorus referring to themselves – descriptions of their dress, dance and other collective attitudes. In the *epinikia*, however, although the scholia often refer first-person plurals in particular to the chorus, Lefkowitz argues that there is no example of the first person that is not applicable to the figure of the poet: 'the content of these passages is in each case better suited to Pindar than to the chorus, since as statements by the poet they have an important structural function in the total context of the ode, but as choral statements they serve only as purposeless interruptions, which do not even perform the function of real choral statements; that is, to portray the physical appearance of the speakers'.[250]

That the vast majority, if not the complete range, of first-person utterances are applicable to the figure of the poet is well demonstrated by Lefkowitz. What does not follow, however, is that therefore all first-person remarks in the *epinikia* must refer necessarily and solely to Pindar, the poet. Rather, it is clear that in many cases a first person is applicable both to a chorus and to the figure of the poet (a point already recognized in Lefkowitz's expression 'better suited'). To argue from cases in which

---

[249] Most (1985) 117 distinguishes 'epinician first-person statements (which refer to the present poem only) and autobiographical first-person statements (which refer outside the poem, may be true and false, and have a function within the poem)'. Such an opposition of 'poet' to 'socially determined individual' too rigidly divides aspects of poetic self-representation – throughout which fictionalization and role-playing have an inevitable part.

[250] Lefkowitz (1963) 235. It is noticeable that at *Nem.* 7.85 Lefkowitz (234) has to accept a far from certain emendation into the text in order to maintain her thesis in this rigid form; on occasions (e.g. *Pyth.* 5.72ff) the thesis is maintained despite the recognition that 'the lines are well suited to the ... chorus' (177).

a first person is only applicable to the poet to the less clear cases seems to depend on the fallacious assumptions first that all examples of the first person must fall into a single category;[251] second, that certain clear examples can and must be used to remove ambiguities in other cases (rather than to contrast with them); third, that even first-person plurals must refer only to single entity and not to a possible – plural – combination of people. What's more, to argue that remarks taken as choral comments in the *epinikia* 'do not even perform the function of real choral statements', is simply – and dangerously – circular. Even if there is a justifiable contrast to be made between the types of first-person utterance found in the *Paians* and the *epinikia*, it does not follow simply that the *Paian* is the 'real' model from which *epinikia* can only diverge.

Yet if there remains an ambivalence or variety in the use of the first person in the *epinikia*, it is not just a (regrettable) lack of clarity on the poet's part. For as much as the variety of social positions adopted and adapted by the poetic 'I' construct an elaborate network of justifications and obligations of praising, so the multiplicity of voices contained particularly in the first-person plural constructs a multiplicity of sources of praise, a multiplicity of ways to praise. Any openness of reference in the 'we' of Pindaric praise is to allow the possibility of including an ever-widening circle of *philoi* in the duty and performance of praise. The generalizing *ego* and the inclusive 'we' invite, even impel, the sharing of a celebration. Indeed, each reader, each performance of the *epinikion* in the first-person utterance can be said to join in the choir of voices praising. And it is in the choir of voices praising that *kleos* is produced.

The precarious search for *kleos* without *phthonos*, then, is formulated in the multiple and complex *loci* of praise made possible by the distinctive developments of the traditions of praise poetry in Pindar's *epinikia*. Yet Pindar's poetry works not merely to praise but also – crucially – to *celebrate*, and the construction of the framework of *celebration* necessarily implicates not merely a network of social roles in performance but also a (developing) system of cultural attitudes that are under construction in and through the poetry, as Pindar weaves the myths of origin and place for the powerful patrons of the fifth-century *polis*. In all senses, the measures of praise, the celebratory performance, produce a frame in which to view the victor.

For the remainder of this chapter I wish to turn to see how these strategies of praise are to be seen in a single poem, *Ol.* 6, an ode which

---

[251] A point made by Most (1985) 200.

has not produced the conflicts and cruces of interpretation that so dominate analyses of the most commonly discussed *epinikia*, such as *Pyth.* 2
or *Nem.* 7, but which does offer an extraordinary view of Pindar's poetry
of *kleos*.

> Χρυσέας ὑποστάσαντες εὐτειχεῖ προθύρῳ θαλάμου
> κίονας ὡς ὅτε θαητὸν μέγαρον
> πάξομεν· ἀρχομένου δ' ἔργου πρόσωπον
> χρὴ θέμεν τηλαυγές. εἰ δ' εἴη μὲν Ὀλυμπιονίκας,
> βωμῷ τε μαντείῳ ταμίας Διὸς ἐν Πίσᾳ,
> συνοικιστήρ τε τᾶν κλεινᾶν Συρακοσ –
>   σᾶν, τίνα κεν φύγοι ὕμνον
> κεῖνος ἀνήρ, ἐπικύρσαις ἀφθόνων ἀ –
>   στῶν ἐν ἱμερταῖς ἀοιδαῖς;

> As when we will establish a shining palace,
>   raising its portal on golden columns,
>   so now we must make radiant
>   the entrance to our song.
>   If it's to praise
>   an Olympian victor,
>   one of those who reared
>   illustrious Syracuse, a prophet
>   of Zeus' mantic altar in Pisa,
>   what glory will he miss,
>   if only he finds
>   his people unenvious amid delightful music?   (1–7)

As in the first lines of *Isth.* 6, where the simile likening the celebratory
song to the libations of the symposium spreads into pervasive, overlapping metaphors of pouring songs like wine and wine like songs, so
here the syntax of these (self-reflexive) opening remarks on opening
interweaves constructing a building and constructing a poem: the poem
has golden pillars; it is (like) a palace hall. The pillars support a porch,
the entrance to a *thalamou*, which normally indicates a 'bedroom' or
'inner chamber'[252] – a room with special associations of generational
continuity and *oikos* stability (the central room which Odysseus in the
Odyssey built around an olive tree 'like a column'). An ode which will
depict a glorious genealogy and establishment of a race (*genos*) opens with

---

[252] As at e.g. *Pyth.* 2.33, though at *Ol.* 5.14 it is often translated in a more general sense as
'dwellings'.

the (self-)representation of the poem as the opening to the sanctum of a glorious house, like a remarkable (*thaēton*) palace. The poet's glorious construction is the frame for the victor's glory, a monument in words.[253]

The first-person plural subject of the verb *paxomen*, 'we will establish', 'fix', is a good example of the difficulty of delimiting the voices of praise in the performance of an *epinikion*. It combines the figure of the poet, whose poetic building is on show; the choir performing; and the group of *philoi* come together for the performance. *Kleos* depends on a collective exercise. Indeed, the strophe continues with a generalization without a specific subject for the verb on the need to establish a *prosōpon tēlauges*, 'a face to be seen from afar', for any new project. As the palace hall is to be seen (*thaēton*), so the façade of a new work – the opening sight – must be strikingly visible (*tēlauges*). In Greek usage (unlike English), however, *prosōpon*, 'face', is applied to a non-anthropomorphic form only as a very rare and thus emphatic metaphor.[254] Here, this shift of semantic field also facilitates the move from the glorious building to the glorification of a man (whose appearance in the building of song, like a cult statue in a temple, is where the rhetorical columns are leading). The appearance of the man is set up as a (rhetorical) question to be fulfilled: if there were to be an Olympic victor who was a prophet at Olympia, and an inhabitant of Syracuse descended from the first founders of that city, what song of praise could he escape? The expression of glory in song, however, with its characteristic combination of Olympic victory, religious position and civic status, is immediately bounded by a condition – that the victor meet with citizens who feel no *phthonos* with regard to pleasant songs. As the song of praise is performed before the citizens, so the song is made dependent on and bounded by the control of the citizens' *phthonos*. In this way, too, *kleos* depends on the community as a social context for poetry.

[253] For the contrast between memorialization in stone and memorialization in language, see Svenbro (1976) *passim* and especially 186–93.

[254] Two examples in Pindar. In *Pyth.* 6.14, it seems to be applied to a 'treasury of songs'; so most commentators, following Wilamowitz (1922) 139–40, who compares Eur. *Ion* 184, where διδύμων προσώπων is used of the temple at Delphi, apparently with an architectural meaning, though the exact sense remains obscure. (Farnell, however, refers πρόσωπον at *Pyth.* 6.14 to the face of a messenger – a figure implied, he suggests, by the verb ἀπαγγελεῖ.) At *Isth.* 2.8, the term is applied to songs pictured as girls, or, perhaps, prostitutes, and so it is not a parallel to the use in *Ol.* 6, as Farnell and LSJ suggest. In each case, the language of the human body is a striking example of what Silk (1974) calls 'intrusion'. μέτωπον, of course, has a regular architectural usage.

Let the son of Sostratos know
  his is the foot
    destined for this sandal.
    A deed done without danger,
      hand to hand,
        or aboard the hollow ships,
          lacks worth, but many remember
          if someone dares and wins.
        Hagesias, ready for you is the praise Adrastus spoke
      rightly for Amphiaraos, Oïkles' prophet son,
                        when the ground
  had swallowed him and his gleaming horses.   (8–14)

The first antistrophe opens with the son of Sostratos proclaimed as
fulfilling the combination of qualities expressed in the opening stanza.[255]
This praise is developed in two directions. First, by the generalizations
that promise memorialization – the poet's task and aim – when success
is achieved through labour and risk: there is no worth, honour (*timē*) for
goodness (*aretē*) without danger either in land or sea battles. The military context for the display of *aretē* and winning of *timē* affiliates athletic
activity in general and Hagesias' success in particular to the tradition of
kleos won on the (epic) battlefield. Furthermore, this military language
prepares for the second development of glorification that follows the first
explicit pronouncement of the victor's name – Hagesias' association with
the *ainos*, 'praise', that Adrastus proclaimed for Amphiaraos after the
battle of the Seven against Thebes. Hagesias, a keeper of the prophetic
altar at Olympia, shares the praise of the great prophet of earlier times,
as the poet contracts the distance between the heroes of the past and the
contemporary victor. The expression of praise is ἕτοιμος, 'ready and
waiting', to be fulfilled in Hagesias. The latency of the past is revealed
in present achievement.

The seven pyres had smouldered for the dead,
when the son of Talaos, later, in Thebes
spoke, saying 'I miss the eye of my army,
a good prophet and a good fighter.'
    The same words fit
this Syracusan, master of the celebration.
    Though I am neither

[255] Kirkwood (1982) ad loc., referring to *Ol.* 3.5, suggests a play between ἀοιδαῖς, the last
word of the first stanza, and πεδίλῳ 'sandal = foot = metrical foot = rhythm': on this
reading, fulfilment is expressed through the poetics established in the first stanza.

quarrelsome, nor too fond of victory, I will
say it clearly, swearing a heavy oath –
and the sweet-voiced Muses will entrust me.   (15–21)

Adrastus' expression of praise (*epos*) after the failed expedition against
Thebes is to regret the loss of the 'eye' of his army, 'a good prophet
and a good fighter'. These exemplary qualities are applied to Hagesias,
described as a 'Syracusan man' – his civic status – and as 'master of the
kōmos', (κώμου δεσπότᾳ) – the celebration that is being performed. The
story of the past, then, provides the paradigm for present achievement,
and the fitness (ἕτοιμος) of the praise is explicitly marked. Yet there
remains a difference and distance between the exemplum and Hagesias'
success, a space in which interpretation necessarily takes place. Is, for
example, the focus on the death of Amphiaraos, a noble moment in a
doomed expedition, itself significant? Is the earth which swallows the
seer to be seen as 'illumined by his φαιδίμας [shining] horses'[256] in a way
which parallels Iamus' emergence into light? And are these two stories,
of a dying, glorious seer, and a glorious seer coming to be, together to
exemplify the generations of seers of which Hagesias is the most recent
epigonos? How much of the narrative of the (epic) figures of Adrastus and
Amphiaraos is to be brought into play by this brief mention of an *epos*?
The tension between frame and mythic narrative – an interplay of difference which always already informs exemplification – requires an activity
of interpretation which, even with the explicit linkage of τὸ καί ('the same
words fit . . .'), joins the reader or audience in the work of constructing
fit praise, of making the fit. It is this logic of exemplification – in which
my example is also inevitably inplicated – that gives rise to so many of
the critical differences in reading Pindar's fiction. It is a logic evident in
this apparently simple and brief use of Amphiaraos in *Ol.* 6, as in the
longer (positive and negative) mythical narratives of the *epinikia*.

The direct assertion of praise once more leads directly to restraint,
however. While he bears clear witness to the suitability of this praise for
Hagesias, the poet does so under the (self-)protection of a strong oath
and with the (self-)assertion that he is neither contentious nor excessively
fond of victory (both Hagesias' and his own). There is a limit of propriety
even to the express desire for victory. The Muses, the creators and guarantors of *kleos*, will thus entrust the poet (who is thus set as the agent of
the divine) in his performance. As the first strophe closes with the
citizens' *phthonos* raised as a possibility to be rejected, so the first epode

---

[256] Stern (1970) 336–7.

concludes with the (self-)positioning of the *sophos* against the poet's negative potential both for strife and for poetry without the divine access to truth provided by the Muses and justified by the oath. The first triad circumscribes its *kleos* with expressions of the proper and improper reception and production of praise.

> But come, Phintis! bridle those mighty mules
> as fast as you can, so that I may mount the chariot,
> drive on the clear road, and reach,
> at last, the source of this clan.
> For they know the way
> better than others,
> having won
> crowns at Olympia.
> I must fling the gates of song
> open before them
> and arrive on schedule
> today, at Eurotas' crossing, home of Pitana   (22–8)

The second triad opens with a change of address and direction. A winning charioteer is invoked elsewhere in the *epinikia*[257] as part of the memorial of victory: so these mules are said to know the route to be taken above others, because they have received garlands at Olympia.[258] But, 'as the sentence proceeds, it gradually emerges that the invocation is a pretext for something else, that we are on a purely metaphorical journey'.[259] Indeed, the charioteer is instructed to yoke 'the victor's chariot to travel into the land of myth'[260] – a clear path to reach the *genos andrōn*, a phrase which may mean, as Nisetich translates, 'the source of this clan', 'the stock of the men' of this celebration, but which also recalls a more general expression, 'the race of men',[261] which implies the more general exemplary nature of the narrative to follow. Thus, in a sentence which links the opening image of the splendid building to the travels of the chariot, the 'gates of song' are to be thrown open and a way is to be found to reach Pitana 'today and in good time'. σάμερον, 'today', and ἐν ὥρᾳ,

---

[257] E.g. *Pyth.* 5.25ff; *Isth.* 2.22ff. On which see Lefkowitz (1984) 37–42.
[258] ἀγεμονεῦσαι (25), 'leading', perhaps suggests an etymology of Hagesias' name. The secondary sources on this poem contain many comments about the seriousness or playfulness of the celebration of specifically mules – animals whose double origin (horse and ass) can lead to no offspring.
[259] Silk (1974) 171.   [260] Segal (1985) 199.
[261] Cf. *Il.* 12.23, and the very common expression *genos gunaikōn*, 'the race of women', on which see Loraux (1981b) 75–117.

'in good time', 'at the proper season', emphasize the (proper) moment of celebration as it happens (and as the instant of glory is memorialized in the present song), and *poron*, 'way', 'route', implies not only the route of the chariot but also the invention of the poet, his negation of *aporia* in his poetic *inventio*. The transition into the extended mythic narrative is made with the imagery not merely of journeying but also of the poet's skill in the 'roads of song'.

> who lay with Poseidon once and bore
> Evadna, violet-braided girl.
>   Her mother had hidden the virgin's
>   birth-pain in her womb
>   until the ninth month, then sent
>   attendants, bidding them give her baby
>   to Aipytos, son of Elatos,
>   lord of Arkadians in Phaisana,
>   with Alpheos in his dominion.
> There Evadna was reared,
>   and there for the first time,
> in Apollo's arms, she knew the sweetness of Aphrodite   (29–35)

The route to the mythic narrative is, as so often in Pindar, through the relative pronoun,[262] as the mention of the city of Pitana translates into the story of its eponymous heroine, the narrative always already immanent in the name. Pitana slept with Poseidon, it is said, and gave birth to Evadna 'of the violet braids'. The mother of Iamos, whose name is etymologized through *ia*, (ἴα), 'violets' (54–8), is described at her birth with another adjective based on the same term. Pitana conceals the birth, a concealment expressed through a paradoxical contraction of phrase παρθενίαν ὠδῖνα, 'a virgin's birth pang' (where to translate παρθενίαν simply as 'unwed', as Nisetich does, unnecessarily reduces the suggested – concealed – narrative of unsuspected liaison and unperceived pregnancy of the daughter of the house). This child of a human and divine meeting is promptly and without further explanation sent away to Arcadia to be brought up in another house – a further concealment which, as

---

[262] See Bundy (1986) 8 n. 27; and, with a more interesting analysis, Hurst (1984) 160–1, who writes (160, 164) 'Le saut vers le temps légendaire est en quelque sorte masqué; il devient l'appendice d'une espèce de scholie attachée au nom de la ville ...'; '... c'est par le rattachement à une figure notoirement située dans le passé que ce procédé syntaxique minimal a la meilleure chance de donner l'illusion d'une sorte de perception du temps dans un continuel présent, présent dans lequel coexisteraient les différents moments d'une chronologie.'

several critics have pointed out, is easily assimilable to a common pattern of Greek mythological narrative:[263] the royal child, with or without his mother, is sent away from his rightful place in order that he might return to reclaim that place in glorious achievement. Iamos will indeed be described in such terms. Evadna, however, goes away as a child to become pregnant by a divine lover (like her mother) and to give birth to Iamos; to have her narrative reach a *telos* in the son whose descendants are being celebrated in this ode. The sending away by the mother, Pitana, of her female child, Evadna, defers by a generation the birth of the male hero that the mythic pattern promises, but thereby creates a double divine fatherhood for the *genos*, as Evadna's upbringing in Arcadia provides a double geographical source.[264] Both doublings are introduced, as we will see, to be instantiated in the narratives of Iamos and Hagesias.

> but could not hide the fruit of the god's seed
> until the end:
>   Aipytos saw and went to Delphi
> to consult Apollo, suppressing with keen determination
> the unutterable anger in his heart,
>   while she
> unloosed her purple-threaded belt, put down
> in the blue shade of the wood
> her silver urn, and bore a godly boy.
> Gold-haired Apollo made Eleithyia and the Moirai attend on her.
>
>   (36–42)

Like her mother, Evadna attempts to conceal her child, but she cannot deceive Aipytos, who none the less suppresses his unspeakable (paternal) rage (οὐ φάτον ... χόλον) and goes to consult the Delphic oracle.[265] Pindar's narrative here progresses in part through hinting towards and suppressing – manipulating – common mythic patterns: 'the mitigation of [Aipytos'] anger makes unnecessary the traditional exile, return and impossible mission of the hero'[266] – a testing and *nostos* enforced by the king's fear of usurpation: 'In the most obvious and mythological sense,

---

[263] See in particular Stern (1970); Nash (1975); Rubin (1980a); Segal (1986b) especially 102, 151; Bonelli (1987) 77–84.

[264] The telling of the myth in this way is related to Pindar's supposed political sympathies by Wilamowitz (1886) and Huxley (1975).

[265] In the phrase ὤχετ' ἴων (38), McDiarmid (1987) 377 n. 35 sees a 'nomen–omen' explanation of the name of Iamos, picked up in ἴμεν (63), an etymology which 'presages many other goings'.

[266] Rubin (1980a) 81.

Aipytos' anger is ... to be explained ... by his fear of destruction or at least exile at the hands of the new born hero.'[267] This is a story line fully demonstrated in, say, the exploits of Jason in *Pyth.* 4, and Aipytos' immediate consultation of the Delphic oracle contrasts markedly with Pelias' reaction to the surprising appearance of the young Jason. Pindar's focus on the unexpressed anger of Aipytos stresses, then, if not a 'tonal ambivalence'[268] in the narrative, at least a pattern of divine and human interaction that Iamos' glorious origin fails to follow.

There is a similar lack of explicit motivation for the siting of the birth in the wood, although again several common mythic patterns may be being suggested. An exile for threatening child or unwed mother (into the wilds)? Or does the detail of the silver pitcher – which is not discussed by the commentators – imply some (royal) domestic or ritual task is being undertaken? Or is it an unutilized recognition token, like the golden snakes with which Ion in Euripides' play is exposed? So, too, the unloosing of the purple ζώναν, 'girdle', suggests the divine seduction(s) whose results are now being seen. If the motivation is left inexplicit, however, the marks of divine favour are clear in Apollo's placing of a gentle Eleithyia (the goddess of birth) and the Fates in attendance on the birth of the boy, who is called θεόφρονα, which implies not merely 'godly' (i.e. 'pious' LSJ) as translated, but also a boy possessed of divine insight through the care of a divinity. Evadna's journey to the wood is set parallel (μέν ... δέ) to Aipytos' journey to Delphi: Delphi's oracle, returned with Aipytos, will lead to a search to return Iamos to the house as Apollo's son and as a prophet for mortals. The narrative of the origin of the Iamidae intertwines a series of journeys with a series of interchanges between the divine and the human action in the foundation of the *genos*: the *genos* is produced between men and gods.

> ἦλθεν δ' ὑπὸ σπλάγχνων ὑπ' ὠδῖνός τ' ἐρατᾶς Ἴαμος
> ἐς φάος αὐτίκα. τὸν μὲν κνιζομένα
> λεῖπε χαμαί· δύο δὲ γλαυκῶπες αὐτὸν
> δαιμόνων βουλαῖσιν ἐθρέψαντο δράκοντες ἀμεμφεῖ
> ἰῷ μελισσᾶν καδόμενοι.

> Without delay, in welcome labour, Iamos
> came from her womb into the light.

---

[267] Stern (1970) 333, who also notes rightly how Pindar does not explicitly bring such motivation into play.

[268] The term of Stern (1970) 334 rejected by Rubin (1980a) 79–84, especially 82 nn. 48, 49.

> In her distress, she left him there
>   on the ground.
>   A pair of grey-eye serpents,
>   by the god's will,
>   took care of him,
>   fed him the bees' inviolate poison.   (43–7)

The first mention of the name of Iamos is pronounced as the child comes to light (from the dark of the womb and the wood)[269] in a 'welcome labour', or, more accurately, a 'pleasant birthpang' – an oxymoron that reinforces the miraculous divine intercession.[270] The rapidity of the narrative and its explicit but insufficient (psychological) motivation continues: 'in her distress, she left him there on the ground'. The child is exposed and the mother distressed, but the relation between the events and the reasons for both are left unexplained. This exposure, however, opens the way for the divinely planned nourishment of the child by two snakes (another doubling). 'The snakes', writes Stern, 'though they are unquestionably meant to establish his powers as a prophet, are even more unquestionably sinister, chthonian animals'[271] (though being awesome and chthonic cannot be in any simple way opposed to being a prophet as, for example, trips to Tiresias in the Underworld show). Moreover, the worship of snakes in shrines also helps make their very appearance a sign of Iamos' miraculous origin and divine favour,[272] that is marked by the further violent juxtaposition of language in the oxymoron of the 'blameless poison' (ἀμεμφεῖ ἰῷ) of bees with which the snakes care for the infant. The term ios, 'poison', is also taken by critics to be an explanatory etymologizing of the name Iamus to match the ion, 'violet' – a double nomen to match his double immortal parentage, the two geographical sites of the origin of the genos.[273] To represent the birth of the liminal figure of the hero – the offspring of a divine and human mingling, fed by beasts – the poet's 'chariot of song' turns to figures of language that meld the boundaries of sense – the combination and transgression of oxymoron and the punning of a double etymology.

---

[269] On the emergence into light in this narrative, see Stern (1970); Rubin (1980a) and especially Nash (1975).

[270] Rubin (1980a) 82 n. 48 takes Wilamowitz to task for missing the point of the oxymoron.

[271] Stern (1970) 337.

[272] The threatening appearance of snakes at the birth of Herakles, while in other respects different, is also a sign of divine attention and the baby's heroic status.

[273] See Ruck (1976).

And the king driving from Delphi's cliffs
   returned,
                     asking all in the house
for the boy Evadna bore: 'He is Apollo's son

and will be a seer pre-eminent
   for mortal men.
      Never will his race fail.'
        So the king declared, but they
          swore they had neither heard
            nor seen
        the five-days' child.
    No wonder, for he lay hidden
      amid tall grass and forbidding brambles,
   his delicate body bathed
               in the yellow
and deep blue rays of violets, from which his mother

then named him Iamos, a name immortal forever.   (47–57)

The narrative turns back immediately to the king returning from
Delphi. The focus is thus on the two journeys of the king, but the
consultation of Delphi is implied in the announcements he is reported to
make to his household: that Apollo is the boy's father, and the double
prophecy that the infant will be an outstanding prophet and his race will
never fail – both prophecies that predict Iamos' descendant, Hagesias.
The child, however, who was not concealed from the king before his
birth, is now hidden in the rushes and briars, 'his tender body drenched
in the yellow and purple rays of violet', ἴων ξανθαῖσι καὶ παμπορφύροις
ἀκτῖσι βεβρεγμένος ἁβρὸν σῶμα. This extraordinary image – though typically Pindaric in its density and complexity of expression – of the rays
blazing from the (colours of) the flowers and drenching the delicate infant
provides another origin: Iamos' 'immortal name', τοῦτ' ὄνυμ' ἀθάνατον,
a phrase emphatically placed by enjambment at the beginning of the
epode (and followed by a heavy stop of grammar and narrative), as
πατρός, 'father', appears first word of the antistrophe. The search for
an immortal name – the pursuit of the poetry of *kleos* – returns to the
glorious, divinely inspired origin of the *genos* and the original act of
naming, as it celebrates the heir of the name.

And when Hebe downed his cheeks in gold
he waded midstream in Alpheos, called

> through the clear night air on his grandfather, Poseidon
> and on Apollo, asking
>> an honour to sustain his race.
> Quickly, his father's voice replied: 'Rise,
> my son, and come this way
> towards my voice, to a place open to all.'   (57–63)

The narrative moves from the naming of Iamos to the moment of his incipient maturity (ἥβας 58).[274] The selectiveness and contraction of the narrative is again noticeable, but the pattern at least is familiar from stories such as Odysseus' scar in the *Odyssey*: birth, naming, entrance to manhood – the rites of passage into adult status. Iamos goes down to the river Alpheos and calls on his progenitors, Poseidon and Apollo. The hero begs for *timē*, as he stands upright in the night. (The details of standing upright in a river at night have often seemed to critics to suggest a ritual performance, but there is no more specific analysis available than Lehnus' comment 'E descritto, con tratti magicosacrali, ... un rito di iniziazione e di transizione dall' adolescenza alla maturità.')[275] Like many heroes, most notably Achilles, Iamos begs a divine parent to fulfil his desire for honour. The child is immediately answered with the voice of the father, which is ἀρτιέπης, 'clearly' or 'opportunely',[276] spoken: an *epos* which summons Iamos to go up and fulfil his vocation of prophet (as Adrastus' *epos* spoke of the loss of prophet under the earth). The child is instructed to follow the father's voice to a place which will be for communal gathering. The voice heard by the boy alone at night enjoins him to return to the community to speak for the father, to take on a role which articulates a privileged access to truth for the community.

> ἵκοντο δ' ὑψηλοῖο πέτραν ἀλίβατον Κρονίου·
> ἔνθα οἱ ὤπασε θησαυρὸν δίδυμον
> μαντοσύνας, τόκα μὲν φωνὰν ἀκούειν
> ψευδέων ἄγνωτον, εὖτ' ἂν δὲ θρασυμάχανος ἐλθὼν
> Ἡρακλέης. σεμνὸν θάλος Ἀλκαιδᾶν, πατρὶ
> ἑορτάν τε κτίσῃ πλειστόμβροτον τε –
>> θυμόν τε μέγιστον ἀέθλων,
> Ζηνὸς ἐπ' ἀκροτάτῳ βωμῷ τότ' αὖ χρη –
> στήριον θέσθαι κέλευσεν.

---

[274] *Hebe* is called χρυσοστεφάνοιο, 'gold-crowned', on which Carne-Ross (1976) 18 comments 'Gold shone at his birth and at his coming of age.'

[275] Lehnus (1981) 103 ad 57–70; see also Carne-Ross (1976) 18–20; Stern (1970) 336 n. 14 with further bibliography.

[276] See Carne-Ross (1976) 19–20. Gildersleeve (1979) ad loc. and Kirkwood (1982) ad loc. note that Apollo normally speaks in riddles, but to his son and prophet is clear.

They climbed the steep rock front of Kronos' hill.
    There Apollo gave him
      a double treasure of prophecy:
        to hear at that time
          the voice of truth, and then –
            when bold Herakles,
              mighty scion of the Alkidai,
          had come and founded
        the Olympian festival, the games
      that draw men in throngs –
                he would become
    priest on the height of Zeus' oracular altar.   (64–70)

Son and father[277] rise to the rock of Kronos (Zeus' father) into the light of the sun[278] – from the dark wood, to the river at night, to the mountain top.[279] The paths of song – Phintis' chariot – have led back to Olympia, the site of their victorious race. (So, the mules were said to know the route since they were Olympic victors.) At Olympia, a 'double treasure' is bestowed on Iamos: first, the gift of prophecy, to hear 'the voice of truth', as he heard his father's injunction, and as the poet hears the Muses; second, to be priest at the oracular altar of Zeus – Apollo's father – when Heracles has founded the Olympic games for his father, Zeus. In this (teleological) gathering of fathers and heroic origins, the double gift continues the 'governing idea of duality'[280] that informs the ode. To a boy with a double divine origin and a double name, a double treasure is given. Iamos' heroic return, then, is to his place by the altar in Olympia, a place now held by Hagesias.

    From that day, the descendants of Iamos
      are famous throughout Greece,
        and prosperity has followed upon them.
          Honouring virtue, they walk in the light.
          Their deeds bear them witness.
          The censure of envious others
          hangs over the man who

---

[277] I take the plural 'they came', ἵκοντο, to imply the arrival of son and father, rather than the vague 'Iamus and his followers' suggested by Fennell, since there is no mention of any followers of Iamos elsewhere in the ode.

[278] On the meaning of the difficult ἀλίβατον, see Nash (1975).

[279] This movement upwards is emphasized as a pattern of the narrative by Stern (1970) and Rubin (1980a).

[280] Norwood (1945) 129.

> rounds the twelfth turn
> in first place, and revered Grace sheds
> the gleam of glory about him.   (71–6)

The route from the mythic narrative is also via the relative pronoun: 'from which time', ἐξ οὖ, the race of Iamidae (*genos Iamidōn*) is famous throughout Greece. The fame 'throughout Greece' that was Odysseus' possession in the *Odyssey*, and the 'immortal' *kleos* of Achilles' desire, are linked in the fame throughout Greece of the *genos*, which, as was prophesied, will never pass away. Prosperity (ὄλβος) follows – the continuing inheritance of a state of plenty where happiness and material well-being are inseparable. The *timē* that Iamos demanded from his father, is maintained by the Iamidae showing *timē* to *aretē*, 'honour to virtue' – a (reciprocal) pursuit and maintenance of honour that is to 'walk in the light', 'go on the brilliant road', ἐς φανερὰν ὁδόν. The journeys that mapped the mythic narrative and the continuation of that paradigm through the generations are linked in a further progression, a way that is clear and splendid (φανεράν), where each act bears witness (τεκμαίρει) to the race's continuing achievement. This celebration of the repeated fulfilment of the glorious origin of Iamos, however, like the praise of the opening stanzas, is immediately set in juxtaposition to the recognition and deprecation of human envy. The *mōmos*, 'censure', 'blame', of those who feel envy (*phthonos*) hangs over the victor, who is described as a man whom *Charis* has transfigured. *Charis* is significantly termed αἰδοῖα, 'deserving of *aidōs*', that value whose observance preserves the bonds between *philoi*, bonds which, we have seen, *charis* promotes and defines against *phthonos*. Even as the *phthonos* and *mōmos* of men is raised as the defining other of the celebration of victory, the expression of the cause of such *phthonos* stresses again the normative ties of the celebrants. *Charis*, indeed, is said to 'drip over' (ποτιστάξῃ) the victor a εὐκλέα μορφάν, a 'shape of fine *kleos*'. The victor's transformation through the Grace that victory brings and instantiates, finds its corollary in the production of *kleos* in the *charis* of song.

> Yet if, in truth, Hagesias,
> your mother's family dwells in Kyllana's foothills,
>
> if with frequent prayer and burnt offerings
> they honour Hermes, god of contests
> and prizes in heroic Arcadia: then he,
> O son of Sostratos, and his thunder-father
> secure your good luck.   (77–81)

After the deprecation of human *phthonos*, the splendour of Hagesias is now set in the context of divine control. The conditional clause expresses the ever necessary condition of divine support for human success. Hermes, born in Kyllana where Hagesias' maternal family lives, shows a special honour to Arcadia, and in his capacity as patron of athletic competition, in return for the pious sacrifices offered to him, guarantees good fortune (with the help of his father). The Iamidae, founded on an association with the divine, depend on such a relation being maintained.

δόξαν ἔχω τιν᾽ ἐπὶ γλώσσᾳ λιγυρᾶς ἀκόνας,
καί μ᾽ ἐθέλοντα προσέλκει καλλιρόοις πνοαῖς
ματρομάτωρ ἐμὰ Στυμφαλίς, εὐανθὴς Μέτωπα,

πλάξιππον ἃ Θήβαν ἔτικτεν, τᾶς ἐρατεινὸν ὕδωρ
πίομαι, ἀνδράσιν αἰχματαῖσι πλέκων
ποικίλον ὕμνον. ὄτρυνον νῦν ἑταίρους,
Αἰνέα, πρῶτον μὲν Ἥραν Παρθενίαν κελαδῆσαι,
γνῶναί τ᾽ ἔπειτ᾽, ἀρχαῖον ὄνειδος ἀλαθέσιν
λόγοις εἰ φεύγομεν, Βοιωτίαν ὗν.
    ἐσσὶ γὰρ ἄγγελος ὀρθός,
ἠυκόμων σκυτάλα Μοισᾶν, γλυκὺς κρα –
        τὴρ ἀγαφθέγκτων ἀοιδᾶν·

> A shrill whetstone that hones my speech,
>   a certain idea I have,
>   drags me, willingly, with lovely flowing airs:[281]
>   the mother of my mother was from
> Stymphalis, fine-flowering Metopa,

---

[281] These lines are particularly difficult and among the most commented on in Pindar. See e.g. Norwood (1941); Woodbury (1955) (with good bibliography of earlier discussions); Dover (1959); Pavese (1964) (surprisingly followed with a small change by Lehnus (1981)); Ruck (1968) (followed by Carne-Ross (1976)), and, most recently, McDiarmid (1987). The text printed in Snell-Maehler's, with, however, προσέλκει rather than προσέρπει, on which see Ruck (1968). My translation is provisional: 'The flute's whistling note' (Nisetich, following Ruck) and 'the smell of a lovely stream' (Dover) are both too specific for πνοαῖς (without a word for 'flute' or 'river'), hence 'airs'. With Ruck and Dover, I take ἀκόνας as an appositional genitive to δόξαν: the δόξα consists in or 'acts as' (Dover) a 'whetstone' to the tongue. δόξα is taken to mean 'idea' by Ruck and others from the scholia onwards. Dover suggests 'reputation'. Lehnus writes '*Ho fama* ...: diversamente "ho l'impressione di ..."' Both translations reflect common concerns of the *epinikia*: the praise of the poet's own reputation and the express marking of a new subject.

> who bore horse-riding Theba,
>   from whose delightful springs I drink,
>   as I plait the intricate song
>   for fighting men.
>   Rouse your comrades,
>   Aineas, and sing first
>   of Hera Partheneia, and then say
>   whether by our words we thrust
>   that old insult *Boiotian sow*
>   aside,
>   for you're a straight messenger, bearer
>   of the Muses' code, sweet bowl of thunderous songs.
>
>   (82–91)

Although the connection between stanzas through the relative pronoun ἅ (85) (and the verb of birth, ἔτεκεν, 'bore') is similar to the transition between, say, the second strophe and antistrophe (29 ἅ ... λέγεται ... τέκεμεν, 'who is said to have borne ...'), this is the first time in the ode that there is no strong grammatical or semantic break at the end of a triad. At the enjambment,[282] the explicit discussion of juncture marks a change of direction, as the poet comments on the poem's development and develops a new connection between himself and the victor, a further genealogical line and linkage. Stymphalos in Arcadia, the home of Hagesias' maternal line, is also the city of origin of Metopa, the nymph whose daughter Theba is the eponymous divinity of Thebes, the poet's city of origin. Speaking as a Theban, the poet claims a compelling and willingly enacted tie between the victor and himself – a kinship, a shared genealogy, an inherited tie of *philia*. The poet is thus willingly drawn 'by the lovely flowing airs', (or 'to the smell of a lovely flow') to 'fine-flowering Metopa'. The language of flowers that surrounds the myth of Iamus, also describes Metopa, the Arcadian origin of Thebes. The language of travelling – of the poet's paths of song, and of the myth's journeys towards a *telos* – progresses in the 'drawing' of the poet to Metopa, a change of (poetic) direction that is also a genealogical and geographical turn. (Pindar's tropes are ever hard to separate from his topography.) The imagery of poetry as a flowing stream and of inspiration as a 'breathing in'[283] also

---

[282] On enjambment in general, see Mullen (1982) 93–7; Carne-Ross (1976) 24–6 sees this enjambment as evidence of the poet's fiction of excitement.

[283] On water and poetic inspiration, see Kambylis (1965); on the 'flow' of words, see e.g. *Il.* 1.249; on inspiration as 'breathing in', see e.g. Hes. *Theog.* 31. See specifically on these lines and with further bibliography Ruck (1968) 132–42; Gildersleeve (1979) ad loc.

makes it especially hard to delineate a metaphorical and a literal sense in the 'airs' by which the poet is drawn. Indeed, the connections between place and inspiration (in more than a poetic sense) make any such attempt at a delineation inadequate, especially when the poet's affiliation to his home city of Thebes is expressed as 'whose delightful water I drink', while 'weaving an involved song for spearmen' (where the connections between the language of water and poetic composition again suggest that the *topos* is to be taken as both a place of origin and a rhetoric of inspiration). This inspiration that comes from a place, forms another link between poet and the (inspired) prophet he celebrates. *Plekōn*, 'weaving', is a common expression for the production of literary texts, as it is for all sorts of fictions, but there is a further particular connotation here, emphasized by the recurrent language of flowers, namely, the weaving of a garland for the victor (in his *kōmos*). The descendant of 'violet-braided Evadna' and of Iamus, lain among flowers, is being woven (in) a victory poem by the poet. The song which is being woven, moreover, is *poikilos*, 'intricate', carefully wrought', 'involved'. The result of the poet's activity of weaving is the (ambivalent) quality of *poikilia* – both the intricacy of art and the deception of fiction – a quality that may seem to be significantly juxtaposed to the values inherent in the 'men of the spear' for whom Pindar sings.[284] Yet, if any negative implications of 'weaving' and 'subtlety' (*poikilia*) are sounded, they are to be repressed in the following praise of the poet's truth and his 'straight messenger'. For to read the fictions of praise against the grain is to read like a citizen with *phthonos*. The self-proclaimed *poikilia* of Pindar's poetic fiction, a truth to set against *phthonos*, also requires a reception that represses *phthonos*, if its truth is to be acknowledged. The poem constantly demonstrates and requires what it announced as a condition in the first stanza: ἐπικύρσαις ἀφθόνων ἀστῶν ἐν ἱμερταῖς ἀοιδαῖς, 'provided that he finds citizens free from *phthonos* amid the pleasant songs'. At this moment of transition into the final triad and of self-reflexive pointing of the poetic process, the song's *poikilos* rhetoric is highlighted (as a performance and exchange between poet, victor and audience).

The assertion of Hermes' support for Hagesias, then, leads in these most densely textured lines – again, the density and complexity particularly associated with Pindar – into a bounding of such praise by the formulation of an especial genealogical linkage between the figure of the

---

[284] On *poikilos* as a value of archaic poetics, see in particular Detienne (1967) especially 30 n. 6; Detienne and Vernant (1978) 25–31, 49–51, 288; Svenbro (1976) 191–3.

poet and the victor, in terms which significantly overlap genealogy with poetic production and which stress the (willingly acknowledged) requirements and achievements of praise (as a continuation of the ties of the *genos*).

Indeed, the remaining lines of the strophe (87–93) go on to set the poet's voice and the choral performance against a background of rejected reproaches. First, in an instruction to another member of the celebration that parallels the earlier address to Phintis, the charioteer, Aineas, the chorus leader or trainer,[285] is told to rouse his companions of the chorus to sing of Hera Partheneia (an Arcadian cult of Hera) – a further divine tutelary for the ode and its celebrants – and then to recognize 'whether by our true words we escape the ancient insult "Boiotian pig"'. *Gignōskein*, 'know' (weakly translated as 'say'), regularly expresses the proper appreciation of poetry: here the Theban poet requires appreciation and acknowledgement of his true words set against an ancient insult. Hagesias instantiates the (ancient) *epos* of Adrastus' praise; Pindar belies the 'the old insult' of his *topos* of birth. As the duty of praise is founded on a (genealogical) placing of the poet, so the reproach of the poet that is to be rejected is based on the poet's place of origin. So, too, the poet in his performance (first-person plural) 'escapes' (*pheugomen*) reproach, as in the opening stanza the victor is to fail to escape (*phugoi*) a proper song of celebration. Here, too, there is enacted the (inescapable) link between poet and victor in the search to avoid falsely constituted evaluation. The truth of the ποικίλος ὕμνος, 'the intricate song', aims to surmount the self-proclaimed precariousness of praise.

Second, the reasons offered for the appeal to Aineas are his qualities as a representative of the Muses. He is a 'straight messenger'. 'Truth' and 'straightness' (ὀρθότης) are regularly correlated throughout fifth-century ideas of communication and particularly in Pindar's writing[286] (and the notion of the false messenger, implied by such a phrase, finds many important instances in tragedy). Aineas, however, is also the *skutala* of the Muses. The *skutala* is a cipher-stick around which a coded message is fitted in order to make sense and guarantee truth: it is a specifically Spartan device. Aineas plays such a role for the Muses, a necessary and enabling intermediary for the *poikilos* poetic exchange. He is, finally, in a bold metaphor the 'sweet bowl of thundering songs'. The symposium, and its sweetness, provide a paradigmatic framework for the the production of praise, as the normative social context for the communication of *philoi*. The figure of the poet and his performers together are invested with a divinely guaranteed access to truth, the human capabilities to express it, and the social context for its proper performance. The prayers and praise for Hagesias that require the poet's self-positioning with regard to the victor, are grounded in the redoubled praise of the poet's voice.

> I have told you to celebrate Syracuse
> and Ortygia, where Hieron is king,
>   with radiant sceptre and straight counsels,
>   priest of red-sandaled Demeter,
>   of her girl
>   borne on white horses,
>   and of Aitnaian Zeus.
> Harps and lyrics know him.
> May time to come never disturb his bliss.
> And may he welcome
>   to the feast
> Hagesias' revelling friends as they come
>
> from home to home, leaving behind the walls
> of Stymphalos, their mother Arcadia, nurse of flocks.
>
> (92–100)

The poet dramatizes his instructions to recall the other base of Hagesias' heritage, Syracuse and its island Ortygia, the kingdom of the powerful Hiero, another patron of Pindar. (It is with the new rulers of the new powers in the Greek world that Pindar's active construction of the myths of origin and place – and the possible tensions in the activity of writing the history of a new power within an ancient tradition and genealogy of heroic achievement – can be most strikingly seen.) Hiero is celebrated for his clear rule, his fit policies and the proper worship of the gods. In his relations with men and with the gods and in his attitudes to such relations Hiero is exemplary. So, he is the beneficiary of the power of song to celebrate, to memorialize (μεμνᾶσθαι 93). The lyres and lyrics (with their dances) know (*ginōskonti* 93) him, as the chorus and Aineas know (*gnōnai* 89) Pindar's poetry for the truth. Recognition – acknowledgement – is a reciprocal process in the community's poetry of memorial. So, after a prayer for the continuing prosperity (*olbos*) of Hiero, to match the *olbos* of the *genos* of Iamidae (72), Pindar asks the king to receive with generous spirit (*philophrosunē*) the *kōmos* of Hagesias, to accept the celebrating *philoi* from the position and attitude of a *philos*. Hagesias, linked with Amphiaraos and his noble forefathers, is now to be joined in celebration by the most powerful figure of Syracuse, as this (projected) acceptance of Hagesias in Syracuse fulfils in the final stanza the condition of 'citizens ungrudging in song' that is raised in the first stanza.

A *kōmos* travels from house to house (οἴκοθεν οἴκαδ' 99); this *kōmos*, however, is journeying not just through a town in celebration, but to a home in Syracuse from a home in Stymphalos, the maternal dwelling. A journey from Arcadia to Sicily, where both houses are of the same man: a *nostos* that is also a departure. The victor, transfigured by victory, is captured at a moment of transition, as the ode has depicted a series of transitions – journeys, births, initiations – in its narrative progression. 'The ode has progressed, like the cortège of Hagesias' revelry, from home to home, from the house of poetry whose columns Pindar sets to the house that must yet be built among the mansions of the victor's peers.'[287] The story of the journey of a *genos* in time is mapped onto a topographical journey, which mirrors the poem's progression (through its *topoi*) – to celebrate the winning of a race. The poem represents celebration as process – the victor being transfigured by praise, the constructing of a εὐκλέα μορφάν, 'a shape of fine *kleos*' – a process in which the audience, the performers and the poet are together implicated.

> On a winter's night, two anchors
> best secure the ship.
>   May god in his favour
> give glory to both these cities.
> Lord of the sea, husband of Amphitrita
> with her golden distaff, grant a safe journey
> to them and new bloom to the song they carry.   (100–105)

The journeys and the pervasive doubling of the poem come together in the generalization that follows: the image of a ship best secured in a stormy night by two anchors. Again, an image of success is constructed through acknowledging and resisting the possibility of failure. The two anchors are proof against the storm. That the two anchors seem to encapsulate the doubleness stressed in the poem's narrative, appears to find an echo in the prayer for god 'in his favour' (*phileōn* 102) to provide a famous (*klutan* 102) fate 'for these men and for those' – the Arcadians

---

[287] Ruck (1968) 141.

and Stymphalians, the two houses of Hagesias' *kōmos* ('both these cities' (Nisetich)). Yet the prayer becomes more specific in the final sentence as a request for Poseidon, the god of the sea, the grandfather of Iamos, to grant a fair voyage free from toil – an image which, although it develops the picture of the ship at anchor, is taken by many commentators to refer to the real voyage of Hagesias to Syracuse.[288] Lehnus' translation captures the possibilities of the phrase more accurately, however.[289] For the phrase could refer to Hagesias' happiness: a prayer for his success (as a son of the two cities and a scion of Poseidon).[290] It may perhaps refer to the two cities, for whom Pindar requests a continuing history of prosperity. It may even include in the wish Pindar himself for whom a final prayer is made: 'make the pleasant flower of my songs grow'. The poet himself is the final bearer of the imagery of flowers and of upward movement: 'the two images, the flowering plant and the motion upward have come together in the person of the victor, the mythic hero, and the poet'.[291] The garland of song forms a community that makes it perhaps unnecessary to delineate the intended recipient of the prayed-for prosperity. The ode that begins with the entrance to the golden building of song closes with a prayer for the growth of the flower of song – an image of the poem that picks up the imagery in the poem in a final self-reflexive gesture.

This detailed analysis of *Olympian* 6 shows how the complex strategies of praise in this poem aim to figure the victor as a bearer of the inheritance of a *genos*' history, and as a heritage for the future to celebrate. The victory is represented in a network of defining and normative contexts: a man's achievement takes place only within the framing powers of the divine, the city, the family, the past, the future – and the poet's ability to memorialize, to capture the transfiguration of the victor in the figures and transitions of narrative poetry. The fiction and practice of performance bind performers, poet and audience in the process of constructing fit praise (and praise of what is fit). The poet's glory – his self-glorification – is a constant grounding for the glorification of the victor, and this

---

[288] E.g. Fennell; Carne-Ross; Myers.

[289] 'Signore patrone del mare, concedi una rotta rapida, scevra d' affanni . . .' For a balanced view of these lines, see Péron (1974) 62–5.

[290] Lehnus (1981) 'Certo la navigazione è anche una metafora dell' esistenza coi suoi affanni.' Hubbard (1985) 141 writes: 'It is also common to find a prayer as a sort of *envoi* at the conclusion of a poem; here it is more common for the subjective wish to follow the objective wish.' He quotes these lines as an example.

[291] Stern (1970) 340.

dynamic, a particular rhetorical interplay of the relations of patronage, is repeatedly bounded by the (self-)awareness of the measures and limits of praise: the controls of the defining and normative contexts in which man's achievements are viewed. The self-representation of the poet, then, plays a crucial role in the voices of praise.

That the declaration and preservation of *kleos* is a crucial function of the poet's voice in ancient Greek culture is a commonplace. What I hope to have shown in this chapter is how such a commonplace cannot hope adequately to delineate what is an intricate literary tradition, involving works of various genres. The texts I have discussed in this chapter from Homer to Pindar reflect different and changing contexts of praise; they demonstrate not merely differing strategies and rhetorics of *kleos*, but also differing ways of constructing and contesting the limits, norms and interplays of power in human exchange. Differing ways of articulating, examining, questioning the network of cultural values are always already implicated in the social performance that is the poetry of praise. In this way, the performance of *kleos* is necessarily interlocked with the questions of representation raised in the first chapter, and with the figuring of the poet as the authoritative voice of representation. For there is no discourse of praise that is not an expression of the changing, normative discourse of what it is to be a(n outstanding) man in society; no discourse of praise that does not engage with the construction of an authoritative position from which to speak. I hope to have shown, therefore, how the developments of this literary tradition cannot be regarded simply as the variations of a poetic, or rhetorical, *topos*. This tradition is made up rather by the continuing responses of the poet's voice to a fundamental dynamic of power and language that is always already in play in the act of 'speaking out', in the representation of man in and to a society.

Poetry in the ancient world returns again and again to the praise – and the problems – of the outstanding: Hellenistic poetry is replete with *encomia* – of which Theocritus' *Idylls* 16 and 17 are perhaps the most sophisticated – and Roman poetry with its self-conscious affiliations to Greek literature, as well as its own highly involved institutions of patronage, further develops the rhetorics of celebration. In each of the following chapters – which include discussions of Aristophanes and comic celebration; of Theocritus and Hellenistic *encomia*; of Apollonius and Hellenistic epic *kleos* – the terms and strategies analysed in this chapter will be rearticulated, as the poet's voice continues to find expression in and against the language of praise and celebration.

3 Comic inversion and inverted commas: Aristophanes and parody

> 'Let's be serious.'
>
> J.Derrida

In this chapter, I shall be discussing the voice of the comic poet in the city and, specifically, Aristophanes. Two interrelated questions provide a focus: how does the comic poet 'speak out' before the city? What is the role of parodic quotation in Old Comedy: the voice within the voice ('speaking out')? I begin with some general remarks about the role of poetry in the fifth- and fourth-century Athenian democratic *polis*, that leads into a discussion of the institution of Old Comedy in the light of modern treatments of carnival and the idea of 'ritual reversal'. The second part of the chapter – focused on the *Acharnians* and the *Frogs* – looks first at the comic poet 'speaking out' to the city through the parabasis in particular, and second at how the poet uses other voices, especially the voice of tragedy, in parodic quotation.

THE CONTEST OF PUBLIC VOICES

When you meet people who praise the poet Homer as the educator of Greece and who say that in the administration of human affairs and education we should study him and model our whole lives on his poetry, you must feel respect and affection towards them as good men within their limits, and you may agree with them that Homer is the best of poets and the first of tragedians. But you will know that the only poetry that should be allowed in a state is hymns to the gods and encomiums in praise of good men; once you go beyond that and admit the sweet muse of epic or lyric, pleasure and pain become your rulers instead of law and the rational principles commonly accepted as best.

(Plato Rep. 10, 606e1–607a8)

As Plato's Socrates concludes his argument both for banishing the poets from the ideal city of the *Republic* and for closely restricting the discourse allowed in such a city, he represents a fundamental aspect of the fifth- and fourth-century *polis* that I will be calling 'the contest of public voices'. First, in most general terms, the Platonic Socrates is aiming to make philosophy the necessary medium for education, especially, though not solely, for those fit to rule in his Republic. As he goes on to say (*Rep.* 608a6–7): ᾀσόμεθα δ᾽ οὖν ὡς οὐ σπουδαστέον ἐπὶ τῇ τοιαύτῃ ποιήσει ὡς ἀληθείας τε ἁπτομένῃ καὶ σπουδαίᾳ,[1] 'We will sing, then, that nothing must be done in earnest with such poetry – as having some claim on truth or being earnest', or, as Lee translates, 'Our theme shall be that such poetry has no serious value or claim to truth.' There is a sharp irony in the use of ᾀσόμεθα, 'we will sing', 'our theme shall be', a word associated precisely with the deprecated poets e.g. at 607c7 – philosophy as a counter-spell to the dangerous charm of poetry. And Socrates' playfulness is further marked in the echo *ou spoudasteon ... spoudaiai*, 'nothing must be done in earnest' – as if poetry were 'earnest'. None the less, there can be little doubt about the importance to Plato's argument of the extensive critique of poetry, representation, education with regard to the criteria of truth and knowledge here in *Republic* 10 and earlier in *Republic* 3. As has been extensively discussed in recent years, poetry's claims to the voice of truth and mastery of fiction – a privileged access to knowledge which authorizes poetry's privileged cultural role – become a particular object of criticism of Plato as he attempts to establish the traditional intellectual and social authority of the *sophos* for the discipline of philosophy (and his own teaching in particular).[2]

This speech, however, also sites Socrates' argument in a network of ideas about public utterance that it will be helpful to investigate briefly. The assumption that poetry could be taken as the prime educative medium conforms both to what is known about the practice of schooling of Athenian young boys, and to what is regularly assumed about the function of poetry by ancient commentators and poets – namely, that poetry has an ethical and normative thrust designed to inform, improve and exhort the citizens, as well as to give pleasure.[3] The emotions of pleasure

[1] The text used here is the *Oxford Classical Text* with Madvig's emendation of the late form αἰσθόμεθα. The irony of the passage would be reduced if αἰσθόμεθα or a similar word of perception is kept.

[2] See e.g. Detienne (1967); Verdenius (1970); Calame (1977); Svenbro (1976); Vernant (1980); Gould (1983); Goldhill (1986a) 138–67. On Plato, see e.g. Nussbaum (1986) especially 122–35, with extensive bibliography 452 n. 2, and for a fascinating siting of Plato within a wide modern tradition Prendergast (1987) especially 1–82. Plato's claim of an 'ancient contest [διάφορα] between poetry and philosophy' (*Rep.* 10, 607b5) is, I take it, a typical strategy of both myth and rhetoric – to construct a teleological historical narrative to explain a present structure.

[3] See e.g. Marrou (1956). I have discussed this material with further bibliography in Goldhill (1986a) 138–67, 222–43. For an extreme thesis that poetry for fifth-century poets has a purely hedonistic aim – a thesis which has difficulty in accounting for the present passage, among many other primary sources – see Heath (1987b) (who surprisingly does not mention Detienne, Calame, Svenbro or Vernant).

and pain that 'the sweet muse of lyric or epic' can arouse, however, are
constructed by the Platonic Socrates in opposition to an intellectual and
moral rigour (that is, philosophy) and this opposition is a basic part of
Plato's rhetorical strategy against poetry: poetry's knowledge and ethical
instruction are reduced to an excitation of the lower emotional faculties
(as philosophy, needless to say, turns the citizen towards the higher
goals). That poetry is recognized and challenged as an educative medium
points to an important source of conflict in Athenian culture of the fifth
and fourth centuries. If in the world of Theognis, say, education depends
to a large degree on 'the company of good men' in situations such as
the symposium, gymnasium and festivals, in fifth- and fourth-century
Athens the formulation, control and dissemination of knowledge depend
not only on such social institutions which conserve and transmit the ways
of the fathers to the young, but also on the possibilities opened by the
new intellectuals whose performance in the intellectual and social life of
fifth-century Athens is so influential. Both the professionalization of
teaching, which facilitates access to knowledge for a less restricted group
than 'the company of good men', and the explicitly questioning and
anti-traditional studies produced by the new intellectuals challenge the
easy development of a common cultural and intellectual framework for
the *polis*, and make education a source of conflict rather than social
stability.[4] In a period of rapid cultural change, like the fifth century B.C.
or the twentieth century A.D., it is inevitably the sources, authority and
control of knowledge that are set in this way at stake. It is within such a
context of the conflicting claims of access to and the nature of knowledge
that Plato discusses the forms of education and the possibilities of discourse to be allowed in the ideal city. When in this chapter I discuss the
institution of comedy and Aristophanes' *Frogs* in particular, the intensity
of the fifth-century questioning of the authorization of a normative,
public voice – the voice of the *sophos* – will prove fundamental. So, more
specifically, conflict about the construction and transmission of knowledge – education – is a fundamental context for Aristophanes' satiric
treatment of Socrates in *The Clouds*.

The sense of shifting educational values can be seen in two further
aspects of Socrates' speech. First, the argument seems to draw in its
vocabulary and phraseology on contemporary literary discussions. The
evaluation of Homer as the greatest poet; the description of those who
make such an evaluation as 'praisers' (*epainetai*) of Homer (where the

---

[4] I have discussed the sophists in the fifth-century *polis* with bibliography in Goldhill
(1986a) 222–43.

critic's evaluation becomes a self-conscious reflection of the poet's practice of praise that I discussed in the previous chapter); the distinctions
between 'hymn' and 'encomiums', and between 'epic' and 'lyric', all show
signs of the contemporary technical discussion of literature.[5] In particular, the description of Homer as *poiētikōtatos*, 'the epitome of poets',
'most poetical' poet, is a striking choice of word, the tone of which
remains hard to judge. Although adjectives in *-ikos* are an especially
common development of late fifth- and early fourth-century language,
particularly in areas of technical expertise, and are parodied by
Aristophanes as a pretentious, intellectual verbal mannerism,[6] the super-
latives of such adjectives are very much rarer; while *poiētikos* is used
commonly enough by Plato in the sense of 'poetic', 'pertaining to poetry'
(there are attested no earlier uses of this adjective in this sense), this is
the only occasion where the superlative is used, and it may be thought to
have an implication of ironic exaggeration.[7] (Plato, like Aristophanes,
typically picks up, ironizes and distorts his opponents' vocabulary). The
description of those who take Homer as a teacher, then, seems to adapt
the contemporary terminology of literary education.

Second, the rejection of those who praise Homer is couched in a
noticeably accommodating manner. 'It is necessary', says Socrates, 'to
treat them with respect and affection because they are good men as far
as they are capable.' Despite the evident possibility of irony here, there
is also a highly relevant social or political point in the manner of expression. The *beltistoi*, the 'good men', those who have the traditional concern
for Homer as educator, are the group of citizens who provide the vast
majority of Plato's and Socrates' pupils and who are also the object of
Plato's rhetorical strategy – which is not one of aggressive alienation.
Indeed, although Plato constantly and inevitably expresses his own complex relationship of attraction and rejection with what he defines as poetry
and rhetoric, it must not be overlooked that such a self-representation of
sympathy with his audience is a precisely articulated rhetorical seductive-
ness (that cannot be adequately reduced to biographical anecdotes about

[5] On early literary criticism, see e.g. Lanata (1963); Pfeiffer (1968) 3–67; Harriot (1969);
Segal (1970b); Richardson (1975); Russell (1981) 18–34, who unfortunately discusses
only Gorgias and Plato at any length.

[6] Chantraine (1956) 97–171 remains the standard treatment of these adjectives. Aristophanes' parody is at *Knights* 1375–81.

[7] *Mousikōtatos*, however, occurs twice *Rep.* 3, 412a6; *Laws* 5, 729a6, with no discernible
sarcasm. Cf. Eur. fr. 224 Nauck. *Mousikos*, however, refers more clearly than *poiētikos*
to a human achievement that allows of gradations. *Poiētikōteros*, the comparative, occurs
at 387b (with the plain form) which may facilitate the use of the superlative here.

Plato's early attempts to write tragedy[8]). The recognition of the *beltistoi* as good and worthy of kindly respect, combined with the invitation to transcend through philosophy the previous limits of 'as far as they are able' (an invitation which simultaneously stresses the possibility of an ironic reading of Socrates' evaluative terms), constitutes a carefully manipulative rhetorical strategy within the framework of the conflicting intellectual and social positions on education in fifth- and fourth-century Athens.

Homer is described by Socrates also as the 'first of the tragedians.' 'First', *prōtos*, is both a temporal and an evaluative term.[9] Homer is the earliest and the greatest of the tragic poets. This link of Homer's epic to what is often regarded as the discrete genre of tragedy may seem surprising (especially since Plato distinguishes epic narrative and dramatic narrative in *Republic* 3, 392c5–398b5). Rather than investigate the ways in which Homer's narrative is 'tragic' or that tragedy is 'Homeric', I want here briefly to juxtapose two public institutions for the performance of poetry, the Great Dionysia and the Panathenaia, which will show in a different way the point of linking Homer and the tragedians as poets in and for the city.

The Panathenaia was an annual festival, with a more grand version, the Great Panathenaia, every four years.[10] Central to the festival was a great procession (*pompē*) of the whole city of Athens – including metics – along the Panathenaic Way to worship Athene on the Acropolis. There, a sacrifice was made for which the altar was lit by the winner of a torch race from the altar of Eros near the Dipylon Gate. At the Great Panathenaia, the procession also presented the *peplos*, a sacred and specially woven robe, to Athene[11] – this is the procession represented on the frieze

---

[8] On the biographical tradition for Plato as tragedian, see Riginos (1976) 47–51, who supposes the tradition to be an invention based on the rejection of poetry in the *Republic*; and for its use in the interpretation of Plato, see Tarrant (1955).

[9] Cf. *Rep.* 10, 595b10–c1: ἔοικε μὲν γὰρ τῶν καλῶν ἁπάντων τούτων τῶν τραγικῶν πρῶτος διδάσκαλός τε καὶ ἡγεμὼν γενέσθαι [sc. Ὅμηρος], 'He [Homer] seems to be the first teacher and guide of all these fine tragic poets.'

[10] For full descriptions of this festival, see Hopper (1971) 68–74; Parke (1977) 33–50; Simon (1983) 55–72; Hurwit (1985) 245–8, 262–4. See also Davison (1958); Brommer (1977) 145ff; Burkert (1985) 135–8; and the not altogether convincing thesis of Figuera (1984) 466–9.

[11] Parke (1977) 38–9 seems to suggest against the weight of modern opinion that the *peplos* was presented every year. Our evidence regularly shows that the *peplos* was presented at the Great Panathenaia, but does not say that it was not presented at the annual Panathenaia (and the ancient sources – like modern critics – often fail to distinguish between the Great Panathenaia and the Panathenaia), so the possibility of a yearly presentation cannot be strictly ruled out.

of the Parthenon[12] – and the celebration continued with both athletic and musical competitions. As well as the standard events of running, wrestling, boxing, pentathlon and pancration (for the three age classes of boys, ephebes and men), the athletic competitions included a contest in 'manly excellence' (*euandria*)[13] and ship races, both of which events were organized and financed on a tribal basis, and extensive horse and chariot races. The athletics, apart from the torch race and the tribal competitions, were open to non-Athenians. So, too, were the musical competitions, which carried, at least by the first half of the fourth century, considerable cash prizes. These competitions were for individual singers and musicians (singers accompanied by the *kithara* (harp) and *aulos* (oboe); soloists on the same instruments);[14] and in particular there was a competition for rhapsodes in the performance of Homer. Each rhapsode was required to pick up the narration where the previous performer had ended so that the poems received a complete telling.[15] With its huge procession and sacrifice, competitions over several days and grand presentation of the *peplos*, the Panathenaia was, as Parke comments, 'a remarkable spectacle even in Greece where this kind of public ceremony was highly developed'.[16]

The great procession clearly 'embodied the united power and glory of Athens'[17] as a *polis*, a community. Nor is it difficult to see how the various competitions in excellence, each placed under the aegis of the goddess, her festival, her city, glorify the *polis* of Athens with splendour and achievement, in the manner discussed in the previous chapter's last section.[18] It is within such a framework that the Panhellenic epics of Homer are recited before the citizens. Although there were many other forums for hearing Homer – a character in a Xenophon dialogue claims

[12] See Brommer (1977), especially 145ff, and for a fine discussion of the relation between the frieze, the festival and the spectator Osborne (1987).

[13] It is not known what this contest consisted in, although 'body-building' has been suggested.

[14] On the musical competitions, see in particular Davison (1958) 36–41.

[15] See Diog. Laert. 1.57; Plato *Hipp.* 288b. It is unfortunately not clear whether Homer was recited every year or only at the Great Panathenaia. Hurwit (1985) 263–4 assumes the latter, but also claims a great influence of these recitals on Athenian artistic life (264): 'The strong Homeric content of Attic vase painting after 520 suggests it was Hipparchos that inserted the *Iliad* and *Odyssey* into the Greater Panathenaia ... and demonstrates the impact words can have on images.'

[16] Parke (1977) 37.

[17] Parke (1977) 37.

[18] Victory in the Athenian games is mentioned by Pindar at *Nem.* 10.33–7.

to hear an extract in performance every day[19] – and although there were indeed opportunities for reading Homer by the fifth century, the Panathenaia provides an illuminating example of the public, normative role of the poet's voice in the city. The introduction of this performance, like many other aspects of the festival, was explicitly linked by fifth- and fourth-century writers to an important political figure of the early *polis*, in this case Peisistratus.[20] The implications of such an institution, however, need not be limited to a politician's desire to win favour from the citizens (as is often assumed). For before what is represented as the whole city – the city representing itself to itself and the outside world – the epics of all Greece are performed. For all Plato's arguments that Homer's text is reduced by such a performance and such a repetition to a vehicle for the performers' manipulation of an audience's emotional responses, such an institution also endows the text performed in and before the community with a considerable normative force for the community (which is, in part, what worries Plato). The work performed in the Panathenaia becomes the shared narrative of all Athenians. In the democratic *polis*, the public space of the festival becomes the site for the collective experience of the poet's work, and an expression of collectivity through such festival activity.

That such an institutionalization of Homer's epics, coupled with its inherited and reinforced normative and privileged status, does not lead simply and necessarily to a single and direct 'normative message', can be seen not only from the critical response of Plato but also and in a most striking manner from the texts of the other great public institution for the performance of poetry in fifth-century Athens, the Great Dionysia. In particular, the tragedies of the fifth century, as I have discussed at length elsewhere,[21] are never less than actively involved with the Homeric poems, as the privileged and normative texts of a tradition against, in and through which the plays of fifth-century theatre are written. The contest of public voices within the city is also a contest with – that is, a contest to appropriate – the past.

The Great Dionysia is, like the Panathenaia, a festival in which the *polis* represents itself to itself and the outside world, and it is in the Great Dionysia that the sense of a contest of public voices takes on an especial force. Not only is the Great Dionysia a contest between poets for the

[19] Xen. *Symp.* 3.5–6.
[20] See Parke (1977) 34 for discussion and references; also Hurwit (1985) 262–4.
[21] Goldhill (1984) 183–95; Goldhill (1986a) 138–67 (with further bibliography).

prize in tragedy and in comedy, but also both tragic and comic drama are structured in a fundamental way around the *agōn* – the contest between figures that makes up both the more formal debates of tragedy and the more physical and uproarious conflicts of comedy. What is more, as I have argued at length for tragedy elsewhere[22] and will be discussing for comedy in this chapter, the public space of the festival becomes not merely the arena for a contest between poets, but also for a contestation of the values, attitudes and beliefs of the citizens. In the Great Dionysia, after the series of rituals and ceremonials, which express and promote the ideology of democratic civic involvement, the tragic and comic plays represent a series of problems for and transgressions of that civic ideology.[23] On the one hand, this willingness publicly to represent conflict and publicly to question the values of a culture can be subsumed *within* democratic ideology: such an institution could exist only in a democracy and in Athens in particular with its values of freedom to speak out, equality before the law, and, above all, the need to place matters of common concern before the city for public discussion, disagreement and decision – that is, to place things ἐν μέσῳ or ἐς μέσον, *in the public domain to be contested*. As we will see, this is an argument explicitly made by Aristophanic characters. On the other hand, the profoundly disquieting questioning of tragedy, as well as the conflicts of comedy, can also be seen as a sign and symptom of the difficulties within the rapidly changing culture of fifth-century Athens. This tension between institutionalization and disruption will prove crucial to the forthcoming discussion of comedy. If the Panathenaia provides an institutional, festival context for Homer to be represented to the whole city as a city, the Great Dionysia provides an institutional, festival context for the (re)dramatization and contestation of the city's *muthoi* for and before the city. When Plato's Socrates talks of Homer as the 'most poetical and first of the tragedians', he is not merely indicating an aesthetic evaluation, but also is referring to the great public institutions of the fifth- and fourth-century democratic *polis* for making the poet's voice heard.

Plato's rejection of poetry as an unwanted emotionalism is further articulated through the specific opposition of 'pleasure and pain' and 'the law and rational principle' as the ruling forces (βασιλεύσετον) over a man. *Nomos* and *logos* are, of course, terms fundamental to the intellectual

---

[22] Goldhill (1984); Goldhill (1986a); Goldhill (1987c).

[23] I have discussed the ceremonials and their relations to the plays in detail in Goldhill (1987c). Such ceremonials were not enacted at the Lenaia where at least five of Aristophanes' extant plays were produced. On the Lenaia, see below 195.

debates of the fifth century, as is the assumption that the laws and rationality
are to be the controlling forces in a man's life. What is more, in the context
of Socrates' search in the *Republic* precisely for the laws and best rational
account of the ideal city, the opposition functions as a neat summation
of the preceding critique. But the reference to the role of *nomos* and *logos*
'in the *polis*' inevitably signals in Plato's writing the context of the
democratic *polis* with the immense importance of the Assembly and
Law-Courts as institutions (of *logos* and *nomos*). These are, indeed, the
institutions where the legitimation and questioning of public utterance,
the public representation of conflict and decision, the public discussion
of policy and development of discourse – what I have been calling in short
'the contest of public voices' – are most obviously tied to democracy as
a political system. The *agōn* here is as basic to the running of the city
as it is to the festivals with their competitions and representations of
conflict. When Plato qualifies the expression τοῦ βελτίστου λόγου, 'the
best rational principle', to read τοῦ κοινῇ ἀεί δόξαντος εἶναι βελτίστου
λόγου, 'the rational principle which has seemed always in general to be
the best', or 'which at any point seems in common best', the adverb
κοινῇ, 'in common', 'in general', recalls how the Republic is established
against the democratic *polis* of Athens, a city for which the principle 'in
common' has a unique and special importance, and a city for which the
processes of finding out what 'seems best in common' are discussed and
institutionalized in such a remarkable way.[24]

I have started this discussion with a paragraph of Plato not in order to
try to investigate the place of the poet's voice in Plato – fascinating though
such an investigation might prove for the history of the poet's voice in
Greek and other culture.[25] As we will see in the next chapter, the development of prose in the fifth and fourth centuries has a lasting and profound
effect on poetry. Rather, I have tried here to show how this brief summary
paragraph in Plato's critique of poetry traces several different social and
intellectual positions for the voice of the *sophos* in the *polis*. This sense
of a multiplication of and conflict between voices of authorization and
legitimation is of particular importance for the discussion of comedy,
since the plays of Aristophanes not only demonstrate an acute awareness
of comedy as a specific type and institution of discourse with the *polis*,
but also parody the other public voices of the city (as if in competition

---

[24] ἔδοξε τῇ βουλῇ καὶ τῷ δήμῳ, 'It has seemed good to the council and people', is the
normal formula for recording the decisions of the state, which may add a further layer
to κοινῇ δόξαντος, 'has seemed [good] in common'.

[25] On Plato and the poet's voice, see most recently Ferrari (forthcoming).

with them): the Assembly, the Law-Courts, tragedy, along with the claims of religious, military and educational experts are each regularly satirized and mocked by the comic poet's drama. What I have been calling the contest of public voices is not only a crucial social and intellectual context for understanding fifth-century comedy: it is also a contest in which comedy plays a leading role.

CARNIVAL AND LICENCE

Once the antinomy is rejected, once the paradigm blurred, utopia begins.

Barthes

How, then, to approach the institution of comedy in the city and in this contest of public voices? Since the literary studies of Bakhtin became available in translation,[26] and since the full range of anthropological studies of ritual behaviour and festivals has become more widely influential in the study of Classics, one model has been extensively and profitably developed for understanding the institution of Old Comedy, namely, the model of carnival. This model needs to be discussed in some detail not only because of the evident insights it has provided for classicists who have seen in Bakhtin's work a way of extending and deepening the common notion of 'comic reversal', but also because the specific circumstances of Old Comedy in the city offer a special case with important implications for the study of the carnivalesque that have not been adequately analysed.

For the purposes of the present discussion, there are two seminal starting-points in the anthropological literature, Van Gennep and Gluckman.[27] Van Gennep's very well-known model of rites of passage develops a tripartite structure for an extensive series of rituals of transition, where in the central period of the ritual – the 'liminal state' – there can be seen a reversal of the norms of the condition into which the initiand is passing. So, the young man, who is about to join the male group of warriors, will be dressed as a woman, or, more specifically, the Spartan youth about to join the *sussition*, the communal mess-hall of adult males, is forced to endure a period on his own in the bush, stealing, and in other ways behaving and being treated as an outcast – the *krupteia*.[28] Van Gennep's

[26] Particularly Bakhtin (1968), but also Bakhtin (1973), (1981).
[27] Van Gennep (1960) (1908); Gluckman (1963), (1965) (preceded by Gluckman ed. (1962)).
[28] On the *krupteia*, see Jeanmaire (1939); Brelich (1969); Vidal-Naquet (1981a) 161–3; and Cartledge (1981).

model has proved extremely productive in the analysis of ritual behaviour, particularly of behaviour during what Leach in his important development of Van Gennep's ideas calls the 'sacred time' of festivals.[29]

Gluckman's studies in south-east African culture focus on a particular set of ritual reversals, where the festival reversals, rather than being specifically initiatory rituals, take the form of political outbursts against, and even overturnings of the established order – what he calls 'rituals of rebellion'. Although there is a lengthy history of anthropological study attempting to explain such rituals in a functionalist manner as a means of society 'letting off steam' (*Ventilsitten*), the detail and depth of Gluckman's analysis have made his work the classic statement of such a position, and his conclusion that while 'these rites of reversal obviously include a protest against the established order ... they are intended to preserve and strengthen the established order'[30] has been often quoted and further developed. Balandier expresses the thesis memorably: 'The supreme ruse of power is to allow itself to be contested *ritually* in order to consolidate itself more effectively.'[31] This sense of a 'ritual contest(ing)' – in the contest of public voices – is a fundamental element in the carnival models of comedy.

The specifics of Gluckman's thesis, however, have been qualified in particular by Turner, Babcock and Geertz. Babcock points out three immediate and necessary corrections.[32] First, such rituals of reversal are not limited, as Gluckman suggests, to 'seasonal rituals'; but, as Van Gennep and others have shown, are an integral component of the liminal periods of rites of passage; second, 'rebellious ritual' does not occur only within an established, secure and unchallenged social order, as Gluckman argues: indeed much work on modern Europe has attempted to demonstrate how 'rebellious ritual" can play a crucial role in the transition from a stable to an unstable social system; third, ritual reversal is not limited to 'primitive' culture nor to 'ritual proper' in the sense of formal, repeated festival behaviour.

Such necessary qualifications, together with a critique of Gluckman's rigid functionalism, have resulted in far more nuanced pictures of rituals of reversal in a culture, epitomized by Turner's studies of the Ndembu.[33] Turner's general conclusion on ritual reversal, however, seems to qualify

---

[29] Leach (1961).   [30] (1965) 109.   [31] Balandier (1970) 41.   [32] Babcock (1978).
[33] Turner (1967), (1969). One of Turner's earliest pieces on the Ndembu appears in Gluckman ed. (1962).

the teleology of Gluckman – that social rituals have as an end the secure maintenance of social order – only by a recognition that such reversals depend on the general possibility of cultural categories of opposition and change; or rather, that such reversals help make such cultural categories recognizable *as* cultural categories (as Geertz and Douglas have also argued[34]): 'This is not simply, as Fortes [following Gluckman] has cogently argued, a matter of giving a general stamp of legitimacy to a society's structural positions. It is rather a matter of giving recognition to an essential and generic human bond, without which there could be *no* society. Liminality implies that the high could not be high unless the low existed, and he who is high must experience what it is like to be low.'[35] Turner introduces, then, a less static view of society than Gluckman or Fortes; but although the anthropologist recognizes a 'potentially subversive character of liminality in tribal initiations, when, in the betwixt-and-between state, social-structure categories are forced to relax their grip on thought and behaviour',[36] it is a strictly limited recognition, a controlled subversion: 'this potentiality never did have any hope of realization outside a ritual sphere hedged in by strong taboos'.[37] For Turner, if Geertz, say, or Meyerhoff can show that such rituals of reversal may make a range of statements about social order – 'to affirm it, attack it, suspend it, redefine it, oppose it, buttress it, emphasize one part of it at the cost of another'[38] – it is because those scholars treat the literary and social products of discrete groups within 'technologically sophisticated and dynamic societies'[39] as opposed to the rituals of agrarian tribal cultures, the stuff of most traditional anthropological study.

The potential for the subversive in rituals of rebellion, however, forms the basis of Bakhtin's extraordinarily influential work. In his analysis of the sources of Rabelais' writing in folk culture, Bakhtin represents the carnival as a populist, utopian vision of the world which provides through its inversions of hierarchy a critique of dominant culture:

As opposed to the official feast, one might say that carnival celebrates temporary liberation from the prevailing truth of the established order; it marks the suspension of the hierarchical rank, privileges, norms and prohibition. Carnival was the true feast of time, the feast of becoming, change and reversal. It was hostile to all that was immortalized and complete.[40]

---

[34] Geertz (1972); Douglas (1966) 114–79.
[35] (1969) 97.   [36] (1978) 281.   [37] (1978) 281.
[38] Meyerhoff (1978) quoted by Turner (1978) 282–3.
[39] Turner (1978) 282.   [40] Bakhtin (1968) 11–12.

For Bakhtin, then, carnival is to be seen as *hostile* to the established order, even as a principle of rejection of the established order.[41] Indeed, the specifics of carnival as background to Rabelais become in Bakhtin's work a delighting in the carnivalesque in general – 'a world of topsy-turvy, of heteroglot exuberance, of ceaseless overrunning and excess, where all is mixed, hybrid, ritually degraded and defiled'.[42] There is, then, between Bakhtin and the anthropologists with whom I began, a marked similarity of interest in cultural categorization and the symbolic value of reversal; but for Bakhtin this leads to a celebration of the possibilities of rebellion rather than a recognition of the multiform ruses of power.

Bakhtin's analysis of carnival has given rise to numerous literary and cultural studies.[43] What is more, detailed investigations of occasions in early modern Europe on the one hand, where rituals of rebellion turned to uncontrolled violence, and, on the other, of systematic attempts by the dominant state authorities to control and indeed suppress carnival activity, have seemed to offer support for Bakhtin's perspective.[44] At the same time, Bakhtin's celebration of carnival as subversive has been criticized precisely because it ignores the *licence* in such an event, that is, the ritual controls and restraints that limit carnival to a specific arena and time.[45] So, Terry Castle, in her fascinating book on masquerade in eighteenth-century fiction, poses the question in general

whether symbolic rituals of disorder function within a culture as safety valves that reaffirm the status quo by exorcising social tensions, or are subversive events that explicitly threaten the prevailing order and encourage the formation of popular consciousness ... To speak metaphorically, the basic question is whether an imagery of inversion – the World Upside Down, for instance – has an inoculating or an infectious effect on collective consciousness.[46]

Although Castle represents accurately the trend towards polarization in the debate I have been tracing, it is a trend which leads to a distorting

---

[41] It should not be forgotten that Marx saw such ritual rebellion as a significant step in the development of a revolutionary consciousness. See Marx (1978) 9–11.

[42] Stallybrass and White (1986) 8.

[43] For a representative list, see Stallybrass and White (1986) 11, and, now, for a good general introduction and extensive bibliography, Hirschkop (1989); specifically on the classical world Rösler (1986).

[44] See e.g. Thompson (1972); Burke (1978); Le Roy Ladurie (1979); Davis (1978); and specifically on the history of prejudice against theatre as an expression of the carnivalesque Barish (1981).

[45] E.g. Eagleton (1981) 143–72; and for a different attempt to place these ideas in a wider Marxist context, Jameson (1981).

[46] Castle (1986) 88–9.

oversimplification both of the festivals in question and of the detailed expositions of the critics. 'Emmanuel Le Roy Ladurie, Natalie Davis and Peter Shaw have all suggested links between historical festivals of misrule and popular rebellion in early modern Europe and colonial America', writes Castle.[47] Le Roy Ladurie in his enquiry into carnival at Romans, after discussing the anthropological case for licence as a controlling or socially normative force, shows how, under the particular pressures of civil unrest, class difference and an attempt by the ruling authorities to quash carnival, the festival becomes the site for a specific outbreak of violent political activity.[48] Davis' brilliant study of early modern France is explicit also in developing a careful relation between norm and transgression in her study of youth groups, the Charivari and the 'Abbeys' of misrule. She writes: 'Licence was not rebellious. It was very much in the service of the village community',[49] and 'the loud and mocking laugh of Misrule [is] intended to keep a traditional order'.[50] In her essay entitled 'Women on top', however, she argues that 'topsy-turvy play had much spillover into everyday "serious" life'.[51] Thus, 'as literary and festive inversion in preindustrial Europe was a product not just of stable hierarchy but also of changes in the location of power and property, so this inversion could prompt new ways of thinking about the system and reacting to it'[52] – an argument which, she says, 'does not overturn the traditional theory about rites and festivities of inversion' (though it also fulfils her hope to 'add other dimensions to it'[53]). Here too, though in a quite different way from the carnival activity at Romans, the ritualized behaviour and imagery of inversion become a (re)source of change – but without losing its conservative aspects: 'The woman-on-top renewed old systems, but also helped change them into something different.'[54] The ritual and imagery of reversal become a *site of conflicting appropriations*.

The adoption of the symbolic behaviour of ritual reversal in political unrest is a focus of Shaw's study of early American rebellion. Flag and effigy burning, despite their evident symbolic function, are not what most anthropologists would regard as 'ritual'. ('Ritualized', for Shaw, 'signifies any incantatory, partly unconscious use of language.')[55] None the less, Shaw does adduce significant evidence, as Burke has for an earlier period, of how 'rebels and rioters employed ritual and symbol to legitimize their action'.[56] The symbolic appurtenances of the festival and

---

[47] (1986) 89.   [48] Le Roy Ladurie (1979).   [49] (1987) 107.
[50] (1987) 116.   [51] (1987) 143.   [52] (1987) 143.
[53] (1987) 143.   [54] (1987) 151.
[55] (1981) 7.   [56] Burke (1978) 203–4.

the carnivalesque can be turned both within an institution and in other (non-institutionalized) arenas to fuel social conflict.

In each of these intensive studies of rituals of reversal and rebellious political activity, there are different histories and different relations of norm and transgression. In the light of the importance of the detailed variables of each case, it is not clear that the possibilities of rebellion instantiated at Romans, for instance, provide an adequate general model for rituals of reversal. Indeed, it seems that Stallybrass and White are right firmly to resist the move to essentialize carnival as *either* intrinsically radical *or* intrinsically conservative: 'The most that can be said in the abstract is that for long periods carnival may be a stable and cyclical ritual with no noticeable politically transformative effects but that, given the presence of sharpened political antagonism, it may often act as *catalyst* and *site of actual and symbolic struggle*.'[57] This scrupulous and exemplary formulation is further developed by the observation that if violent social clashes seem to coincide with carnival, 'to call it a "coincidence" of social revolt and carnival is deeply misleading', since for Western Europe it is only in the late eighteenth and nineteenth centuries and then only in delimited cases that 'one can reasonably talk of popular politics *divorced* from the carnivalesque at all'.[58] The carnival is a specific ritual practice, closely bound up with the laws of church and state – but 'carnival' also refers to 'a mobile set of symbolic practices, images and discourses which were employed throughout social revolts and conflicts before the nineteenth century'.[59] There is, then, a changing history of conflict in and around carnival and the carnivalesque. These detailed investigations into particular events and into the possibilities of generalizing about carnival offer a far more complex picture of the institution than Bakhtin and most of his critics have sketched. As Stallybrass and White conclude, 'the politics of carnival cannot be resolved outside of a close historical examination of particular conjunctures'.[60]

Now, all drama, in that it requires and creates a ritual space in which the norms of social discourse are suspended, can be approached through these models of carnival, but it is particularly comedy that has been explored in such terms,[61] and the particular conjunctures of Athenian

---

[57] (1986) 14.   [58] (1986) 14.   [59] (1986) 15.   [60] (1986) 16.

[61] Shakespeare, and, of course, Jonson in particular have been influentially discussed in such terms. See e.g. Barber (1959); Donaldson (1970); Salingar (1979); McCanles (1977); Haynes (1984); and especially Bristol (1985) (with extensive discussion of contemporary carnivalesque). That Jonson draws on Aristophanes as a model is argued by Theyer (1963) (see index *sub* Aristophanes), but on Jonson's use of the phrase *vetus comoedia* see Donaldson (1970) 26.

comedy, difficult though they are to approach because of the paucity of evidence (especially in comparison with early modern Europe), raise some fascinating questions. Notions of ritual release – *Ventilsitten* – are common to many critical interpretations of Aristophanes' work, and there are excellent examples of more specific analyses of the logic of inversion in particular plays, particularly with regard to gender,[62] but the most developed treatment of carnival and Old Comedy is that of Jean Carrière (1979) (a book that has not had the wide influence of several other general introductions to the genre). Carrière discusses (23–4) the (probable) carnivalesque origins of comedy in Dionysiac ritual,[63] how this ritual becomes part of the festival which is, in all senses, political, and how comedy none the less retains a (transformed) force of the carnivalesque in this more complex setting of the city festival. Indeed, he argues (24) that it is the tension between the carnivalesque and its politicization that provides the constitutive ambiguity of comedy that is evidenced in Aristophanes' plays and that results in the particular nature of modern Aristophanic criticism, which constantly debates the seriousness of Aristophanes' commitment in the political arena. The idea of *renewal* (that many critics have seen as central to Aristophanes and to comedy in general) helps specify the ambiguous drive of comedy (42):

cette politicisation demeure ambiguë parce que le genre comique est tourné à la fois vers un passé mythique ou idéalisé qui doît être restauré, et vers le présent qui va être régénéré, où l'âge d'or doit renaître d'une manière fictive. La Comédie est donc prête à se tourner non seulement contre les 'vieilles' autorités en place, mais aussi contre les 'excessives' nouveautés qui rompent avec le passé.

Thus Aristophanic comedy can appear at the same time violently critical and strongly conservative ('à la fois aggressivement critique et puissamment conformiste' [42]). On the one hand, because of its criticism both of the established order and of novelty, comedy 'semble prédisposée à fonctionner comme une sorte de régulateur social et politique' (42); on the other, because of its constant recourse to the fantastic, the grotesque – the world of inversion and reversal – comedy seems to function in a spirit of ludic release.

---

[62] See in particular the fine work of Zeitlin (1982a) from which I have learnt on all aspects of Aristophanes; Foley (1982); Rosellini (1979); Saïd (1979); Auger (1979); Loraux (1981b) 157–96.

[63] The ritual origins of comedy are much discussed: see Herter (1947); Pickard-Cambridge (1962) 132–229; Giangrande (1963); Adrados (1975); Landfester (1979) 361–7; Reckford (1987) 443–51.

It is particularly instructive that Carrière stresses the tensions
constitutive of Aristophanic comedy rather than attempting, as so
many critics have done, to resolve these tensions into a single and
oversimplified portrait – Aristophanes the critic, Aristophanes the joker,
Aristophanes the artist, Aristophanes the historical source. So, too,
Carrière's unwillingness to demand a single level of 'politicization' in the
Aristophanic corpus (and in the history of comedy) is a refreshing rejoinder to the formulas of much Aristophanic criticism.[64] His treatment
of modern carnival, however, is less than satisfactory, and his consequent
distinctions between modern carnival and the fifth-century festival need
further discussion.

The brief description Carrière offers of modern carnival is perhaps best
represented as a weakened version of Bakhtin: he describes carnival as
having (30) 'une ambivalence remarquable'. This ambivalence is constituted by a negative aspect – the destruction of the old, in which process
is included carnival's obscenity, grotesqueness and overturning of the
hierarchies of social institutions; and by a positive aspect – the (re)genera-
tion of the new, in which process is included the temporary delights of
an abundance of food, sex, festival celebration. There are, however,
several problems with the construction of such an opposition – how, for
example, can carnival's obscenity be *opposed* to carnival's 'liberté sex-
uelle'? – but most striking in Carrière's formulation is the reduction of
the question of carnival's political import. This is especially relevant
because, as Carrière notes but does not adequately explore, the political
system of democracy is the very condition of possibility for Old Comedy
and is integral to its understanding.

Indeed, the major difference between carnival and ancient comedy that
Carrière outlines immediately indicates what is at stake in such a reduction of the political. Unlike carnival, he writes (31), 'le "rituel" comique,
aux Dionysies, est officialisé ... il fait l'objet d'une élaboration, littéraire
et cérémonielle, et se trouve ainsi fortement organisé'. As we have already
seen, the relation between modern carnivals and the established political
order is far more complex than Carrière suggests. Not only is the carnival
proper legitimated by the church's calendar but also the range of responses of authority to carnival – from a recognition and manipulation
of such licence as a ruse of power, to violent attempts to suppress the
carnivalesque – suggests that 'official organization' will be too blunt a
term to account for the difference between carnival and comedy in the

---

[64] E.g. Koch (1965); Schwinge (1975).

city. Indeed, while it is the case that the Great Dionysia and the Lenaia are festivals sponsored and funded by the city and the playwrights are selected by a city official and comic plays are a late introduction by the city into the city festival, what little we know of responses to comedy also suggests the possibility of a more tense relationship. There appear to have been laws passed to limit abuse of individuals by name in comedy;[65] Plato is prepared to write of comedy influencing the people's willingness to have Socrates executed. The relation between comedy and the democracy, which is its subject and context, is not simply one of licensed transgression.

Now carnival, especially as Bakhtin formulates it, is inherently dependent on a class system. It is the rebellion of the repressed. Old Comedy, however, is the product of and for the citizens of a radical democracy and takes place in a festival of citizens. The plays may represent on occasions slaves outwitting masters and, more often, women subordinating men; but these remain representations by male citizens for male citizens (and the (male) ambassadors of foreign cities and metics). It would be wrong, of course, to deny that there were any distinctions of class in Athenian society – and, as we will see, Aristophanes often mentions and manipulates such distinctions – but its proclamations of equality of citizens and its instantiation of such equality in its festivals crucially inform any public representation of the city.[66] When Dicaeopolis in the *Acharnians* retorts to the general Lamachus that (595) he is no beggar but 'a good citizen', πολίτης χρηστός, he is drawing precisely on the idea(l) of a democratic *polis* in which to be a citizen is to assert a status of equality (for all that the term *hoi khrēstoi*, 'the good', is itself appropriated as a (self-)representation of class within certain areas of political discourse). The remark of Dicaeopolis – whose name means 'Just City' – is part of a fictional representation of the city to the city, for sure, but it is crucial that the framework of Old Comedy is citizen pronouncing to citizen, the democratic citizens playing (for) the democratic citizens. It is a framework which inevitably establishes the alignments of conflict, the possibilities of reversal, quite differently from carnival.

One way in which these different alignments of conflict can be approached is by contrast with the construction of praise that I discussed as a function of the poet's voice in the previous chapter. One trait typical

---

[65] A vexed issue, however; see Sommerstein (1986); Radin (1927); MacDowell (1978) 127–9; and the highly sceptical Halliwell (1984a).

[66] The rhetorical strategies of the orators have been recently analysed from this perspective stimulatingly by Ober (1989).

of Old Comedy is the practice of *onomastikōmōdein*, the verbal assault or mockery of particular citizens by name.[67] In Aristophanes, we see (as well as particular jokes at the expense of individuals) whole plays, such as the *Clouds* or *Knights*, based on such personalized abuse. This practice draws on traditions of 'blame poetry', such as the *iambos*, and on such rituals as the *gephurismos*, the ritual insults of the Eleusinian procession;[68] but it also has a specific force in the city festival. For comedy proclaims a sort of negative *kleos*. As much as citizens strive (even within the democratic *polis*) for the individual success of *kleos*, so comedy attacks individuals within that system of personal honour. A great fear regularly expressed in all periods of Greek culture is the fear of becoming a laughing-stock for one's enemies – a fear that derives its power from the system of personal public reputation so important to any ancient Greek sense of self. Comedy again and again entails not just laughter (γελᾶν) but laughter against (καταγελᾶν). This aggressive conflictual laughter is within the boundaries of the festival, but it both represents itself as having a cutting edge among the citizens (so Aristophanes depicts Cleon as responding in kind – with personal aggression – to his comedies); and is represented by e.g. Plato's Socrates as having had a damaging effect on his public standing. Public, personal enmity as a cause and motivation runs through many aspects of Athenian democratic institutions, not merely comedy. *Onomastikōmōdein* is not so much 'the ordinary man's protest ... against all who are in some way stronger and better than he'[69] – the rebellion of the repressed – nor simply 'festive mockery' which '*did not count* in the ordinary world' because 'the victim could not really lose face'.[70] For all its ritualization, *onomastikōmōdein* remains a contribution to the contests of personal status in the *polis*. The comic poet is not merely the 'allowed fool' of democracy but a citizen *sophos* whose utterance raises *a question of the limits of licence.*

If the constitution of the participants in the festival – the shared status of audience, actors, poet – is crucial to understanding its sense of licence, so too is the fact that the plays *represent the city to the city*. For the work

[67] For trenchant discussion on this practice and bibliography, see Halliwell (1984a). See also for more general discussion Reckford (1987) 461–82.
[68] On the nature and types of this tradition of *aischrologia*, mocking and shameful talk, Fluck (1931); Reckford (1987) 461–7 (with further bibliography). On Aristophanes and this tradition, see Henderson (1975) especially 13–18. On the *gephurismos*, see Richardson (1974) 213–17.
[69] Dover (1970) 270. A more tempered version in Dover (1972) 41.
[70] Reckford (1987) 479.

of representation allows for a far wider range of fictional strategies than merely 'reversal' or 'fantasy'. The full range of possibilities – including idealization, nostalgia, parody of institutions and of other (idealized, nostalgic, fantastic) representations of the city – are incorporated in Aristophanes' texts. The opening scene of the *Acharnians*, for example, begins with Dicaeopolis alone, waiting for the Assembly to start. He despairs in the tone of a tragic monologue (ὅσα δὴ δέδηγμαι τὴν ἐμαυτὴν καρδίαν, 'How often have I bitten my own heart . . .' (1)) and in less tragic tones (ἃ δ' ὠδυνήθην ψαμμακοσιογάργαρα, 'my times of pain have been sand-grain-hundred-loads-full' (3)). His despair is in general for the city of Athens (ὦ πόλις, πόλις, 'O City, City' (27)) and its behaviour in the Assembly (19–27), and his feelings are expressed both through references to contemporary events (the mishap of Cleon (6–8)) and through re-collections of contemporary drama (poetics are never easily separated from politics, especially in Aristophanes). As Dicaeopolis takes up his role here at the beginning of the play as a spectator of the political actors in the Assembly, he depicts himself as an audience member in the theatre waiting for a play to begin (προσδοκῶν τὸν Αἴσχυλον, 'Waiting for Aeschylus' (10)). The play begins, then, with a (fictional) audience waiting for a beginning. Part of comedy's discourse is a marked self-awareness and self-projection of its own fictionality. Aristophanes' plays inevitably include self-referential comments on the construction of theatrical fiction – such as the slave in the opening of *Peace* announcing (50) that he will tell the audience the plot (*logos*) of the drama, or the chorus in the parabasis of the *Clouds* (518ff) praising the author's sophistication and skill. There is, however, a further manipulation of reference in the opening scene of the *Acharnians*. For once a year in the Athenian political calendar the Assembly did meet in the theatre instead of its usual place on the Pnyx.[71] As Dicaeopolis settles himself as a (fictional) political actor (in the theatre), the representation of the institution is performed in a space in which the institution annually acts – a fiction which playfully intertwines the dramatic and political roles of the audience in the theatre. The self-awareness of and comment on its own fictionality produces in the *Acharnians* a complex interplay of dramatic and political *écarts*, as the city is represented in the city to the city.

The Assembly opens in the theatre as on the Pnyx with the herald's formula (45) τίς ἀγορεύειν βούλεται, 'Who wants to speak?' – a formula which 'implying as it did that all citizens had an equal right to advise the people, regardless of birth, wealth or position, was regarded as one of the

---

[71] See Dem. *In Meid.* 8–10, discussed by Pickard-Cambridge (1968) 67–9.

touchstones of democracy'.[72] It is in part against the ideals incarnated in
this ritual address that the Assembly which follows derives its ironic
humour. Dicaeopolis dramatizes his democratic participation in the Assembly with a series of running comments on the business and then by
taking a hand in the scrutiny of the returning ambassadors – a parody of
an enquiry into the conduct of state officials (another procedural touchstone of democracy), as it is also an ironic comment on the material benefit
of being a state official. It is from this (mis)representation of an Assembly
that Dicaeopolis' plan of a private peace treaty takes shape as an answer
to the difficulties set up in this scene. And the play contains – is made up
by – a series of further transformations of this opening scene: Dicaeopolis
makes his orator's defence before the chorus of Acharnians – a speech I
will discuss in detail below; the *agōn* of the latter part of the drama replays
Dicaeopolis' cross-examination and maltreatment of the ambassadors.
Indeed, the parodic and distorted public exchange of the Assembly finds
a series of analogues in the exchange of costumes (as Dicaeopolis takes
a role and a costume from Euripides – which looks forward to the
final scenes where Lamachus and Dicaeopolis dress for their respective
expeditions to war and to the table), and the exchanges that follow
Dicaeopolis' treaty (where, for example, a Megaran wants to exchange
his daughters, dressed as pigs, for salt and garlic; where a Boeotian
exchanges eels for a sycophant). The comic inversion of the (symbolic)
exchange of words, of goods, of women, of roles, performs a (carnivalized)
repertoire of the city's operations. The opening scene's version of the
Assembly constructs the need for a (re)solution: the narrative moves
through a series of parodic and inverted transactions as Dicaeopolis
realigns his position in the system of exchange (by formulating a private
international treaty). The tension between the (mis)representations of
the social situation that is to be rectified and the ludic and transgressive
narrative (re)solution that Dicaeopolis enacts is a constitutive element of
the difficulty of evaluating the position from which Dicaeopolis speaks –
a difficulty often formulated as the attempt to balance judgements of
Dicaeopolis' 'unpatriotic selfishness' and his 'triumphant individualism'.
To view Dicaeopolis is to site Just City within the city – a framework
that is, however, itself manipulated, distorted, mocked in its comic
representation.

This combination of depictions of a contemporary Athens in various
forms of (mis)representation is typical of Aristophanes' writing. Although the play's central motif of a private peace treaty shows all the

[72] Sommerstein (1980) ad loc.

signs of a fantastic inversion of norms and leads to a carnivalesque
triumph of abundance, the opening scene and its transformations through
the narrative of the *Acharnians* show how the play fictionalizes Athens
for the citizens in the theatre in a complex network of superimposed
(mis)representations. It is not simply that the parody of the Assembly,
like all good parodies, comes close to the Real Thing, nor that the play's
fictional representations include 'reality effects'[73] to ground its fiction.
Rather, throughout the play, different (self-)representations of the city
construct the possibility of different (self-)recognitions in the citizen
audience. The shifting levels of fictional representation – a hallmark of
comedy – cannot be reduced to mere 'comic inversion'. In the interplay
of comic fictions, 'transgression' is not necessarily the polar opposite
of 'norm'. Comedy in and as performance tests – *negotiates* as well as
celebrates – the possibilities of transgression.

The models of carnival, then, are illuminating for the licence and
celebration of the Dionysiac festivals of fifth- and fourth-century Athens,
but the constitution of the social group of participants, and the nature of
the literary representations of Old Comedy, provide different constraints
and possibilities for the carnivalesque. In particular, the combination
of Aristophanes' self-awareness and manipulation of levels of fictional
(mis)representation makes the performance of Old Comedy a constant
renegotiation of licence, a constant rediscovery of the possibilities and
boundaries of inversion. It is this sense of testing the limits of licence
that gives comedy its constantly active role in the contest of public voices.

SPEAKING OUT

In principle I'm against manifestoes as I am also against principle.   Tzara

A citizen before the citizens, how does Aristophanes speak out in his
dramas? This question – the evaluation of the voice of the poet in comedy
– has been one of the most debated issues in Aristophanic criticism.[74] It
must first be stressed that by its very nature drama fragments the poet's

---

[73] For the phrase 'reality effects' (effets du réel) see Barthes (1975) 101–2 and (1984)
141–9.
[74] A massive bibliography could be given here: I have learnt in particular from Gomme
(1938); Forrest (1963); Koch (1965); Vaio (1971); de Ste Croix (1972) appendix xxix;
Dover (1972); Schwinge (1975); Lenz (1980); Edmunds (1980); Nussbaum (1980);
Henderson (1980); Newiger (1980); Konstan and Dillon (1981); Moulton (1981); Cassio
(1982); MacDowell (1983); Bowie (1982); Konstan (1985); Heath (1987); Reckford
(1987) and the works cited in n. 59 above.

voice into a chorus of speaking parts, which inevitably places difference at the heart of dramatic communication. Aristophanic comedy, however, raises the issue of 'the message' of drama in a particularly striking manner not only because of the tension in its apparent function between social-and-political criticism and ludic release, but also because the role of speaking out to the city is so often dramatized as a part of Aristophanes' plays both through the roles of the leading figures of each comedy and through the device of the parabasis, where the chorus addresses the city. What is more, it is precisely in such speaking out scenes that the violent varieties of expression demonstrate most forcibly the tension between criticism and release. In the following pages, I intend to approach these problems first by considering one particular scene, namely, Dicaeopolis' self-defence before the Acharnian chorus,[75] and second, more briefly and in slightly more general terms, the parabasis as an institution.

Dicaeopolis, as we have seen, in response to the transactions around him, has concluded a truce with the Spartans. Now he is faced by the wrath of the chorus of Acharnians, warlike citizens of the Athenian deme of Acharnae. He prepares to speak out for the Spartans and his own actions. The defence will culminate in a formal speech which splits the Acharnians into two groups – those who are persuaded and those who remain hostile and summon Lamachus the general to continue their martial cause. The preparation for this formal speech is extensive, however. First (355–67), Dicaeopolis, at the instance of the chorus, brings out a butcher's block so that he can speak with his head literally 'on the block'. Such literalization of a metaphor is used with great tragic effect by Aeschylus – Agamemnon crossing the tapestries in the famous carpet scene, for example, instantiates the chorus' deprecation of 'trampling the grace of things not to be touched' (*Aga.* 371–2). Here, however, where the literalization is both of a common idiom and of the lines of Euripides which utilize the idiom (and so functions also as a first sign of the extended *Telephus* parody to come), the effect is both to point towards the extraordinarily risky nature of the speech to come – to defend publicly the city's enemies at a time of bitter military conflict – and also to place the speech under a (typical) sign of comic inversion and exaggeration.[76] This preparatory piece of comic business immediately establishes, then,

---

[75] Helene Foley's important article (1988) appeared after this chapter was completed. I have added references where her work bears most closely on mine.

[76] For the literalization of metaphor as a typical comic (ludic) device, see Stewart (1978) especially 77–81. On Aristophanic metaphor, see Newiger (1957).

what Carrière calls Aristophanes' 'constitutive ambiguity' between social (and artistic) criticism and comic inversion.

How literally to take Dicaeopolis' speech from the block remains a question ... He continues his worries with a representation of the difficulties of speaking to such an audience (370–4):

> Yet I've ample cause for fear. I know the ways
> of country folk – all too happy if some fraud
> of an orator spouts eulogies on them and the city,
> the truth and its opposite.

These remarks return to a *topos* of Aristophanic writing, the gullibility and fickleness of the mass of citizens (before whom and for whom he plays). This cannot be taken simply as proof that the aristocratic Aristophanes believed 'it was intolerable when ignorant and ill-educated men demanded a share of the delicate art of government'.[77] On the one hand, it must be seen within the logic of (self-) representation to provoke (self-)recognition – though how amusing the self-recognition of collective folly proves might depend on an audience member's (sense of) perspective. On the other hand, the description of his audience as ἀγροίκων, 'countrymen', 'rustics', misled by an ἀλαζών, 'rogue', 'fast talker' – as he himself prepares to dress up in Euripides' clothes and words to manipulate the chorus of countrymen – both ties his remarks to the specifics of this scene, and further turns his representation towards a self-aware and ironic exaggeration.

The following lines, however, further complicate the sense of the place from where Dicaeopolis speaks (375–82):

> And I know the minds of the old men, that
> they hanker after nothing but biting with their ballots.
> And I know about myself, what I suffered from Cleon
> because of last year's comedy.
> For he dragged me before the Council, and began
> to slander me, and tell glib lies about me,
> roaring like the Cycloborus, swilling over me, so that
> I very nearly perished in a sewer of troubles.

Dicaeopolis continues with a gibe at the old men, the jurors, who look only to 'bite with their votes' (ψήφῳ δακεῖν[78]) – the central conceit of the

---

[77] As the Oxford Marxist de Ste Croix puts it (1972) 357.
[78] To read the morphologically less likely ψηφηδακεῖν, as does the *Oxford Classical Text*, makes little difference to the point here.

Wasps; a remark which joins the possibility of the laughter of self-recognition and the laughter at the folly of others (for the audience as a body). The gibe moves, however, into a tale of personal experience ('I know about myself . . . ') of an attack on the speaker by Cleon . . . for last year's comedy. Dicaeopolis here has often been said to speak in the voice of 'Aristophanes, the comic poet', since he refers to Cleon having recourse to law in response to the previous year's drama and Aristophanes appears to have been so treated for his *Babylonians*.[79] This apparent shift in persona raises in a most striking form the problem of speaking voice. Several critics have argued as follows: the speech appears and has regularly been taken to refer to the experience of the historical individual Aristophanes; it is only in this play – here and at 500ff with a reference to the same events – that a character speaks in the guise of the poet in this way;[80] the joys of peace are a constant theme of the other plays of Aristophanes; and Dicaeopolis puts the argument for peace at a most developed political level. Thus, it is to be concluded, 'Dicaeopolis, "Just City", proves to be Aristophanes, the comic poet';[81] 'Aristophanes is identifying himself with Dicaeopolis, making it quite clear that Dicaeopolis is speaking for him';[82] 'It is obvious that the words are spoken by the actor on behalf of the poet.'[83] The bizarre dramatization where a character speaks as if he is the poet is therefore in order to give a particular authorization to the views expressed by the character. Aristophanes speaks out in the guise of Dicaeopolis speaking out.

There have been several responses to this argument. The first is to question the extent of the identification between Dicaeopolis and the author, Aristophanes. Even if here, as later at 501–3, Dicaeopolis speaks as or for Aristophanes, because of the freedom with which characters in comedy move between registers or levels of fictionality, such identification proves nothing about the overall role of Dicaeopolis or about any other specific remark of Dicaeopolis. So Whitman writes cautiously: 'It would be unsafe to conclude that Aristophanes means everything that Dicaeopolis says, as it would be to accept as sober truth some of the

---

[79] For the evidence, see Norwood (1930).

[80] De Ste Croix's strong statement (1972) 363 that Dicaeopolis 'alone of Aristophanes' characters of whom we know anything is *carefully and explicitly identified by the poet with himself'* is criticized (and *à la mode aristophanique* wrongly quoted) by Bowie (1982) 29 n. 14 for ignoring forms of 'identification of poet and hero in the early plays'. This passage, however, remains in need of special treatment for Bowie, too, because of its specific and close identification. Foley (1988) seems happy to accept an identification of Dicaeopolis and Aristophanes.

[81] Edmunds (1980) 9.   [82] De Ste Croix (1972) 363.   [83] Sifakis (1971) 14.

hair-raising assertions which occur in many a parabasis';[84] and as Forrest
(writing of the later speech (496–556)) puts it more strongly: 'The speech
is parody from beginning to end. We cannot with confidence take it
seriously at any level.'[85] Dover, however, goes further and resists the
identification of poet and hero even in these lines. He suggests that when
Dicaeopolis speaks in the first person here, it is '"I, the comic hero" or
– looking at the same person from a slightly different standpoint – "I,
the comic protagonist"' who speaks and that thus 'Aristophanes treats
Dicaeopolis as if he were an annual visitor to Athens who got into trouble
on the last occasion he attempted to δίκαια λέγειν [say what's right].'[86]
If it is difficult to accept the specific idea of Dicaeopolis speaking 'for
comedy', Dover's analysis usefully recognizes that Dicaeopolis also has
a more general exemplary role (as a victim of Cleon, as an attacked
defender of democratic free speech). Thus, Bowie, despite the recognition that the link between 'the real Aristophanes and his hero is especially
close', seems to suggest that the separation of hero and poet must be
maintained: 'Dicaeopolis has ... spoken of his prosecution by Cleon the
year before for a comedy he had written, and this is exactly what
happened to Aristophanes.'[87] Dicaeopolis speaks, then, as *a* poet, not *the*
poet, for Bowie. It would seem that the similarity of Dicaeopolis' and
Aristophanes' experience(s) create(s) an ironic tension in the comic characterization which allows Dicaeopolis and Aristophanes to share an exemplary function as victims of Cleon but which does not mean 'Dicaeopolis is speaking for Aristophanes.'[88] For each of these critics, then, to
stress a rigid identification between the poet and one of his characters is
to underemphasize the playful manipulation of comic characterization
which resists precisely such a unified persona. The (biographical) role
that Dicaeopolis adopts in order to speak out would seem to construct a
specific critical problem of discovering the place from which Dicaeopolis
speaks. Which 'I' does the persona impersonate?

What is more, as Frances Muecke and Froma Zeitlin have each discussed,[89] disguise and fictionality are in themselves a thematic concern
of Aristophanic drama in a way that is important for the *Acharnians* and
this scene. In the Assembly, for which I have already discussed some
aspects of the manipulation of representation, the central action is the

[84] Whitman (1964) 22.   [85] Forrest (1963) 8–9.
[86] Dover (1963) 15.   [87] Bowie (1982) 30.
[88] Bowie (1982) 29 n. 14. Bowie (1988) goes so far as to suggest that Dicaeopolis represents
Eupolis, another poet. (These two Bowies are not the same.)
[89] Muecke (1977); Zeitlin (1982a). It is surprisingly little discussed in Kowzan (1983).

piercing of the disguises of the envoys; Dicaeopolis is about to dress up in a Euripidean costume on stage[90] (to deceive the chorus as the Assembly had been deceived by the envoys); the Megaran disguises his children as piglets; as Lamachus is dressed for battle, Dicaeopolis dresses himself and his table for festive celebration. This concern with disguise and *mimēsis* is perhaps not as dominant in the *Acharnians* as in the *Thesmophoriazusae* or *Frogs*, but it does signal the playful manipulation of fact and fiction in the drama or rather what Muecke calls 'the superimposition of conflicting fictions'.[91] As Aristophanes produces the (fictional) representation of Dicaeopolis, Dicaeopolis produces the (fictionalized) representation of his author, or of an experience the same as his author's.

Indeed, the speech concludes with lines that have implications for each of the readings of the earlier remarks in it (383–4): 'So, first of all, before I speak, please let me dress myself as piteously as I can.' 'So' suggests that this final remark is the conclusion of the previous self-representation and that 'let me speak' refers to the same figure as 'I know about myself' (377–8). Aristophanes represents himself, then, in a highly self-conscious manner by a double fictionalization of Dicaeopolis in a (theatrical) disguise? Yet, it is precisely the fact that the disguise is borrowed (in yet another level of fictionalization) from Euripides and consists in props and lines purloined from Euripides' *Telephus* that leads to the critics' unwillingness to accept the identification of Dicaeopolis and Aristophanes, or to take Dicaeopolis' potted Euripides as an Aristophanic attempt to teach the citizens. Do these lines, then, mark the retreat from such identification (as they mark the juncture with the comedy of the Euripides' scene)? The logic of Aristophanic self-reflexivity here reaches a bizarre limit case, where the separation of a character's and the author's self-representation becomes difficult to determine with any security.

This recollection of Dicaeopolis also bears significantly on the question of the limits of licence. Aristophanes' Dicaeopolis refers to the previous year's drama which, he claims, sufficiently upset Cleon to be raised as an issue in the Council. This tells of comedy's failure to maintain the safe – ritualized – boundaries of its occasion – a representation which is

---

[90] 'We have an actor (who might be Aristophanes) who is playing a comic figure, Dicaeopolis, surnamed "Just City", who is playing the Mysian prince Telephus, who is pretending to be a Greek beggar in order to argue his own (Telephus') case before the members of a comic chorus who are playing old Acharnian charcoal-burners who are now going to be treated as Achaean dignitaries – if all this doesn't teach the audience to become aware of role-playing and deception, then what will?' Reckford (1987) 179.

[91] Muecke (1977) 61.

destined itself to repeat the previous fault[92] by such a recollection, as it sets out to be different by the new circumstances that Dicaeopolis is to establish in the first place by dressing as piteously as possible. The play knowingly *re-presents*, then, what is seen as the transgression of the previous year with the added control of being (only) a story about another transgression. In this way, Aristophanes' writing is (self-consciously) involved with the process of (re)negotiating the possibilities of comic freedom. The citation of the previous year's event (like the citations from Euripides' verse) retells the story, playfully recreates and renegotiates comedy's licence.

Indeed, these constant manipulations of levels of fiction and the difficulty of securely placing the play's speaking voice actively involve the audience in the process of what I have called 'negotiating the licence' of comedy. For comedy – to be comedy – depends on the shared recognition of the space for comedy, a shared recognition of what counts as comic – a shared recognition, that is, of the *boundaries* of the comic. (A joke out of place – say, at a funeral – becomes offensive, as a joke about certain topics will not be funny in certain circles.) As Aristophanes, like all great comic writers, explores and extends the boundaries of the comic (and self-consciously discusses such exploration), so the definition of the acceptability of his comic transgression becomes a shared process of collective and individual negotiation. The modern critics who disagree so strongly about the seriousness and comedy of Aristophanes' writing are involved in the self-same procedure (albeit from a different perspective) of defining the boundaries of acceptability in the transgression of comedy. How far, how serious, how comic, how literal, how applicable to me, to us, to them, to you are questions that Aristophanes' writing constantly poses for its readers and audiences; or, to be more scrupulous, Aristophanes' writing constantly raises for its audiences and readers the (playful) worry of how seriously (etc.) to pose the question of how serious (etc.) (the) play is.

The formal speech of defence that Dicaeopolis finally makes shows a similar difficulty of placing the speaker's voice. It is a parody of a speech from Euripides' *Telephus* and is delivered by the figure of Dicaeopolis dressed up in the rags borrowed piecemeal in the previous scene from Euripides himself. It announces comedy to be parallel to tragedy in its knowledge of right (500): τὸ γὰρ δίκαιον οἶδε καὶ τρυγῳδία, 'comedy too knows about justice'. *Trugōdia*, translated here 'comedy', is probably a

---

[92] 'By alluding to the affair here ... Aristophanes is rubbing his antagonist's nose in the ineffectualness of his attack' (Heath (1987a) 17).

coined word, 'trugedy', from *trux*, 'wine lees', to sound like 'tragedy' (hence the translation of καί as 'too' rather than 'even').[93] It promises just but terrible words, δεινὰ μέν, δίκαια δέ (501). From the beginning, it claims 'to speak about the city before the Athenians' (498–9). It recalls the self-defensive remark about Cleon's slander, as Dicaeopolis again seems to take on his poet's role or experiences (502–3):

> This time Cleon will not spread the slander that
> I foulmouth the city in the presence of foreigners.

What might have been a passing slur on Cleon's repressive and vindictive political activity becomes, because of the echo of the previous tale of Cleon's slander, a similar shift of persona to the poet of last year – now dressed as an Aristophanic Euripidean character, with a speech culled from that character. The speaker also, however, places himself firmly in the dramatic context of the Lenaian festival (504–8), where, he says with what might seem an ironic comment on the difficulties of disguise and speaking out in this scene, αὐτοί ... ἐσμεν, 'we are ourselves'. (It is as citizen to citizen that he speaks – a fiction of immediate address?) The biographical gloss rather than determining the position from which the speaker speaks forms a component in a shifting network of fictionalized representations, the glossolalia of Aristophanic characterization.

This elaborate proem, however, leads to an explanation of the Peloponnesian war,[94] which attempts to explain Spartan behaviour by showing how Athenians would behave in the same way: the defence of the Spartans turns repeatedly to a description of the city to the city with a plea for self-recognition. It is a tale which not only echoes Euripides (and perhaps Herodotus[95]) but also parodies such causal narratives with a hilariously trivializing account of the processes of war and diplomacy. Is this lengthy and brilliant parody of rhetoric and history to be seen through, like Dicaeopolis' rags, to reveal a kernel of the serious expression of truth? Or does the parodic narrative comically undercut the (self-important) truth-telling claims of comedy in the proem? Is comedy to be found in the claims to speak out what is right? Serious commentary

---

[93] For an excellent study of these lines, see Taplin (1983).

[94] On which, of course, historians have written at length. For poles of the debate see Forrest (1963) and MacDowell (1983), and for the most detailed study de Ste Croix (1972) 231–44, 355–67.

[95] The common assumption that Aristophanes echoes Herodotus here has been challenged by Fornara (1971) who argues for a later date for Herodotus' first publication in Athens; his arguments are accepted by Heath (1987a) 17 n. 28 who categorically denies an allusion to Herodotean narrative.

in the comic triviality of the explanations? The play of different voices infects each voice with an instability, an uncertainty that cannot be resolved into carefully delimited 'serious utterances' and 'comic utterances'.

This scene of Dicaeopolis speaking out demonstrates, then, in a most striking manner how the different levels of fiction in Aristophanes' dramatic writing can produce a vertiginous destabilization of the poet's voice. The effect of such destabilization – how seriously, how comically it is taken – involves the audience's or critic's *negotiation* (of the boundaries of comic transgression). In comedy, there is no secure – uninvolved, unmediated – place outside the contest and test of public voices. (No spectator is safe.) The ritual space of comedy is constantly being individually and collectively (re)determined.

The element of Old Comedy on which the discussion of the poet speaking out as a *sophos* has focused in particular is the parabasis. Critical discussion of the parabasis has been extensive.[96] There has been considerable analysis of its formal structure, which has been complemented by much speculation from negligible evidence about its role in the history of the dramatic structure of comedy.[97] There has also been much discussion of the parabasis as a key indication of the views of the poet. Certain formal qualities of the parabasis stress this sense of a poet speaking out to the city. The chorus is usually alone on stage: the chorus is a fundamental medium for the poet's role as *sophos*. The parabasis often deals with contemporary issues. The parabasis addresses the audience. If these factors suggest that the parabasis is a component of the drama designed for the poet directly to address the city, a more detailed analysis quickly reveals a more complex picture. First, although it may seem that 'the chorus is doffing its persona to speak for the comic poet',[98] it must be remembered that the chorus does not merely step out of character and address the audience directly with their advice and exhortations. Rather, as Sifakis comments, 'it is the freedom of the chorus to change the

---

[96] See for good coverage of earlier debates Herter (1947) 31ff; Sifakis (1971); also Dover (1972) 49–53; Fraenkel (1975); Bowie (1982) (with further bibliography); Hubbard (1986) and Reckford (1987) 483–91.

[97] See Bowie (1982) 28 for bibliography and a sensible side-stepping of the issue.

[98] Edmunds (1980) 15. He adds 'just as Dicaeopolis has already done'. That there was an actual stripping of costume or mask has been argued by Ketterer (1980). There is, however, as Edmunds (1980) 15 and Reckford (1987) 188 note, no way of telling from our extant evidence. What would the audience see if the chorus did take off its masks? As Stewart (1978) 109 writes of Nabokov's self-representations: 'The mask ... when stripped off covers another mask, which covers another mask and so on to infinity.'

viewpoint from which it speaks'.[99] So the chorus regularly speaks as the dramatic chorus. The chorus of the *Knights* concludes in the persona of knights with a eulogy of their horses; and the first parabasis of the *Birds*, to take the most remarkable example, combines a cosmological tale of how the birds are older than the gods, a eulogy of birds' usefulness to man, a utopian picture of the inversions of the world of the birds compared to the human city, and a picture of the usefulness of wings for humans in the city ('Nothing is better or more sweet than to grow wings...'). Although the bird chorus' remarks are addressed to the audience and mention individuals by name, there is no talk of the poet nor any indication that there is a (didactic) message beyond the pleasant fantasy – fantasy is always to a degree instructive if not normative – and the 'sweet muse' of choral lyric. But if the chorus regularly speaks in its dramatic persona, then, it is also the case that its remarks are only rarely linked in an explicit fashion to the dramatic action, and are often sufficiently general that Dover writes that 'they speak and sing not as if they were involved in a fictional situation ... but as if they were visiting Athens on the occasion of a Dionysiac festival'.[100] In particular, the hymns to the gods that are regular elements in the structure of the parabasis draw the comic chorus close to the other choruses who sing in religious celebration at the festival. Sifakis analyses each parabasis, section by section, to outline the persona which the chorus adopts in order to speak, and if his diagrams offer an excessively formalist picture, his conclusions that there is great 'freedom of these changes of point of view, even within the same part of the parabasis',[101] and that 'the standpoint from which the chorus speaks each time is sometimes clear and sometimes not'[102] indicate that as the parabasis claims the privilege of the chorus to speak the words of the *sophos*, so it draws on the manipulation of levels of fiction that produces the difficulties of siting the speaking voice in Dicaeopolis' address. 'The reader of parabases studies works of fiction.'[103]

It is particularly important that the chorus remains a figure in the play who speaks of rather than merely for the poet (*Knights* 507–10):

> If a comic producer of the old school tried to compel us
> to come forward to the audience and speak,
> he would not easily have gained his wish. But our poet
> deserves it, because he hates the same men as us, and
> dares to say what is just ...

---

[99] Sifakis (1971) 36–7.   [100] Dover (1972) 49.   [101] Sifakis (1971) 37.
[102] Sifakis (1971) 28.   [103] Harriot (1986) 25.

Here, the chorus describes itself as speaking the words of the poet but
also, in a fiction of external evaluation, describes and praises the poet in
comparison with the producers of an earlier generation (as if the chorus
when allotted to another poet would refuse to speak . . .). So in the *Wasps'*
parabasis the chorus tells of the audience's ingratitude. They rejected his
offering of last year, despite all his previous benefits to them by helping
other poets and by raising comedy to new levels of sophistication. This
(self-)representation of the poet in the mouth of the chorus, no less than
the personal remarks of Pindar discussed in the previous chapter, creates
a fictional biography, which includes not merely the fantasy, the narrative
stereotyping and the self-conscious image creation of the genre of autobiography, but also the (comic) mixture of irony, wild exaggeration and
wilful distortion.[104] As Harold Bloom writes 'Defense, for poets, always
has been trope' and 'a person tropes in order to tell many-colored rather
than white lies'. . . .[105] So, in the *Acharnians'* parabasis, the chorus first
defends the poet's brilliance in showing up how the Athenians could be
easily misled by orators from the allied states (as Dicaeopolis unmasked
the ambassadors in the Assembly scene) (636–40):

> Previously, when the foreign ambassadors tried
> to deceive you, they began by calling you 'violet-crowned'.
> When someone said that, at once the word 'crowned'
> made you sit on the edge of your little buttocks.
> If someone flattered you by calling Athens 'shining',
> he could get anything by that 'shining', applying to you
> the honour of sardines.

The claim to have benefited the citizens is made with characteristically
humorous and trivial examples and a deflating picture of the Athenians
as easily inflated by mere words. (Part of the parody here is directed at
the clichés of the pose of 'city's adviser and defender' struck in the public
rhetoric of the Assembly and Law-Court.)[106] The parabasis continues,
however, with the claim that the ambassadors from the allied states bring
tribute to Athens just to hear such a wonderful poet, who takes the risk
of speaking out what's right before the Athenians (εἰπεῖν ἐν Ἀθηναίοις
τὰ δίκαια). This wilfully distorting self-aggrandizement and parody of

---

[104] So Harriot (1986) 24 writes 'The poet uses the techniques of persuasive (mis-)informa-
tion to create a persona for Cratinus as fictitious, conceivably, as the one the composer
of these "anapaests" was endeavouring to create for himself.'
[105] Bloom (1982) 119, 124. Bloom's use of the term 'trope' is discussed by de Bolla (1988).
[106] See Halliwell (1984b) especially 17.

the Athenian exercise of imperial power leads into the fantasy of the poet's *kleos* being so great that the Persian king makes his military and political decisions according to which city, Athens or Sparta, has the most ships and is most abused by Aristophanes (649–51):

> Then he asked which city this poet greatly abused.
> For those people, he said, have been made much better
> and will win the war decisively, with him as adviser.

The good that the poet offers is speaking ill. That's what gives strength and indeed promises victory in war. The very process of the poet giving advice is the subject of this comic fantasy of profound Persian respect for Greek abuse. In a play which pictures the delights of a private peace won against the privations of war, the chorus steps forward to assert that the comic poet's abusive advice promises victory in war – or so the Persian king claims. In the parabasis, the giving of advice and discussion of giving advice are part of a (fantastic) fiction of the poet's voice.

The third-person description of the poet is common in the parabasis (see also e.g. *Knights* 507ff; *Wasps* 1015ff; *Peace* 734ff), but in the *Clouds* the parabasis opens (after a brief farewell to the actors) with a speech in which 'the first person singular throughout is the poet',[107] that is, in which the chorus speaks as and for the poet – with a description of the failure of the first version of the *Clouds*, and reasons for re-presenting it. In the remaining sections of the parabasis, however, the chorus speaks as clouds and describes the benefits they bring as clouds for men. This is perhaps the most striking and complete disjunction in the position from which the chorus appears to speak in the extant parabases. In the *Frogs*, however, as we will see, there is a move away from any depiction of the poet as a figure in this his drama, as the chorus declares its role to be that of the sacred chorus coming forward to teach the city. With each parabasis, we see what Reckford calls 'an experiment in self-exposure'.[108]

In a great variety of ways, then, and with a great variety of effect, the parabases of Aristophanic comedy develop and play with the tensions and disjunctions between the roles of the chorus as a character in the drama, as a medium for the words of the *sophos*, as a celebrant of the festival of Dionysus, as the performer of lyric poetry – and with the possibilities of poetic self-representation through such choric roles. As with Dicaeopolis' speech, it is not simply that there is a series of discrete fictions, but rather that these fictions are superimposed, conflict with

---

[107] Dover (1970) ad 518–62.   [108] Reckford (1987) 188.

each other, and infect each other. The parabasis, as a chorus coming forward to speak for the poet to the city, cannot be read apart from the ironic multiplication and fragmentation of voices with which the comic poet endows it. As Angus Bowie concludes: '"Aristophanes the man" the social commentator ironically viewing the events of the play from without, is not to be found ... His "personal" statement in the parabasis is no more than the play in miniature; he is as much a literary construct as his hero.'[109] The search to discover the place from which the figures of comedy speak will not uncover an author's voice speaking out from beyond the boundaries of comic interplay.

The formal structure of the parabasis encourages critics to see it as a discrete section of the drama; this tendency is reinforced by what critics have often seen as its thematic separation: in the parabasis, 'we might have expected to see him [Aristophanes] using this privilege [of the *sophos*] in order to preach directly whatever lessons the rest of the play implies but this is exactly what he does *not* do'.[110] Angus Bowie, however, (in an important recent article which is a prolegomenon to a longer study (Bowie (1982))) has questioned this *communis opinio* by a detailed study of the *Acharnians* and its parabasis, which attempts to show the significance of the parabasis for the play both in general thematic concern and in specific verbal parallels. Indeed, the parabasis, he argues, 'indicates and emphasizes those themes and ideas of the play that are the chief bearers of meaning'.[111] In particular, the 'notions of violent reaction and hasty suppression of opponents'[112] can be seen to link all the various scenes of the play, which also provides a political commentary in the form of a critique both of Athenian reactions to overtures of peace, and of its policy towards Megara and Boeotia. Bowie is also quick to stress that the ambivalence of the hero, Dicaeopolis, with his trickery and his 'selfish and unpatriotic transactions',[113] as well as the association of 'Aristophanes the poet' with this ambivalent figure, is a key factor that prevents such thematic links developing into a 'simple sermon': 'it would, I think, be a mistake to see the play simply as a moral fable, enshrining Aristophanes' deepest convictions'[114] – if only because 'there exists a tension between the implied "message" that a peace treaty would be a good idea and the terms in which this is embodied'.[115]

Bowie's recognition that the perception of thematic links between sections of the play does not lead to the reduction of the ambivalence of

---

[109] Bowie (1982) 40.   [110] Dover (1972) 52.   [111] Bowie (1982) 37.
[112] Bowie (1982) 37.   [113] Bowie (1982) 39.   [114] Bowie (1982) 38.
[115] Bowie (1982) 29.

the interplay of voices is crucial. Above, I discussed how Aristophanes' writing constantly poses the question of how seriously, how comically, how literally to take (the) play. And how far to go with such questions. The parabasis is crucial to that questioning not merely because of its necessarily privileged place in a discussion of 'serious communication' in Old Comedy, but also because its framing within the drama inevitably raises in starkest form the question of *how applicable, how relevant* (to me, to us, to them, to you) Aristophanes' dramatic fictions are. The problem of whether or to what extent the concerns and representations of the parabasis are in a significant relation with the framing dramatic action establishes precisely the question of what is to be taken (as significant, relevant, applicable, serious) in and from Aristophanic comedy (as a whole or in part). This determination of relevance or significance depends on the active involvement of an audience, its work in constructing or ignoring possible significant links between parts of the play, and between the play and its audience, and between the citizens in the ritual frame of the festival theatre and the citizens in the life of the *polis* outside the festival . . . as the frames of reference multiply to an ever wider context for comedy's relevance. Negotiating the licence and limits of comedy is drawing the line (somewhere), that is, framing a response. What is to be taken from Aristophanes inevitably remains a question replayed with every audience member's or reader's engagement with the comic. When the traditional wish is expressed 'to find some kind of external control, evidence independent of our reading of the plays that would help us calibrate our estimation of their tone or mood',[116] it is precisely this sense of individual and collective negotiation in and of comedy that makes this wish so misconceived, finally so unfulfillable. The parabasis, a chorus stepping forward to address the audience, does not obviate but rather emphasizes the audience's involvement in negotiating the boundaries and transgressions of comedy. Indeed, the framework of comedy requires ritual because the freedoms of comedy pose a problem for the work of framing by which social order is maintained.

PURLOINING THE POET'S VOICE

The last word in stolen telling.   James Joyce

The parabasis of the *Frogs* is a crucial example for the discussion of the poet's voice and the framing of the parabasis. Aeacus invites Dionysus and Xanthias inside the house (668–71) and thus the stage is emptied.

[116] Heath (1987a) 8.

Xanthias will return after the parabasis for a piece of dialogue with the servant of Aeacus[117] which prepares the audience for the *agōn* between Aeschylus and Euripides. The parabasis divides, then, the arrival in Hades and the business to be conducted there. It is a simply and symmetrically constructed piece which consists in a short ode and antode, each of ten dactylo-epitrite verses, alternating with the epirrhema and antepirrhema, two short (twenty line) addresses to the audience in trochaic tetrameters. There is no farewell to the characters (*kommation*), no *pnigos* and no anapaests (though the initiates in the parodos have a passage (354–71) in this metre which has some similarities to the expected range of subjects for the anapaests of a parabasis). As I have already mentioned, there is no explicit mention of the poet as a figure in this parabasis, which makes the lack of an anapaestic section, in which the chorus often talks about the poet, seem to be not merely a variation of form. Although it refers to itself as a 'holy chorus' (686), there is no further indication that it speaks especially in the persona of a chorus of initiates – ἱερός, 'holy', may refer to the role of the chorus in this festival; or to the roles of choruses in general. This parabasis is marked, then, in comparison with the parabases of earlier plays, by its lack of formal complexity and variety.

The ode and antode both attack a single individual by name (Cleophon and Cleigenes) in terms that are obscure to modern scholars, except for certain constants of Aristophanic abuse – foreign birth, humble occupation, small stature, drunkenness. The epirrhema and antepirrhema address the political issue of re-enfranchisement of those citizens exiled for their role in the oligarchic coup of 411: in the epirrhema, the chorus directly appeals for the re-enfranchisement, with reference to the fact that even slaves had been offered the same rights as the Plataean allies after the battle of Arginusae in which *in extremis* they had taken part; in the antepirrhema, the problem is approached more generally by the suggestion that the city fails to make use of its best citizens – a general point expressed through the famous extended conceit of the comparison of old and new money. The chorus speaks up for using the citizens imbued with the traditional, aristocratic virtues. The symmetrical structure of the parabasis, then, alternates (i) a political argument on the specific issue of re-enfranchisement and the general issue of which citizens the city ought to use with (ii) personal abuse of two particular

---

[117] It is unclear who the interlocutor of Xanthias is. Whitman (1964) and Reckford (1987) are among the few to suppose it is Aeacus who discusses the joys of slavery with Xanthias. I have assumed it is a servant, but, for my present argument, little hangs on the identification.

citizens, both associated – though in the case of Cleigenes, only on the strength of this passage – with 'populist' politics, so that even the structure of sung abuse and recited advice has seemed to produce consistent political advice to the city in need.

The specificity and consistency of this parabasis have resulted in it being seen as a perfect example of what the chorus announces to be its role (686–7):

> τὸν ἱερὸν χορὸν δίκαιόν ἐστι χρηστὰ τῇ πόλει
> ξυμπαραινεῖν καὶ διδάσκειν.
>
> It is right for the holy chorus to advise and teach
> the city what is good.

It has also made for a largely uncritical acceptance of the remarks in the *Hypothesis* that the play was so admired *because of its parabasis* that it was given a second performance – a unique honour for comedy. The story is attributed to Dicaearchus. It must remain highly doubtful, however, whether the parabasis was the reason offered for a second performance by the Athenians, officially or by any individual; or an explanation, guessed by Dicaearchus, writing many years after the event; or indeed a proposal by the writer of the *Hypothesis*. That the parabasis tapped, if it did not influence, contemporary Athenian public opinion, has been argued from the fact that shortly after the play was produced – and after the defeat at Aegospotami – a decree of re-enfranchisement was enacted.[118] It is also the case, however, that the general, conservative political stance expressed in the parabasis is commonly endorsed with feeling – and instantiated – by (ancient) commentators.

It would seem, then, that if any parabasis demonstrates the role of the unmasked chorus speaking to the citizens on behalf of the poet on a matter of common political concern, it is here in the *Frogs*. Yet, this is not the whole story. The relation between the parabasis and the framing drama establish a more complex picture – and it is noticeable that in the *Frogs* in particular the parabasis is treated by critics as a discrete dramatic unit. Now, the parabasis praises the nobles for their qualities of birth, sense and justice, produced by a traditional upbringing of athletics, the chorus and the arts (727–9):

> τῶν πολιτῶν θ' οὓς μὲν ἴσμεν εὐγενεῖς καὶ σώφρονας
> ἄνδρας ὄντας καὶ δικαίους καὶ καλούς τε κἀγαθοὺς
> καὶ τραφέντας ἐν παλαίστραις καὶ χοροῖς καὶ μουσικῇ ...

[118] An argument found e.g. in Dover (1972) 53.

> The citizens whom we know to be noble and sensible
> men, just, and real gentlemen, trained
> in the wrestling-school, chorus and arts ...

Bring back the nobles, use the good (*khrēstoi*), is the advice. The first lines after the parabasis run as follows (738–40):

Serv.   By Zeus the saviour, your master's a noble man.
Xan.   Of course he's a noble. All he knows how to do is
        to drink and to fuck.

From the holy chorus' view of nobility we return immediately to a comic slave's view – the noble (*gennadas*) is the man who knows only how to drink and to fuck (*pinein kai binein*, a word play that gives the sentiment an air of catch-phrase or proverb[119]). This brief dialogue is significant, however, not only because it refers immediately to the subject of the parabasis but also because it draws its relevance and humour from the scene immediately before the parabasis, where Dionysus and Xanthias, slave and master, after a series of role changes, are beaten in the hope of determining which is the real god and master and which the mortal and slave. That scene ends with Aeacus at a loss and they enter the house with the promise that his master (the god of the Underworld) and Persephone will know the truth. What's more, Aeacus actually calls Xanthias a 'noble man', *gennadas* (640), as indeed Dionysus earlier refers to his slave as (179) 'a good fellow [*khrēstos*] and a noble man [*gennadas*]' – precisely the values praised by the parabasis. Now Xanthias comes out of the house and his companion's comment places him in the persona of slave, as Xanthias' comment jibes at the master whose role he no longer usurps.[120] As so often in Aristophanes, an apparently serious piece of advice is set in tension with jokes on the self-same subject. The controlled seriousness of the parabasis remains in control only by framing it as an entirely discrete scene.

The parabasis indeed appears closely tied to the play by more than such immediate and humorous comments. For if the chorus states clearly its role to teach and advise the city, it is a chorus of a play whose central conceit is the search for a poet to perform such a role. Indeed, Dionysus, who has gone to find Euripides, in an act of glorious narrative reversal,

---

[119] Which is not to say, as Ehrenberg (1951) 102 does, that in Aristophanes 'the gentleman, the *gennadas*, was generally characterized by his inclination to drinking and sexual pleasures' – a view quoted with ridicule by Chapman (1978) 67.

[120] On the shifts between master and slave, see in particular Whitman (1964) especially 236–41.

returns with Aeschylus – the figure of traditional, archaic tragedy who speaks up (in a parodic and comic manner) for virtues similar to those praised by the chorus in the parabasis. That literary values and political worth are inherently linked is a *topos* of this, as of other, Aristophanic dramas. As the chorus speaks out in the parabasis, its self-aware adoption of role is set firmly within the thematic texture of the work: 'whom to bring back? Who is the good citizen for the city in the time of need? What values are needed?' are the questions which motivate both the parabasis and the dramatic narrative. To view the parabasis as separate from the play of which it is a constitutive part is, then, a critical strategy with crucial implications for understanding the drama. How is the search for a tragedian to save the city to be related to the comic poet's claim to offer saving advice?

The central conceit of the *Frogs*, then, is the search for a poet by the god in whose festival the play is acted, the god under whose aegis tragedy and comedy are produced in the city. A god of the theatre as a character in search of an author ... In the *Thesmophoriazusae* (produced 411 and the closest extant play to the *Frogs* (405)), Euripides is a central figure, and a series of parodies of Euripidean drama structure the final scene of the play, as a discussion of Euripides and the Woman Question motivate the *agōn*. *Gerytades* (probably 408) probably included an embassy of poets sent to Hades to bring back the goddess of poetry.[121] The *Phoinissae* (409 or later) appears to have parodied Euripides' play of the same name. Other fragments suggest that Euripides was a character in other plays too. Parodies of tragedy recur throughout Greek literature and particularly comedy, but there is a further emphasis in Aristophanes' writing. For, as with 'the writer' in post-Romantic fiction, 'the poet' or more generally 'the *sophos*' becomes for Aristophanes a central figure; the tragedian and his tragedies become a comic hero, a subject of drama.

The poet's voice, then, is a focus of Aristophanic writing not merely in the self-reflexive comments on the production of comedy, but also in the way in which Aristophanic comedy regularly stages and upstages the tragic poet's voice.

Aristophanes' staging of Aeschylus and Euripides in the *Frogs* is the paradigm of this focus on the poet's voice. Not only does he bring the archetypal figures of old and new style tragedy on stage for an *agōn* that

---

[121] Some have thought that the commentary (*CGF* 63.85–7) from which we learn this plot detail, is on the *Geras*, which was probably produced in 409. Koerte ascribes it to the *Gerytades*. On the date of *Gerytades* see Sommerstein (1980) 25 n. 22.

parodies the competition for tragedians, but also the *agōn* specifically concentrates on the nature of each man's poetry. (It is a scene, it need hardly be added, that has had an extraordinary – a comically dispro-portionate – influence on the history of literary criticism.) From my start with the irony of the Platonic Socrates' attempt to control tragedy within philosophic discourse, it is finally to Aristophanic comedy's parodic staging of the value of tragic poetry that my discussion turns.

Now parody as a rhetoric and as a genre has been much discussed in recent years, particularly with regard to twentieth-century literature and art, for which the mode has often seemed a defining characteristic.[122] These discussions, on which I have liberally drawn in the following pages, not only help specify the nature of Aristophanic parody but also will help tie the discussion of parody to the earlier consideration of the carnivalesque and the institutions of comedy as (a negotiation of) trans-gression. Now, parody and comic inversion are inherently linked: in the Aristophanic 'World Upside Down', as I have already discussed, institu-tions such as the Assembly and Law-Courts, public figures such as poets, generals and orators, rituals of social behaviour and rituals of religious observance, all fall under the general rubric of an inversion or distortion of an assumed model, set in a new context, for comic effect – a rubric that remains the starting-point for definitions of parody. Although in its representation of the figures of Euripides and Aeschylus and in its version of a tragic competition the *agōn* of Aristophanes' *Frogs* shows that these disparate forms of inversion inevitably and inextricably come together in the comic theatrical representation, my concern here is more specifically with the linguistic element of literary parody which is both a crucial part of Aristophanes' writing and a crucial focus of modern criticism.

August Schlegel wrote – in a discussion of Aristophanes – that 'Parody always implies a relationship with and dependence on its object.'[123] Schlegel draws on a history of criticism of parody (as well as a particular set of Romantic notions of individuality and truth) that emphasize par-ody's *parasitism* on its models with all the ambivalence such a relation-ship can imply.[124] Indeed, the 'combination of respectful homage and

---

[122] 'Parody, once considered anti-normative and hence also anti-generic, now represents the discontinuity characteristic of modernism' (Rose (1979) 185). I have learnt in particular also from Hutcheon (1985), Genette (1982a), Stewart (1978), each of which have further bibliographies.

[123] Schlegel (1966) 132 'Parodie setz immer eine Beziehung auf das Parodierte und Abhän-gigkeit davon voraus.' This is comically translated by Rose (1979) 34.

[124] The best introduction to this relationship remains Miller (1979).

ironically thumbed nose'[125] – the fact that 'all parody is overtly hybrid and double voiced'[126] – opens the possibility of an extraordinary range of possible relations between parodist and the object of parody that goes far beyond the ancient scholiasts' usual explanation of mockery towards what has become in the twentieth century a prime artistic mode of seeking *Aufhebung*, the subsumption and transcendence of traditional form, in writers such as Joyce and Beckett. The first point I wish to make on parody, then, is the simple observation that the relation between parodist and object of parody is not one of simple mockery or contempt. Indeed, when Aristophanes parodies Euripides, as many critics have pointed out, he does not merely poke fun or merely despise.

The ambivalent 'double voice' of parody, moreover, has often been directly connected to the carnivalesque, particularly with regard to the interplay of revolution and authority that is fundamental to carnival and its criticism. For, on the one hand, parody can be seen as a transgressive force that 'disrealizes and dethrones literary norms',[127] a mocking voice which for Bakhtin speaks of fertile rebellion (but for Leavis, perhaps more threateningly, of philistine opposition to creative genius and originality). On the other hand, parody requires 'a certain aesthetic institutionalization which entails the acknowledgment of recognizable, stable forms and conventions'.[128] Parody is a licensed transgression, or, in Kristeva's fine phrase, 'a principle of *law anticipating its own transgression*.'[129] The various uses of parody from (self-)defence against political repression to literary parlour game are each formulated within the ambivalent possibilities of authorization and rejection: 'parody presupposes both a law and its transgression, or both repetition and difference, and therein lies the key to its double potential: it can be both conservative and transformative'.[130] Like (the politics of) carnival, parody is constituted in an interplay of norm and transgression (differently articulated by different practices and institutions). As the parodist has an ambivalent relation to the object of parody, so parody functions with ambivalent social and literary effect.

My second area of concern is with the act of recognizing and interpreting parody. For parody entails a particular and complex process of recognition (which is a constitutive element in its ambivalent effect). On the one hand, parody entails a recognition – in and through the parody – of a presupposed model, that is, the *object* of parody. As we will see,

[125] Hutcheon (1985) 33.   [126] Hutcheon (1985) 28.   [127] Shlonsky (1966) 799.
[128] Hutcheon (1985) 75.   [129] Kristeva (1980) 71.   [130] Hutcheon (1985) 101.

this does not imply that the model or process of recognition is the same for all readers or audiences; merely that a parody – to be a parody – presupposes a 'modelled reality'[131] as object (as Aristophanes' representation of Euripides assumes a recognizable construct 'Euripides' as the basis and object of parody). On the other hand, parody also requires a corollary recognition that its representation changes or distorts that 'modelled reality'. Aristophanes' representation of Euripides must also be recognizably other than the presupposed model 'Euripides'. Parody's mimesis, in other words, *traces* a model from which it always already *differs*. Reading parody, then, constitutes a particular example of the always complex process of recognizing similarity and difference.

Let me use an ancient anecdote to make this discussion more specific. There is a story reported in Aelian (*VH* ii. 13) that at the performance of Aristophanes' *Clouds*, when foreigners were whispering 'Who is this man Socrates?', Socrates stood up in silence that he might be seen. The historical veracity of the story is unimportant. What is relevant for my purposes here is what the story tells about the process of recognition in parody. First, there is an evident assumption that the foreigners recognize that there is an object presupposed in the parody of which they are the audience. Their question is designed to specify the target of the parody more closely than 'a man', 'a *sophos*'. That they are foreigners who ask this question also implies that the model is (more) recognizable to the Athenian audience. Second, the question arises of what sort of recognition is involved when Socrates stands in silence. It is sometimes assumed that this narrative is proof of the use of portrait masks in the theatre and that Socrates is offering a comparison of the actor's caricature and the original.[132] Such a juxtaposition may imply a self-aware and amused act of reappropriation (as when a politician, presented with a cartoon of him/herself, may be photographed holding it for the newspapers). It may imply – to take a different perspective – a dignified correction of a distorted and hurtful portrait.

For the knowing Athenian audience a more complex recognition is required than physical resemblance. For Socrates, as he stands in the theatre to face his parodic portrait, raises by such a striking juxtaposition a question of similarity and difference, of how close, how distorted, how biased a representation Aristophanes has produced. A requirement of

---

[131] This term is borrowed from Ben-Porat (1979).
[132] On portrait masks and this passage, see Dover (1975) especially 167–9.

negotiation. The anecdote of Aelian stages in the (silent) juxtaposition of model and parody the problematic question of recognition (of difference, of similarity) that is replayed in each performance of parody.

Parody is inherently a critical mode of discourse: the recognition of difference is also a recognition of critical distance. Parody's representation exposes its target by representing it. In particular, parody works by making explicit, by drawing (critical) attention to the conventions, strategies and characteristics of its object. (Literary parody conventionally shows how literature requires that its conventions be taken seriously.) This activity of exposing or making explicit the strategies of the parodied model is inevitably a highly self-conscious process: literary parody is always self-reflexive in this sense of a heightened awareness of the modes of representation with which it works. My second point, then, is that the reader's negotiation of both the recognition of difference and the self-reflexivity in parody precludes a simple and straightforward hermeneutics of parody.

My third general point is to make explicit another factor in this anecdote from Aelian, namely, that the different knowledges of different audience members are a crucial element in the functioning of parody. Parody shows in the clearest form how the readers' presuppositions, attitudes, information are a necessary component in the activity of interpretation. Certainly there are signals that facilitate the recognition of parody, implicit and explicit markers of which the drama festival itself is the most developed institutional form.[133] But the differences within an audience necessarily produce differences in the possibilities of comprehension. When Aristophanes' Dicaeopolis parodies Euripides' *Telephus*, the depth and detail of an audience's knowledge of the Euripidean play alter the understanding of the parody. Parody, as with all poetics of allusion, raises not merely a question of recognition but also a question of how developed a recognition is to be. Whether Dicaeopolis is seen merely to be acting in a tragic way for comic effect or constructing an elaborate and significant network of allusions with Euripides' *Telephus* necessarily depends on the knowledge and attitudes with which an audience member approaches the *Acharnians*. What is more, audiences and readers may be quite self-aware of this *complicity* in parody's criticism, and this self-awareness is a source of the pleasure parody can provide:

[133] These are discussed in general form by Rose (1979) 25–8 and, for Aristophanes, by Schlesinger (1936) and (1937).

'The pleasure of parody's irony comes . . . from the degree of engagement of the reader in the intertextual "bouncing" (to use E.M. Forster's famous term) between complicity and distance.'[134]

It is not merely the case, however, that 'different readers read differently'. For parody, like irony, establishes an unsettling possibility of *reading otherwise* that becomes finally difficult to control. The question of how developed a recognition is to be becomes a question for each reader. The boundaries of parody require negotiation. An example: Margaret Rose in her important book on parody begins her lengthy discussion of the problems of defining parody with the issue of etymology, for which she returns to the Greek evidence. She concludes this section with the following remark: 'The word "parodos" was also used in the time of Aristophanes to describe the side entrance to the right of the stage in the ancient theatre.'[135] The knowledge each reader brings to this remark is, of course, crucial. The reader who knows no Greek might well be misled into thinking that this word 'parodos' is the same word as the term also transliterated 'parodos' and translated by Rose earlier in her discussion as '"singing in imitation" or an "imitating singer"'.[136] Readers who know some Greek will immediately recognize two wholly distinct words πάροδος and παρῳδός, transliterated in the same way. Now the reader who recognizes this disparity – and the recognition of disparity is crucial to Rose's definition of parody – is faced with a difficulty. It could be simply that this remark is at best an irrelevancy, at worst an egregious error in the etymological search. But Rose is a sophisticated critic, who is well aware of modernist games with etymology often for parodic effect; nor does she develop any significance for this definition of 'parodos', but lets it stand like a throwaway line, as she proceeds to her next section, 'The Comic Effect in Parody'. Could it be, then, that her comment is a parodic jibe at her own antiquarianism in a book focused on modern literature and art? The self-awareness of parody provokes a self-awareness in the knowing reader, which incites doubt and a consciousness of duplicity to flourish in the act of reading. Recognizing parody can involve the reader or audience in the unsettling (and comic) process of recognizing how things can be taken otherwise – and how each reader's complicity remains integral to that process.

These four general points developed from the theorists of parody – the ambivalent relationship between parodist and object of parody; the pro-

---

[134] Hutcheon (1985) 32.   [135] Rose (1979) 19.
[136] Rose (1979) 18. Her discussion starts from the standard work of Householder (1944).

blems for interpretation that are produced by parody's self-reflexive 'repetition with a difference'; the function of an audience's complicity in comprehending parody; the disruptive process of reading otherwise that parody evokes – provide an important framework for the analysis of the specifics of Aristophanic parody in the *Frogs*, to which I now turn.

'Le style, c'est l'homme même', is a basic principle of Aristophanic parody: Euripides and Aeschylus are represented as incarnations of their poetic productions, as (parodic) images of the characteristics of poetry overlap into (parodic) pictures of the poets (830–4):

Eur.	I could not relinquish the throne. No advice, please.
	For I declare that I am in my art better than he.
Dio.	Aeschylus, why are you silent? You hear his words.
Eur.	First, the dignified silence, the device he tried
	every time in his tragedies for Grand Effect.

Aeschylus' silence in reaction to the hectoring Euripides is explicitly marked as a trait of his tragic practice by Euripides (whose self-con-sciousness of tragic technique and appeal to contemporary criteria of criticism are in themselves expressions of Euripidean dramaturgical modernity).[137] The opening dialogue of the *agōn* immediately establishes poetics as the means and matter of the exchange.

The *agōn* is announced by the chorus as 'the great contest in *sophia*' (νῦν γὰρ ἀγὼν σοφίας ὁ μέγας 882), a competition in and of words (818–29), which places at stake both technical skill and the right to address the public as a *sophos*. The *sophia* of both poets is subject to Aristophanes' parody. Aeschylus and Euripides are set in opposition to one another in a way which comically undercuts both. So, for example, Euripides' modernity is seen as an adoption of the new (and ridiculous) gods of 'Air, my nourishment, Twisting of Tongue, Sophistication, Taste', αἰθὴρ ἐμὸν βόσκημα καὶ γλώσσης στρόφιγξ καὶ ξύνεσι καὶ μυκτῆρες ὀσφραντήριοι (892–3), before which, for maximum comic con-trast, Aeschylus prays to sober Demeter, 'the nurse of his mind' (886). The prayer to 'Air, my nourishment' not only echoes Aeschylus' prayer to his nurse Demeter – Aeschylus was born in Eleusis, the home of Demeter's mysteries[138] – but also combines a finely pretentious sense of

---

[137] Whitman (1964) 242–3 makes the contrast between Aeschylean silence and Euripidean jabbering the key to the play and in particular to Dionysus' decision to take Aeschylus.
[138] The mysteries, and initiation in general, are discussed as a theme of the play by Segal (1961); Whitman (1964) (on these lines, 242–3); Konstan (1986); Reckford (1987) 433–9; see also de Vries (1973); Byl (1980).

the habitat of the high-minded poet with the deflating sense of 'living on air', that is, on nothing. In a similar parodic twisting, Aeschylus' traditional values are seen as the need for long words to match great thoughts (1058–60):

Aes.   But, wretch, grand ideas and concepts must
        give birth to words of equal size.
        In the same way, it is right for heroes to use bigger words.

The double sense of *megas* when applied to words – both 'proud' and 'long' or 'big' – is used to turn Aeschylus' assertion of his heroes' grand discourse into a rationale of polysyllabic language.

This undermining of each poet's claims of *sophia* is particularly relevant in the discussion of the moral teaching of poetry, a discussion which constantly returns in the arguments over *sophia* but which is especially marked in Aeschylus' self-defence (1004ff). His explanation of how his poetry makes citizens better is punctuated with sardonic remarks by Dionysus who regularly adds incisively comic counter-examples to Aeschylus' grand claims (1034–37):

Aes.   Why does divine Homer have honour
        and fame, except because he taught good things –
        military strategy, virtue and preparation for men.
Dio.   He doesn't seem to have taught Pantacles much.

The *topos* of Homer's value as a paradigm for the poet's voice, set in the Aristophanic context of the comic *agōn* and combined with the Dionysiac trivialization, becomes subject to parody's repetition with a difference. Indeed, these Aeschylean claims demonstrate well the problem of recognition and the strategies of negotiation that such repetition with a difference entails. Aeschylus continues (1039):

Aes.   Among his many other noble products is the hero Lamachus.

Lamachus is a butt of Aristophanic satire particularly in the *Acharnians* and *Peace*. Here, he is Aeschylus' crowning example of poetry's military education – a hero. The standard commentaries note that Lamachus died in the Sicilian expedition and thus here 'he is cited with respect'[139] as a

---

[139] Stanford (1963) ad loc. At *Thesmo.* 841 the mother of Lamachus is contrasted with the mother of Hyperbolus, and the scholia's comment there (that Aristophanes praises Lamachus now) starts the tradition of Lamachus' *post mortem* rehabilitation (though Stanford does not refer to the *Thesmo.* passage). Yet is there no hint of a *paraprosdokian* joke there also? The speech is a parodic claim that mothers should have public honours in respect of their sons' achievements, so Hyperbolus' mother should not be allowed to sit next to ... Lamachus' mother. Serious praise?

hero of the city: the reference is 'una sorta di palinodia, nell' esaltazione dei valori patriottici'.[140] Yet the very phrase 'O hero Lamachus', 'Ὦ Λάμαχ' ἥρως, is a running joke of Dicaeopolis' ironic scorn in the *Acharnians* (575–9), a parallel surprisingly not adduced by Stanford or Del Corno. Nor does Aristophanes' treatment of Cleon or the setting of the *agōn* in the Underworld suggest that *de mortuis nil nisi bonum* is a principle with much purchase in Aristophanic comedy. Is there, then, really no suggestion of a *paraprosdokian* joke in Aeschylus' account of the teaching of poetry, as Lamachus – the hero – is named as the epitome of Homer's pupils? Is there no parodic humour in having Aeschylus claim as his example the figure Aristophanes had elsewhere so often mocked? Does Aristophanic parody allow Aeschylus (here as so often in the scene) to undermine the seriousness of his own argument? The 'seriousness and respect' that critics have read as Aristophanes' voice here and elsewhere in Aeschylus' speeches are the result of a particular critical negotiation of the ambivalent potentialities of parody, a particular complicity (which rarely reproduces Aristophanic self-awareness). The unsettling possibility of taking words otherwise constantly introduces into Aristophanic drama a playful uncertainty (that is repressed at the cost of the subtlety and force of his comic writing).

Within the logic of polarization typical of the *agōn*, both Euripides' and Aeschylus' appeals to *sophia* work as much through (personal) attack as through self-justification (959–68):

Eur. I introduced familiar affairs, which we use, are
at home with, which I could be taken up on. For these
men could test my art from shared experience.
I didn't stun them with bombast, nor did I terrify
by writing Cycnoi or Memnons with bell-snaffled horses.
You'll recognize his pupils, and mine on the other side:
his are Phormisas and Megainetos the Manian,
long-beard-lance-and-trumpet men, flesh-rippers-with-the-pine.
Mine are Cleitophon and the sophisticated Theramenes.
Dio. Theramenes? Aye, a clever man and extraordinary at everything.

Euripides establishes his 'homely poetics' in opposition to Aeschylus' antique heroes in antique garb. Unlike Aeschylus, he shares a world and an art with his audience. Euripides' claim of a 'democratic art' (952) is the corollary of Aeschylus' abusive accusation that he reduced the grandeur of tragedy to the level of the mob, as his justification is set

---

[140] Del Corno (1985) ad loc. But see Halliwell (1982) 154 for a reading which approaches mine.

in contrast with his own parody of Aeschylean grandeur in the vast portmanteau terms σαλπιγγολογχυπηνάδαι, σαρκασμοπιτυοκάμπται, 'long-beard-lance-and-trumpet-men, flesh-rippers-with-the-pine'. The last term with its derivation from *sarkazein*, 'to tear asunder', also echoes with the ridicule (*sarkasmos*) that it is performing.[141] Euripides' defence, then, proceeds in part through sarcastic attack. Yet even as the parody of Aeschylus is being conducted by the Aristophanic Euripides, the Aristophanic Euripides is also the target of parody in his claims of the educative power of verse. As he compares his own pupils with those of Aeschylus, he boasts of prize students 'Cleitophon and the sophisticated Theramenes' – two of the leaders of the four hundred, the oligarchic coup. The democratic tragedian produces, it would seem, the sophisticated oligarch. The joke is pointed by Dionysus' sarcastic rejoinder, where the phrase σοφός γ' ἀνὴρ καὶ δεινός, 'Aye, a clever man and extraordinary . . .' focuses attention on the *sophia* at stake in the debate.

There is, then, a complex layering of parody here, with the Aristophanic Euripides – a parody of Euripides – parodying the Aristophanic Aeschylus – a parody of Aeschylus. So, the Aristophanic Euripides, with a fine piece of 'new rhetoric', accuses the Aristophanic Aeschylus of roguery and deception in his artistic manipulation of the dolts that constitute the old-fashioned audience (908–10):

> First I will prove him to be
> a rogue and deceiver – how he tricked
> the audience of idiots he had, brought up on Phrynichus.

The announcement of the opening move in a rhetorical strategy (πρῶτ' ἐλέγξω, 'first I will prove') and perhaps even the notion of deceiving (ἐξηπάτα) the audience which plays such a part in Gorgias' arguments on *logos*, mark Euripides' parodied modernity, which in itself parodies the tragedy and audience of a former generation as old-fashioned and unsophisticated. In the double-speak of this parody, the poetry of the past is viewed both with a nostalgic idealization and with a mocking of its outmoded pomposities, as the poetry of the present is seen both as a sophisticated advance and as a corrupt and trivializing pursuit of novelty.

This *agōn* of parodied poets parodying each other produces some dizzying effects for the poet's voice (1152–9):

Aes. 'Prove saviour for me, and an ally as I pray.
For I have come to this land and returned . . .'

---

[141] As Stanford (1963) ad loc. suggests.

Eur. The wise Aeschylus has said the same thing twice.
Dio. How twice?
Eur. Look at the expression. I will expound.
      For ' "I have come" ', he says, ' "and returned." '
      'Have come' is the same as 'returned'.
Dio. By Zeus, it's just like if someone said to a neighbour
      'Lend me a stirring bowl, or, if you wish, a mixing bowl.'

The Aristophanic Aeschylus correctly re-cites lines from Aeschylus' *Choephoroi* (or at least that are now in modern texts of Aeschylus[142]). The quotation is interrupted by the Aristophanic Euripides to announce that Aeschylus, the *sophos*, 'the wise' – an adjective used sarcastically but also to stress the term being fought over – has said the same thing twice. The Aeschylean re-citation contains, he claims, a tautology, a doubleness that is to be remarked by Dionysus: 'How twice?' 'Look at the speech', demands the figure of Euripides – literary parody's typical self-consciousness of the material of literary production – 'I will expound.' And the Aristophanic Euripides re-quotes the Aristophanic Aeschylus' quotation of the *Oresteia* to show its error – of saying the same thing twice: ' " "I have come" " is the same as ' "I have returned" " '.' Euripides' critique is in itself recognizable as a parody of contemporary linguistic criticism (particularly Prodicus and Protagoras[143]), a parody brought down to earth by Dionysus' replication of the argument with the less elevated example of *maktran*, 'stirring bowl', and *kardapon*, 'mixing bowl' (both terms mean 'large vessels for kneeding dough'). The figure of Aeschylus, however, goes on to reassert the significant difference between ἥκω, 'I have come', and κατέρχομαι, 'I have returned' (1160–5). The parodic critical discussion (on lines quoted and requoted from the targets of parody) itself turns on whether two expressions are the same or different. Recognizing difference is both the subject and the interpretive requirement of this parody. Hutcheon's description of parody as 'repetition with a difference' can scarcely do justice to this vertiginous self-reflexivity of *sophos* parodying *sophos* parodying *sophos* parodying ...

Aeschylus' famous final assault on the Euripidean prologue is the disruptive insertion of the phrase ληκύθιον ἀπώλεσεν, 'he lost his little bottle', into Euripides' recitations (1197–250). Again, the parody depends on a brilliant variation of the play of similarity and difference, as

---

[142] The placing of the lines in the *Choephoroi* is disputed. See Garvie (1986) ad loc.; Blumenthal (1984); West (1985).
[143] See Segal (1970b) for discussion.

the Aristophanic Aeschylus makes the Aristophanic Euripides seem more
and more ridiculous by completing the different prologues with the same
(Aristophanic) phrase, the humour of which increases as each attempt of
Euripides to escape ends the same way. The addition of this one same
phrase, a repetitive *reductio*, aims to set Euripides' different prologues in
a different, parodic light of assumed sameness. (The more he adds, the
more he takes away ...) Aeschylus' repetition of the same phrase threatens the semantic security both of the Euripidean prologues – which all
say the same thing, finally ? – and of the phrase itself, whose brief triviality
may seem significantly pregnant with sense or inevitably empty (as the
critics' negotiations in reading this piece of parodic comedy demonstrate
all too well[144]). Indeed, this uncertainty, this loss of control in and of
language, turns the critics to seek for the (lost) dramatic gestures, which,
they believe, might contain the scene's significance. Or to seek for a (lost,
but secure) other meaning for ληκύθιον, the container that keeps getting
lost. Or, with the greatest sense of humour, to prove from the shape of
ancient bottles that there could be (no) sexual innuendo here ...[145]
Aeschylus' repeated expression of loss destroys or mimes the loss of
language as a container of value, significance, truth. As comedy ever
demonstrates, language leaks. The poets' *agōn* of and on words provides
a paradigmatic case of comedy's archetypal practice: to explore and
explode the limits of language both as signifying system and as medium
of social exchange.

Dionysus himself is drawn into the play of poet's voices. The second
example of this Aeschylean semantic hooliganism is directed against the
prologue of the *Hypsipyle* (1211–14):

EY.   'Διόνυσος, ὃς θύρσοισι καὶ νεβρῶν δοραῖς
      καθαπτὸς ἐν πεύκῃσι Παρνασσὸν κάτα
      πηδᾷ χορεύων ...'
ΑΙ.   ληκύθιον ἀπώλεσεν.
ΔΙ.   οἴμοι πεπλήγμεθ' αὖθις ὑπὸ τῆς ληκύθου.

Eur. 'Dionysus, who, equipped with thyrsus and skins
      of fawns, leaps dancing down Parnassus,
      amid the pines ...'
Aes.   Lost his little bottle.
Dio. Alas, we are struck again by that little bottle.

---

[144] See Whitman (1969); Griffith (1970); Hooker (1970); Henderson (1972); Penella (1973);
      Henderson (1974); Penella (1974); Snell (1979); Anderson (1981).
[145] Anderson (1981), with pictures, attempts to trump Henderson (1972) 135 n. 10.

Euripides – with perhaps a touch of special pleading? – quotes a prologue that begins with Dionysus, his judge, celebrating on Parnassus, but again his syntax inevitably opens the way for Aeschylus to add the phrase again. Dionysus' tragic reaction, however, as Rau, following Stanford, suggests, echoes that most famous cry of Aeschylean dramaturgy, the off-stage death of Agamemnon.[146] The echo combines and manipulates the two lines of the dying king. αὖθις, from the second cry of Agamemnon, indicates that this is the second time that the Aristophanic Aeschylus has struck with his bottle. οἴμοι πεπλήγμεθ᾽, 'alas, we are struck', however, recalls ὤμοι πέπληγμαι, 'alas I am struck' of Agamemnon's first cry. The change in Aristophanes from first person singular to plural is significant, as it widens the reference to include 'Dionysus' as quoted by Euripides' prologue (and cut off in his dance by Aeschylus' ληκύθιον ἀπώλεσεν, 'lost his little bottle') and also the figure of Euripides whose prologue has been disrupted. Dionysus' tragic reaction to Aeschylus' attack on Euripides' prologue on the subject of Dionysus parodies the paradigmatic reaction to attack in Aeschylean theatre. The tragic poet's voice is disseminated throughout the parodic *agōn*.

The process of critical judgment itself seems to be the focus of the final parodic conflict of the *agōn*, where lines of poetry are weighed on a scale (1377–410). In each case, the poet quotes a line and in each case the scale inclines to Aeschylus, and Dionysus offers a comically argued reason for the greater weightiness of Aeschylean verse. The brilliant comic invention of the scene shows a typical device of parody in the literalization of metaphor and also in the naive misprision of poetic convention that is demonstrated by the submission of both poets to a process of judging poetry by the weight of the referents of each verse. Yet the scene is also important for setting Dionysus centre stage as judge of the *agōn*.[147] Throughout the scene, Dionysus acts the role of audience to the poets' claims. (As so often in parody, the role of reader is mirrored in the text.)[148] His commentary plays a crucial part in articulating the *agōn*, as it is his remarks which comically deflate, maliciously exploit or naively support the protagonists (thus dramatizing a range of responses to the poets for the audience, as well as offering his own particular style of divine wisdom). Yet the conclusion of the *agōn* requires a decision from Dionysus. At first, he seems unwilling to make a choice and earn the hostility of one

---

[146] Rau (1967). The lines are Aeschylus *Agamemnon* 1343, 1345.
[147] On the transformation of Dionysus in this play, see Segal (1961).
[148] See Rose (1979) 61ff for discussion and examples.

poet (1413):

> τὸν μὲν γὰρ ἡγοῦμαι σοφόν, τῷ δ' ἥδομαι

> For I think the one wise, the other gives me pleasure.

His playful or tactful unwillingness to specify which of the two is *sophos* and which gives pleasure leads to a final test in which each poet is asked two questions: what to do about Alcibiades, and what to do to save the city. On Alcibiades, both poets react with tragic generalizations – Euripides with a political aphorism which expresses hatred for the citizen who puts self-interest before the city; Aeschylus with an allusive fable that echoes the tale of the lion in the house in (Aeschylus') *Agamemnon*. Again, Dionysus' reaction to these two forms of tragic wisdom is uncertain; and his expression of the difference between the poets scarcely induces certainty in the audience (1433–4):

> νὴ τὸν Δία τὸν σωτῆρα, δυσκρίτως γ' ἔχω·
> ὁ μὲν σοφῶς γὰρ εἶπεν, ὁ δ' ἕτερος σαφῶς.

> By Zeus the saviour, I certainly find it hard to decide.
> For the one spoke wisely, the other clearly.

The pun *sophōs/saphōs*, 'wisely'/'clearly', adds a verbal similarity to the difficulty of determining the significant difference.

On the question of the city, Euripides begins with a fantasy of military success by aerial bombardment of the enemy with vinegar (1437–41);[149] but then, with a change of tack and tone, he offers a general political solution, which first provokes Dionysus to ask for something 'less learned and more clear' (ἀμαθέστερον ... καὶ σαφέστερον 1444–5), but then prompts the god to exclaim (1451): εὖ γ' ὦ Παλάμηδες, ὦ σοφωτάτη φύσις, 'A fine solution, O Palamedes, O nature most wise' (*sophos*). It might seem, then, that Euripides is the *sophos* poet, and is not the *saphēs* poet: Dionysus eulogizes Euripides (or is Dionysus' extreme praise highly sarcastic?) first as Palamedes, a paradigm of ingenuity and Gorgianic rhetoric, and second as a nature 'most wise'. Euripides' proposal is that, if the city through putting itself into the hands of certain individuals is in difficulty, then its fortunes will change when it puts itself into the care of other citizens. Euripides' advice broaches the same subject as the parabasis: 'which citizens should the city use (χρᾶσθαι)?' His answer, like that of the chorus, is not to trust those who are now being trusted.

---

[149] On the textual problems in these lines, see MacDowell (1975). For further discussion of the political import of this scene, see Foley (1988).

This answer is now, however, in the mouth of the Aristophanic Euripides (who is immediately asked (1452) if he thought of such a plan himself: it turns out Cephisophon is responsible for the vinegar). Does the repetition in this different context, in this different voice, further emphasize the seriousness of the advice of the poet?[150] Or does the repetition (re)introduce doubt about the seriousness of the poet's voice?[151] Is Dionysus' (eulogistic or sarcastic) response a comment also on the chorus' advice, or only on Euripides' version of it?

Aeschylus, too, expresses his lack of respect for the citizens who lead the city, but offers his advice in a highly Delphic manner that has provoked much critical discussion.[152] Its mention of wealth, however, leads Dionysus to raise a laugh at the expense (in both senses) of the pay for jurymen.[153] Can Aeschylus' argument be said straightforwardly to confirm the seriousness of the chorus' position? Or does the context of the comic *agōn* also affect this figure as the *sophos* for the city? Is his advice the policy of a previous generation and how seriously should another piece of old-style wisdom be taken? Can Aristophanic parody be read to resolve the negotiation of ambivalence that it sets in motion?

The debate reaches its climax in Dionysus' decision to take Aeschylus. Yet Dionysus' critical reasoning here once more shows the purloining of the poet's voice that is so in evidence in the *agōn*. Euripides reminds him of his oath to take him back to earth, and Dionysus replies (1471):

ἡ γλῶττ' ὀμώμοκ' ... Αἰσχύλον δ' αἱρήσομαι.

My tongue has sworn, but I will take Aeschylus.

The god purloins the infamous line of Euripides' *Hippolytus* in order to desert its author. He uses a Euripidean argument to prefer the other poet. Indeed, in a process repeated three times, Dionysus shows the benefit of the *sophia* of Euripides – to choose the *sophia* of Aeschylus. Is this the ultimate criticism of Euripides, to show how his own lines can be turned

---

[150] As e.g. Sommerstein (1974) 24 assumes without argument: 'Euripides in 1446–50 has offered what Aristophanes clearly thinks a highly relevant and essentially correct piece of advice, since it is advice already given in the parabasis.'

[151] 'Euripides' cleverness is shown up finally as frivolous and irresponsible' (Reckford (1987) 430 following Wills (1969)). On the scene as a whole, see MacDowell (1975) and, on Dionysus' decision, Erbse (1975).

[152] For a useful survey of the question, see Sommerstein (1974).

[153] Sommerstein (1974) 26, however – reading otherwise – fails to find anything funny in this line, which, for him, 'is not so much a buffooning comment as a serious remark on the treatment of a sacred cow, even in times of crisis, of the daily pay of thousands of jurors'. And the *Wasps*?

against him? Or is this Dionysus learning from the poet, using (χρᾶσθαι) the poet's *sophia*? Which poet has the last word?

In the *agōn* and its final judgment, then, there is a highly complex dissemination of tragic poetry through the various levels of parody, a dissemination which constantly works to destabilize the poet's voice (as the production and expression of a stable identity). 'Who speaks?' – as Barthes asks[154] – is a question posed in all its complexity by Aristophanes' play with its search for a poet and for the evaluation of a poet's *sophia*.

The question 'Who speaks?', however, is also the focus of the scenes immediately before the parabasis, which I have already briefly mentioned. Dionysus and his servant swap and reswap the costume of Heracles – each time to the detriment of Dionysus – and this scene of dressing and re-dressing on stage, like the costuming of Pentheus by Dionysus in Euripides' *Bacchae*, has been often seen by critics as a perfect example of drama's ability to reflect its own processes, to act out its own strategies of fictional representation. Indeed, the conclusion of this scene consists in master and slave both being beaten so that the identity of the immortal and the mortal can be distinguished. The blows are meted out in turn with increasing violence and increasingly violent reactions. Yet there is no difference apparent between human and god in response. Indeed, Dionysus is moved to call on his brother (659–61):

Dio.   Apollo! ... 'you who hold Delos or Pytho'.
Xan.   He was hurt. Didn't you hear?
Dio.   Not I.
        I was just remembering a verse of Hipponax.

Once again, the recitation of poetry is a mask of parody, as Dionysus attempts to prove his identity (but disguise his pain). In this similarity of reaction between the figures of Dionysus and Xanthias, is there a suggestion of the common and ineluctable physicality of two human actors – each trying to maintain his role of a figure trying to maintain his role?

The very opening lines of the play show this self-reflexive manipulation of the question 'Who speaks?' (1–2):

Xan.   Shall I say one of the usual things, master?
        The things the audience always laughs at?

Both the (self-)awareness of the theatrical event and the presupposed model of parody – the 'usual thing' must be assumed by each audience

---

[154] (1974) especially 48–9.

member – pave the way for Dionysus to refer to those 'usual things', quoting catch-phrases in, as it were, inverted commas (and so the Oxford Classical Text and Budé print) (3):

ΔΙ. νὴ τὸν Δί᾽ ὅ τι βούλει γε, πλὴν 'πιέζομαι'.

Dio. By god, what you want, except 'I'm loaded'.

Dionysus cites one of the usual lines, in order to preclude it being told: the archetypal comic appropriation – which purloins in order to mark its own superiority, the *Aufhebung* of the practice of others, only to remake the joke by the parodic repetition with a difference. So Xanthias complains about the unfulfilled potential of his entrance – a self-rectifying complaint (12–14):

Xan. Why should I carry these bags, then,
      if I'll do none of the things Phrynichus
      usually does, and Lykis and Ameipsias,
      when they carry bags every time in their comedies?

And this comic editorial comment in the script is turned finally to the utilization of the cliché – suitably fenced with ironic self-awareness – in order to tell the joke again (19–20):

Ξα. ὦ τρισκακοδαίμων ἄρ᾽ ὁ τράχηλος οὑτοσί,
      ὅτι θλίβεται μέν, τὸ δὲ γέλοιον οὐκ ἐρεῖ.

Xan. O thrice unfortunate is this neck, then,
      that it gets the rubbing, but not the joke.

This opening exchange, then, is a paradigmatic demonstration of the logic of the comic purloining of the poet's voice. The inverted commas of comedy are both an act of appropriation and the mark of the ever present potential for reading otherwise – comic inversion. Pursuing the signature of Aristophanes in this writing can never escape the design of comedy which by these comic inverted commas both parades and parodies the act of speaking out.

The public production of poetry in a city whose institutions are dominated by the contest of public voices provides the framework for Aristophanic comedy, and in the *Frogs* in particular forms the basis of its subject-matter and plays of comic parody. Through Aristophanic writing, the role of the poet – speaking out as a *sophos* – is claimed, manipulated, parodied, undermined in a series of dizzying variations. If in the *Frogs* the comic poet appears to appropriate the role of the *sophos* over and above the tragic poets, it is an appropriation which cannot evade its ambivalent formulation and context – the inverted commas of comic inversion. (The comic and the serious are not opposed in Aristophanes' writing but mutually infect each other's status). Aristophanic comedy and the *Frogs* in particular, with its search by the god of theatre for a poet, its depictions of poets, its parodic dissemination of tragic poetry, is a fundamental body of writing for the consideration of the poet's voice. For Aristophanic comedy shows most vividly how, as I wrote in the introduction to this book, the search for the poet's voice entails the negotiation of the interrelated problematics of representation, self-reflexivity and intertextuality . . .

4   Framing, polyphony and desire: Theocritus and Hellenistic poetics

> How could you say I do anything so foul and abject as to state?
>
> Henry James

σικχαίνω πάντα τὰ δημόσια, 'I loathe everything to do with The People', writes Callimachus, and this (public) turning away from the public poetry of the fifth century is a stance, a gesture, repeated in a multiformity of guises throughout the texts of the Hellenistic period. Although the practices of literary production, performance and circulation are known in even less detail for this period than for the fifth century (and many questions about, say, the constitution of the public of Hellenistic literature are simply not answerable with any security), none the less there are much discussed and highly significant shifts both in the conditions of literary production and in the presentation of the poet's voice which require some brief introductory remarks.

While in the fifth century 'citizenship' is the sign through which the boundaries of the racial, cultural, economic group are articulated, in the Hellenistic writers a sense of community, a sense of to whom poetry is addressed and from what position poetry is produced, is quite differently formulated and contested. The poet's gesture of withdrawal from the persona of the public *sophos*, who speaks out to the citizen body, finds an institutional analogue in the Mouseion and Library in Alexandria (from where much of the poetry I shall be discussing in this and the next chapter is written). The *polis* as context and community for the major cultural products of the fifth century is supplanted by the Library, which is the first and largest attempt in the ancient world to create an inclusive archive of the writing of the past and present, and by the Mouseion, in which scholars from the Greek-speaking world were collected to pursue research and teaching. This cultural enterprise proceeded under the patronage of successive monarchs of the Ptolemaic dynasty, whose courts formed the small Greek elite in Alexandria – which at that time was the largest city in the world with a huge population of which Egyptians and other non-Greeks constituted the vast majority. Social and intellectual exclusivity, then – however wide the readership for Alexandrian poetry is supposed to have been – is as integral to the contextualization of Hellenistic writing as the values and institutions of collectivity and open-ness are to fifth-century theatre.

Writing from within the archive profoundly informs the role of the Hellenistic *sophos*. Crucial aspects of scholarship and its apparatus are established at this time and become deeply involved with the sense of poetic *sophia*. It is not merely that, as for the English Metaphysical poets or the fifth-century *sophoi*, writing poetry is a cultural activity that is not dissociated (to use Eliot's term) from physical, medical, philosophical and historical research. It is rather that the institutions of the Library and the Mouseion construct literary and scientific knowledge *as institutions*: the categorizing, collecting, cataloguing of material; the prescrip-tive rules of literary method; the critical annotation of past texts – emble-matic activity of the Hellenistic scholars – develop even further than did the Athenian Academy the possibilities of institutionalizing knowledge (both in the sense of formulating knowledge in and as disciplines, and in the sense of setting a group of individuals within an institutional frame-work for pursuing knowledge). At all levels of writing, the formulation of *sophia* within such an institutionalization of knowledge is a distinc-tive element of the Hellenistic poetry to be discussed in the following chapters.

The archive as context for poetic production is also seen in the con-stant, even obsessional, awareness of past texts. The poet, as Posidippus puts it, has a soul ἐν βύβλοις πεπονημένη, 'worked out in books'. This is seen not only in the fascination with details of earlier writing but also in a search for novelty in narrative and technique through an active response to and manipulation of the texts of the past. The past is in all senses *written through*. Indeed, this constant interplay with the texts of the past is a mark also of a self-awareness of position within a poetic tradition, a self-reflexive concern for the composition of poetry, expressed within poetry, that makes the Hellenistic writers fundamental for my discussion of the poet's voice.

This self-aware sense of belatedness in poetic tradition, coupled with the particular claims of Hellenistic poetic *sophia*, produces a complex concern with poetic authority that is further fuelled by the recognized importance of prose as a medium for serious communication. After Herodotus' and Thucydides' contributions to the narratives of war, Plato's analysis of desire, Aristotle's investigation of the natural world, the authority of, say, Homer, the lyric poets, Hesiod as privileged exposi-tors of the world (and the authority of those writing within such a poetic tradition) becomes subject to less certain validation. In the Hellenistic era, to write as a poet and with a self-conscious affiliation to a tradition of poetic *sophia* necessarily involves negotiating a problematized conception of intellectual, social and literary authority – as it involves the complex task of self-representation within such contests of authorization.

Exclusivity, scholarship, self-reflexiveness, acute awareness of the poetic past – these characteristics have provided a framework for many recent discussions of Hellenistic poetry, and, as several commentators have stressed (since each of these traits can be found to varying degrees in earlier poets), it is both the particular combination and the particular intensity of such characteristics that distinguish the poetry of the Hellenistic period. My brief and very general remarks here are intended as an introduction – and context for – the detailed studies of the following two chapters, which will extend, qualify and explore such generalizations through readings of particular Hellenistic poems. In the present chapter, I shall be investigating the problem of the poet's voice in some poems of Theocritus, with particular attention to the interlocking concerns of irony, distancing and the multiplication of speaking voices in the construction of a poetic stance. In the final chapter of the book, I will return to epic and, specifically, the *Argonautica* of Apollonius Rhodius, to discuss in particular the relations with the past inscribed in Hellenistic poetics.

THE PROGRAMMATIC VOICE

I wish to start with a poem that has long been recognized as basic to understanding the poetic voice in Theocritus, *Idyll* 7. It is the most closely studied of Theocritus' poems, and that the poem has a certain programmatic force has been regularly and persuasively argued by the many critics who have used this work above all others to demonstrate the 'essential nature' of Theocritus' pastoral poetry.[1] Indeed, the explicit discussion in the poem of how poetry is to be written (conjoined with the two examples of Lycidas' and Simichidas' songs); the echoes of the

---

[1] See in particular the articles of Cataudella (1955) (with bibliography of earlier discussion 159–61); Kühn (1958); van Groningen (1959); Puelma (1960); Cameron (1963); Luck (1966); Giangrande (1968); Williams (1971); Seeck (1975); Miles (1977); Segal (1981) 110ff; Berger (1984); E. Bowie (1985); Walsh (1985); Goldhill (1986b); and the relevant sections of Rosenmeyer (1969); Ott (1969); Serrao (1971); Halperin (1983), who shows how these discussions are intimately connected with the definition of 'pastoral'.

famous scene in Hesiod where Hesiod is invested as a poet (the so-called *Dichterweihe*); the image of the journey itself; have all been seen as creating this sense of a programmatic statement. That Theocritus becomes the founding figure of the genre of pastoral adds further significance to such a sense of programme.[2] Yet it is a poem that continues to provoke extended discussion and disagreement – a debate which stems in part at least from the elaborate ironies surrounding the idea of poetic persona in this poem.

The poem is a first-person narrative and it opens by setting this narrative in the past (1–2):

> Once upon a time, I and Eukritos were going
> from the city to Haleis, and Amyntas made up the party.

'Once upon a time', ἧς χρόνος ἄνικα, represents the narrator 'as looking back on something which has become remote to him either through lapse of time or through great change of circumstances'.[3] It is a personal narrative but one from which the narrator immediately distances himself. (So, too, the journey, as befits a pastoral programme, sets a distance from and an origin in the city.) If there is a certain specificity, an *effet du réel*, invoked by the use of the proper names of both the place of destination, the narrator's companions and, in the following lines (3–6), the deity of the harvest festival and its hosts and their lineage,[4] there remains an uncertain significance, an air of 'remoteness', conjured by the poem's temporal framework. This opening combination of precision and blurring[5] of the marks of placement and recognition is repeated at key junctures of the poem and bears significantly on the programmatic construction of the poet's voice.

The honorific lineage of the harvest festival's hosts leads back to Chalcon, the creator also of the spring at Bourine (6–9):

> Χάλκωνος, Βούριναν ὃς ἐκ ποδὸς ἄνυε κράναν
> εὖ ἐνερεισάμενος πέτρα γόνυ· ταὶ δὲ παρ' αὐτὰν
> αἴγειροι πτελέαι τε ἐύσκιον ἄλσος ὕφαινον
> χλωροῖσιν πετάλοισι κατηρεφέες κομόωσαι.

---

[2] See Poggioli (1974); Empson (1960); Rosenmeyer (1969); Van Sickle (1976); Ettin (1984); and, for the most detailed discussion of the development of the genre with regard to Theocritus, Halperin (1983).

[3] Dover (1971) 150–1 ad 1. Wilamowitz (1924) 142 calls it 'eine unbestimmte Ferne'.

[4] The geographical specificity has prompted much discussion of a positivist type: see Arnott (1979) and most recently Zanker (1983); but also, more promisingly, Krevans (1983).

[5] Segal (1981) 163 calls it a 'blending of imprecision and specificity'; Lasserre (1959) 324 'volontairement imprécise et cependant réelle'.

> Chalcon, who made the spring Bourine by his foot
> when he set his knee against the rock. By the spring
> poplars and elms weave[6] a well-shaded grove,
> waving, overarching with green leaves.

Halperin[7] compares this passage with the description in the *Odyssey* of a spring (κρήνη) on Ithaca – also man-made and also surrounded by a grove – by which the disguised Odysseus and Eumaeus, journeying from the country to the city, meet and argue with Melanthius, the evil goatherd (*Od.* 17.204ff). The violence of Homer's scene – an exchange of insults between herdsmen – is replayed in Theocritus as a poetic competition between herdsmen: 'the tension in the Homeric narrative, with its careful character drawing, its anticipation and artful postponement of Odysseus' revenge, is diffused in Theocritus' richly evocative narrative with its new set of challenges and rivalries'.[8] So, Homer's description of the grove – a topography replete with normative, social significance, as with all the geography of the *Odyssey* – is diffused through Theocritus' narrative. Homer mentions an altar to the Nymphs, where wayfarers make offerings, above where the cold water of a stream pours down (*Od.* 17.210–11). Simichidas, the wayfarer, claims to have learned his poetry in the hills from the Nymphs (91–3), and ends at the harvest festival sitting where the sacred water pours down from the cave of the Nymphs (135–7), and finally addressing the Nymphs in prayer and libation (148–54). The *Odyssey*'s conjunction of a rural setting and an epic scale provides a source of thematic continuity – a literary genealogy – for Theocritean pastoral, as well as a model to be rewritten and turned away from in the Hellenistic resistance to epic grandeur.

Yet by recalling this Homeric description of a grove not as the setting for action but as the end of a genealogy the narrative has taken another direction also. In Homer, a figure briefly mentioned (in a genealogy or even in an *aristeia*) is often characterized with a short, vivid description. Here, however, the physical details of the hero's knee on the rock and the creation of the spring turn to a lengthier portrayal of the grove (as if

---

[6] ὕφαινον is an emendation by Heinsius accepted by most editors, but recently Hatzikosta (1982) ad loc. has defended the manuscript reading.

[7] (1983) 224–7. Hatzikosta (1982) 35 ad 8 writes – apparently without irony – that 'localities with springs shaded by trees' constitute 'a topos'. For this observation he amusingly cites Giangrande *CR* 79 (1965) 279, which is merely a statement of approval for the work of Seelback (1964)! On the *locus amoenus* in this poem, see now Pearce (1988) and on the name Bourine as a play on the poetic associations of the Hippocrene fountain, see the fine work of Krevans (1983) 210–12.

[8] Halperin (1983) 227.

the hero's tale is a foil to the description of the natural surroundings). Whereas the genealogy of the Homeric Glaucus finds an analogy and contrast in the world of trees and leaves, here the grove forms the conclusion of the genealogical narrative (as the opening lines of the poem arrive in a *locus amoenus*). The genealogy ends in a pastoral scene as does the programmatic journey of the poem. Indeed, this first description of a 'green bower' establishes a focus, a direction that will be returned to throughout the poem.

The encounter with Lycidas forms the centre of the poem (10–131). As befits the poetic significance of the meeting, it is placed under the aegis of the Muses: ἐσθλὸν ξὺν Μοίσαισι Κυδωνικὸν εὕρομες ἄνδρα: 'we fell in with a good man of Kudonia by the grace of the Muses'.[9] This figure of the goatherd, Lycidas, is a character whose façade critics have loved to pierce.[10] There are many hints that Lycidas is not what he seems; in particular, critics have pointed to the pervasive parallels with encounters with disguised divinities in the *Odyssey*, the strange smile (19–20), the authoritative gift of the staff (43ff). It is important to note, however, how Theocritus points towards the possibility of hidden identity while studiously avoiding any direct statement (13–14):

> ἦς δ᾽ αἰπόλος, οὐδέ κέ τίς νιν
> ἠγνοίησεν ἰδών, ἐπεὶ αἰπόλῳ ἔξοχ᾽ ἐῴκει.

> He was a goatherd, nor could anyone fail
> to recognize him by sight, since he appeared extremely like a goatherd.

No one could fail to recognize Lycidas as a goatherd because he looked extraordinarily like one. The suggestion of appearance in ἐῴκει, 'looked like',[11] may imply an opposition to reality, particularly with the qualification ἔξοχ᾽, 'extremely', 'especially', which as Gow notes, often 'involves a term of comparison expressed or implied' and which 'if pressed here ... would possibly lend a little colour to the universal view that Lycidas is not a goatherd at all'.[12] The suggestion that Lycidas looks just like what he seems – with the descriptive details of shaggy coat reaking of rennet, broad belt and wild-olive staff (16–18) – introduces a

---

[9] Segal (1981) 128 suggests ξὺν Μοίσαισι may also qualify ἐσθλόν, 'good by the grace of the Muses'. Lycidas is later called 'dear to the Muses' (95).

[10] See in particular Segal (1981) 119–29; Williams (1971); Brown (1981); Bowie (1985) and, for a survey of the earlier literature on the topic, Cataudella (1955) 159–61.

[11] On this word in epiphanies, see Cameron (1963) especially 303.

[12] Gow (1950) 135 ad 14. Williams (1971) shows well how some of the hints in this passage suggest that Lycidas may be 'like' Apollo in his epiphany as poetic inspirer.

series of hints that he may not be what he seems. A doubt is introduced? Yet precisely what is not provided is adequate, clear information to move with certainty beyond that doubt.

The nature of the first-person narrative is important to this hesitation in secure recognition. The picture of Lycidas and the poetic exchange is developed only through the viewpoint of one of the participants: there is no authoritative narrative persona. So there is no narrator to strip the disguise (as there is in Homer), no narrator to evaluate the exchange between the smiling Lycidas and the narrator. So – and this is paradigmatic of the difficulties introduced by a first-person narrator – when the narrator first replied to Lycidas, he describes himself as speaking (42) *epitades*, 'purposefully'. Yet what the purpose is remains a question for the reader's interpretation. This lack of a controlling overview not only restricts our secure understanding of the narrative, but constantly gives the impression of observing a strangely playful encounter where we can never quite grasp the rules of the game.[13]

The status of the first-person narrative is further put at stake in Lycidas' opening address (19–21):

> And with a quiet grin he spoke
> with smiling eyes, and laughter hung on his lips:
> 'Simichidas, where now are you walking at midday ...?'

The *ego* of the poem, so far unnamed, is now identified as 'Simichidas'. With such a delayed naming in the first-person narrative, Theocritus both hints at an autobiographical tale but refuses to place himself in the poem. It is a *Dichterweihe* where the *Dichter* has absented himself. Since the time of the scholia at least, the question as to whether 'Simichidas' is to be taken as representing Theocritus has been earnestly considered. On the one hand, that poets can be referred to by such patronymics or other sobriquets is exemplified by the scholia's identification in this poem of 'Sicelidas' (40) as Asclepiades. (There is similar evidence for other Hellenistic and earlier poets.)[14] On the other hand, as I have discussed in chapter 2, there are acute difficulties in the assumption of many ancient and some modern critics that the poet's use of the term 'I' necessarily refers to the figure of the poet himself (as autobiographical exposure). Ancient biographical writers have certainly taken 'Simichidas' as a mask for Theocritus, and it is reported in the scholia to this line that some

---

[13] 'Hier wird uns ein Geplänkel vorgeführt, dessen Spielregeln wir nicht ganz durchschauen' (Seeck (1975) 198).

[14] See e.g. Gow (1950) 127–9; Dover (1971) 146–8.

claim 'Simichos' to have been the name of Theocritus' father, and that others treat 'Simichidas' as a sobriquet for Theocritus because the poet was snub-nosed (*simos*). There is even a counter-suggestion that if Theocritus is represented in this poem it is in the guise of Eukritos, the companion mentioned in the first line, whose name differs in only one letter from one possible Coan form of the poet's name: *Theukritos/ Eukritos*. The name of Theocritus' father is given in his own *Epigram* 29 and – hence? – in the Suidas as Praxagoras, and there seems little reason to doubt that the ancient explanations of the name 'Simichidas' are prompted by the assumption that 'Simichidas' and '*ego*' refer directly to Theocritus. So, too, since this poem is set on Cos, biographers, ancient and modern, have tried – from meagre evidence – to construct a biography that includes Cos as well as Sicily (where Theocritus claims and is claimed by other writers to come from) and Alexandria. This debate on the identification of Simichidas with Theocritus is strictly speaking unresolvable. (Even if the assumption is made that Simichidas represents Theocritus, the question must be reframed as to why the poet represents himself through another name, a 'comic *persona*'[15].) And this uncertainty – which is demonstrated by the very earliest comments on the poem – is important. On the one hand, this is a *Dichterweihe* – an encounter which normally represents the poet's instruction by a divine figure – where the identity of both participants is opened to question. A playful distance is introduced, a move away from direct (self-)representation[16] (as there is a temporal distance marked from the present and a distance from the city). On the other hand, this sense of uncertain identity is also instrumental in diffusing the scene of instruction within the programmatic narrative: as we will see, Lycidas and Simichidas exchange songs and commentary on the songs; and the relation between these elements and the definition of poetic instruction has been endlessly debated by critics. It is in part the suggestion of ironic masking and disguise that creates the difficulty of securely positioning the programmatic force of this poem.

The identification of the characters in the *Dichterweihe*, then, is playfully laid open to a certain doubt. What of the exchange itself? Lycidas laughingly questions where Simichidas is going (21–6) and his final

---

[15] Halperin (1983) 245. The comic side of Simichidas is emphasized by Hatzikosta (1982) and Giangrande (1968).

[16] See Seeck (1975) 199–200; Segal (1981) 125. Rosenmeyer (1969) 63 writes 'We may wish to identify the narrator with Theocritus himself; but the author wards off the identification, or rather plays cat and mouse with it, by interposing the name Simichidas, which is not a *Shlusselname*, but a device to bar the ego ...'

remark introduces what becomes a constant association of bucolic poetry
– the pathetic fallacy whereby the natural world is not merely the subject
or inspiration of song but the producer of it (25–6):

> As you go, every stone
> flying by your feet sings at your shoes.

Simichidas' reply – spoken, as we have seen, 'purposefully' (42) – not
only answers the question (31–3) but also frames this response with
comments on poetry and singing. He immediately recognizes Lycidas as
an outstanding musician (28–9) (though one with whom he hopes to
compete on an equal basis). So, he claims himself to be (37) the 'clear
mouthpiece of the Muses' (Μοισᾶν καπυρὸν στόμα) – a representation
which may seem to connect him to the sources of archaic inspiration, to
the image of the poet as the conduit of the Muses' outpourings; at the
same time, he qualifies his boast that 'all call me the best singer', by
professing his inferiority to Sicelidas (Asclepiades) and Philetas – contemporary or at least modern poetic figures. This self-representation
within competitive, poetic terms frames an invitation, a challenge to sing
(35–6):

> But come: a common road and a common day:
> let us sing bucolic songs. Each, perhaps, will profit the other.

The common road and time, the promise of common benefit, will lead
to an exchange of songs: βουκολιασδώμεσθα: 'Let us sing country/
bucolic songs'. As Halperin (1983) most recently and in greatest depth
has shown, this term seems to be marking the development of a new generic impulse, a claim of a new poetic voice. The surprising expression of
Simichidas' challenge suggests that it is in the exchange of songs that this
new generic impulse will – in part at least – be instantiated. Simichidas'
challenge, however, leads Lycidas first to offer him his staff (43–4). This
gesture, as many critics have noted, echoes Hesiod's famous verses in the
Theogony (22–35) where he is invested by the Muses with his poetic
vocation by the present of a sceptre.[17] Yet the relation to Hesiod's poetry
here needs to be specified. For the scene Theocritus represents is not so
much a Hesiodic moment of truth as a meeting between apparent poets/
herdsmen which is consciously likened to such a moment by one of its
laughing participants: it is only after the agreement to exchange bucolic

---

[17] See in particular Puelma (1960); Serrao (1971) 44–5; Giangrande (1968); Segal (1981)
112ff; Zagagi (1984). For the affiliation of Hellenistic poetics to Hesiod in contradistinction to Homer, see in general Reinsch-Werner (1976); Van Sickle (1976).

songs that Lycidas promises Simichidas the gift of the staff, and the very offer is constituted as a pun (43–4):

> 'τάν τοι', ἔφα, 'κορύναν δωρύττομαι, οὕνεκεν ἐσσί
> πᾶν ἐπ' ἀλαθείᾳ πεπλασμένον ἐκ Διὸς ἔρνος.'

> 'I grant you my staff', he said, 'because you are
> a sapling made up by Zeus wholly for the truth.'

'I grant you my *stick* because you are a *sapling*' (*ernos*). The Hesiodic sceptre of the Muses becomes a shepherd's staff, the authorization of the poet's voice becomes in Lycidas' mouth a play on words between poets.

What, however, does πᾶν ἐπ' ἀλαθείᾳ πεπλασμένον –translated above 'made up . . . wholly for the truth' – mean? Dover comments that 'Lycidas treats Simichidas as a young tree "moulded" into the right shape by Zeus – the god of the weather' – though, as he himself notes, ἐπ' ἀλαθείᾳ, 'for truth', does not fall into the metaphorical field of ἔρνος, 'sapling', and ἐκ Διός, 'by Zeus'. πεπλασμένον, 'made up', 'moulded', may also have the connotation of 'fabricated', which gives an almost paradoxical feel to the phrase ἐπ' ἀλαθείᾳ, 'fabricated for truth', 'made up for truth'. The expression ἐπ' ἀλαθείᾳ is also rare and hard to construe with any certainty.[18] Here Dover suggests that it merely implies Simichidas is a young man who has 'grown up to tell the truth'. Gow translates more suggestively 'fashioned all for truth', and Walsh glosses the line 'Simichidas is a "made up" character created with an eye to the truth.'[19] What none of these commentators stresses, however, is that here we see the Hellenistic writer referring back to the traditional claim of the poet. It was the Muses' power that gave Hesiod his privileged access to truth; so, too, authorization for the special potency of the sceptre is traced to the king of the gods. Here, the echo of the grandeur of the past – by another process of affiliation and distancing – is significantly in the mouth of the goatherd as he promises his stick to the young, already composing Simichidas. Simichidas is described as 'fabricated for (or with) truth' rather than proclaiming himself the authorized singer of the truth of things. There may also be a certain ironic devaluation – or at any rate redirection – of 'truth' from what is Hesiod's divine access to cosmogony and cosmology to Simichidas' description of his friend Aratus' love affair. The construction of the poetic voice within the poetry in terms of truth

---

[18] I have discussed the linguistic problems of this line at greater length in Goldhill (1986b) 50–1.

[19] Walsh (1985) 19.

and valorization is carefully fenced with evasive ironies here at the very moment of its apparent authorization. The phrasing of Lycidas' courtesy, then, with its evident alignments with the past language of poetic vocation, by its very manipulation and reordering of such language draws attention to its rhetoric of poetics (beyond mere courtesy) and opens a question of its significance which is hard to answer with certainty (precisely because of its *playing* with the clichés of poetic authority). Such evasive strategies of praise, courtesy and authority will be returned to, especially in the fourth section of this chapter.

Lycidas introduces his own song with a statement of poetic principle that sets his verse clearly in terms of the metaphors of the small scale, of the modern and of the distance from Homeric grandeur that typify the so-called Callimachean contribution to Alexandrian poetics. The verb he uses to describe his composing is *exeponasa*, 'I have fully toiled away at' – that is, the careful activity of the poet rather than the unmediated inspiration of the Muses. He marks his acceptance of Simichidas' invitation with a phrase that echoes the offer closely (49): ἀλλ' ἄγε βουκολικᾶς ταχέως ἀρξώμεθ' ἀοιδᾶς, 'come let us begin a bucolic song', 'a song of the country', and the echo in terminology (*boukoliasdōmestha/boukolikas ... aoidas*) seems to restress the new generic impulse. The definition of this 'bucolic' poetry, however, and what constitutes pastoral as such has been a recurring problem of Theocritean studies (as well as literary criticism in general). What is, then, the truly pastoral voice here? Is it that of the townsman on his way to the pastoral festival with his description of the leafy bower (7–9) where the trees, like poets, weave a grove? The discussion of Simichidas and Lycidas seems to be anchored in contemporary poetics both in its terminology and in its specific reference to recent poets. The 'bucolic song' is introduced here by Lycidas as such and it is a song within a song. Is it, then, Lycidas' carefully worked set-piece (52–89) which is to be regarded as the new bucolic poetry promised by the programmatic poem? In its delicate sophistication it is indeed easy to see this poem as the work of the modern poet and critics have been quick to catalogue elements in it that become commonplaces of the pastoral tradition.[20] Lycidas' song is a *propemptikon*, a song for the occasion of the beginning of another's journey – in this case, Ageanax's trip to Mitylene. Lycidas pictures himself by the fire celebrating the safe arrival of Ageanax, his lover (63–70). Two shepherds will flute and Tityros will sing how Daphnis the cowherd once loved Xenea (71–3). The song

[20] For discussion and survey of the literature, see Segal (1981) 135–48.

within the song turns to a further embedded song of another (pastoral) love affair. The song of Tityros, what is more, seems to suggest a different mythical level from the frame: it is no longer contemporary poets like Philetas and Asclepiades but the 'mythical' pastoral singer Daphnis sung of by Tityros in Lycidas's song. And for Daphnis a song of mourning is sung by the natural world (74–7):

> χὣς ὄρος ἀμφεπονεῖτο καὶ ὡς δρύες αὐτὸν ἐθρήνευν
> Ἱμέρα αἵτε φύοντι παρ' ὄχθαισιν ποταμοῖο,
> εὖτε χιὼν ὥς τις κατετάκετο μακρὸν ὑφ' Αἷμον
> ἢ Ἄθω ἢ Ῥοδόπαν ἢ Καύκασον ἐσχατόωντα.

[He sung]   Also how the mountains toiled in grief, and how the oaks
            which grow on the river Himera's banks, sung a dirge,
            when he was melting away like snow on high Haemus
            or Athos or Rhodope or the farthest Caucasus.

Ampheponeito, 'toiled' (in grief) (like *exeponasa*, 'thoroughly toiled' (51)) and *ethrēneun*, 'sung a dirge', imply the poetic laments which form part of what becomes the standard pastoral poetic fallacy of exchange of songs between poet and landscape – a poetic fallacy already hinted at in the stones that 'sing' at Simichidas' feet. Is this song of Tityros, then, the pastoral song – with its recognizably pastoral characters, Daphnis and weeping nature, its mythic distance from the present?

A further song will be sung: ἀσεῖ δ' ὥς ποκ' (78), 'he will sing how once', repeats ἀσεῖ δ' ὥς ποκα (72–3), 'he will sing how once'. This second song of Tityros will be of a goatherd (like Lycidas) who is another famous singer, another mythic figure, Comatas. Are Comatas – a name which appears in less exalted circumstances elsewhere in Theocritean verse[21] – and Lycidas inhabiting the same mythic world? What is the connection between the two songs of Tityros – the dying cowherd Daphnis and the dead goatherd Comatas? This Comatas, a singer within the song within the song within the song is within ... a box (78–82):

> He will sing how once a wide box received that goatherd
> alive – through the evil presumption of a king;
> and how the blunt-faced bees came from the meadow
> to the fragrant cedar chest and fed him on soft flowers
> because the Muse had poured sweet nectar on his lips.

---

[21] See *Idyll* 5, where a Comatas and a Lacon argue about buggery and theft and even (45ff) which *locus* is the suitably *amoenus* one for their singing match: a sort of inverse of *Idyll* 1.

The chest is part of a veritable Chinese box effect of songs within songs, frame upon frame, as each song's content becomes the frame for the next song. The description of Comatas' boxed-in existence is also a network of images of poetic composition, as once again the programmatic poem brings the language of poetics to the fore. The bees bring honey to the sweet cedar chest, because of the nectar the Muse had poured on Comatas' lips[22] – an image of composition strikingly different from Lycidas' self-representation as the toiling, working poet (as it recalls Simichidas' claim to be the clear mouthpiece (στόμα 37, στόματος 82) of the Muses). The next lines seem playfully to manipulate this difference (83–5):

> ὦ μακαριστὲ Κομᾶτα, τύ θην τάδε τερπνὰ πεπόνθεις
> καὶ τὺ κατεκλάσθης ἐς λάρνακα, καὶ τὺ μελισσᾶν
> κηρία φερβόμενος ἔτος ὥριον ἐξεπόνασας.

> O blessed Comatas, yours is this sweet suffering.
> You too were shut in a coffer; you too, fed on honeycomb,
> fully toiled away the springtime of the year.

The blessed Comatas' sweet suffering (*peponthas*) is described as 'fully toiling away' the spring: *exeponasas* is the same verb as Lycidas markedly used to express his process of composition (51). Is this, then, the expression of the poetic work of Comatas? Does it link the figures of Lycidas and Comatas (as pastoral poets in a poetic affiliation)?[23] Is the singing of Comatas the pastoral voice we are seeking out?

The address 'O blessed Comatas' is recalled in the final words of Delphis' song (86–9):

> If only you had been numbered among the living
> in my day, so that I might have herded your fine goats
> on the mountain, listening to your voice, as you lay
> under oak or pine sweetly singing, divine Comatas!

The two vocatives frame the final lines of the song, but it is hard to tell the provenance of the apostrophe. Is it a quotation of Tityros' song, a more vivid expression than the reported speech with which the song began? Or is it Lycidas' own wish to have heard Comatas? In the reces-

---

[22] On bees see e.g. Waszink (1974), which is more useful than Usener (1902), though neither discuss this nor any Theocritean passage; on nectar Poliakoff (1980); on sweetness Edquist (1974) and Hunter (1983) (primarily on later material).

[23] καί ... καί suggests Comatas has a parallel figure, which, as Hatzikosta (1982) ad loc. suggests, may link Daphnis and Lycidas and Comatas within a tradition of poetic suffering and support by the Muses.

sion of voices that constitutes this song within a song within a song, the possibility of securely attributing the final lines to a certain, unified poetic voice is undercut. The referent for ἐμοῦ, 'I', 'in *my* day', is uncertain. We are left merely with the expressed desire to have heard (in a pastoral setting) a former (pastoral?) poet, whose honeyed words are concealed within the box-like recession of other poets' (pastoral?) songs.

Lycidas' song, writes Dover, 'is essentially bucolic in character as is made plain not only by its interest in Daphnis and Komatas but also by the name "Tityros"'.[24] A more sophisticated analysis is required. For there seems to be with the various singing herdsmen a series of different levels, a recession towards a lost mythic world where *once* Daphnis loved, where *once* Comatas was put in a cedar chest. As the opening words of the poem mark a remoteness, so Lycidas' song of an imagined party after his lover has gone sings of another lost world (or worlds). It is as if the instantiation of bucolic poetry in the programmatic poem comes complete with a history of past pastoral, or as if an essential part of the 'bucolic muse' is the desire for what is *lost*, from Lycidas' desire for Ageanax, through Daphnis' pining love for Xenea, through nature's loss of Daphnis, to the poem's loss of Comatas. The sophisticated city hankering for the absent world of the country finds expression in this recession of songs of desire and loss.

Seeck has well observed that the very device of a song within a song can be seen as a reaction to the problematic status of writing poetry in the Hellenistic age: 'in der Zeit Theokrits ist das Dichten problematisch geworden, und das Gedicht im Gedicht ist ein Reaktion auf die kritische Verunsicherung; die Position des Dichters war fraglich geworden und wird reflektierend wiederhergestellt'.[25] Two of Seeck's arguments are particularly relevant here. First, he claims that the poet's self-conscious adoption of a persona (or personas) develops a multiplicity of points of view rather than an authoritative viewpoint; second, he argues that in this way the poet distances himself from concrete reality – an unwillingness to seem to offer a direct, unmediated portrayal of things. Both of these points are crucial to understanding how the form of this poem – the song within the song(s) – introduces a tension into its programmatic expression.

Simichidas' reaction to Lycidas' song is to offer as a gesture of honour to Lycidas his own outstanding work (94–5), which, the traveller from

---

[24] (1971) 155 ad 52–89.
[25] Seeck (1975) 203. I have discussed Seeck's article in more depth in Goldhill (1986b) 31–2.

the city explains, the Nymphs taught him while he was herding in the hills (91–3):

> 'Dear Lycidas, many other songs
> have the Nymphs taught me too, herding [*boukoleonta*] in the hills;
> fine songs, of which report has perhaps reached even to Zeus' throne.'

In view of the invitation to sing country songs (*boukoliasdōmestha* 36) and Lycidas' announcement of a *boukolikas aoidas* (49), a 'country song', the expression *boukoleonta*, 'herding', may indeed be a hold metaphor, as Gow translates, 'I too have bucolic inspiration.'[26] That his songs have reached the throne of Zeus, however, has often been taken to suggest not simply hyperbolic self-promotion (scarcely tempered by *pou*, 'perhaps', 'I suppose'), but more specifically that Simichidas' poetry has had the attention of Ptolemy Philadelphus. (Praise of the Hellenistic monarch, particularly in *Idyll* 17, seems elsewhere to assimilate his rule to that of the king of the gods.)[27] As Simichidas seems to mark his new bucolic muse, so his self-praise draws on the associations of poetry, praise and the patron that, as I have discussed in chapter 2, is so important in the ancient Greek tradition.

One may expect, then, that Simichidas will sing a 'bucolic song' of similar scope to that of Lycidas. His song, however, calling on Pan to help Aratus in an unhappy love affair shows the sophistication, literary allusiveness and elusiveness of other Hellenistic love poetry. Dover, once again looking for the pastoral essence, comments that the bucolic element 'is constituted essentially by Pan ... because of his association with the countryside',[28] and indeed Pan is mentioned, among other things, as tending a flock (113). None the less, much of the song may well seem far in tone and content from what Dover calls the 'essentially bucolic' and quite different – as many critics have noted – from Lycidas' elegant yearnings. Is Simichidas' proffered song another aspect of 'bucolic poetry' (lost love, failed desire)? Or is it rather the evident differences in tone and subject matter between the two songs that should be stressed (e.g. to indicate Simichidas' failing 'attempt to appear a convincing "campagnard"'[29])? Or is 'the bucolic' to be located *in the relation between* the songs of the goatherd and the man from the city? Once again, the framing of a song within a song leads not to the control and order of an argument and exemplum but to a more problematic *interplay of difference*.

---

[26] See on this word Giangrande (1968) 509–11.
[27] See Dover (1971) 159 ad 93 for the arguments and evidence.
[28] Dover (1971) 159 ad 96–127.   [29] Hatzikosta (1982) 148 ad 97.

Both songs appear under the aegis of *boukoliasdōmestha*, 'let us sing country song'. Yet rather than exemplifying the 'essentially bucolic' in any straightforwardly programmatic manner, the multiplicity of exemplary voices invokes a complex network of differences (that has opened the way to much interpretative effort).[30] Indeed, it seems that the attempt to draw up criteria for the 'essentially bucolic' by which each poem's bucolic content can be calculated seems destined for failure precisely because of this multiplicity of voices within the programmatic stance.[31] Theocritus absents himself from his programmatic poem and multiplies the programmatic utterance into a polyphony of voices, voices against voices, voices within voices. Can the assertion of a unified, single poetic voice – the 'essentially bucolic' – do more than oversimplify this polyphony?

In response to Simichidas' poem, Lycidas presents him with the staff (as the guest-gift of the Muses (129–30)), and in an extraordinarily swift transition (130–1) the scene shifts to the pastoral festival (131–57). We are in another *locus amoenus*, and if there was the smallest hint of the poetic, inspirational aspect of the landscape in the earlier description of nature, this closing description is full of suggestive echoes. The holy water of the Nymphs bubbles (137).[32] The cicadas 'chatter' (λαλαγεῦντες 139) and toil (ἔχον πόνον 139): the cicada is often associated particularly with Callimachus' self-representation in the prologue to the *Aetia* but it is also associated with poets' singing elsewhere.[33] 'Toil' (*ekhon ponon*) what is more, seems to echo 'toil thoroughly' (*ekponein*) of Lycidas' composition and Comatas' 'work' in the box. The nightingale (139) 'murmurs' (τρύζεσχεν 140); the birds 'sing' (ἄειδον 141); the dove 'moans' (ἔστενε 141). The bees – associated with Comatas and the Muses earlier – fly around. Once more, the landscape seems invested with a mythopoetic force.[34] How does this description relate to the song of

[30] For examples and discussion see Segal (1981) 135–153.

[31] Dover (1971) 159 ad 96–127, in what seems almost a parody of positivism, says that the 'bucolic element' of Simichidas' song is to be located in 'twelve lines out of thirty-two'.

[32] On water and inspiration, see Kambylis (1965) 110–24.

[33] See Crane (1986). On the *tettix* (cicada) in general, see King (1986) and the reply of Segal (1986a).

[34] On possible poetic associations of σχοῖνος, the 'reed' (133) on which they lie, see Goldhill (1987a) and, from a different perspective, Cairns (1984a) 104 and 110. It is difficult to know what Dick (1968) 33 means when he writes that 'The only Greek Pastoral poem which uses the pathetic fallacy for symbolic purposes is the pseudo-Moschus *Lament for Bion*.' For a general discussion of the representation of the country in Theocritus, see now Reinhardt (1988).

nature mourning Daphnis' death? On the one hand, the journey that began at the beginning of the *Idyll* finds its conclusion in a pastoral *locus* that is not only resonant with metaphors applicable to poetic composition, but also criss-crossed with references and allusions to the poetry of the past, both at the level of linguistic detail[35] and in the references to Heracles, Chiron and the Cyclops with which Simichidas praises the wine at the festival (149–53). As a programmatic journey it ends suitably in a poetic grove. But on the other hand, there is also a significant uncertainty, introduced by this heightened metaphoric description, particularly after the song of Lycidas. Is Simichidas' experience of the festival, or rather, his *representation* of this experience of the festival, to be thought of in the same way as nature's mourning for Daphnis, that is, as if Simichidas and Delphis may be thought to inhabit the same pastoral world? Or, to take a radically opposed view, is this passage merely a heightened, even a 'sham ... overzealous',[36] way of saying that there was singing at the country festival? Or – a third view – is this passage designed to show the connection between the pastoral world of Daphnis and the pastoral world of Simichidas (while maintaining a difference between the two)? How do the references to the lost world of Cyclops, Heracles and Chiron function here? Are they on a par with Daphnis and Comatas? Can the repetition of pastoral pathetic fallacy and the citations of earlier poetry not introduce the divisions and divisiveness of difference into the *locus amoenus*?

There is, in other words, considerable difficulty in determining a secure frame of reference in this poem. The interplays of metaphorical and mythical language seem deliberately to problematize the development of a single, unified level of enunciation. It is hard to agree with Segal when he writes 'In *Idyll* 7 ... Theocritus is able to generate an inclusive mythical frame for his bucolic world';[37] and harder still to agree with Snell when he writes: 'Theocritus' scene is mythical and he keeps that atmosphere free of any intrusions.'[38] Rather, the mythological world of *Idyll* 7 shows a tendency towards fracture and polyphony that can be repressed only at the expense of the subtlety of the poetry. Indeed, as I shall be arguing in further detail in the second section of this chapter, Theocritus' pervasive strategy of framing is precisely (and at first sight paradoxically) what rules out *inclusiveness* for Theocritus' pastoral pic-

---

[35] Well catalogued in the editions of Gow (1950); Dover (1971); Hatzikosta (1982).

[36] Hatzikosta (1982) 200 ad 139; he is following Giangrande (1968) somewhat overzealously here, as in many other places in his edition.

[37] Segal (1981) 190.   [38] Snell (1953) 283.

tures. The self-awareness of – and the difficulties introduced by – the gesture of framing (with its questions of exclusivity, inclusion and fragmentation) are crucial to Hellenistic poetics, and here provide a fundamental element of the irony, complexity and evasiveness that inform Theocritus' programmatic stance.

The programmatic journey of *Idyll* 7, then, is crucial for a discussion of the poet's voice in Theocritus. It seems to be leading us towards the establishment of a new pastoral poetics, but the songs within songs, the recession of frames, the ironic fragmentation of the programmatic statement, all seem to undercut the clear and straightforward progression of that journey, all seem to resist the direct and comprehensive – inclusive – statement of poetics. Perhaps we should regard this very fragmentation and polyphony as the final poetic imperative of Theocritean writing.

The first *Idyll* of Theocritus also holds a special place in the criticism of the Theocritean corpus and stands in a particular relation to *Idyll* 7. For although it does not have the explicit discussions of poetic technique of *Idyll* 7, this poem has also been taken as demonstrating in a privileged way the nature of bucolic song. In particular, the form of the poem – a dialogue between two herdsmen – has been seen as paradigmatic of Theocritus' representation of shepherds' song.[39] What is more, the dialogue – set in a *locus amoenus* – includes an exchange between the two figures, Thyrsis and a goatherd, where the goatherd describes and presents Thyrsis with a decorated cup (as well as a goat) in return for a song. This description of a work of art within a poem (an *ekphrasis*) both in the manner of representation and in the scenes represented has seemed to offer a particular picture of the Theocritean 'pastoral world', much as the shield of Achilles in the *Iliad* – which stands at the head of a poetic tradition of *ekphrasis* – plays a crucial role in the narrative of the *Iliad* and its sense of the boundaries, limits and nature of human activity. So, too, the song which Thyrsis sings marks its genre by repeating three regular refrains, each of which uses the term βουκολικᾶς ἀοιδᾶς, 'song of the country', 'bucolic (*boukolikas*) song' – and the song's subject is Daphnis, the archetypal herdsman, who forms the first theme of Tityros' song to Lycidas in *Idyll* 7. Each of these elements, then, has led to *Idyll* 1 being considered as especially instructive for understanding the bucolic voice of Theocritus and I wish to discuss this poem very briefly by way of conclusion to this section on the programmatic voice.

---

[39] For discussion of this with bibliography, see Halperin (1983) 162–2; Cairns (1984a).

The bucolic song of Thyrsis is elaborately framed. It is introduced by the goatherd's praises for Thyrsis' singing (7–11), and in particular for Thyrsis' skill in bucolic song (19–20), and it prompts similar remarks at the end (146–8). The specific subject of Daphnis is requested by the goatherd (19 and 61 'desired song'). The goat and the cup are offered for the song, described at length (23–61) and then presented after the song (149–50). The *locus amoenus* is described in similar terms at the beginning and the end of the *Idyll*.[40] Thyrsis begins with the first use of the refrain ἄρχετε βουκολικᾶς, Μοῖσαι φίλαι, ἄρχετ' ἀοιδᾶς, 'Lead, Muses dear, lead the bucolic song', and the first stanza opens with a signature and brief self-praise for the poet's voice (65): 'This is Thyrsis from Aetna and the voice of Thyrsis is sweet.' The song itself is of the mortal woes of Daphnis, as requested, and the death of this herdsman prompts a response not merely from the natural world (pathetic fallacy) but also from the gods themselves who attend and take part in his final scene. Like *Idyll* 7, then, the 'bucolic song' is explicitly set off from the surrounding scenario: it is a song within the poem marked generically by the term 'bucolic' (*boukolikas*), and it is a song of a past (pastoral) world, a poet lost to the present. As we will see, like *Idyll* 7's bucolic songs, the song of Thyrsis also produces questions about its relations with the framing scene.

Yet there is a further crucial strand to the (programmatic) force of this song within a song. There are three successive refrains in the song: ἄρχετε βουκολικᾶς, Μοῖσαι φίλαι, ἄρχετ' ἀοιδᾶς, 'Lead, Muses dear, lead the bucolic song' (64, 70, 73, 76, 79, 84, 89): ἄρχετε βουκολικᾶς, Μοῖσαι, πάλιν ἄρχετ' ἀοιδᾶς, 'Lead, Muses, lead again the bucolic song' (94, 99, 104, 108, 114, 119, 122); λήγετε βουκολικᾶς, Μοῖσαι, ἴτε λήγετ' ἀοιδᾶς, 'Cease, Muses, come cease the bucolic song' (127, 131, 137, 142).[41] Part of the originality of Theocritus' writing is to form a piece around such a repetitive motif, which seems to be a mimesis of the most traditional, least personal of poetic voices (in a poem the poetics of which seem aligned to ideals of delicacy, subtlety, sophisticated variation – a contrast established by the opening juxtaposition of a refrain with its appeal to the Muses as source and a signature with its claim of a proper name's

---

[40] Segal (1981) discusses at length what he calls (40) these 'heavily articulated enframing motifs'.

[41] Gow (1950) 15–17 ad 64–142 discusses the surprisingly solid manuscript tradition for the irregular spacing of these refrains and resists all attempts at transposition or regularization.

individuality and individual performance).[42] The mimesis of song –
a mimesis around which so much of Theocritean poetry revolves –
alternates the allusive and elusive tale of Daphnis with a repetitive marker
of 'simple country song-making'. Indeed, each voicing of the refrain
punctuates the narrative of Delphis' melting away (τάκειν 66, 82, 88, 91),
thus producing a series of fragments, each framed by a pair of refrains.
One refrain even interrupts the course of a sentence (81–5):

> Priapus came and said
> 'Poor Daphnis, why are you melting away? The girl
> wanders through all the springs, through all the groves; for you –
> begin, Muses dear, being the bucolic song –
> is she searching. Ah, you are too crossed in love and helpless!

On the one hand, this fragmentation, by offering selected aspects of
what is apparently a more extensive narrative, forms a fundamental
element of the sense of mystery that pervades the story of Daphnis: both
the details that are offered (such as Daphnis' final 'going to the stream'
to die (139–40)) and the gaps in the narrative (such as a lack of a coherent
pattern of cause and effect for Daphnis' woes) constantly brook a reader's
attempt to produce a simple, coherent story for Daphnis, and, as critics
from the scholia onwards have found, while many elements of Daphnis'
tale find suggestive parallels in other mythic narratives, no one other
story of Daphnis or any other figure matches – and thus could explain or
control – all the details offered here.[43] As in *Idyll* 7, the pastoral song
within the song hints towards a pastoral world, only discontinuous fragments of which it offers: the song of Daphnis (melting away and finally
sinking into the river in death) dissolves at critical junctures into suggestive uncertainty. The repeated refrain, then – as a performative utterance,
as a marker of rustic singing – contrasts with the particular obscurity of

---

[42] A brief refrain is sometimes found in hymns, paeans and other choral poetry – though
nowhere to the extent of this Theocritean example. It is regularly assumed that such
refrains are part of a folk tradition utilized by Theocritus for his fiction of the bucolic.
In *Idyll* 2, discussed below, the refrain is taken as a sign of the unsophisticated, ritual
magic of Simaetha, though refrains are an important aspect of many religious performances in Greek culture. See Fraenkel (1950) 73–4 ad 121; Fantuzzi (1985) 25–9 ad 1
and 2; 158–9.

[43] Segal (1981) 25–65 discusses with bibliography these problems. He concludes (36) that
'If Theocritus is aware of the traditional version … he has … transformed it within
his own narrative to make its familiar content virtually unrecognizable.' He also notes
rightly how even Ogilvie (1962), who argues that a traditional story can be perceived in
Theocritus' version, concludes that the poet (108) 'has veiled the whole story in a cloak
of allusive obscurity'.

the narrative of the loss of Daphnis, its gaps, its uncertainties, its studied uncanniness.

On the other hand, such fragmentation must also be seen as part of the evident complementarity of cup and song (as objects of exchange) in this *Idyll*. For one element that has been repeatedly seen by critics as paradigmatic of Theocritean poetry is the representation of the three scenes on the cup, where the very form of fragmentary vignette (as well as the focus of the vignettes) has been taken as an indication of Theocritean affiliation to Hellenistic poetic of discontinuous, sophisticated lightness (especially in contrast with the apparently inclusive cosmological representation of, say, Achilles' shield).[44] In different ways, then, the representation of the song and the representation of the cup significantly manipulate the framed vignette, the poetic fragment. Indeed, in as much as the *ekphrasis* and the song within the song can be seen as framed, discrete elements, the *Idyll* itself demonstrates a narrative which 'se déstructure, s'atomise en une site lâche de morceaux brillants, juxtaposés selon une modèle rhapsodique' (as Barthes defines the rhetorical *topos* of *ekphrasis* itself) – Theocritus' *Idyll*, like the *ekphrasis*, is 'un fragment anthologique'.[45]

Much as the figure of Daphnis, the pathetic fallacy and the active involvement of deities are elements that recur in Theocritean verse and in the later pastoral tradition, many elements of the cup's three ivy-framed scenes of the lovers arguing, the old man fishing and the child plaiting a grasshopper cage, while two foxes plunder his vineyard and steal his lunch, have been seen to express the stylistic and thematic range of Theocritus' *Idylls*. For example, critics have emphasized the rejection of the grand heroic paradigm in favour of the marginal figures of the old and the young, engaged in tasks far from heroic; the variation between the old man's *ponos* (where it is the lowly task and its physical strain that are brought into focus) and the child's concentration on plaiting while being gulled (where the image of the child, the brief humorous episode of pastoral work and the suggestion of an image of poetics in weaving are all significant); the humorously distanced scene of failed *eros*; the choice of a cup itself (rather than a shield or temple doors).[46] In each of these

---

[44] For extensive discussion and bibliography, see Halperin (1983) especially 161–89.

[45] Barthes (1970) 183. So Segal, in a fine phrase (1981) 7, calls the Hellenistic poets 'bold collagists of heterogeneous fragments'.

[46] These points are drawn from Halperin (1983) 161–89 with bibliography 161 n. 50; Segal (1981) 25–46; Lawall (1967) 28ff; Walker (1980) 30ff; Rosenmeyer (1969) 91; Fabiano (1971).

aspects, the representation of the cup has been taken to map a 'distinctive geography',[47] programmatic for Theocritus' poetry. Yet this complementarity of song to cup, the shared poetic of the vignette, cannot be allowed to efface completely the differences between the pastoral worlds represented. For there is, as Segal in particular has emphasized, a disjunction between the paradigm of a pastoral fiction that makes up Thyrsis' song, and the paradigmatic fictions of pastoral represented on the cup: the doom-laden, uncanny narrative of Daphnis, a past world and dying poet *contrasts* with the brief amusing pictures of workaday life in the country. Both Thyrsis' song within the poem and the *ekphrasis* of the cup, then, seem to offer privileged images of pastoral scenes, and also to pose a question of difference and complementarity – much as do the bucolic songs of *Idyll* 7.

What, then, of the *locus amoenus* in which the exchange of cup and song takes place? The *locus amoenus* – represented in the opening exchange of Thyrsis and the goatherd – constitutes a frame for the framed vignettes.[48] The complementarity of singer and the natural world in the *locus amoenus* is immediately stressed (1–3):

> Sweet is the whispered music which that pine makes,
> that one, yonder, by the spring; sweet too do you
> pipe.

This version of pathetic fallacy is conjoined with the performers' elaborate compliments which compare their poetry and playing to that of the Muses and the gods (3–4, 8–11); and the gods play a further part in the pastoral scene (15–18):

> It is not right, shepherd, it is not right for us at noon
> to pipe. We fear Pan. For at that time he rests

---

[47] Segal (1981) 27.

[48] In the treatment of *ekphrasis* in rhetorical theory, there exists a tension between on the one hand regarding such descriptive passages as mere ornamentation to the work of narrative, even as scandalous delay and flippancy; and, on the other hand, placing such passages under the rubric of *ut pictura poiesis* – where the sister arts of painting and poetry support each other's pictorial capacity (*enargeia*) as crucial factors of persuasion. The difficult opposition of description to narrative is rendered quite unstable for a poem such as *Idyll* 1, where the dramatic dialogue and series of frames of description constitute the poem's narrative as an exchange of *ekphrases*. For a history of the treatment of *ekphrasis* see Hagstrum (1958) who emphasizes Lessing's reworking of classical models as a turning-point in the modern era, for which see also Todorov (1977) 161–78; Lee (1967) 8 n. 29, 20–3, 66, 68–9. For *ut pictura poiesis*, see also Lee (1967) *passim*; Praz (1970); and in particular Baxandall (1971). For modern attempts to treat the rhetorical status of ecphrastic description, see e.g. Hamon (1981); Beaujour (1981). I discuss the relevant topic of framing with further bibliography in the second section of this chapter.

> tired from the hunt. He is bitter,
> and sharp anger is ever ready in his look.

Is this recitation of pastoral lore about a divinity of a piece with the divine drama of the woes of Daphnis, where divinities also walk the pastoral stage? Or is the exchange of shepherd and goatherd itself a vignette similar rather to the scenes on the cup and to be set in contrast with the absent frame of Daphnis' world?[49] The cup and the song constitute pastoral fictions within the frame of the pastoral fiction of the *locus amoenus*, and these representative fictions offer contrasts and similarities that are hard to resolve into a single pastoral scene, a single frame of reference. As in *Idyll* 7, the recession of frames produces a complex multiplicity of pastoral voices, a polyphony within the pastoral scene(s).

The closing lines of Thyrsis, however, raise in a fascinating way the question of the complementarity and difference of pastoral frames. After the death of Daphnis, and a last refrain, Thyrsis continues (143–5):

> And you give me the goat and the cup, so that I may milk it
> and pour a libation to the Muses. O farewell, Muses,
> many times farewell. I will sing more sweetly for you in the future too.

Dover and Halperin treat this passage as simply the final lines of Thyrsis' song. Certainly the farewell to the Muses and the promise of a further song are traits typical of the closure of hymns (the *khaire(te)* formula). The address to the goatherd, however, the indication that Thyrsis has performed his side of the bargain, and the suggestion that another ritual, a libation, is now to take place suggest that the song ended with the final refrain (as it had begun with the first use of the refrain). (So Gow and Segal suggest 142 is the final line of the song.)[50] Are these lines part of the mimesis of a pastoral song? Or are they part of the herdsmen meeting and exchanging a cup and a goat for a song? Or are the remarks to the goatherd to be taken as an interruption of the song, which then continues until the final word ᾄσω, 'I will sing'? Can a difference between Theocritus' representation of the pastoral exchange and Theocritus' representation of the bucolic song be heard? In *Idyll* 1, as in *Idyll* 7, a question remains of how similar and how different – *how* complementary – the voices in the poem's dialogue(s) are.

Both *Idyll* 1 and *Idyll* 7, then, contain songs explicitly marked as

---

[49] Segal, who discusses the divine in this poem at length, writes also (1981) 27: 'Each of these *loci* is, in a sense, unreal and artificial, but there are gradations of unreality.'

[50] Segal actually varies in his article between calling 141 and 142 the final line of Thyrsis' song, which may show the discomfort many critics feel with the refrain in this poem.

pastoral, bucolic songs and other elements of programmatic expression. Yet both poems show a multiplying of pastoral scenes, a multiplying of pastoral voices. The profession of poetic voice for Theocritus is constantly being made through this fragmentation, ironic distancing and polyphony. Where the profession of poetic voice, poetic affiliation, may seem to be most evident, then – the *Dichterweihe*, the *ekphrasis*, the 'bucolic song' – the profusion of the voices is most marked. And this tension is a constitutive difficulty in tracing Theocritus' programmatic voice.

THE PASTORAL FRAME

In the previous section of this chapter I have talked about the devices of framing that structure Theocritus' *Idyll* 1 and 7 – the *locus amoenus*, the songs within the poems, the ivy-edged vignettes. There is a further sense of framing that seems to be crucial to Theocritean poetry, namely, the frame constructed by the invocation of an exclusive group as audience, producer and commentator on the pastoral scene. As critics on many periods of pastoral poetry have discussed, pastoral poetry is a response from the city (court) for the city (court) – a varied response, for sure, that ranges across the idealistic, nostalgic, amused, dismissive etc. An implied reader is (in different ways) a construction of all poetry,[51] but both the projection of exclusivity that I have discussed as a typical trait of Hellenistic poetry, and the focus of much of Theocritean poetry on scenes removed from the exclusive group make Theocritus' inscription of an implied reader especially important.

The sophistication of the implied audience of Theocritus' poetry has become a commonplace of modern criticism. The constant resort to esoteric pun, etymological plays and the minutiae of scholarship, allusively manipulated, has led to many critical studies that take for granted in Theocritus' writing (as for Callimachus and Apollonius) a complexity of linguistic playfulness and subtlety that seems to require an audience especially attuned and alive to such intricacies.[52] Yet the dynamics of this

---

[51] The expression 'implied reader' is taken in the first instance from Iser (1974), a study with many *epigonoi*. Two interesting collections of essays are Suleiman and Crossman (1980) and Tompkins (1980), both with extensive further bibliographies to this much-discussed field.

[52] Many of these studies appear under the rubric of *arte allusiva*, a phrase coined by Pasquali in 1951 and passionately defended by Giangrande (1967) and Giangrande (1970) (with bibliography 46 n. 3).

implied sophistication and framing cannot be adequately treated simply by describing Theocritus' poetry as 'written for a fabulously learned court élite'.[53] For, as we will see, Theocritus' framing of a pastoral scene raises crucial questions of how bucolic simplicity can be a model for (literary) sophistication – which in turn raises a question for the sense of hierarchy and difference integral to claims of 'sophistication'.

Idyll 3 is a fine example of how the pastoral scene can invoke a sophisticated audience. It is a dramatic monologue that announces in its first word (κωμάζω) that it is to be a *kōmos*, a revelling, singing procession to serenade a lover. The goatherd requests Tityros to pasture his flocks (1–5) and turns (6) to address Amaryllis. His address is replete with the *topoi* of the *paraclausithyron*, the lover's serenade outside a locked door,[54] but the transposition of this practice of the city to the rustic world makes the performance ironically inappropriate to the setting – the hindrance to his approach, for example, is provided not by a locked door, but by a cave's surrounding of ferns and ivy. So, too, as several critics have pointed out, it is precisely the distortion of the poetic conventions of the genre that creates the poem's humour: so the herdsman moves from a threat to hang himself (9) to the (bathetic) complaint of a headache about which Amaryllis does not care (52); similarly the mythological exempla to which he appeals are recondite stories of successful wooing which are not 'out of place in the mouth of [this] rustic goatherd' only in as much as they are 'wholly in keeping with the poem's basic incongruity of theme and setting'.[55] What is more, not only do each of the goatherd's exemplary male lovers 'go into a decline of one sort or another after achieving union'[56] with the object of desire, but also the exempla – with their suggestions of religious cult and grand religious myth-telling – contribute importantly to the 'poem's juxtaposition of the sombre and the ridiculous'.[57] The poem parodies, then, the self-representations of a lover: it parodies first by the general transposition of a city convention into a bucolic setting (much as *Idyll* 18 depends, in part, first on the irony of composing a wedding song for what will prove to be the most famous example of an adulterous couple[58]); it further parodies the lover by the deliberate trivialization and bathetic articulation of the conventions of erotic self-expression in this goatherd's performance.

---

[53] Hutchinson (1988) 6.
[54] See Cairns (1972) 145–7 for the details.
[55] Lawall (1967) 40, 74.   [56] Rosenmeyer (1969) 174.
[57] Segal (1981) 71.   [58] See Stern (1978) *passim*.

As I have argued with regard to Aristophanic parody in chapter 3, however, it is insufficient to regard such parody merely as 'patronizing humour'[59] directed at the herdsman's 'naively blundering way' of wooing.[60] That is, the 'double reading' required by the double voice of parody inevitably provokes 'the difficulty of recognizing similarity and difference'. Or, in the case of *Idyll* 3, is it only the rusticity of this goatherd that is the object of parody's amusement? When the lover's strategies of self-representation are read – with all the burlesque and distortion of convention – is there to be for the reader no ironic self-recognition of an investment in such conventions? What sort of sophistication is it that finds only patronizing distance (and no self-recognition) in such a satire of the desiring subject?

This question of the exemplarity of even – especially – the parodied figure of desire is posed in *Idyll* 13, which begins not only with an explicit invocation of an audience, but also by the explicit supposition that the audience is to be set parallel to the figure(s) of the poem's erotic narrative (1–5):

> Not for us alone, Nicias, as once we thought, was
> love begotten by whichever god did beget him.
> Not for us first of mortals who do not see tomorrow,
> does the beautiful seem beautiful;
> but even Amphitryon's iron-hearted son . . .

The opening words 'Not for us alone', οὐχ ἁμῖν . . . μόνοις, join the poet and his addressee Nicias: 'as we thought', ὡς ἐδοκεῦμες, points to a shared past of discussion or reflection. The reference to the unknown progenitor of desire – an idea which finds an echo certainly as early as Plato's *Symposium*[61] – also may imply (as a *topos*) a shared world of literary allusion. The repetition of 'not for us', οὐχ ἁμῖν (3), broadens the outlook from Nicias and the poet to the world of humans, which is contrasted with the world of heroes or even divinities with the introduction of Heracles, the figure of desire on whom this *Idyll* focuses (though both the Nymphs and the soon to be deified Hylas also can testify to the power of *eros*). The power of desire over even the heroes and gods, however, is itself a commonplace that stretches back to the *Iliad* with the seduction of Zeus and finds regular expression throughout the fifth century, not least, with regard to Heracles, in Sophocles' *Trachiniae*. It is not only for Nicias and this poet that this argument finds poetic expres-

---

[59] Dover (1971) 113.   [60] Segal (1981) 71.   [61] See *Symp.* 178b.

sion. Indeed, if this poem is didactic advice, starting from the principle that 'a man seriously in love is inclined to feel that no one can ever before have been so afflicted',[62] the erotic message is explored through the 'reassessment of a time-honored hero who is here measured against a contemporary poetic sensibility'.[63] The hero 'does not fit into an erotic situation without losing his heroism',[64] or, at least, in Theocritus, without both the erotic situation and the idea(l)s of heroism being significantly and ironically manipulated. As Heracles rages round the island's undergrowth like a ravening lion, chasing the ever distant voice of Hylas (58–63) – another fading voice, lost in the *locus amoenus* – the (re)inscription of the epic simile in the archetypally allusive, playful Hellenistic narrative can only stress the discontinuities, the disjunctions, with which Theocritus is working in his erotic narrative. The question posed by this poem is in what ways Heracles might be exemplary, in what ways Heracles as an example for Nicias might be exemplary. The figure of Nicias – as implied reader – is part of the figural language of this questioning, this juxtaposition of modern and inherited poetic and erotic languages.

Idyll 11 is perhaps the best example of the critical difficulties produced by the framing of pastoral song, particularly with regard to the question of sophisticated and naive readings. The central section of the *Idyll* and its main claim to the status of pastoral poem is the love song of the lovesick Cyclops, Polyphemus. The brutal monster of the *Odyssey* is taken back to his green youth, and the song itself is an amusing fantasy of what happens to the standard *topoi* of love poetry in the mouth of such a bucolic grotesque: 'whiter than cream cheese', λευκοτέρα πακτᾶς (20), the Cyclops begins his wooing compliments to Galatea, and with the classic line of the ugly but wealthy, he attempts to bribe her with the promise of his rustic riches of a cave and unlimited cheese (34–7). There are numerous lovely touches: the monster's desire to have been born with gills (54–5), for example – a charming addition to his physical attributes – or his fussy pedantry about winter and summer flowers explaining why he can't bring lilies and poppies in the same bouquet (56–9). In particular, his hopes and aspirations are set against the *Odyssey*'s depiction of the monster. 'If only a stranger would come', he muses, 'to teach me how to swim' (60–2), then he would reach his love who may 'burn even his soul and his one eye dearer to him than anything' (52–3). The stranger – a key term in the Cyclops episode in the *Odyssey* – is Odysseus and he

[62] Dover (1971) 181 ad 1.   [63] Mastronarde (1968) 275.   [64] Mastronarde (1968) 288.

will not teach the Cyclops how to swim. Rather, the metaphor of the burning of love, or the rhetorical exaggeration of Polyphemus' extreme willingness to suffer, will be horribly literalized in the putting out of the Cyclops' one eye.

This song of the Cyclops is set within a frame of the poet's address to Nicias, a doctor and a friend – presumably the same Nicias as in *Idyll* 13 – for whom Polyphemus' song is offered as an example of the power of poetry with regard to desire, *eros*. The poem opens with a statement of the potency of the Muses as opposed to drugs and ends with a dig at Nicias' profession with the reprise that Polyphemus fared more easily in this way than if he had paid for medical treatment.

This poem has been extensively discussed in terms of its relation to Hellenistic poetry. The playful metamorphosis of the Homeric monster to a lovesick youth, the discussion of the value of poetry itself, as well as the highly self-conscious parody of the love song genre, the detailed manipulation of earlier, especially Homeric, language have all been seen as typically Hellenistic strategies.[65] The song within the song, as we have seen, is a common technique of Theocritean poetry. In general, however, this device of the framed song within the song has been treated by critics as a formal strategy which makes the meaning of the poem clear. 'First the moral of the poem is set out quite explicitly; the only cure for love is song. This vital clue is picked up in the last lines';[66] 'Theocritus is very explicit ... Polyphemus composed a song ... and this song cured him';[67] 'He organizes his poem as a miniature treatise, complete with thesis (1–6), demonstration (7–79) and recapitulation (80–1).'[68] Cairns' influential reading marks the steps of the argument with admirable clarity:

At the end of the song (80–1), we are told that by singing it Polyphemus cured himself. Theocritus must therefore show the cure occurring in the song. Had Polyphemus behaved like a normal komast, Nikias might well have been unable to see how the Cyclops was helped by singing. The change of mind is therefore both required and guaranteed by the use to which Theocritus puts the story of Polyphemus.[69]

---

[65] On the metamorphosis, see Goldhill (1986b); on the value of poetry, Erbse (1965); Holtsmark (1966); Spofford (1969); Brooke (1971); Horstman (1976) 85–110; Segal (1981) 224–9; on parody and genre, see Legrand (1898) 111–13; Cairns (1972) 143–7; DuQuesnay (1979).

[66] DuQuesnay (1979) 45.   [67] Walker (1980) 41.   [68] Brooke (1971) 73.

[69] Cairns (1972) 147. I will analyse Cairns' argument in depth because it has been especially influential and seems paradigmatic of a range of approaches.

As I shall demonstrate, at each step this argument begs the question. The frame, indeed, rather than establishing a closed structure of generalization and example may be seen as the source and site of the poem's most interesting complexities. For the frame is not merely composed in order to constitute the ironic distance between the world of the sophisticated Nicias/Theocritus and the world of the naive Cyclops (despite their similar afflictions of desire). As we have seen, the sophisticated reader may be implied without such an explicit frame, as in *Idyll* 3. So, in *Idyll* 11, it is insufficient to see the marking of Nicias' talent in all nine Muses (5–6) merely as introducing a need for a close, sophisticated reading of the rapid shifts of tone and the subtle or more obvious jokes of Polyphemus' song. Nor is the frame simply in order to tie the poem to the circumstances of contemporary social life – although the relation between Polyphemus and Nicias will remain important. There is more at stake in the frame.

Gow points to a primary crux of interpretation. He focuses his reading on the last word of line 13, ἀείδων, 'singing'. He comments as follows: 'Song, says T., is the only cure for love as Polyphemus found when in love with Galatea. He was distraught with passion and neglected all his affairs, but he discovered the remedy and thus would hymn his love. T. is here describing the symptoms of Polyphemus' affliction and if one of them is singing, his whole paragraph which asserts that it is not a symptom but a cure, falls to pieces.' Can song be a symptom as well as a cure for desire? Dover tries to find his way around the apparent impasse by glossing the phrase as 'by *persisting* in singing he *eventually* found a remedy he could not have found in any other way'.[70] Neither of the words that Dover needs to emphasize are in the Greek, or even hinted at (unless he is commenting on Theocritus' remark that the cure is not easy to find (4–5)). This solution, however, is worked out in more detail by Holtsmark (1965) and Erbse (1965), who see this poem as a sort of 'talking cure' – a catharsis for Polyphemus who reaches self-knowledge and self-enlightenment finally through his poetry.

Much depends in Erbse's and Holtsmark's readings – as for Cairns, DuQuesnay and Dover – on the final lines of Polyphemus' song (72–9):

ὦ Κύκλωψ Κύκλωψ, πᾷ τὰς φρένας ἐκπεπότασαι;
αἴ κ᾽ ἐνθὼν ταλάρως τε πλέκοις καὶ θαλλὸν ἀμάσας
ταῖς ἄρνεσσι φέροις, τάχα κα πολὺ μᾶλλον ἔχοις νῶν.

---

[70] Dover (1971) ad 13.

τὰν παρεοῖσαν ἄμελγε· τί τόν φεύγοντα διώκεις;
εὑρησεῖς Γαλάτειαν ἴσως καὶ καλλίον᾽ ἄλλαν.
πολλαὶ συμπαίσδεν με κόραι τάν νύκτα κέλονται,
κιχλίζοντι δὲ πᾶσαι, ἐπεί κ᾽ αὐταῖς ὑπακούσω.
δῆλον ὅτ᾽ ἐν τᾷ γᾷ κἠγών τις φαίνομαι ἦμεν.

Ah, Cyclops, Cyclops, where have your wits flown?
You would show more sense if you would go and plait
cheese-baskets and gather greenery for your lambs.
Milk the ewe that's by. Why pursue one who flees?
Another and fairer Galatea you will find, perhaps.
Many a maiden bids me sport the night with her,
and they all titter when I hearken to them.
It is plain that on land I too am a somebody.

The Cyclops rhetorically questions his sanity and explains in a potential clause that he *would* be more sensible *if he were to* go and plait cheese-baskets. There is no sign that he actually does leave or that this question 'Where have your wits flown?' is anything but a rhetorical expression of misery.[71] The lover as madman. A *change* of mind, then? It would seem a strangely indirect way of expressing it. 'Why pursue one who flees?' is a constantly articulated question in Greek love poetry which regularly turns to precisely such unfulfilled and unfulfillable desire as the basis of the erotic encounter. In general, 'love poetry' in Greek is poetry of the *sickness* of *Eros*, poetry of unfulfilled desire. The Cyclops' question marks the continuation of a generic expectation as much as any change of mind. The suggested answer to his questions (finding another and prettier Galatea) is not only undercut by the addition of ἴσως, 'perhaps' – which may be hopeful, or perhaps is despairing or a threat, or just plain doubtful – but also by the flight from one Galatea to the next. The cure for desire seems to be ... another desire. But not quite: for Polyphemus goes on to explain the basis of his hope for a more successful pursuit this time. Many girls call him out to play in the night. συμπαίσδεν, 'to play together', 'disport', is a word whose erotic connotations are common; so too is the giggling with which they greet his attempt to obey them: κιχλίζοντι, 'titter', is used of seductive, lewd or lascivious laughter in particular.[72] Does it follow, however, as DuQuesnay supposes, that 'the giggling of the girls should be understood as genuine enticement: it is sexual laughter

[71] The same expression occurs at *Id.* 2.19, where Simaetha upbraids her servant with the same question: 'Are you mad?'
[72] See Gow (1950) ad loc. for examples.

not mockery'?[73] Is Polyphemus' understanding of an erotic encounter
(presumably, as yet, unfulfilled) to be so trusted? *He* may describe their
laughter as wanton and lascivious, and regard it as genuine enticement,
but is there no possibility that he may have misread (with his one eye)
the girls' expressions – especially when we recall his misunderstanding
of Odysseus? He sees himself as being seen as the object of desire, but
how does he seem in the girls' eyes? As the scholion on the passage
comments ἴσως δὲ καταγελῶσιν αὐτοῦ, 'Perhaps they are laughing at
him'. There may, then, be thought to be something of an irony in
Polyphemus' use of their laughing to show that on land at any rate he is
a somebody. The irony of this final assertion to seem to be a somebody,
however, is not merely because of the character he has displayed throughout the song, but also because of the echo of the famous joke in the
Odyssey. Polyphemus may use the girls' laughter to prove that he seems
a somebody: but it will be Odysseus' joke on the difference between being
a somebody and a nobody which will make him finally a laughing stock.
The Cyclops' assumed status ironically looks forward to his future humi-
liation at the hands (or words) of Odysseus.

So, can we be sure that we are seeing a development of cathartic
self-awareness through song in these final lines? Is this song really a
serious proof of the eventual healing powers of song? What sort of an
example is the Cyclops for the efficacy of love poetry? Indeed, Horstman
and Brooke suggest in different ways that the song demonstrates rather
a necessary self-illusion or self-delusion (that saves the Cyclops from the
despair of thwarted passion).[74] Not so much a cure as a necessary deceit.
To keep going. Is the Cyclops approaching desire with open eye(s) now,
or with careful averting of the gaze of truth? Turning a blind eye?

It is interesting at this point to return to Gow who pointed out the
problem that the song appears to be a symptom of what it was meant to
cure. He goes on to suggest that if we delete lines 1–7, 17–18, 80–1, then
there is nothing in the poem to 'provoke suspicion'.[75] Gow's bizarrely
Draconian solution to his critical problem develops a fundamentally
different line from the critics on whom I have been focusing so far. For
by removing these particular lines, Gow removes any hints that the poem
is about the *cure* for desire at all. For him, Polyphemus' song is a sign
and symptom of desire: 'The whole content of the song ... shows Polyphemus very far from cured.'[76] We would seem to be, then, in a situation

---

[73] (1979) 213.   [74] Brooke (1971) *passim*; Horstman (1976) 95–110.
[75] Gow (1950) ad 13.   [76] Gow (1950) ad 13.

where the exemplum is taken by critics as certain and explicit proof of mutually exclusive and contradictory generalizations. There is certainly something more to be said here.

Yet does not the frame in which Theocritus explains the point of the poem make all 'clear', 'explicit'? How perversely must we read against the grain of the poem to see the song as anything but a demonstration of the efficacy of poetry against desire? The final two lines of the poem are taken as a restatement of the opening expression of song as the only cure for song.

> οὕτω τοι Πολύφαμος ἐποίμαινεν τὸν ἔρωτα
> μουσίσδων, ῥᾷον δὲ διᾶγ᾽ ἢ εἰ χρυσὸν ἔδωκεν.

> So Polyphemus shepherded his desire
> by singing, and fared better than if he had spent gold.

So Cairns, 'We are told that by singing it Polyphemus cured himself.' So, too, DuQuesnay who writes that the conclusion of the poem allows 'the reader no room to doubt that the Cyclops has been successfully cured'.[77] *No* room? Certainly the end of the poem echoes the beginning. ἔρωτα (80), 'desire', echoes ἔρωτα (1), 'desire'; ῥᾷον δὲ διᾶγ᾽ (81), 'fared easier', echoes ῥᾷστα διᾶγ᾽ (7), 'fared most easily', and μουσίσδων (81), 'singing' (and playing), picks up Μοίσαις (6), 'Muses', as well as the sense of Πιερίδες (3), 'Pierian maids', ἀείδων (13), 'singing', ἄειδε (18), 'he used to sing'. So, too, the mention of spending gold (81) may be thought to relate to the rejected use of unguents and salves in the first two lines. But the main verb of the final couplet contains a notable ambiguity which is repressed by most critics in order to maintain their position of certainty: ἐποίμαινεν τὸν ἔρωτα, 'he shepherded his desire'. Polyphemus is doing to his desire what he is not doing to his sheep. In 65 the same verb is used in the expected context of a shepherd and his flock, and, indeed, when ποιμαίνειν, 'shepherd', is used in a metaphorical manner elsewhere it is generally taken to imply 'tend', 'care for', 'nourish'.[78] Can we really see this verb here as implying simply and explicitly the removal, the destruction or even cure of desire? Theocritus' witty final use of *poimainein*, 'shepherd', scarcely resolves any uncertainty whether the love poem really demonstrates the shepherd's cure. As

---

[77] Cairns (1972) 147; DuQuesnay (1979) 47.
[78] See LSJ ποιμαίνω II.1. Cf. the common Homeric expression ποιμένα λαῶν, 'shepherd of the people'. Gow (1950) ad loc. notes the scarcely paralleled sense of 'cheated' – I have discussed this in Goldhill (1986b) 49 n. 64.

Alpers writes, 'The wit largely involves the opacity of "shepherded" (*epoimainen*) which suspends divergent interpretations by saying in effect "saw it through by behaving like the shepherd he was".'[79] The conclusion of Theocritus' moral tale, then, scarcely reduces the problematic nature of the exemplum. What sort of cure is poetry if by singing it Polyphemus is said to 'shepherd his desire'?

Let us return to the beginning of the poem where the problem was first diagnosed by Gow in the form of the awkwardness that both the symptom and the cure for the desire seemed to be singing or writing poetry. Perhaps now that doubleness is beginning to take on a more significant guise. 'Is poetry to be taken as a cure or symptom for desire?' may be more of a question than the critics have allowed for. The key word that occurs in 1 and 17, framing by its repetition the argument which Gow found disturbing, is φάρμακον, *pharmakon*: οὐδὲν ... φάρμακον ἄλλο, there is 'no other *pharmakon*'; ἀλλὰ τὸ φάρμακον εὗρε, 'But he found the *pharmakon*'. So far I have used the translation 'cure', 'remedy', but it is time to mark the doubleness of this key term also. *Pharmakon* means not merely remedy but also poison; not merely cure but also harmful drug, dangerous spell. It develops such meaning particularly in the context of desire.[80] Phaedra's nurse in Euripides' *Hippolytus* promises her a *pharmakon* (516) for her desire for Hippolytus, but it turns out to be a fatal advancement of the tragic chain of events that destroys Phaedra – through *Eros*. So Deianeira in Sophocles' *Trachiniae* smears a *pharmakon* (685) on a robe to win back her husband's love. It proves, however, to be the destruction of Heracles, who cannot escape the poison. One should be very careful about taking a *pharmakon* for love in a naively straightforward way as a cure. It quickly turns to a curse. When Odysseus smears a *pharmakon* on his arrows (*Od.* 1.262 – the only time in Homer that *pharmakon* is used with χρίεσθαι, 'smear', the verb from which ἔγχριστον (2), 'unguent', is derived), it is a poison and a method of attack that no decent man would adopt. What, then, about Aphrodite's weapons fixed in the heart of Polyphemus? Is poetry a love philtre or love cure, then? Read the poem and see ... And the systematic uncertainty we traced particularly at the end of the poem mirrors the doubleness we are finding in the opening statement of poetry as *pharmakon*.

Perhaps a closer look at the opening lines of the *Idyll* is now called for.

---

[79] (1979) 123.
[80] Though not, of course, only desire. My argument inevitably draws on the famous discussion of the *pharmakon* in Plato by Derrida (1981).

No other *pharmakon* is there for desire, Nicias,
neither unguent, it seems to me, nor salve,
but the Muses. This is a light and sweet thing
for mortals – but it is not easy to find.

The *pharmakon* is 'light and sweet' and indeed the poem we are reading
is both 'light' (*kouphon*) and 'sweet' (*ādu*): both terms, especially *ādu*,
'sweet', can be seen as descriptions of Theocritus' Hellenistic poetics
which reject the grandeur and heaviness of the epic and tragic poetry of
the past[81] – but it is also proving, as Theocritus says, 'not easy to find' –
as we try to specify the relation between writing and desire in this text.
The warning's there. This will not be easy.

γινώσκειν δ' οἶμαί τυ καλῶς ἰατρὸν ἐόντα
καὶ ταῖς ἐννέα δὴ πεφιλημένον ἔξοχα Μοίσαις.

I think you know this, as a doctor
and beloved exceedingly by all the nine Muses.

Nicias should be able to recognize the truth of Theocritus' statement
because he is a doctor and the favourite of all the Muses. Nicias' status
as doctor and poet make him especially capable of recognizing the interplay of desire and the *pharmakon* that is poetry. The double status of
Nicias makes him the perfect recipient of the demonstration of the
pharmakon.

οὕτω γοῦν ῥᾶιστα διᾶγ' ὁ Κύκλωψ ὁ παρ' ἁμῖν,
ὡρχαῖος Πολύφαμος, ὅκ' ἤρατο τᾶς Γαλατείας,
ἄρτι γενειάσδων περὶ τὸ στόμα τὼς κροτάφως τε.
ἤρατο δ' οὐ μάλοις οὐδὲ ῥόδῳ οὐδὲ κικίννοις,
ἀλλ' ὀρθαῖς μανίαις, ἁγεῖτο δὲ πάντα πάρεργα.

Thus, at least, my countryman, the Cyclops, ancient
Polyphemus, fared most easily, when, with the down
new on his lips and temples, he loved Galatea.
He loved not with apples or roses or ringlets,
but with genuine frenzy, and he thought all else but trifles.

So, at any rate, the Cyclops, ancient Polyphemus – whose name means
both 'much talked of' and 'of many voices', 'many auguries' – the one
from down the road (Gow's translation 'my countryman' is perhaps a

---

[81] On ἁδύ see Edquist (1974); Kühn (1978) 43 n. 16. I have found no example of κοῦφος in
the context of poetics: but Latin *levis* by which it may be translated is the commonest
term in poetics for those Latin poets affiliating themselves to Callimachus and Theocritus. On treating such terms as 'families', see Hinds (1987) 141 n. 58.

shade too formal for ὁ παρ' ἀμῖν), spent his time most easily when he was in love with Galatea. Poetry is 'not easy' to get hold of, but the Cyclops fared 'most easily' with it. He loved, too, not with apples or the like, but with real frenzy. The apples and roses mark the traditions of the narrative of *Eros* in Greek poetry.[82] But for the Cyclops it is not a question of the signs and demonstrations of love according to the narratives of love poetry. For him, it is the real thing. ὀρθός, 'right', 'real', 'genuine', is a central term in fifth- and fourth-century intellectual discourse. In linguistics and literary criticism it connotes the proper and certain connection of words and the world – the etymological, semantic or phonetic 'rightness' that guarantees the proper use of language.[83] In political language, it implies the right and proper organization of the laws of the state. In less specific terms, it can indicate simply 'right', 'correct'. Perhaps most importantly for my argument here, ὀρθός is a term that can authorize the poet's voice as the voice of truth, that can authorize the poet to speak publicly to citizens as educator, adviser, seer. It is, however, typical of Theocritus, as we have seen, that such a protestation of truth, such a self-authorization of poetic discourse, is fenced and framed with irony. Here, Theocritus prefaces his parodic love song, which draws precisely on the *topoi* of love poetry for its humorous effect, with a denial that Polyphemus' love was just love-token, love-song love, and with the claim that it was the real, proper madness of desire. The parodic is introduced by the claim of the genuine and the real. What's more, the Cyclops may not deal in apples and roses and ringlets; but he does offer cheese and the fruit of the vine and lilies and poppies, and he discusses his facial hair at some length. The 'real thing' is not so far removed from the devices of love poetry as it may at first seem. It is not a straightforward thing to relate the song of Polyphemus to its explanatory frame in terms of the genre of love songs, or to relate παρῳδία to ᾠδή, parody to ode. The sense of 'genuine frenzy' rather than explaining the song to come is set in ironic tension with it. The frame finds itself framed by its contents.

At first sight, this *Idyll* may seem to demonstrate the simple form that the critics have assumed, that is generalization followed by example: truth followed by proof. A thus-we-have-seen conclusion to seal the exchange. On this reading, the humour lies primarily in the grotesque in-

---

[82] Apples are thrown towards a beloved one; the rose is a gift or sign of desire (perhaps because – as Gow suggests – the flower is sacred to Aphrodite, and has its colour from the blood of Adonis). It is less certain what 'ringlets' refers to – I have discussed this further in Goldhill (1986b) 49 n. 68.

[83] See e.g. Pfeiffer (1968) 39–40, 74–5; Guthrie (1969) 205–25.

appropriateness of making a bestial monster the example of the curing power of poetry, and in the parodic nature of the song itself (both of which have rarely seemed to critics to set at risk the possibility of any too serious point about the nature of poetry in this poem). Let us return and see how Cairns frames his argument for this reading: 'At the end of the song (80–1) we are told again that by singing it Polyphemus cures himself.' This represses any suggestion of doubt in the phrase 'shepherded his love', or any sense of development through the poem which might change our sense of the repeated phrases. 'Theocritus must therefore show the cure occurring within the poem.' Despite the 'must' and the 'therefore' this statement does not necessarily follow from the first remark; it ignores any possibility of tension between frame and song, and fails to consider any ambiguity or irony in the final lines in which the cure is supposed to be demonstrated. 'Had Polyphemus behaved like a normal komast' (difficult to imagine) 'Nicias might well have been unable to see how the Cyclops was helped by singing.' It is important for Cairns that there should be no hint of uncertainty in anyone's reading of this poem. 'The change of mind is therefore both required and guaranteed by the use to which Theocritus puts the story of Polyphemus.' Because he thinks it *should* be there, Cairns claims a change of mind *must* be there. But 'the use to which Theocritus puts the story of Polyphemus' is what we may hope to discover by reading the poem, not that by which a reading of the poem is to be judged or authorized. In other words it can be shown that, in order to develop this reading, at each step of his argument Cairns must carefully frame from his view a series of what can be seen as worrying doubts and questions.

What we may term the naive reading of the poem, then, can be maintained only by a systematic glossing over of a certain doubleness in the text. In one guise, it is the doubleness of song as both symptom and cure, song as *pharmakon*. It is the uncertainty whether the song shows the Cyclops as cured or maintaining, even creating, his love. This makes the joke neatly double-edged, particularly if we care to assume that the *Idyll* is written for a lovesick Nicias, as most critics do. The figure of fun in the poem is not merely Polyphemus, but also Nicias, the implied, inscribed reader. Not merely in the unflattering comparison with Polyphemus as lover, but also and more precisely in the suggestion that in performing love poetry – like this *Idyll* – the lovesick reader is fostering his love even if he approaches the text as an attempt to cure his desire. The general frame of reference implied by 'among mortals' (4) or by placing the Cyclops amongst us as 'our countryman' is relevant. We –

the sophisticated Nicias and us – may read *Idyll* 11 for an expression and example of the cure for desire. What we get also, however, if we do not adopt the blinkered naivety of a Cyclopean reading, is the surprising suggestion that in the very act of reading or singing the poem, we, like Polyphemus, are actually fostering and helping to maintain our desire. It is not only Polyphemus who is framed by Theocritus' poem. The joke, then, is not on the naive reader – finally – but on the *sophisticated*. As we perform by singing a poem which professes to tell us what happens to those who sing poems, the superiority of the sophisticated reader to the naive is twisted to mark the uncertainty of even the sophisticated control over the poem (and over desire). As Wright puts it in another context, 'Instead of the reader getting hold of the story . . . the reading effect is that of the story getting hold of the readers, catching them out in a fiction of mastery'[84] – a fiction I will be discussing at further length in the following section of this chapter. It is the canny, intelligent reader who finds himself for all his suspicion repeating the passage of the text. The figure of fun is inverted.

This specific analysis leads to a more general reflection on framing – and framing is a gesture integral to pastoral poetics: the *locus amoenus*, the embedded songs, the *ekphrasis*, the implied audience of an exclusive group. For the relation between generalization and example that I have been tracing in this *Idyll* shows how a certain excess, a supplement, is produced in the interplay of difference between frame and framed – which is the source of the interpretative difficulties of the text. Jacques Derrida, in one of the most scrupulous analyses of the devices of framing, calls this problematic interplay the 'logic of the parergon',[85] and argues that 'the structure of framing effects is such that no totalization of the border is even possible. The frames are always framed: thus, by some of their content.'[86] Indeed, we have seen in *Idyll* 11 that, for example, the song of the Cyclops necessarily becomes the defining *frame* of reference for its own (defining) introductory phrase ὀρθαῖς μανίαις, 'genuine frenzy'. The frame in *Idyll* 11, in other words, cannot be treated as Polyphemus treated all his work, as a *parergon* to the *ergon* of the love song.

---

[84] Wright (1984) 131.

[85] Derrida (1978) 21–168; also (1975) 99. 'Framing' has become an important area of literary research: see Dällenbach (1977); Caws (1985) with further bibliography; and of sociological research, particularly after Goffman (1974); and, of course, in art, see e.g. Bryson (1981).

[86] Derrida (1975) 99. From which Ulmer (1984) 102 concludes simply and directly, 'The logic of the parergon, then, defeats conceptual closure.'

By which I mean that the framework cannot be considered simply as an explanatory preface and summing up conclusion, as if it were somehow outside the poem proper, as if Theocritus' explanation, his signature, *in* the poem were not *part* of the poem. And/or as if there could be a critic's explanation outside the poem that did not partake in the same game of framing, the same glossing contagion of text on text, frame on frame – as the implied reader becomes the implicated reader, as the figure of fun turns and turns about. The frame, then, cannot be treated as if it were a figure of clarification, control and order (through the rigid delimitation of inside and outside, argument and example); rather the frame, as the source and site of difference, is the figure which always already undermines the rigid determination of the boundaries of sense, the sense of boundaries. As Barbara Johnson writes: 'The total inclusion of the frame is both mandatory and impossible. The frame thus becomes not the borderline between the inside and the outside, but precisely what subverts the applicability of the inside/outside polarity to the act of interpretation.'[87] There is, then, a certain interplay between the naive and the sophisticated readings of this poem which cannot be regarded simply in terms of a hierarchical opposition. The sophisticated reading finds itself framed, entrapped, as does the naive. It is not simply a question of a complex poem's ambiguities, but rather – more scrupulously – an ambiguity about how ambiguously the poem should be read. To quote Barbara Johnson again from her brilliant piece "The Frame of Reference':[88] 'The "undeterminable" is not opposed to the determinable; "dissemination" is not opposed to repetition. If we could be sure of the difference between the determinable and the undeterminable, the undeterminable would be comprehended within the determinable. What is undecidable is whether a thing is undecidable or not.' How serious an example is Polyphemus' song, then?

The interplay, the *oscillation*, between naive and sophisticated readings – *how* serious a reading to offer, *how* far to go – seems a constant outcome of the framing inherent in pastoral poetry (dramatized forcibly in the framing opposition of the world of Nicias and Theocritus and the world of Polyphemus). The attempt to comprehend the naivety of bucolic life within the textual artifice of poetry or painting not only requires a framing gesture but also replays again and again the divisions and divisiveness set in motion by the logic of the frame. The bucolic masque always divides us from the picture it invites us to see ourselves in: a never-never

---

[87] Johnson (1980) 128.   [88] Johnson (1980) 146.

or always-already land of sameness *and* difference in which the Cyclops has to be ὁ παρ' ἁμῖν, one who is *para* to us, who parodies, is a parody, who displays the (paradoxical) parergonal logic of the frame.[89] Of being relative. (Relatively sophisticated. More or less wealthy.) Of what the frame is . . . about. Or (to put it otherwise) there is always a *pharmakon* in the green cabinet.

Framing, then, is both fundamental to pastoral poetics – and a fundamental source of the interpretative difficulties and the pleasures pastoral poetry provides.

THE LOVER'S VOICE: THE SUBJECT OF DESIRE

The subject of *eros* is central to much of the poetry of the Hellenistic era. The *Odyssey* is, as I have discussed, concerned with the proper ordering of sexual relations within the *oikos*, and tragedy again and again turns to the destructive capabilities of desire within the structures of the tragic city. Sympotic poets, such as Anacreon and Theognis, chart the twists and turns of the narratives of *eros* with irony and self-aware humour (as they develop a normative model for erotic interaction). And Plato's *Symposium* can be seen as philosophy's encounter with such a social and intellectual institution. Yet even within such an extensive tradition Hellenistic poetry seems to show a particular and heightened concern for *eros* as a topic for poetry. Not only is *eros* the explicit focus of a great number of poems of different genres from epic to epigram, but also the acute awareness of the tradition of writing on *eros*, coupled with the self-aware and ironic framing of the act of speaking out, makes the scene of desire fundamental to Hellenistic poetics.[90] Each of the *Idylls* I have discussed so far in this chapter frames *eros* as the theme of its inset songs, and in each case this prompts a question of the relation between song and singer, song and audience. I wish now to look at a further *Idyll* which highlights the writing of desire in Theocritus and which is regularly treated as a masterly psychological portrait of desire, namely, *Idyll* 2.

Idyll 2 is a dramatic monologue (whose urban setting has been the cause of much debate about the sense of the terms 'pastoral', 'bucolic poetry'[91]). The *Idyll* opens with the mimesis of Simaetha, a young woman, prepar-

---

[89] These senses of *para* are explicated by Miller (1979).

[90] The social changes in the Hellenistic world with specific regard to sexual behaviour are discussed by Foucault (1984a), (1984b); Pomeroy (1984).

[91] For useful discussion with bibliography see Halperin (1983) 118–37, especially 126–9.

ing and performing a magic rite – with ritual instructions to a maidservant
and an incantatory refrain – a rite which is designed to draw back the
man, Delphis, to her house. Then, alone (64), Simaetha turns to lament
her story to the moon – a narrative also in short stanzas punctuated by a
refrain which is addressed to the moon. The final passage of the poem
(136–66) continues this story and finally bids farewell to the moon – but
now without a refrain. The first-person narrative in the voice of a young
woman of uncertain status and background immediately indicates a shift
in the alignment of possibilities of poetic self-expression. Without the
explicit framing device of *Idyll* 11 or the dramatic form of, say, *Idyll* 1 or
15, this story of personal desire is spoken in a first person resolutely other
than the *ego* of the poet (like *Idyll* 3). I make what may seem an obvious
point about the portraiture of this *Idyll* to stress a crucial factor in this
poem (which links it to the other *Idylls*), namely, the *distance* inscribed
between the author as the one who speaks out and the voice he imper-
sonates. As the pastoral frame establishes and questions the distance
between the world of the city and the world of the country, so in representing desire in this urban poem, there is a gap engendered between the
(male) poet and his subject – a gap which helps produce the distance
between the poem's (unreliable) narrator and the readers' understanding.

Indeed, this sense of 'ironic distance' informs the critical readings of
Idyll 2, especially of Simaetha's self-representing narrative of her love
affair with which I wish to begin. C.P. Segal in particular has offered a
range of readings of the poem which, under the rubric of Northrop Fry's
'ironic mode', focuses on the gap between 'reader–author sophistication
and speaker–participant naivety'.[92] This gap is seen to operate on several
levels. First, Simaetha's echoes of grand literature – particularly Sappho
and Homer – establish a pattern of ironic similarity and difference between Simaetha's self-representation as heroine and the all too unheroic
frame of reference for this representation. So, when Delphis, as he is
about to speak, is described by Simaetha with 'he looked at me, the
loveless man, and fixed his eyes on the ground', καί μ᾽ ἐσιδὼν ὥστοργος
ἐπὶ χθονὸς ὄμματα πάξας (112), the description recalls Antenor's famous
description of Odysseus as orator in the *Iliad* (*Il.* 2.217 ὑπαὶ δὲ ἴδεσκε
κατὰ χθονὸς ὄμματα πάξας, 'he looked down and fixed his eyes on the
ground'). Unlike the political rhetoric which Odysseus pours forth 'like
snow flakes', Delphis – 'a calque on the wily Homeric orator'[93] – enters
into a long manipulative speech of erotic persuasion. If looking at the

ground may seem to be a gesture of assumed modesty in an erotic scene (as Gow suggests) – a gesture already differently understood by Simaetha in her recognition of him as ὥστοργος, 'the loveless man' – 'the gesture also connotes the deceptive appearances and the premeditation and skill of Odyssean craft'[94] for the sophisticated reader. The allusive description, then, contains the echo of the speaker's own later disillusionment – but in whose voice? Segal argues that 'the effectiveness of the patterns behind the participants' attitudes in fact depends upon their ignorance of the models which they are following. The reader sees, as the speaker does not, the discrepancies between those ancient parallels and the bourgeois setting in the present.'[95] So, when Simaetha describes her symptoms of desire in words that so strongly recall Sappho's famous self-representation (106–13), 'if the reader discerns the similarities that unite Simaetha with Sappho in the experience of love, he also has to traverse the differences'.[96] The lyric passion of Sappho and the heroic world of Homer both are in ironic and humorous tension with the scene of bourgeois seduction, and also, Segal argues, deepen by such an interplay of similarity and difference the understanding of the scene of seduction – '(pathetically) ennobling as well as ironizing'.[97] Thus, Segal concludes, Theocritus 'exploits a threefold set of tensions in ascending order of complexity as we penetrate beneath the pseudo-simplicity of the mimetic surface to the underlying artifice. First, there is the pathetic contrast between Simaetha's trust and Delphis' manipulative skill. Second, there is the contrast between the two literary, quasi-mythical models for the scene, Sappho and Odysseus. Third, there is the contrast between the reader, who grasps the echoes, and the girl who uses them without understanding the pattern she is creating.'[98] There is, then, an analogy between on the one hand the pathetic contrast of Simaetha's trust and Delphis' manipulative skill, and, on the other hand, the contrast between the ignorant Simaetha's self-representation and the 'attentive, sagacious and suspicious reader'.[99] Indeed, Simaetha's naivety, Segal argues, is composed to entrance, to pleasure the sophisticated superiority of the ironically aware reader (who 'grasps' the echoes and 'penetrates' the poem). It is this sense of mastery over this masterpiece that I wish to investigate a little further, and I intend to approach such questioning through another important aspect of the poem, the manipulation of the conventions of erotic poetry and erotic behaviour.

[94] Segal (1984) 204. [95] Segal (1984) 206. [96] Segal (1984) 205.
[97] Segal (1984) 205. [98] Segal (1984) 206–7. [99] Segal (1984) 207.

264 Framing, polyphony and desire

It has often been observed how Simaetha's narrative depends on a distortion or manipulation of the generic expectations of love poetry, not least in the female's pursuit of the male at the gymnasium. Both Griffiths and Segal, for example, two of the most sophisticated critics to have written on this poem, have commented on how Simaetha and Delphis in their different ways draw on the *topoi* of love poetry (as well as on more precise literary predecessors), and how important a knowledge of such *topoi* is for understanding this poem.[100] An excellent example of this and one which has not been sufficiently commented on is Delphis' first entrance, where the effect of his speech depends precisely on an audience's awareness of the conventions of love poetry. For, after Simaetha's blunt invitation (through her maidservant), Σιμαίθα τυ καλεῖ, 'Simaetha summons you', Delphis' address, as represented by Simaetha, precisely recalls in a series of potential constructions an expected order of events that has been resoundingly ignored by Simaetha (118–28):

ἦνθον γάρ κεν ἐγώ, ναὶ τὸν γλυκὺν ἦνθον Ἔρωτα,
ἢ τρίτος ἠὲ τέταρτος ἐὼν φίλος αὐτίκα νυκτός,
μᾶλα μὲν ἐν κόλποισι Διωνύσοιο φυλάσσων,
κρατὶ δ' ἔχων λεύκαν, Ἡρακλέος ἱερὸν ἔρνος,
πάντοθι πορφυρέαισι περὶ ζώστραισιν ἑλικτάν.

φράζεό μευ τὸν ἔρωθ' ὅθεν ἵκετο, πότνα Σελάνα.

καί κ', εἰ μέν μ' ἐδέχεσθε, τάδ' ἧς φίλα (καὶ γὰρ ἐλαφρός
καὶ καλὸς πάντεσσι μετ' αἰθέοισι καλεῦμαι),
εὗδόν τ' εἴ κε μόνον τὸ καλὸν στόμα τεῦς ἐφίλησα·
εἰ δ' ἄλλα μ' ὠθεῖτε καὶ ἁ θύρα εἴχετο μοχλῷ,
πάντως κα πελέκεις καὶ λαμπάδες ἦνθον ἐφ' ὑμέας.

For I would have come, by sweet Eros, I would,
as night fell, with two or three friends,
cherishing apples of Dionysus in my bosom,
on my head white poplar, sacred plant of Heracles,
twisted all about with crimson bands.

Show, Lady Moon, whence came my desire.

And if you had received me, that would have been nice
(for I am called easy and beautiful by all the lads);
and I would have slept, had I but kissed your beautiful mouth.

---

[100] Segal (1984); (1985); Griffiths (1979b); (1981).

But had you thrust me elsewhere, or barred the door,
then truly axes and torches would have come against you.

Delphis explains how he would have come in a *kōmos* at night with his
philoi; he would have brought love gifts – the statutory apples; he would
have been garlanded: he would, in short, have played the *exclusus amator*
to perfection. Delphis' fiction of desire represents the expectations of a
pursuing lover – as he finds himself the object of pursuit. There is an
expressive tension here, a distance, between Delphis' fiction of desire –
an unfulfilled story that would have, should have, consisted of a series of
attempts to find an elusive fulfilment – and Simaetha's retelling of her
fleetingly found and now lost fulfilment that makes up the poem. It is a
tension neatly and ironically marked in the juxtaposition of Delphis'
rhetorical expectation of what is sufficient fulfilment for a lover and
Simaetha's earthier euphemism for how the sequence of events concludes: Delphis, as he sits on Simaetha's couch (113), asserts how, had
he been able to gain entrance – in his fiction of desire – a mere kiss would
have sufficed. Simaetha – avoiding, she says (142), going on and on – sums
up what happened as ἐπράχθη τὰ μέγιστα, 'we went all the way', 'the
whole hog'. This tension or disjunction is replayed as Simaetha finally
tells us (149–54) how she has been told by her friend – another story
within the story – that Delphis is now 'drinking an unmixed measure of
wine' and 'decorating a door with garlands' – the completely conventional
behaviour of the unfulfilled sympotic lover, back satisfyingly in the
narrative groove.

If the sophisticated reader sees the manipulation and transgression of
the conventions of love poetry in this encounter of mismatched narratives
of fulfilment, that is not the end of the story, the end of the game of erotic
narrative's fulfilment. For the first-person narrative, as several critics
have pointed out in a variety of ways, with its particular and selective
perspective, its unstated alternatives, its self-representation as agent and
victim, inevitably moves each reader to attempt to establish a framing
and controlling narrative. To see through the unreliable narrator's story
to a more secure level. The gaps between Simaetha's self-representation
and her report of Delphis' self-representation seem to provoke a desire
to produce a master version of events, by which the manipulation and
deception of erotic rhetoric can be evaluated and determined *as* manipulation and deception. A master version that determines what was 'really
going on' from what the poet leaves unstated – the 'mastery temptation',
as Felman aptly calls it.[101] Yet this is a desire that can only be fulfilled

[101] Felman (1985) 240.

by the reader filling in the story – with an (erotic) fiction of his or her own, that is, with the reader's own expectations, stereotypes and narrative patterns. The potential constructions of Delphis' fiction of desire and Simaetha's search for control through magic seem to lead to the sophisticated reader's (erotic) construction of the potential of Theocritus' fiction. Indeed, the sophisticated reader's mastery and pleasure can be said to come from an indulgence in the erotic fictions that the poem represents with such ironic distance. As each reader, faced by Simaetha's representation of Delphis' words, aims to be less ταχυπείθης, 'swiftly persuaded', 'gullible', than Simaetha, each reader repeats Simaetha's drama of interpreting and implicating one's own and others' expectations of erotic fiction.

There are three ways I wish to consider this praxis of complicity, this way in which the narrative of desire lures the reader's 'mastery temptation'. First, I shall look at one word in Delphis' speech of seduction, by way of providing a paradigm of the problem involved in reading this elaborately layered language. Second, I shall discuss the end of the poem – where the narrative of mismatched fulfilments culminates. Finally, I shall return to the question of literary allusiveness raised by Segal, Griffiths and other commentators on this poem.

When Delphis explains how, if he had been let in by Simaetha, it would have been nice, he glosses his remark as follows (124–5):

(καὶ γὰρ ἐλαφρός
καὶ καλὸς πάντεσσι μετ᾽ ἀιθέοισι καλεῦμαι),

(for I am called easy and beautiful by all the lads);

How one reads such a boast – the representation of a desperate lover's *topos*? Smug self-satisfaction? Ironic banter? – will depend to a degree on the reading of the term *elaphros* (which I have translated unsatisfactorily as 'easy'; Gow translates 'nimble'). *Elaphros* is a rare word in Hellenistic writing and a surprising term to be conjoined with *kalos*, 'fine', 'beautiful', 'noble'. Gow notes that it is glossed ἀστεῖος, 'witty', 'sophisticated', in the Antinoa papyrus, and adds that it may have a good sense when applied to moral or mental qualities, '*genial* or the like': indeed, Plato (*Epist.* 13.360c) describes a pleasant and balanced person as ἐλαφρὸς καὶ εὐήθης, '*elaphros* and of a good disposition'. Gow concludes, however, that 'it is more probable that Delphis is advancing only his physical attractions'.[102] Dover, too, regards *elaphros* as a matter of phys-

---

[102] Gow (1950) ad loc.

ique, though for him it refers specifically to his ability at running: Delphis
boasts earlier (114–15) how he has beaten Philinos (one of the greatest
contemporary athletes) and *elaphros* meaning 'nimble', 'swift of foot',
'light', is a common epic usage. Is this, then, a mark of Delphis' self-
heroization to parallel Simaetha's own epic turns of phrase? If it is such
a heroic term, how is it to be read? Is it Delphis' pompousness or naive
boasting? Or self-deprecating humour? Or the poet's irony at Delphis'
expense? *Elaphros*, however, can also mean 'light' in the sense of
'fickle'.[103] Is there a suggestion here, then, of the outcome of the seduction, Delphis' 'easy' transference of affection elsewhere, his inconstancy?
If *elaphros* does imply an ironic hint of what's to come, at what level is
the irony, in whose voice is it spoken? Is it Delphis recalling what others
call him without recognizing the *double entendre*, that is, an irony for the
reader in the poet's (or Delphis' friends') voice(s)? Or is it Delphis
manipulating the double sense for his own amusement? Is it the poet
putting into Delphis' mouth a self-undercutting and self-fulfilling remark? Can it even be Simaetha adding a gloss – like ὥστοργος, 'the
loveless man' – after the event? (We have no adequate way of telling how
(un)reliable this narrator's telling is.) What is more, when Simaetha first
searches for a cure for the onset of desire, she says (92) it was οὐδὲν
ἐλαφρόν, 'no light matter' or there was 'no easy solution'.[104] Delphis, the
object of her (sickness of) desire, ironically describes himself with the
same term she had used for the longed for cure. The evaluative term,
then, is framed in a recession of voices – the comment of the 'young men',
represented by Delphis, represented by Simaetha, represented by the
poet, echoing in the poem. From whose voice does *elaphros* take its
significance? As much as the mimesis of Simaetha's magic seems to lead
the reader to read through the representation to determine a reality
against which the representation can be judged and thus mastered, at the
same time the monologue form with its voices within voices prevents the
security of that process. The poem's readers share with the figures

---

[103] So ἐλαφρόνοοι are opposed to σαόφρονες by Phocylides; Philemon calls the race of
women ἐλαφρόν apparently in this sense; Polybius 6.56.11 calls the mob (τὸ πλῆθος)
'fickle', 'changeable'; so Dodds translates *Bacchae* 851 ἐλαφρὰν λύσσαν, 'dizzy, in-
constant frenzy' (though there it may be an ironical or paradoxical usage – 'light' in the
sense of 'easy' for Dionysus, but disastrous for Pentheus). κοῦφος has a similar range
of senses, including the surprising description of a drunken man having a κοῦφον νόον
in Theognis 497–8. Latin *levis* regularly implies 'fickleness' also.

[104] If, that is, *elaphros* can have a transitive sense, 'lightening', which Gow, rightly to my
mind, doubts.

dramatized in and by Simaetha's monologue a desire for mastery over the narrative of desire.

Nor can the continuation *kai kalos*, 'and beautiful', determine the sense of *elaphros*. While *kalos* is a broad term of positive evaluation, the *kai*, 'and', marks a range of possible connections between the two adjectives from the close equivalence (on Dover's reading) of physical prowess and physical appearance, to the possible tensions between the appearance of physical or social worth and an inconstancy of mind. (And does *kaleumai*, 'I am *called*', especially with a hint of a pun with *kalos*,[105] suggest the possible slippage of language in such evaluative description?) 'And' need not imply equivalence.[106] Putting together a discourse of evaluation remains a site of dissension in this poem.

What I wish to stress here is not the common complaint against a particular tradition of classical scholarship that it strives to reduce complex ambiguity to univocal simplicity, but that each reader of this word *elaphros* makes choices and evaluations according to feelings about what is proper, natural, probable, inherent in the language, the fictions of desire. Each reader tells a story. There is no neutral, no clean position from which to read (of) the language of desire; no secure position outside the *topoi* of *eros*. Reading the fiction of the naive voice of the girl draws in and implicates the sophisticated reader as the victim, the dupe, seduced by his own *topoi*. The veiling of the poet's voice in the recessed voices of this dramatic monologue provokes the reader into the unfulfillable role of omniscient narrator. The desire for mastery over the fictions of desire is not lightly, not easily to be eluded.

It is at the end of the poem, however, where critics have most strongly disagreed about what this narrative tells of desire. Simaetha concludes her story with a threat of still stronger magic (159–62):

> Now I will bind him with these charms. If he still
> pains me, he will, by the fates, beat on Hades' door.
> In my box I vow I keep for him such evil drugs,
> that I learned of, mistress, from an Assyrian stranger.

This threat leads, however, to a final farewell to the moon and a final statement of her condition that has caused much discussion (163–6):

> ἀλλὰ τὺ μὲν χαίροισα ποτ' ὠκεανὸν τρέπε πώλως,
> πότνι'· ἐγὼ δ' οἰσῶ τὸν ἐμὸν πόθον ὥσπερ ὑπέσταν.

---

[105] The scansion of καλός here notwithstanding.
[106] For a fine and sophisticated analysis of 'and', see Gallop (1982) 1–14.

χαῖρε, Σελαναία λιπαρόθρονε, χαίρετε δ' ἄλλοι
ἀστέρες, εὐκάλοιο κατ' ἄντυγα Νυκτὸς ὀπαδοί.

Farewell, lady, and turn your horses towards the ocean.
I will bear my longing as I have endured it.
Farewell, Moon of shining throne, farewell you other
stars, companions of the chariot of quiet night.

For Hopkinson, who follows Gow, this ending indicates that Simaetha 'has achieved only resignation, which we feel will be short lived. She still wants Delphis, and we know he will not come again.'[107] The resignation is indicated by line 164, which he renders: I will bear my longing 'as I have undergone it ⟨hitherto⟩'; but her preceding threats are but a 'delusion of power' – a self-delusion that is an attempt 'to deal with helpless and hopeless desire by using song as a substitute for action'. For Segal, however, these lines 'convey an impression of nascent capacity for objectively distancing the experience'.[108] 'The poem depicts a movement, albeit unsteady . . . towards a more human perspective and a more rational clarity.'[109] Such 'self-knowledge' is for Segal not the 'delusion of power', but the 'real hope of salvation'.[110] So the final two lines suggest for Segal 'lucidity, calm, mastery of passion';[111] for Dover, the passage shows a 'descent into darkness and melancholy'.[112] Crucial to each of these readings is the understanding of line 164. Gow, followed by Hopkinson, translates 'I will bear my longing as till now I have endured it.'[113] There is, however, no word in the Greek for the crucial qualifier 'as till now' – as Hommel has pointed out. Segal also notes that 'the problem with Gow's translation is that Simaetha has not in fact "borne" or "endured" her love "hitherto", but has been very impatient and intolerant of it'.[114] Thus, he goes on to suggest tentatively the translation 'I will endure this love with the suffering of my past subjection to it' – a less stoical reaction, but none the less one replete with a recognition of suffering. Dover suggests a contrast is to be seen between the moon, who leaves, and Simaetha who must continue in her love: 'it was I, not you, mistress Moon, who fell in love; and I who will endure it while you depart'.[115] Hommel's version runs 'I will endure this love, as I have undertaken, taken it upon myself, to endure it.'

---

[107] Hopkinson (1988) 156.   [108] Segal (1985) 117.   [109] Segal (1984) 42.
[110] Segal (1985) 117.   [111] Segal (1984) 43.   [112] Dover (1971) 94.
[113] Parry (1988), most recently, goes so far as to elide the difference between the two verbs: he translates 'I will endure as I have endured'.
[114] Segal (1985) 117 n. 35.   [115] Dover (1971) 112 ad 164.

Simaetha's assertion supposes an understanding of her past and a projection into her future dependent on that understanding: the ambivalence of the term ὑπέστην ('I have endured', 'I have undertaken', 'I have been subjected to') is not merely because of its complex semantic possibilities but also because, as a self-representation, its comprehension depends on a perception of that self, that subject and the desire to which she is subjected. Understanding her remark is necessarily affected by whether the narrative is understood as a move towards 'mastery of passion' or as a continuing expression of a 'delusion of power'. Her assertion is preceded by a threat of more and more destructive magic, if Delphis continues to grieve her (159–60). Is this juxtaposition designed, as Segal argues, to indicate a move away from a 'final surge of anger and determination for revenge' in order that the poet might show how Simaetha finally learns that 'she lacks the magical power to move Delphis from his unbounded erotic adventures outside',[116] even, as Griffiths claims, in order that 'the wild passions of the poem seem finally to have distilled themselves into aesthetic sublimation'.[117] Or is this final self-representation a promise to continue the search to control Delphis and her desire for him 'as I have undertaken' or 'as I have been subjected' – that is, continuing pain? The monologue both provokes the reader to read through the self-representations and misrepresentations to find a controlled comprehension of the fluctuating expressions of Simaetha's desire, and at the same time prevents the secure fulfilment of that reading.

Segal remains the critic most aware of the tension between the formal closure of the poem – with its gestures of farewell – and the 'interminable and unbounded . . . emotions of the speaker'.[118] He writes: 'The very inconclusiveness of the ending entices [us, the readers] to relive and rethink this experience and, of course, to reread the poem.'[119] So let us return to the representation of Delphis' approach and reconsider the language of allusion there (112–13):

καί μ' ἐσιδὼν ὥστοργος ἐπὶ χθονὸς ὄμματα πάξας
ἕζετ' ἐπὶ κλιντῆρι καὶ ἑζόμενος φάτο μῦθον.

He looked at me, the loveless man, and fixed his eyes on the ground;
he sat on the bed, and sitting there spoke this speech.

As we have seen, the echo of Homer's Odysseus for the sophisticated reader tells of deception, untrustworthy words. Segal writes: 'These inter-

---

[116] Segal (1985) 114.   [117] Griffiths (1979b) 262.
[118] Segal (1985) 118.   [119] Segal (1985) 119.

textual echoes ... are one-directional only; they operate for the benefit of the reader, not the speaker',[120] (despite the fact that 'the loveless man' already cues the recognition of fickleness). If, however, the allusiveness of Simaetha's language raises a question of where the significance of her remarks is properly to be found, where it is directed, this question comes about not merely because of the gap between the sophisticated reader and the ignorant speaker, but also because of the particular nature of the language of desire. For as Theocritus writes in *Idyll* 13, οὐχ ἁμῖν ... μόνοις, οὐχ ἁμῖν ... πράτοις, 'not for us alone, not for us first': the language of desire in particular is always already layered with allusion, informed with normative, paradigmatic expression (especially in the case of the literary representation of desire). To utter – to write – 'I love you' – to take an extreme modern example – can never be simply a personal utterance, the property of an individual. As an utterance – 'too articulated to be no more than an impulse, too phatic to be a sentence'[121] – 'I love you' is inevitably overdetermined – or, as Heidegger's famous apophthegm puts it, 'Die Sprache spricht'. Indeed, the formulation of the problem can be reversed to ask to what degree desire can be spoken (of) outside the (over)determining framework of language, replete with its proprieties and normative constructions. (And much contemporary analysis is concerned precisely to chart the ways in which the speaking subject is subject to language.)[122] When Simaetha's allusive language reveals more than she appears to control, does the sophisticated reader find only the obverse of his superior mastery? The 'mastery temptation' is precisely the temptation to believe oneself beyond the lures and duping of the language of desire, to believe one can 'penetrate' and 'grasp' the language of desire without complicity, without implication.

When Simaetha sings her repeated refrain, then, φράζεό μευ τὸν ἔρωθ' ὅθεν ἵκετο, πότνα Σελάνα, 'Indicate, lady Moon, whence came my desire', both the question of 'the whence of desire'[123] and the act of narration in response to the question set this *Idyll* within the tradition of what Tony Tanner calls 'necessarily a central topic of all literature' – that is, literature's attempts to chart 'the diffuse genesis of desire ... to track

---

[120] Segal (1984) 206.
[121] Barthes (1978) 149 – his whole discussion of 'I love you' (147–54) is instructive.
[122] See e.g. Wilden (1968); de Man (1971); Derrida (1976), (1981); Coward and Ellis (1977); Kristeva (1980); Johnson (1980); Silverman (1982); Gallop (1982), (1985); Felman (1985) – each with further bibliography.
[123] I cite this phrase from Tony Tanner's quotation ((1979) 87) of Anthony Wilden's quotation of Lacan.

out its operations and strategies in their complex, devious and diverse manifestations'.[124] As Simaetha's magic spells and erotic narrative together attempt to control, determine and explain the passage of desire, and yet seem to founder on the inability of her language to control, determine, explain the object of her desire, so the readers of Simaetha's story may find their attempts to explain, control, determine the passage of desire foundering on the resistance of her entrancing language to penetration and grasping, its resistance to certain and final comprehension. Reading the lover's voice, then – especially this voice of the deserted and desiring young woman, searching for 'the whence of desire' – cannot finally elude the ways in which, as Felman puts it, 'The joke is on us; the worry, ours.'[125]

COURTING FAME

I wish to conclude this chapter with a brief consideration of a set of Theocritus' poems that has received less attention than those I have been discussing so far, namely, the poems associated with Theocritus as a court poet, and in particular *Idylls* 15, 16, 17.[126] Although patronage in Renaissance Europe, and particularly in Renaissance England, has been the subject of much recent and sophisticated criticism,[127] the legacy of the Romantic movement's profession of poetry as the 'spontaneous overflow of powerful feeling' has been hard to escape in the discussion of the classical poetry of patronage (as indeed it has been for Shakespeare and his contemporaries[128]). What is more, for the Hellenistic age, the analysis of the poetry is further hampered by the paucity of information about

---

[124] Tanner (1979) 87 and 100.   [125] (1985) 247.

[126] Since we know so little about the circulation and production of Theocritus' verse, it may well be wrong to regard these poems (as opposed to any others) as specifically produced for the court. I am discussing them together here because of their explicit language of encomium and patronage. Although such discussion could have been placed in chapter 2, it seemed more profitable to set it after the consideration of Theocritus' other output.

[127] For the institutions of patronage, see MacCaffery (1961); Stone (1965) 385–504; Greenblatt (1975); and the fine collection of essays in Lytle and Orgel (1981); and on the later Renaissance, see Foss (1971).

[128] For a fine essay on the repression of the discourse of patronage and the editing of Shakespeare, see Barrell (1988) 18–43. For studies of the rhetoric of encomium, see Hardison (1962), which attempts to link Classical and Renaissance theories of encomium to Renaissance literature (in a somewhat formalist manner); Lewalski (1973), which is more attuned to the possibilities and precariousness of praise; and in particular Tennenhouse (1981).

the institutions of patronage that exist in such abundance for Elizabethan and later English culture, and, to a lesser degree, for Augustan Rome. In particular, the details of performance and circulation that have been so instructive for English texts of the Renaissance,[129] are simply lacking for Hellenistic Greek writing: although *Idyll* 15 dramatizes the attendance at a festival and a song performed at it, there is nothing but speculation about the performance of the *Idyll* itself (and the other poems of Theocritus).[130] The assumption regularly and plausibly made that such mimetic poetry was 'written for recitation before an educated audience associated with the royal court at Alexandria'[131] is far too general to be of much use, and even this relies on tenuous evidence.[132] The counter-assumption that this is 'Buchpoësie' – to be circulated in manuscript for private reading – has equally negligible evidence in its favour, though it, too, is an assumption regularly supported.[133] The brief anecdotes of a tyrant's patronage are unreliable and lead largely to arguments from silence.[134]

---

[129] See e.g. on performance Tennenhouse (1986); Berry (1989); Montrose (1977); Sinfield (1983); and in particular the brilliant study of Orgel (1975). On circulation, see e.g. Saunders (1951); Greenblatt (1975) 56–98; and more generally Helgerson (1983).

[130] Even with the mimes of Hero[n]das the most detailed study (Mastromarco (1984)) can only conclude (95–6) that 'one can believe that the "publication" of the mimiambi took place *by means of stage performances*' but also that 'it is obviously possible – and in fact highly likely – that ... Herondas' mimiambi were also read as texts'. For a convenient collection of the (minimal) testimonia, see Cunningham (1971) 3–17. The studies of e.g. Sidney's *Lady of May* by Montrose (1977) and particularly Berry (1989) or of the masques discussed by Orgel (1975) show the insufficiency of this level of generalization most strikingly.

[131] Bulloch (1985a) 8.

[132] See in general n. 130 above. A more specific example: Cairns (1984b) supports the claims of Hardie (1983) to have shown that *Idyll* 16 is a performance piece: the 'good reason' he cites is that 'It concludes with an address to the Charites of Orchomenos.'

[133] Though the different possible implications of such circulation are not considered. Compare the detailed studies of Greenblatt (1975) 56–89; Tennenhouse (1981); and Saunders (1951).

[134] The case often cited is that of Sotades (told in Athenaeus 621a), put to death for writing a less than encomiastic line about the incestuous marriage of Ptolemy and his sister. Compare the detailed treatments of the careers of Sidney, Ralegh and Lyly in Berry (1989); Greenblatt (1975); Montrose (1977) for the complex reasons for the failures of encomium and patronage. Orgel (1975) 43–5 tells the story of William Prynne who, for his book's index entry 'Women-actors, notorious whores', was (44) 'convicted by the Star Chamber [of high treason] and sentenced to life imprisonment, fined £5,000, pilloried, expelled from Lincoln's Inn, deprived of his academic degree, and his ears were cut off by the public executioner'. Orgel's detailed treatment of this case shows how a single model of 'the tyrant patron' is unlikely to do justice to the complexity of the social interaction of power and praise.

And as we have seen in chapter 2, the history of praise poetry in Greek culture is sufficiently complex and changing to make the assumption of unchanging generic rules an insufficient guide to particular poems in particular circumstances, important though such generic awareness is to set against the Romantic and post-Romantic trivialization of encomiastic verse. It is, in short, the poems themselves that have been read by critics to uncover the rhetoric and performance of praise and patronage in the Hellenistic age – and as one might expect from the arguments of this chapter already, the poetry of praise further demonstrates the problem of articulating the place from which the poet speaks.

Idyll 15 has often been called an 'urban mime': it dramatizes two women meeting and going to view the Adonis festival sponsored by queen Arsinoe at the palace in Alexandria. It is also a poem that enacts praise for Ptolemaic rule, not merely in the explicit comments particularly of the two women, Praxinoa and Gorgo, but also in the representation of the Adonis festival itself: 'the homage to Adonis is clearly an homage to the Ptolemies as well'.[135] Indeed, the representation of the song to Adonis – another inset song in Theocritus – 'draws the Idyll beyond the simple and traditional form of mime',[136] and this (generic) movement makes possible the complex work of praise.

I have three points I wish to make about this *Idyll* for my present argument. The first is to stress the indirectness of the strategies of praise: although it has been said that 'the encomiastic poets wrote, for the most part, as individuals, assuming no other personality',[137] in this poem the dramatic form splits the voice of the poet and puts the most explicit praise into the mouths of the two suburban women (44–50):[138]

> Heavens, what a crowd! How and when are we to get
> through this plague? Ants! Countless, innumerable.
> You have done many fine deeds, Ptolemy, since
> your father was among the gods. No thug
> slips up to you in the street and hurts you in that
> Egyptian way, the trick those men packed with deceit
> used to play, as bad as one another, terrible tricks, all cursed.

---

[135] Griffiths (1979a) 65.

[136] Griffiths (1979a) 128. On mime, see Cunningham (1971); Mastromarco (1984).

[137] Hardie (1983) 30–1. This is notably different in later traditions: see e.g. Berry (1989); Javitch (1978).

[138] 'Theocritus entrusts his praise, covert and open, to a variety of voices very unlike his own' (Griffiths (1979a) 82).

The threatening crowd, like innumerable ants, acts as a foil to the praise of Ptolemy for ruling the city in such a way that the Alexandrians do not behave in an Egyptian fashion. Both the Hellenizing – civilizing – of the population, and the recognition of the divinity of Ptolemy's father – which is introduced as a temporal marker, as something taken for granted – celebrate Ptolemaic rule. Yet the distance that such praise in the voice of another introduces, it must be noted, also opens the possibility of a less secure reading: for Griffiths, this passage may indicate 'the real affection felt by the populace for the royal family' (even if 'Theocritus clearly shares some of the irony of the Ptolemies themselves towards the façade that they presented to the masses'[139]); for Dover, however, this praise 'sounds stilted and ornate in the mouth of Praxinoa and betrays the desire of the poet to capture royal favour by flattery'.[140] Perhaps what the difference between these two readings indicates is first the tension that arises inevitably from the composition of such an indirect expression of praise – how to control the distance between the voice of praise and the poet himself? How committed to this voice of praise is the poet? In whose voice is it spoken?[141] And second, the tension that can be seen throughout Theocritus' court poetry in discovering the correct strategy to praise a king, within a Greek tradition that regularly stigmatizes tyranny; in Alexandria, an Egyptian city – in a tradition that regularly valorizes Greekness over foreignness; in a vast polyglot city – within a Greek tradition that promotes the *polis* as the context of praise; for a family that is incestuous and proclaims itself divine – in a tradition of the praise of limits that abhors *hubris* and sexual transgression. Now the Greekness of Praxinoa and Gorgo is asserted not only in the dismissal of Egyptian behaviour (in this Egyptian city), but also explicitly in the following lines. A man at the ceremony tries to stop the women chattering (κωτίλλοισαι) an *ekphrasis* (80–6) in such broad accents (πλατειάσδοισαι) and Praxinoa responds (89–93):

> My! Where does this man come from? What's it to you, if we chatter?
> Give orders where you're master. You're ordering Syracusans.
> Let me tell you this too. We're Corinthians by descent
> like Bellerophon. We talk Peloponnesian;
> it's allowed, I suppose, for Dorians to talk Dorian.

---

[139] Griffiths (1979a) 82, 83.
[140] Dover (1971) ad 46.
[141] See Javitch (1978), especially 141–62, for an interesting discussion of indirect praise in Spenser.

The claim of Greekness – with descent to match Bellerophon's – and specifically of a Peloponnesian and Dorian birthright may be 'emotive words in Dorian colonies throughout the Greek world',[142] but there is also an ironic twist putting such terms in the mouths of these women arguing in a crowd at a festival. Do these lines indicate how 'Theocritus seems to participate . . . in a conspiracy never to reveal that Egypt is not a Greek land'?[143] Or does the need to emphasize descent in this way, with its grand claims of equivalence with the hero, Bellerophon, highlight such a fiction of Hellenization? Does the 'chatter' of the women stress the 'real affection' in the praise of the royal family, or make the praise seem 'stilted' and (mere) 'flattery' from the poet? The ironic detachment of Theocritus from the voice of praise needs to be carefully controlled if the encomiastic project itself is not to fail.

One way in which Theocritus can be seen to turn 'the variety of voices very unlike his own' towards the establishment of a strategy of praise is in the narrative procession to the palace itself (and this is my second point). For the inset song to Adonis, framed by the *ekphrasis* of the bier of Adonis, provides a focus for the crowd, as it does for the two main figures of the poem. The old woman, the two men, join Praxinoa and Gorgo to form an image of the people of Alexandria celebrating the ritual of the royal palace. In Pindar's *epinikia* and in the sympotic poetry discussed in chapter 2, we saw how the individual voice of praise also works to construct a community, a choir of voices celebrating. So Gorgo in the last line of the poem concludes (as she prepares to go home and cook her husband's lunch) 'Farewell, beloved Adon, and come to us as we rejoice', χαῖρε, Ἄδων ἀγαπατέ, καὶ ἐς χαίροντας ἀφικνεῦ (149). The echo of the formula of closure for a hymn – which is absent from the Adonis song itself – as well as the plural χαίροντας, 'as we rejoice', 'farewell', represents Gorgo as a celebrant, participating in the ritual. The festival of Adonis, sponsored by the royal family and set in the royal palace, is the focus that structures, centres, the multiform characters of the poem. It celebrates the palace and its royal household as that which gives order and festival to the city.

The Third aspect of *Idyll* 15 I wish to investigate is the framing technique of the embedded Adonis song. (Both the framing device and the focus on erotic relations find echoes in the poems I have already discussed in this chapter – again marking a degree of continuity in the corpus of Theocritus.) The Adonis song has provoked much discussion

---

[142] Dover (1971) ad 92f.   [143] Griffiths (1979a) 85.

whether it is to be taken as a parody or not – a discussion which re-emphasizes the difficulty of simply determining the discourse of praise in the mouths of Praxinoa and Gorgo in particular, who expresses her strong approval of the performance (145–6). Yet here I wish merely to note the disjunction and similarities promoted by frame and song – that is, by the domestic and daily routine and complaints of the women with their husbands, and the lament for the lost Adonis, Aphrodite's doomed lover, whose death is mourned in counterpoint with a celebration of Aphrodite's immortalization of Berenice and Arsinoe's glorious sponsorship of the festival. The splendid celebration of Adonis by Berenice and Arsinoe as represented in the *Idyll*, and the celebration of Adonis by Gorgo and Praxinoa in the context of their marital households, can be seen as an amusing but none the less serious expression of the communal project of social order through family life, state festival and royal majesty: a celebration of the controlled diversity of Ptolemaic Alexandria. 'Things experienced mundanely in the household find their supreme idealization here in Arsinoe's palace' and the 'social relationship of the rulers and their subjects' is 'seen as harmoniously interdependent' where 'absolute power can be seen as benign and constructive'.[144] Yet this careful encomiastic reading cannot recognize – or must repress any recognition of – too great an ironic distanciation between the daily life of the women and the festival offered for them; or between the incestuous and wealthy palace, and the families outside, proud of their Greekness.[145] The siting of the praise in the voices of these women articulates a fine division between ironic distance and a divisive recognition of the political manipulation and exploitation of religious events. The discomfort, to which many modern critics attest in reading the court poetry of Theocritus, is not merely because of a modern distaste for the explicit mechanisms of patronage and praise, but more precisely because the discourse of praise seems finally able only to veil the difficulty of discovering a strategy of celebration which is adequate to the new circumstances of the Ptolemaic dynastic rule, but which is not diminished in contrast with the great tradition of Greek encomiastic verse. Or is the *veiling* itself a courtly strategy of praise, revealing the work of encomium as artfully dissembled?[146]

---

[144] Griffiths (1979a) 255, 257.   [145] See Reinhardt (1988) 99–107, especially 106–7.

[146] See Javitch (1978), especially his discussion of Puttenham's extended gloss on *qui nescit dissimulare nescit regnare* 50–75. On the need for dissembling rhetoric and a classical context, see Ahl (1984).

The formulation of the new and changing political requirements of the Ptolemaic dynasty develops a new and changing discourse of praise, and the sense of that change, the sense of that reformulation of the language and context of praise in and against the language of the past, is constantly expressed by Theocritus' encomiastic poetry.

The problem of the reformulation of the language of praise is perhaps most in evidence in *Idyll* 17, the encomium to Ptolemy. At a generic level, the poem appears at first sight to be a hymn of a Homeric type, particularly in the opening and closing formulas and in its vocabulary of song; it also appears to manipulate the *topoi* of prose encomium.[147] This combination of forms – another typical Hellenistic trait – is, however, also a crucial factor in the rhetorical strategy of the poem, which takes its start and finish from Zeus, but works to assimilate Ptolemy into divine status; or rather, through the extensive description of Ptolemy's birth that is explicitly made parallel to the birth of Apollo, and through the promise finally that he is to be sung (135–6) 'no less than other demi-gods' (ἡμιθέων) the suggestion of Ptolemy's more than human status can be read, without the explicit statement of divinity ever being made. The final lines of praise before the closing formula of farewell show both the thrust of this assimilation towards divine status and the possible difficulties of this reformulation of a (Greek) encomiastic discourse (126–34):

> He burns many fat thighs of oxen
> on the reddening altars as the months come round,
> he and his noble wife; there is no better woman
> who clasps in her arms a husband in their palace,
> loving with all her heart her brother and spouse.
> Thus was accomplished the sacred marriage of the gods
> whom Queen Rheia bore to be rulers of Olympus.
> Iris, virgin still, with her hands cleansed with oils,
> spreads a single couch for Zeus and Hera to sleep.

Ptolemy is depicted first as a pious ruler, sacrificing to the gods. The gods in question, however, are his mother and father; Ptolemy, alone of mankind (121–3) established shrines to his parents, a piety which sepa-

---

[147] See Cairns (1972) 100–14 for detailed analysis; also Meincke (1965) 85ff. Cameron's analysis of later praise for kings (Cameron (1965)) shows not merely a tradition of encomium, as Hardie (1983) 15–36 argues, but also the important differences within such a tradition: it is noticeable, for example, that precisely what appears to be lacking for *Idyll* 17 is the formal, civic framework described by Cameron for the Byzantine poets. I note that Van Dam (1988) 705 argues that Hardie's position is 'unfounded and seldom persuasive'.

rates him from the traditional norms of Greek religious life and praise poetry. He sacrifices together with his wife, who is his sister. The incestuous union of brother and sister, a Pharaonic and at least later Egyptian norm,[148] is immediately likened to the (Greek) *hieros gamos*, 'sacred marriage' of Zeus and Hera, the king and queen (βασιλῆας) of Olympus. The assimilation of the Alexandrian royal union to the Olympian 'sacred marriage' not only continues the construction of a more than human status for Ptolemy but also aims to normalize the marital status of Ptolemy and Arsinoe as the accepted exception (like the 'sacred marriage') – 'the culmination of the equally unique social order that they have established on earth ... the well-spring of the praeternatural good fortune of Egypt'.[149] That many other common associations of the 'sacred marriage' – Zeus's adulteries, the constant arguments between god and goddess, the deception of Zeus by Hera, Hera's threatened punishment by Zeus etc. – are not surprisingly not (to be) invoked indicates first the difficulty of constructing a secure, unimpeachable discourse of praise especially under changing historical circumstances and in an extensive literary tradition of encomium; and second, the need for selective, controlled reading of such encomium – a reader's necessary participation in the social performance of encomium. The need to control the dangerous uncontrollability of (Theocritean) irony and such allusiveness within a tradition demonstrates most strikingly the precariousness of the response of the poet's voice to the dynamics of power and language set in play by the performance of praise.

The moment in the *Idyll* of the apparently most traditional assertion of poetic voice also manifests the precarious relationship of this rhetoric to the poetic past (115–20):

> The spokesmen of the Muses celebrate Ptolemy
> for his benefactions. What could be finer for a man
> of wealth than to win fine renown among men?
> This lasts for the Atreids too. But the countless
> treasure won when they took Priam's great halls lies
> hidden somewhere in the darkness whence there is no return.

The plural 'spokesmen of the Muses', Μουσάων ὑποφῆται, creates a community of poets singing, but also conceals the individual poetic voice of praise within such a community, a 'formal, bardic anonymity',[150] expressing gratitude on behalf of poets in general (and not for his specific

---

[148] See Hopkins (1980).   [149] Griffiths (1979a) 79.   [150] Griffiths (1979a) 81.

patronage). The rhetorical question is posed as to what could be finer than 'fine *kleos* among men' – the stake of the poetic exchange. The exemplum offered is a surprising one, however. For the Atreids' lasting fame – in contrast to the perishable treasure won at Troy – is also fame for being destroyed and cuckolded (as the *Odyssey* and tragedy recall). And 'from where there is no return', 'no *nostos*', seems to hint at the great epic of return, the *Odyssey*, Odysseus' return precisely from 'the darkness'. What is more, these lines lead directly into the announcement that Ptolemy alone founded shrines to his parents, and the praise of Ptolemy's piety and marriage that I have been considering. How does this immortality relate to the immortality of poetic fame? Is the divinization of the dynasty of the Ptolemies to be taken as the answer to the rhetorical question of what could be finer than 'fine *kleos*' among men? Is the role of the poet's voice projected only to be subsumed to the promise of a divine dynastic future for the royal household?

The final poem of Theocritus I wish to consider – most briefly – is *Idyll* 16, the court poem which has been most extensively treated in recent scholarship.[151] It is a poem that focuses on the exchange that is patronage, and the possibilities of praise in changing circumstances and against a literary tradition. It is a poem that begins as a petition for patronage and with a critique of the treatment that his 'Graces' (*Charites*) receive from contemporary society; it moves through an assertion of the Muses' immortalizing power to praise of Hiero in the form of a series of wishes and hopes for his reign: it concludes with an expression of the poet's willingness to sing if bidden, but otherwise to stay with the (i.e. his) Graces. The shift from an attack on contemporary support for (his) poetry to praise for Hiero has been the focus of much critical discussion. The transition – marked, as so often in Pindar, by the language of journeying

---

[151] See especially Treu (1963); Meincke (1965) 31–84; Austin (1967); Horstman (1976) 119–37; Kühn (1978); Griffiths (1979a) 9–50 with extensive treatment of earlier discussions; Gutzwiller (1983). This is a poem that is probably not written at or for an Alexandrian audience in the first instance. Cairns (1976) 303, (1979) 160 believes it to be written to a commission from Hiero: his claim (1976) 303 that 'Theocritus' reader knew that by convention such requests were already fulfilled. So he would see in *Idyll* 16 not a genuine plea for patronage but a commissioned poem ingeniously posing as a request for a commission', is based on no evidence (even if it is, of course, a possible reading): he cites no other examples of his 'convention'. In (1979) 160, he merely quotes 104–9 as the (self-evident) proof of a commission, translating ἄκλητος μὲν ἔγωγε μένοιμί κεν·, 'I would stay at home if I were not invited abroad'! The addition of 'abroad' shows the strain in Cairns' reading: for a different version of these final lines, see Austin (1967) 18; Gutzwiller (1983) 235; Griffiths (1979a) 44–50.

(7, 28, 47, 51, 58, 69, 93, 98–100, 106–10)[152] – seems to dramatize an accession to the possibilities of patronage (as it outlines the possibilities of praise and as the poetic *ego* develops the position from which the poetry is spoken[153]). So the downcast and jeering Graces of the opening despair finally appear as the revered goddesses of Orchomenus, companions and inspiration of the poet. The self-representation of the poet proclaiming vividly his lack of success; the shifting poetic persona; the indirect and understated praise; the subtle manipulation of encomiastic technique[154] have helped produce a critical evaluation of this *Idyll* which is the reverse of that accorded to *Idyll* 17. Gow calls it 'strikingly and unexpectedly successful'[155] and Griffiths describes it in terms germane to my project: 'a poetry of evasion, full of startling turns, dazzling ποικιλία [variations], and the assumption of many different voices which combine to leave the poet's own vantage point irretrievably hidden'.[156] The precariousness of the rhetoric of praise is articulated – staged – in the poet's expressions of rejection and then accession to a place from which praise can be uttered – a move which in itself constructs Hiero as a figure who enables praise. That the poem ends with deferral – the decision to wait for the summons to praise[157] – veils the work of celebration in the poem as a priamel awaiting its climax.[158]

The self-conscious affiliations to the poetry of the past is – in typically Theocritean fashion – a key way of expressing both the sense of poetic tradition and Theocritus' novel position within it. In particular, the poetry of both Pindar and Simonides has been rightly and repeatedly seen by critics as crucial to this poem's argument and form. Not only is Simonides' praise of the Scopadae – a double-edged paradigm[159] – the first example of the need for poetry if wealth is to have 'immortal *kleos*', but also the Simonidean recognition of a double sense of *charis* – as gratitude and as financial reward – has been seen as a pun that underlies the poem's shifting representation of the *Charites*.[160] Pindar hymned the

---

[152] See Hardie (1983) 34.
[153] As Griffiths (1979a) 33 writes of the change from opening despair to encomium: 'The poetic ἐγώ differs markedly from what we first heard of Theocritus as a beleaguered individual, for now he is not anxious about money, but quite the opposite.'
[154] For this see Austin (1967) and Gutzwiller (1983) in particular.
[155] Gow (1950) 305.   [156] Griffiths (1979a) 50.
[157] On the 'bidden/unbidden' theme in encomium, see Hardie (1983) 30–6.
[158] Gutzwiller (1983) 236 suggests that by such rhetoric this poem deserves an important place in the history of the *recusatio*.
[159] See in particular Austin (1967) and Gutzwiller (1983) 221ff.
[160] See in particular Griffiths (1979a) 22ff.

Graces of Orchomenus (*Ol.* 14) and celebrated Hiero I: Theocritus manipulates both the language and the strategies of the epinicean cele-bration.[161] Pindar and Simonides are regularly set in opposition to one another as the noble and the mercenary poet.[162] Theocritus, however, sets himself in relation to both – without any gesture of simple affiliation – in a poem whose dramatic focus is the rewards and performance of encomiastic verse. The poet appropriates the poetry of the past: on the one hand, in a way that particularly in the opening section distances the present circumstances from the earlier conditions and assumptions of praise – the present no longer matches (up to) the past; on the other hand, in a way which transcends the past in the potential of Sicily's glorious future under Hiero. The past poetry of praise is used not merely to site Theocritus within a literary tradition but also as a strategy of praise – the past becomes the foil to Hiero's and the poet's future. The discussion of poetics becomes part of a (manipulative) discourse of celebration, where the potential of the future becomes the glory to outshine the past, where the concealment of poetic success becomes an ironic evasion that is also the possibility of establishing future triumphs. That the representation of poetic failure can be a tactic of praise (as the direct statement of achievement can fail in its encomiastic purpose) articulates once more the complex process of exchange and reading, veiling and revealing, that praise necessarily involves. The opposition of a concern for poetry as such and a concern for the work of praise – an opposition around which much of the discussion of this poem has polarized – is, then, inadequate to Theocritus' writing, where the self-consciousness of the literary artist and the self-consciousness of the encomiastic poet necessarily overlap in the precarious establishment of a poetic voice.

The manipulation of the poet's voice that distinguishes Theocritus' poetry is, then, crucial to his development of a language of praise. The novel circumstances of encomium within a Greek tradition – which could be expressed as the move from the context of the *polis* to the context of the court – requires a transformation of the discourse of praise, for which Theocritus' indirect, varying and self-dramatizing articulation of voice is both a symptom and a condition of possibility. As with the case of the

---

[161] On the Pindaric language of this *Idyll*, see Clapp (1913); Perotta (1925) 9–25; Meincke (1965) 79–84; Cairns (1976) 303–4; and for a lengthier discussion of these echoes Gutzwiller (1983); Austin (1967); and at greatest length Griffiths (1979a) index s.v. *Pindar*.

[162] The testimonia are collected by Pfeiffer (1949) ad fr. 222.

pastoral tradition, the later traditions of praise poetry must not be used to efface the specificity of the Theocritean project.

In this chapter, I have traced the highly complex sense of the poet's voice in the varied output of Theocritus, and in particular the pervasive multiplication and framing of voices and the representation of desire. One area that I have regularly hinted towards but not developed is the Hellenistic poets' acute awareness of the past and in particular the literary traditions to which they are heirs. It is to that sense of the past and the great epic of Apollonius Rhodius, the *Argonautica*, that I wish to turn for the final chapter of this book.

5   The paradigms of epic: Apollonius Rhodius and the example of the past

The avant-garde writers of the Hellenistic period demonstrate an acute sense of literary tradition. In the previous chapter we have already seen some of the ways in which Theocritus develops his distinctive fragmented and polyphonous voice in relation to the past. In the programmatic narrative of *Idyll* 7, the search for an exemplary voice recedes through a series of lost poets' songs towards an always already distanced model of excellence. So in *Idyll* 11, the much-discussed Hellenistic technique of reversing and restructuring the phraseology of earlier writing finds a parallel in the appropriation and manipulation of a Homeric figure: the Cyclops is taken back to a green and loving youth, back to a time before Homer's writing of him as a paradigm of monstrous brutality. Indeed, in Hellenistic poetry we see again and again a search for an original and originating moment in the past 'before Homer wrote'. In part, this move can be seen as a response to an awareness of the modern poet's epigonal status – an awareness of what Walter Jackson Bate (1970) calls 'The Burden of the Past'. Like Seferis, the Hellenistic poet can truly say 'I awoke with this marble head in my hands.'[1] The awareness of the effects of the monuments of the past on the possibilities of the creative act are not limited in the ancient world to the Hellenistic writers, for sure, but writing from within the archive – the Hellenistic condition ἐν βύβλοις, 'amid the books' – provides a heightened perception and concern that 'the word is not his own word only, but has whored with many before him'.[2] Many of the traits that are regarded as typical of Hellenistic

---

[1] ξύπνησα μὲ τὸ μαρμάρινο τοῦτο κεφάλι στὰ χέρια (*Mythistorema* 3).

[2] Bloom (1973) 65. It has become an article of faith recently that the classical world does not show an 'anxiety of influence': Conte (1986) 26–7; Bing (1988) 61 ('non-agonistic'); Rosenmeyer (forthcoming). Yet, for Conte at least, this depends on the surprising counter-assertion that in the ancient world there is an 'essentially neutral meeting' (27) with tradition – tradition defined as 'a single organic body of once individual but now institutionalized choices, a system of rules and prescriptions'.

poetry can be seen as functions of 'the remorseless deepening of self-consciousness before the rich and intimidating legacy of the past':[3] the construction of new and hybrid poetic forms – what Kroll calls 'die Kreuzung der Gattungen'; the refocusing of poetic subject matter onto what in earlier traditions had been the margins of interest; the repeated use of aetiology; the elaborate word games with the language of the past; the parodic refiguring of earlier representations; the shattering of generic expectations; and, of course, the extensive collecting and cataloguing of and commentary on the texts of earlier generations can all be seen as products of the self-conscious distancing from and dependence on the work of the past. Peter Bing, in a fine recent study of Callimachus' relation to the past, has well observed that it is significantly concomitant with these gestures of 'rupture and revival' that the theme of mourning a long dead poet, or writing an epitaph for him, becomes a *topos* of epigrammatists.[4] So, too, one might add, does the description of earlier works of plastic arts – the ecphrastic epigram (which may also include praise of the artist).[5] There are even encomiastic descriptions of the books themselves of earlier writers.[6] In these many epigrams – an important form of cultural expression for the Hellenistic writer – the present's response to the art of the past becomes the explicit theme of composition.

The paradigms of the past are integral to Apollonius' writing. On the one hand, he shows with striking clarity – as we will shortly see in more detail – the strategies I have just presented in very general terms. The subject of his great poem, the *Argonautica*, is Jason's quest for the Golden Fleece, and not only does this take place in the generation immediately before Homer's *Iliad* – we observe the child Achilles watching his father's departure – but also the story of the Argo is expressly mentioned in Homer as a well-known song (*Od* 12.69–70). Apollonius goes back to a time before Homer's to write – as it were to *rediscover* – the story already old for Homer. And Apollonius' awareness of his epigonal status, his manipulation of the linguistic and cultural artefacts of the past, are crucial to this text: his games with literary language, his confusion of generic expectations, his parodic representations of the heroic figures of the past, his self-consciousness, have indeed become standard topics of recent criticism of the *Argonautica*.

On the other hand, to write epic is to write within a genre which cannot

---

[3] Bate (1970) 4.   [4] Bing (1988) 56–72.

[5] E.g. Antiphilus 35, 48, 49; Antipater 36, 38.

[6] E.g. Antipater 103; Antiphilus 36. Argentarius 15 is an amusing late variation on the theme.

escape the past. It is, first, the genre whose subject matter is – in a privileged way – the past. Description in the preterite tense of events in the past is the *modus operandi* for the epic (unlike, say, love lyric, elegy, epigram). The memorializing function of epic for Homer was discussed in chapter 2, and it is not by chance that Apollonius announces the subject of his epic as παλαιγενέων κλέα φωτῶν, 'the famous deeds of people *born long ago*.' Yet, and this is a second point, the inevitability of mentioning Homer in a description of Apollonius arises because epic in the ancient world comes with a particular and highly articulated notion of literary tradition – the genre's past. The interconnected praise of Homer as 'greatest poet' and of epic as 'noblest genre' leads any self-conscious affiliation to the genre of epic into a remarkably developed sense of a paradigm. To write a Hellenistic epic, then, is to be inscribed in an especially intricate, overdetermined relationship with the literary past.

This chapter will consider one particular facet of this problem in some depth: the exemplarity of the past – that is, how the past becomes an example, a paradigm, for the present, and how these paradigms of the past may affect the present. I need hardly add that this subject is fundamental not only to Apollonius, but also to the classical tradition itself, which takes the Classics as its example, which calls the texts of the ancient world 'the Classics' precisely because of their exemplarity. I hope that in exploring exemplarity in Apollonius, I will be illuminating also an idea crucial to the functioning of Classics as a discipline.

Before I turn to the more detailed treatment of the topic of exemplarity, however, there is a need to outline a more general framework by way of introduction to this tantalizingly difficult and still insufficiently studied and read text. And as I began my discussion of the *Odyssey* with the proem, so, too, here I wish to begin at the beginning.

OPENING AND CLOSING THE TEXT: SINGING AND SIGNING

Ἀρχόμενος σέο, Φοῖβε, παλαιγενέων κλέα φωτῶν
μνήσομαι, οἳ Πόντοιο κατὰ στόμα καὶ διὰ πέτρας
Κυανέας βασιλῆος ἐφημοσύνῃ Πελίαο
χρύσειον μετὰ κῶας εὔζυγον ἤλασαν Ἀργώ.

Beginning with you, Phoebus, I will recount the famous deeds
of people born long ago, who, at the behest of King Pelias,
down through the mouth of the Pontus and the Black Rocks
drove the Argo in search of the Golden Fleece.

The relation of 'rupture and revival' with Homeric epic is strongly marked in the opening lines of Apollonius' work, at the level of the word and at the level of generic expectation. The first words of both the *Iliad* and the *Odyssey* are key indications of the thematic structure of each narrative. So, too – but in a different way – is the first word of the *Argonautica*. As many critics have noted, the phrase *archomenos seo, Phoibe*, 'beginning with you, Phoebus', echoes the opening phrases of hymns: *archom' aeidein*, 'I begin to sing', is a common formula through-out the corpus of hymns (as is *mnēsomai*, 'I will recount'),[7] and there is also a particular (regularly cited) close parallel with the closing formula of the *Hymn to Selene* (18–9) σέο ἀρχόμενος κλέα φωτῶν ᾄσομαι, 'Begin-ning with you, I will sing the famous deeds of people.' This hymnic invocation at the beginning of the epic is often taken as a wilful 'mixing of genres' – an effect which turns the familiar recognition of a generic sign to a defamiliarized recognition of difference. Yet the performance of Greek epic poetry was normally preceded by a short hymn, and the *Theogony* of Hesiod – an author to whom the Hellenistic poets indicated an especial affiliation – offers a fine example of the hymnic proem as an integral part of a hexameter poem.[8] As Callimachus' *Hymns* can be seen as 'mimetic poetry',[9] so the signs of hymnic language here trace a perfor-mative scenario. Moreover, when the epic, as we will see, abruptly ends with the closing formulas of a hymn, framing the narrative, it is as if the complete *Argonautica* has been a (hymnic) prelude; as if the pretext to end is – playfully – an epic to come.

In the light of such manipulation of the language of commencing and closure, it is also significant that the beginning word of the epic is 'beginning'. It focuses attention on the act of narration; and this self-reflexiveness is without doubt programmatic. (We see here how 'the level of the word' and 'the level of generic expectation' are separable only for heuristic purposes.) For the journey of narration and the journey of the narrative are constantly and in a most self-conscious manner intertwined by Apollonius (and notice that the subject of 'beginning' is the *ego* of the narrator). This emphasis on narration itself as a thematic is followed by the announcement of the most traditional performative aim of epic,

---

[7] *Archom' aeidein*, e.g. *H. Dem.* [ii] 1; *H. Art.* [ix] 8; *H. Dio* [xxvi] 1; *H. Ath.* [xi] 1; *mnēsomai*, e.g. *H. Dem.* [ii] 495; *H. Ap.* [iii] 1, 546; *H. Herm.* [iv] 580; *H. Aph.* [x] 6.

[8] See West (1966) ad 1; Richardson (1974) 3–4. On Hesiod and Alexandrian poetry, see Reinsch-Werner (1976); Kambylis (1965) 110–24; Pfeiffer (1968) 117; Halperin (1983) 245–8.

[9] This phrase is borrowed from Bulloch (1985a); Hopkinson (1984).

namely, *kleos*. Yet here, too, the rewriting of epic language is marked. First, the phrase *klea phōtōn*, 'the famous deeds of people', although it closely parallels the *Hymn to Selene*, also varies the famous description of Achilles in the *Iliad*, singing the *klea andrōn*, 'the famous deeds of men'; and the shift is significant. For while the plural term may suggest that this is the epic of a group rather than an individual[10] – and the catalogue of heroes will begin as soon as line 23 – the selection of the general term 'people' as opposed to the valorized heroic term *anēr*, 'man', also opens a question on the one hand about the qualities of 'manliness' of the figures of this epic and on the other about the gender of its leading figures. 'The famous deeds of people' programmatically indicates the epic's concerns with the relations between Jason and his crew, the disfigurements of heroic models of behaviour, the role of Medea.

Second, the adjective 'born long ago' introduces at the outset an added emphasis on the distance of the figures of the poem from the narrator's present.[11] The tension between 'this hypothesized past age and the very Alexandrian concern of much of the poetic material'[12] of the *Argonautica* is integral to the epic narrative. It is demonstrated from the first line.

The address to Apollo (within the hymnic language) fills the place of the invocation to the Muse of the opening of the *Iliad* and the *Odyssey*. Apollo is associated with poetry, of course, both in general and specifically, say, in the prologue to Callimachus' *Aetia* (which is so often taken as a founding statement of Hellenistic poetics). Here, however, the god's involvement as a figure in the narrative is stressed at line 8, where Jason arrives 'not long after your oracle . . .', and the god plays a role repeatedly afterwards.[13] The opening address to a divinity constructs a source of authority which actively enters and figures in the narrative (to be authorized).

The opening lines of the *Argonautica*, then, are hard to read adequately without a recognition of the *arte allusiva* at work in them. This writing in and through the language of the past has regularly been seen – and often (within a Romantic poetics of originality and 'spontaneous overflow of powerful feeling') censured – as a sign of belatedness. Bing writes: 'The allusiveness of these poets . . . reflects the profound desire to compensate for a perceived epigonality and artistic disjunction . . . The un-

---

[10] So, in particular, Carspecken (1952) 110–12; also Beye (1982) 77–79 (with qualifications); Lawall (1966).

[11] Giangrande (1976) 273 notes that *palaigeneōn* means 'born long ago' i.e. 'old' (of alive people) in Homer, but 'born long ago' i.e. 'of another age' here.

[12] Hunter (1988) 452.   [13] See Hunter (1986) for discussion and bibliography.

derlying hope of these poets' allusiveness is meaningful continuity ...
[But] the very mastery that the Hellenistic poets are so zealous to establish and display is itself a sign of rupture.'[14] Yet, as we saw in chapter
3 with parody – and, as Butor comments, 'la citation la plus littérale est
déjà dans une certain mesure une parodie'[15] – there is also a complex
double hermeneutic at work in reading such allusive writing. Indeed,
there is an active involvement, an implicating, of the reader at work also
in this Hellenistic *arte allusiva* (an involvement that was associated in the
previous chapter with the proclaimed esotericism of Hellenistic poetry,
an esotericism which is often equated precisely with the literary knowledge suggested by such a poetics of allusion). For, as Compagnon comments on literary allusion in general: 'la citation est un élément privilégié
de l'accommodation car elle est un lieu de reconnaissance, un repère de
lecture':[16] that is, the process of recognition also invites a self-recognition
as a knowing reader, a sharer of knowledge. The rhetoric of allusion
marks the poet's self-representation as an epigonal voice, then, but also
requires the reader's collusion. As we will see, Apollonius time and again
playfully manipulates the relation between allusion and collusion – in a
way which raises questions both for the poet's voice and for the reader's
engagement with it.

The narrative of the proem 5–17, which is to explain (γάρ) the announcement of the quest for the fleece (2–4), scarcely follows the norms
of Homeric causality (and the traces of similarity with hymnic and
lyric narratives serve further to emphasize the strangeness of this epic
formulation[17]):

> For such was the oracle Pelias heard, that in the future
> a hateful doom awaited him – to perish by the devices of the man
> whom he saw come from the people in one sandal.
> Not long after your pronouncement, Jason
> crossed the stream of wintry Anaurus on foot;
> he saved one sandal from the mud, the other he left
> in the depths, held back by the current.
> He came straight to meet Pelias
> at a feast, where he was sacrificing to his father Poseidon
> and the other gods; but he ignored Pelasgian Hera.
> The king immediately saw him and recognized the omen; and he devised
> a test of a voyage of many cares, so that Jason might lose his return
> either at sea or among foreign men.

[14] Bing (1988) 75.   [15] (1968) 18.   [16] (1979) 23.
[17] See Fränkel (1968) 31–2; Fusillo (1985) 32–4; Beye (1982) 19–21.

290 The paradigms of epic

The figures are presented with little contextualization: no genealogies, nor even a patronymic; on spatial co-ordinates; no mention of the relationship between Jason and Pelias, nor its history. There is no indication of why Jason accepts the mission; nor of the significance of how he lost one sandal. Even the structured pattern of oracle and fulfilment and the suggestion of transgression and punishment in the king's ignoring of Hera at the sacrifice are expressed so barely that it is as if the narrative of explanation is reduced to (merely) some fragments, some sign-posts. The Aristotelian recommendation of commencing *in medias res* becomes – without a developed pattern of Aristotelian causality – a series of extracts 'aus der Vorgeschichte'.

Yet this disjunctive narrative itself turns out to be a function of the rhetoric of *praeteritio*, of passing over (18–22):

> νῆα μὲν οὖν οἱ πρόσθεν ἔτι κλείουσι ἀοιδοὶ
> Ἄργον Ἀθηναίης καμέειν ὑποθημοσύνῃσιν.
> νῦν δ' ἂν ἐγὼ γενεήν τε καὶ οὔνομα μυθησαίμην
> ἡρώων, δολιχῆς τε πόρους ἁλός, ὅσσα τ' ἔρεξαν
> πλαζόμενοι.

> Now as for the ship, the songs of former bards celebrate
> how Argus built it with the guidance of Athene.
> But as for me, I wish to tell the races and names
> of the heroes, the long journeys on the sea, and all they did
> on their wanderings.

The proem is but a priamel to the catalogue of heroes which begins the tale of the Argo's route and her crew's adventures. Earlier poets have sung – and the song lives on[18] – of the construction of the *Argo*. The continuity of epic's celebration becomes part of the reasoning for the selection of a different subject for poetry, for not repeating the *kleos*, as the narrator passes over the Argo (which ship, as Gaunt points out, famously can talk for itself[19]). Where Homer can ask that *he too* should hear and repeat the Muses' song (*kai hēmin Od.* 1.10), in the *Argonautica* there is an opposition between 'the former bards' and the present narrator. This is, however, not merely another response to the burden of the past (as he sings of the past). For the rhetoric of the *praeteritio* also marks the (wilful) entrance of the narrator into the narrative (and I have already commented on the programmatic focus on narration as practice in the

---

[18] On the readings ἔτι κλείουσι and ἐπικλείουσι, see Giangrande (1973) 1.
[19] (1972) 118.

opening lines of the epic). Indeed, *praeteritio* is a repeated rhetorical strategy in the *Argonautica*. As the story of Hylas unfolds, the relation between Hylas and Heracles is expressed (genealogically) through the encounter of Heracles and Theiodamas, Hylas' father. As this tale expands – again so allusively that to follow it, Vian suggests,[20] requires prior knowledge of the story that is recounted, significantly, in Callimachus' *Aetia* – the narrator comments (1220): ἀλλὰ τὰ μὲν τηλοῦ ἀποπλάγξειεν ἀοιδῆς, 'But this would wander far from my song.' The 'paths of song' is a common expression in Greek and we have seen how Pindar develops such terminology as a structuring element of the discourse of praise and its limits. Here, as Hylas wanders off – which leads Heracles and Polyphemus also to wander off into a different set of toils – the language of wandering song is not merely a moment of self-reflexive humour about the direction (in all senses) of the narrative.[21] Rather, the entrance of the narrator points towards a different Hellenistic construction of the question of what is to come into a narrative. The *praeteritio* not only reinforces the allusiveness of the preceding narrative – and its elusive significance for the tale to come – but also self-consciously marks such abrupt changes of narrative direction as part of the narrator's role in (the aesthetics of) this epic. For Homer, not even ten mouths could exhaust the Muses' omniscient account of the forces mustered for Troy; he – a human conduit of the divine voice – recounts only the leaders and the ships. For Pindar, the boundaries and limits of fitting praise are fundamental to the act of praise and are thematized within the songs of praise. The Hellenistic writers and Apollonius in particular manipulate different protocols of inclusion and exclusion. The set of intellectual, rhetorical and aesthetic concerns of the *Argonautica* constitutes the framework for the rhetoric of *praeteritio*. The self-reflexive and ironical narrator's comment on narration implies – and plays a part in – the development of a set of Hellenistic criteria for writing epic.

This rhetoric of *praeteritio* is linked also to the language of epic memorial in the description of the herald Aethalides (640–49).[22] Aethalides is the son of Hermes (the tricky god of communication) and Hermes has given him μνῆστιν ... πάντων ἄφθιτον, 'an immortal memory of all things'. *Aphthitos*, 'immortal', it will be remembered, is the especially valorized epithet that qualifies Achilles' object of pursuit, his *kleos*. What for Achilles is the search for a (passive) 'immortal renown' on the lips of

---

[20] (1974) 46–8.   [21] So Beye (1982) 16.
[22] On Aethalides, see Ardizzoni (1965); Beye (1982) 37; Hurst (1967) 149–53.

men becomes for Aethalides an (active) 'immortal recall'. Indeed, 'even now', ἔτι νῦν περ 644, even in Hades, Aethalides answers mens' enquiries – and, like the demi-gods, Castor and Polydeuces, lives partly in the Underworld, partly among living men. The phrase ἔτι νῦν περ, 'even now', is a repeated expression in the *Argonautica* that links a narrative of the past with the present (it is, as we will see, a particularly significant sign of crossing the gap with the past in the *Argonautica*'s pervasive aetiologies). Here, the figure with 'immortal recall' lasts on, to the present incarnation of song. At this point, the narrator comments (648–9): ἀλλὰ τί μύθους Αἰθαλίδεω χρειώ με διηνεκέως ἀγορεύειν;, 'But what need is there for me to tell the *muthoi* of Aithalides continuously?' Both the stories about Aethalides and the speech he makes as herald to queen Hypsipyle are repressed, as the narrator cuts himself off from a continuous telling of the *muthoi* of the figure whose memory continues still. If, as Beye suggests, the adverb *diēnekeōs*, 'continuously', indicates an affiliation to a poetics of discontinuous, disjunctive narrative,[23] it has a particular, ironic significance here as a comment on the 'immortal memory' of the herald Aethalides and the immortalizing role of the bard's poetry.

The intervention of the figure of the narrator – focusing the reader's attention on the act of narration itself – is a well-known feature of the self-conscious literary stance of the Hellenistic poets. What each of these examples of *praeteritio* further demonstrates is that these authorial comments are not isolated moments of humour or irony but linked to the widest problems of the poet's voice and constructed within and against the literary tradition of such problems.

Hence, the relation of the poet to the Muses becomes especially relevant. The proem (which I am still glossing) ends (22): Μοῦσαι δ' ὑποφήτορες εἶεν ἀοιδῆς, 'May the Muses be the interpreters of my song.' As Paduano notes, both the delayed mention of the Muses – preceded by Apollo – and their position, apparently subordinate to the poet, as suggested by *hupophētores*, 'interpreters', constitutes an inversion of the Homeric model.[24] Yet the narrator and the figure of the Muse have a more complex and varied relationship than Paduano suggests. In the invocation at the beginning of Book 3, Erato, a single Muse, is asked both to stand by the poet (παρά θ' ἵστασο) and to speak

---

[23] Beye (1982) 37.
[24] Paduano (1970). For the most recent discussion with full bibliography, see Fusillo (1985) 365–6 with n. 16, n. 18.

to him (καί μοι ἔνισπε).[25] In Pindar's fourth *Pythian*, the Muse is asked 'to stand by a dear man' – the comastic celebration for Arcesilas, which is also, of course, to narrate Jason's expedition and return. The similar language points to the very different sense of poetic production in the two narratives of the Argo's trip. Here, then, the Muse seems to be an authoritative co-voice (as Apollonius marks his distance from the literary tradition). What is more, Erato is also a cause of the erotic narrative. It is Erato who 'bewitches unwed young girls with the cares of desire' (3–5). As with the opening address to Apollo, a divinity is apostrophized who enters and affects the narrative to come. In Book 4, however, in the opening invocation, the poet now appeals to the goddess to tell him an authoritative tale, as he professes his doubt about the causes of Medea's flight from Colchis. The narrator's mask of uncertainty – where in contradistinction to Homer's and Pindar's rhetoric of doubt, 'the ignorance is now not of action but of interpretation'[26] – not only may mirror the complexity of human motivation and (self-)perception of motivation, as Richard Hunter rightly argues,[27] but also produces for the reader a parallel difficulty of interpretation, a difficulty of determining the reason – the cause – for such a rhetoric of indeterminacy at this turning point in the narrative. (Behind the mask of uncertainty is ... ?) So, the Muses' authority becomes a sign in Apollonius' game of epic 'believability': like Callimachus, Apollonius writes in and against an Aristotelian commitment to the plausible, and nowhere with more complexity and irony than when the values of 'truth', 'likelihood', 'persuasiveness' are explicitly broached.[28] Thus at 4.1381–2, as the Argonauts decide to carry the Argo across the Libyan desert, the narrator comments: Μουσάων ὅδε μῦθος· ἐγὼ δ' ὑπακουὸς ἀείδω Πιερίδων, καὶ τήνδε πανατρεκὲς ἔκλυον ὀμφήν, 'This is the *muthos* of the Muses; I sing obedient to the Pierides, and I heard this message with absolute certainty.' The role of epic bard as conduit of the Muses' voice is proclaimed ... as if it were a disclaimer. The obedience of the poet to the Muses' *muthos*, and the absolute certainty with which he claims to have heard it, sets an ironic distance between the narrator and the tale he reports. The fact that this story of heroic endurance is also told in Pindar, however, raises a question of the degree to which 'the Muses' and 'literary tradition' are to be interrelated.

---

[25] On this and the other invocations of the Muses, see in particular for discussion and bibiography Hunter (1987); Fusillo (1985) 367–75.

[26] Hunter (1987) 134.   [27] Hunter (1987).   [28] See Goldhill (1986b) 26–30.

So, earlier in the same book, the narrator cuts off his story of Kronos' castration with a plea to the Muses to be gracious, since he is reporting the song of former poets (4.984–5): ἵλατε Μοῦσαι, οὐκ ἐθέλων ἐνέπω προτέρων ἔπος, 'Be gracious Muses; I sing unwillingly the *epos* of earlier generations.' The (innovative) poet appeals to the Muses now for forgiveness for his unwilling repetition of an old story.[29] Literary tradition becomes a (mask of) compulsion, even as the interruption marks the rupture from the past.

Such examples could be multiplied; there are two brief general points that I wish to make, however. First, in the narrative of the *Argonautica* there is a *developing series* of comments on the process of telling the story: there is a narrative of its narration. Second, this shifting relationship of control and direction between the Muses and the figure of the narrator is a sign and a product of a shifting sense of authority in Hellenistic poetry. As there is a turn towards different criteria of inclusion and exclusion, so there are different possibilities of valorization: whereas for Homer the catalogue of the ships is sanctioned by the divine Muses' omniscience, for Apollonius it is the (man-made) catalogues of the library, the scientific, anthropological, literary critical studies of the scholars of the Mouseion that provide the intellectual and institutional framework of poetic *sophia*. The rise of prose, the importance of philosophy as a cultural as well as an intellectual force, the changing social conditions of poetic production, as I argued in the previous chapter, make the position from which the poet speaks profoundly ambivalent – especially for the epic poet within the epic tradition. The claims of poetic *sophia* are realigned. The intricate and shifting relation between the Muses and the narrator must be seen within the movement towards poetry's new strategies of authorization.

This discussion of the narrator's self-representation in the narrative puts a different light on the final lines of the poem. I have already mentioned that the epic ends with a bold, even scandalous,[30] and certainly abrupt return to the hymnic formulas with which it began (4.1772): ἵλατε ἀριστήων μακάρων γένος,[31] 'be gracious, O race of blessed heroes'. This invocation of the subjects of the poem (rather than the god Apollo) leads to a prayer that 'these songs might be sweeter year by year for men to sing' (1772–4). The Homeric hymns regularly conclude with a prayer for

---

[29] On this passage, see in particular George (1977); Fusillo (1985) 371–2.

[30] The term 'scandalous' is taken from Livrea (1973) ad loc. See also Fränkel (1968) 622–5.

[31] Fränkel's emendation of ἀριστήων is plausibly rejected by Livrea and Giangrande.

prosperity and the promise of future song: here, however, the prayer is for the song's increasing success over the years – thus combining the hymnic terminology of closure with a sense of epic memorializing among men, and, in *glukerōterai*, 'sweeter', a term closely associated with especially lyric poetry's self-description. The narrative, typically enough for Apollonius' writing, approaches its end with a complexly allusive announcement of its own continuing performance. (From its past to ... now, ἔτι νῦν.) What is to be made of this frame of the hymn? Beye essays a sophisticated answer to this question: 'Apollonius at last wishes to call the poem finished as a creation, like a painter who finally signs his canvas and hangs it on the wall. Then just as the painter stands and gazes upon his creation, so Apollonius takes his stand with the reader, bidding his heroes and his poem farewell.'[32] The self-reflexiveness of the *Argonautica*'s marking of itself as a work of art is indeed strongly marked here, especially in comparison with the endings of the *Iliad* or *Odyssey*, as it is throughout the narrative. So, too, the apostrophe does change the relation between narrator and the figures addressed. Yet what sort of signature is there here? How does the poet 'stand with the reader'? The expression of ending is intricately turned (1775–6): ἤδη γὰρ ἐπὶ κλυτὰ πείραθ᾽ ἱκάνω ὑμετέρων καμάτων, 'for now I reach the famous termination of your toils'. The first-person verb *joins* the figure of the author to his subjects' toils. I have already described how the narrative of narration runs with the story of the journey: the telling and toiling are joint subjects of the epic. Here, Apollonius and the Argonauts reach a conclusion together. Thus, as the first word of the epic is *archomenos*, the poet 'beginning', so the last word is (1781) εἰσαπέβητε, 'you disembarked', the heroes' ending. (In this ring composition, to purloin a caption from Stephen Hinds, the return trip is, precisely, *booked*.)[33] The description of the termination of the toils as 'famous', *kluta*, is also pointed. It stresses the *kleos* of the (prayed for) telling and retelling of the Argonauts' story, the subject announced in the opening line and here affirmed in the conclusion of the epic. (*Kleos* is both the medium and the result of epic performance.) *Kluta*, too, then, marks a *poetic* arrival. Rather than 'signing the canvas and standing back', the author depicts himself in the frame (as a figure). The poet cannot slough off the masks of self-representation to 'stand with the reader'. The signature is part of the design.

The abruptness of the ending, however, is also given a nicely ironic colouring by a certain deflationary logic in the final paragraph's journey.

---

[32] Beye (1982) 14.   [33] Hinds (1985).

After the multiform adventures of the previous four books, the 'famous termination' is reached because (γάρ, 'for' (1775); ἐπεί, 'since' (1776)) 'no adventure happened, no storm' on the final stage from Aegina to Pagasae. Yet this amusingly negative description of the final voyage will take us to the heart of the *Argonautica*'s narrative composition. Fränkel notes well that despite the evident and emphatic ring composition of the poem and the return journey ('the author brings his heroes to the threshold of their homecoming but not a step further'), the epic has 'with respect to the narrative action, an open ending'.[34] Indeed, there is no mention of Jason's return to the city with the fleece, or of any of the subsequent murderous developments. Fränkel relates this abrupt ending to Orpheus' song in Book 1 of the *Argonautica* (494–515) – a performance of the 'ideal singer' which leaves its audience leaning forward eagerly and in silence to catch the enchantment of the just finished song. This he takes as the image of poetic performance towards which Apollonius aspires. We have, however, also seen the importance – within the different protocols of inclusion and the different constructions of authority – of Apollonius' repeated rhetoric of *praeteritio*, to which the abruptness and negative expressions of the final paragraph can easily be assimiliated: the ending depends on a refusal to tell the *muthoi*. The tension that is created here between the possibilities of narrative expansion and the boundaries of the structuring provided by the round-trip is integral to the progress of the epic. As Fusillo writes, in one of the most developed, if overly formalistic, studies of this technique, 'la presentazione dello schema dell'*iter* ... contribuisce alla coesione dell'opera, e rappresenta un anti-doto dalla spirita centrifuga originata dalla framentazione degli episodi collaterali e dalle varie forme di deviazione'.[35] (Like an encyclopaedia or catalogue – those privileged models of Hellenistic intellectual achieve-ment – there is a taxonomy (the round-trip) but within it, there is the possibility of an unending expansion of entries or of any one entry, the exhaustiveness that 'not even ten mouths' could compass.) Indeed, the different diversions and divagations that articulate the round-trip con-stantly provoke a question of whether – or how – the various landfalls and sea-passages are to be connected other than by the geography and chronology of return: 'the poem', as Hutchinson writes, 'deliberately plays on the reader's conception of its unity as it develops'.[36] The ironic

---

[34] Fränkel (1968) 624–5, my translation.
[35] Fusillo (1985) 102. See also Hurst (1967).
[36] (1988) 105. See also Fusillo (1985) 172–5.

wilfulness of the end, therefore, like the other direct and directing comments of the narrator on his protocols of inclusion, only make explicit what is an informing narrative strategy of the *Argonautica*. The narrative of the *Argonautica* is articulated between the teleological linearity of a journey – where the *iter* (of ship and text) depends on *praeteritio*, passing by and passing over – and the fluid and intricate possibilities of the *muthoi*, the representations (histories, descriptions, explanations) that delay each stage of the journey. The highly self-reflexive development of the figure of the narrator within the *Argonautica* serves to mark this tension in the narrative and the different responses to it.

The mise-en-abŷme effect of representing the poet within the poem is not limited to the figure of the narrator, however. As with the profusion of bards and songs in the *Odyssey*, so in the *Argonautica* the performance of song is highlighted and in particular through the figure of Orpheus who heads the catalogue of heroes. I have already mentioned his song in Book 1 (494ff) which Fränkel describes as the representation of the ideal Hellenistic composition. In Book 2, Orpheus sings a paian to Apollo; it is (as with the songs in *Odyssey* 8) described in indirect speech (704–6): 'Orpheus began the song; how once on the rocky ridge of Parnassus ...' But the text immediately turns to direct invocation (708–10): ἰλήκοις · αἰεί τοι, ἄναξ, ἄτμητοι ἔθειραι, αἰὲν ἀδήλητοι · τῶς γὰρ θέμις ..., 'May you be gracious! Always, lord, is your hair uncut; always unspoilt. For that is right.' This comment is a correction of the previous line, where the youthful Apollo is described as '*still* rejoicing in his curly locks', as if the god would grow up to have them cut off and dedicated (to himself?). Yet, as Fränkel asks, in whose voice does this interruption come? Beye assumes that this is the 'poet's direct speech' – a 'sudden breaking of the illusion' that is 'breathtaking', 'extraorḍinary'.[37] Fränkel outlines a more subtle game of masks here, however, where the poet, as if he were a singer in performance, let slip an error which must be hastily corrected – a fiction of immediacy that once more emphasizes the literary self-reflexiveness of Apollonius' *Buchtext*.[38] This invocation could, then, be the narrator's intervention, correcting the error of his most famous predecessor – a pleasantly ironic representation in the form of a religious scruple of the self-imposed and competitive precision of Alexandrian literary techniques. So, the narrator takes the song's last words as the *aition* for the name of the hymn to Apollo, a scholarly afterword on the history of a religious (and aesthetic) term. Or, as Fränkel himself would have it, the

[37] (1982) 19. [38] (1968) 227–8.

correction could be the poet playing a Callimachean game with his own *sophia* – wittily apologizing for the mistake he has committed in Orpheus' name rather than attributing a bêtise to Orpheus, the son of a Muse. Or, despite Fränkel and Beye, the prayer could also be the more vivid representation of Orpheus' own performance – appealing to Apollo (as Orpheus had announced the performance with a direct appeal for epiphany – with the same term (693), 'be gracious, lord, be gracious', ἵληθι, ἄναξ, ἵληθι[39]). As in the *Odyssey*, the interlacing of direct and indirect speech in the song within the song produces a complex overlaying of poets' voices. Here, however, the interlacing is made even more difficult to disentangle because of the pervasive intervention of the narrator himself as a figure and the note of correction that the shift to direct speech brings.

The narrative of the *Argonautica* shows many signs of experimentation with techniques of summary and of direct and indirect speech.[40] But if there is a single image that captures the complexity of the representation of the performance of song/speech in this work, it is the Argonauts' encounter with the Sirens (4.893ff) – a passage rarely discussed by critics. The Sirens, whose enchantments Odysseus describes to the Phaeacians and whose promises of omniscience he represents in direct speech, form an important image of poetic production in the *Odyssey*, it will be recalled. As so often, an Odyssean scene provides a paradigm for the *Argonautica*. Apollonius opens with a description of the Sirens that markedly varies from Homer's version. Many of these variations have been noted by the commentators. The genealogy for the Sirens that Apollonius offers – there is none in Homer – chooses one of several lineages attested in ancient authors.[41] The name of the Sirens' island is culled from Hesiod – but there is no name in Homer.[42] The use of the term *molpē* to mean 'song' seems to refer to a scholarly discussion on its sense in Homer in which Aristarchus in particular was involved.[43] Apollonius connects the Sirens with Persephone, as Euripides does: in Homer, there is no mention

---

[39] Hutchinson (1988) 89–91 notes this echo: he regards the second invocation as a 'parody' of the first. See also Hunter (1986) 53–4.

[40] 3.579–605 has been much discussed (most recently by Hunter (1989) ad loc.), all too often without reference to *Od*. 23.300–43; *Od*. 8.499–520. It is an experimental passage, for sure; but perhaps not 'quite unlike anything in Homer' as Hunter suggests.

[41] See Livrea (1973) ad loc. for the testimonia.

[42] Homer calls the place where the Sirens sit a 'meadow' (λειμών); the island is called here 'Flowery', Ἀνθεμόεσσα.

[43] See Livrea (1973) ad 894.

of a connection between the Sirens and any other figure. Apollonius describes the Sirens as part girl, part bird (888–9), the result of a transformation that Apollonius, like later writers, also refers to the Sirens' association with Persephone.[44] Where the Sirens' victims in Homer have become 'a pile of rotting bones and shrivelled flesh' (*Od.* 12.45–6), in Apollonius, the Sirens 'wear them down with a wasting disease' (902). Apollonius has, then, fleshed out the Sirens with an Alexandrian intellectual aparatus of genealogy, history, physical description (and perhaps reduced the physicality of the description of the victims). It is, however, the encounter itself that shows Apollonius' wit – and the point of these variations (903–9):

> The Argonauts were ready to cast
> their hawsers from the ship onto the shore –
> had not Thracian Orpheus, son of Oeagrus,
> strung his Bistonian lyre in his hand
> and let the forceful melody of a quick-moving song ring out
> so that all at once their hearing might roar with the beat
> as he spread confusion. The lyre defeated the virgins' voices.

Rather than listening to the Sirens, and thus being able, like Odysseus, to repeat the ineluctable seduction of their song (to an enchanted audience), and rather than having their ears blocked, like Odysseus' crew, the Argonauts are saved by Orpheus' overlaying of sound. Apollonius, the 'ideal poet' within the poem, plays over the voices of the earlier figures of knowledge and song. As Apollonius rewrites the earlier representations of the Sirens, he depicts the expedition's descendant of the Muses drowning out the descendants of the Muses who threaten the expedition, so that the reader too cannot hear what the Sirens sing. Yet the verb κανάχησεν, 'ring out', occurs only once in Homer (*Od.* 19.469), when the bronze bowl hits the ground as Eurycleia recognizes Odysseus' scar. Even as the contest of voices is represented, it is expressed through a unique Homeric turn of phrase from a significant juncture of memory and recognition. It is not only Homer's voice, however, that Apollonius has Orpheus sound out. The sailors' ears roar, and the phrase used *epibromeõntai akouai* (908), 'their hearing might roar', echoes the famous description of the effects of desire on Sappho, *epirrombeisi akouai*, 'my hearing whirred' (fr. 31 11–2) (especially since *peribromeousi akouai*, 'her hearing roared around', is used of Medea's symptoms of desire/panic

---

[44] Again, for testimonia, see Livrea (1973) ad loc.

4.17). As the lyre defeats the maidens' voice (as if in literary competition or violent assault, *ebiēsato* 909), the confusion echoes with the most famous female lyric poet's voice. Echoes – and distorts: *epibromeō*, Apollonius' verb, metamorphoses Sappho's *epirrombeō*, so that between 'roaring' and 'whirring' the confused overlaying of sound is performed as it is described.

The rewriting of the Siren scene, then, is replete with images of drowned out sound and echoes of past voices. The waves, too – unlike the uncanny calm of Odysseus' encounter – make noise, indeed 'echo' (910–11): 'the west wind and the echoing wave (ἠχῆεν κῦμα) rushing past the prow, carried them on'. And Apollonius follows this melée of sounds with a pun (911): 'the voice that the Sirens sent forth was *akriton*'. *Akriton* has two senses: 'unceasing' – hence Seaton's translation 'The Sirens kept uttering their ceaseless song': but also, 'indistinct'; hence Vian: 'Les Sirènes ne laissaient plus entendre que des sons indistincts.' At the end of a passage where both the sense of literary tradition and the images of confused sound are marked, the pun's mixing of the meanings 'unceasing' and 'indistinct' seems remarkably pointed and acutely self-reflexive.

One man, however, a certain Boutes, despite these barriers to his hearing, leaps into the water, only to be saved instantly by Aphrodite, who sends him 'to dwell on the heights of Lilybaion' (918). The story ends, as so often in Apollonius, with a tale of foundation, the start of another story.

This scene provides a wonderful model of the ways in which, at all levels of representation in the *Argonautica*, the past is *written through*. The changing depictions of the narrator and of poetic performance within the poem form a crucial element both of the narrative strategies of the epic – marking in particular the shifting criteria of inclusion and the realignment of authorization – and also of the sense of 'rupture and revival' with the literary traditions in and against which Apollonius' writing works.

It is worth noting finally how in this discussion I have returned to major concerns of the earlier chapters – the (self-)representation of the poet in a narrative of return; the devices of framing and the poet's position in the frame; the masks, humour and parody of rewriting and quotation; the language of *kleos*. This is not simply because the final chapter of my book leads me to wish to end with arguments that form a unifying conclusion: it is rather another sign of how deeply Apollonius' concerns are intertwined with the traditions to which he is an heir.

I wish to begin this discussion of exemplarity with what I take to be a paradigmatic example of the use of mythological exempla in Apollonius. In Book 3, Jason and Medea meet for their first and fateful tryst – to talk inspired by 'the breezes of desire' (972). Jason breaks the charged silence of their encounter with a speech that is glossed by the narrator as *hupossainōn*, 'fawning', 'wheedling'. He promises he is not a 'misleading boaster' (δυσαυχής) like other men (976–8); asks her not to show any modesty in speaking out what pleases her (978–9); but rather, since it is not right to sin in the holy place where they have met, to speak openly, and not to deceive him with charming words (980–3). As so often, a scene of rhetorical manipulation begins with claims of truth and an explicit focus on the dangers of misleading language. The rhetoric of rhetoric. As he leads Medea on, Jason depicts himself as the possible victim of deceit, in a position of weakness from which he supplicates Medea (985–9). He holds out the promise of the thanks suitable for those who are far separated – the glorification of her 'name and noble fame', *ounoma kai kalon kleos* (992). For the wives and mothers of heroes, as well as the heroes themselves, will sing her praises (κλήσουσιν) if the expedition returns (990– 96). This scene is clearly constructed to recall Odysseus' meetings with Nausicaa (and to signify through the echoes and differences).[45] The phrasing here may be designed (with its emphasis on 'separation' and 'return') to have a 'powerful effect on Medea's emotions':[46] but it also recalls specifically the farewell of Nausicaa and Odysseus (*Od.* 8.460–8), where Nausicaa asks to be remembered, and Odysseus promises to pray to her 'as to a goddess' since she saved his life. The promise of *kleos* that is Homeric epic's *raison d'être* becomes in Jason's words a sign of deceptive manipulation.

Jason then offers this extended example to support his plea (997–1005):

> Once Theseus too was saved from a terrible contest
> by kindly Ariadne, Minos' virgin daughter,
> whom Pasiphae, daughter of the Sun, bore.
> When Minos put his anger to rest, she left her homeland,

---

[45] See e.g. for discussion and bibliography Fusillo (1985) 69–73, 307–10; Paduano (1972) 171–200; Clausen (1977); Weber (1983); Bulloch (1985b) 594–5; Hunter (1989) ad 997–1004; also Campbell (1983) who writes (60) 'The Nausicaa–Medea equation is not an equation at all. It is carefully set up only to be swept aside by the evocation of an atmosphere of menace (883f), then duplicity (891f), then neurosis (948f).'

[46] Hunter (1989) ad 990–2.

seated on Theseus' ship. The immortals themselves also
loved her, and there is a sign in the middle of the heavens,
a crown of stars, which men call Ariadne's Crown,
which all night long rolls around the heavenly constellations.
So for you too will there be gratitude from the gods . . .

Odysseus uses the example of the ideal marriage to persuade Nausicaa.
Jason's choice is markedly different, though it, too, may be thought
to hint towards a future (idealized) alliance for persuasive effect. The
connections between the exemplum and Jason's case are precisely drawn:
Theseus, like Jason, is faced by a 'terrible contest' (κακῶν ἀέθλων 997,
ἀέθλων 989); like Ariadne, Medea is a *parthénos* (παρθενική 997,
παρθενική 975); and both are (exhorted to be) 'kindly' (εὐφρόνεουσ' 998,
εὐμενέοντες 980); in both cases there is an angry father, a ship waiting to
take the girl away. Yet Jason's tale is, I take it, revealingly disingenuous.
Ariadne was deserted by Theseus; she was discovered by Dionysus
(hence the 'habilement ambiguë' (Vian) expression 'the immortals themselves also *loved her*' (*philanto* 1002). What exactly would be the proper
term for the relation between Ariadne and Dionysus? What expression
would not show a certain linguistic slippage in describing such a 'habilement ambiguë' liaison?). The god turns her bridal crown into a star. The
careful veiling of crucial links in the story and the selectivity of the details offered produces a fine example of the manipulation involved in
exemplification. The seductive rhetoric, playing with what is stated and
unstated, works both on the innocence of Medea and on the sophistication of the reader, whose understanding of the allusions to a significantly
untold story is a necessary collusion in the humour of the scene.

Yet it is not only the knowing observation of Jason's seductive rhetoric
in action that produces this scene's effect. Nor is it only the distortion of
the model of Odysseus and Nausicaa, and of the story of Theseus and
Ariadne, that is significant. First, the mention of Ariadne is part of a
structured series of references to a continuing family history. Hypsipyle,
the queen on Lemnos whose affair with Jason prefigures his relations
with Medea,[47] is the granddaughter of Ariadne and Dionysus; Jason
performs the magic ritual prior to the tasks in which he wins the fleece,
wearing a robe which is still imbued with the divine odour of the love-
making of Dionysus and Ariadne – which Hypsipyle had given to Jason.
Each of the male-female liaisons in this sequence (Jason/Hypsipyle,

---

[47] This prefigurement is discussed by e.g. Zanker (1979); Beye (1969); George (1972);
Levin (1971a).

Jason/Medea, Theseus/Ariadne, Dionysus/Ariadne) in different ways expresses a doomed disjunction between the sexes. (Perhaps the ambiguous *philanto* is the only term that could do justice to this variety of mismatches?) As Jason prepares to speak this wheedling speech to Medea he recognizes that she has 'fallen into divinely inspired disaster' (ἄτη ... θευμορίη 973–4). On the one hand, this is a perception of the influence of the gods in Medea's emotional disturbance, and even perhaps in her arrival alone and at night in such a place. On the other hand, it is an indication of the continuing history of (erotic) disaster in which this scene plays a part.

This leads to a second point. For as much as Apollonius takes us back to a time before Homer's narratives, so his Medea is, of course, a younger representation of one of the most famous figures of the fifth-century tragic stage. Many critics have sketched ways in which Apollonius' figure of Medea is played off against the great and violent witch of Euripides' play.[48] The future for Medea is an important background here. 'The name and fame' she will have in Greece will be as an infanticide and violent hater of her deceptive husband, who tries to desert her for a new bride. The humour of this passage may lie in Jason's rhetorical seduction of an innocent Medea. But Jason is also the dupe, as his language unwittingly reveals him to be the future victim of an attempt to treat Medea like Ariadne. Jason is seducing his way into tragedy.

This double edge of seductive rhetoric is further explored as Medea opens Jason's example to scrutiny. After she has explained the magic drugs and ritual to him, she begs him – with a strong echo of Nausicaa – 'to remember the name of Medea' (1069–70), and then asks Jason first where he comes from and second who is this distant relative of hers, the daughter of Pasiphae (1071–6). Jason offers in response an extended account of his glorious genealogy (1079–95), which ends abruptly with a gesture of *praeteritio* that again shows clearly enough the far from innocent practice of exclusion enacted by such rhetoric (1096–101):

> But why do I tell you of all these things to no avail,
> of my home and the daughter of Minos,
> far-famed Ariadne, by which glorious name
> they called the lovely virgin of whom you aske :
> If only, as Minos made agreement with Theseus
> for her sake, your father might be reconciled to me!

[48] See e.g. Phinney (1967); Paduano (1972) 61–239; Clack (1972/3); Barkhuizen (1979); Beye (1982) 33–4, 132ff; Hunter (1987) with further bibliography.

Since he has not in his reply yet mentioned Ariadne, this (mere) repetition of Ariadne's name and glory constitutes a refusal to tell the tale whose further details could suggest the difficulty in his earlier use of the exemplum. (There is a nice irony in the representation of the fawning speaker covering his tracks with another rhetorical strategy, one which mimics the narrator's own repeated gesture! What Jason does to the story of Ariadne, the narrator ...) So, the prayer with which Jason concludes is set to reinforce but not to expand his parallel between Ariadne and Medea. Medea, however, although his speech is strikingly described as 'stroking her down with gentle blandishments' (μειλιχίοισι καταψήχων ὀάροισιν 1002), replies with vehement grief (1103–4) as she marks the *difference* between the exemplum and the present situation (1105–8):

> That is fine, I suppose, for Greece – to honour agreements.
> Aietes is not such a man as you say
> Minos, the husband of Pasiphae, was. Nor am I the same
> as Ariadne. So do not speak of 'proper hospitality'.

There is, of course, bitter irony in these lines as they look forward to the history of broken agreements to come, especially in Greece.[49] But it is the particular phrase 'Nor am I the same as Ariadne', οὐδ᾽ Ἀριάδνῃ ἰσοῦμαι, that shows the double edge of the exemplum most strikingly. It indicates at one level Medea's unwillingness to leave with Jason: the doubt about the causation of Medea's flight at the beginning of Book 4, that I have already mentioned, is in part occasioned by the shifting of Medea's motivation throughout Book 3. On another level, it indicates how Medea will indeed be different from Ariadne, not least in her murderous response to the possibility of abandonment, after she imitates Ariadne's elopement to Greece. Where Ariadne's crown becomes a star in the sky, Medea will leave the tragic stage rising into the sky in the chariot of the Sun. The explicit language of 'likeness', 'sameness', points precisely to the interplay of similarity *and* difference in the logic of the example. As the frames of reference shift, there are different ways in which Medea can be recognized as like and unlike Ariadne.

Jasons's manipulation of Medea by the use of the exemplum is itself, then, to be recognized as Jason being always already framed by the literary tradition he cannot escape (for all his way with words) – a figure Euripides' Medea will make an example of. The reader's recognition of the exemplum's multiple frames of reference is integral to the working

---

[49] So Hunter (1989) ad loc.

of this scene. Yet, if Jason's speech is introduced by the narrator as *hupossainōn*, 'fawning', 'flattering' – a mark of its manipulativeness – it is glossed finally (1008) as κυδαίνων, 'praising', 'glorifying', her. Terms that the tradition of praise poetry repeatedly express the need to keep separate together frame Jason's rhetoric.[50] As Medea is faced by the difficulty of seeing through Jason's words, and as Jason talks of the dangers of deception with words, the narrator's glosses form a question for the reader of the similarity and difference between these evaluative terms as descriptions of this speech. Is Jason's speech an example of 'flattering' or of 'praising' or of both? How is the difference to be formulated?[51] The narrator introduces a play of difference into his framing of Jason's speech, and thus turns back on the reader the problem of reading (through) the seductive rhetoric of exemplification. It is not only Jason and Medea who are being manipulated here.

There are three general points, then, that arise from this scene's self-aware representation of the rhetoric of exemplification. The first is this: the relation between exemplum and case is not one of exhaustive similarity, but also always of difference and excess. The exemplum depends on all levels of its formulation and reading on selectivity. (This means that an example, however simple, is never innocent.) The gap between the exemplum and the case is the condition of possibility of rhetorical manipulation and misrecognition. This leads to the second point: the logic of the exemplum depends on a gesture of framing – the boundaries selectivity imposes. As we saw in the previous chapter with the Cyclops' song, an example presupposes a frame, but the relation such framing constructs is far from simple. In particular, as with Jason's manipulation, different frames of reference produce different possibilities of comprehension. The range of implication that an exemplum may offer is, as we will see, further explored in the *Argonautica*. Yet – and this is my third point – as the reader's position is crucial to the functioning of the exemplum, so there is no possibility of discussing exemplification without

---

[50] Neither Hunter (1989) ad 396 and ad 973–4 ('Like κυδαίνων ... ὑποσσαίνων stresses how Jason's words both please and flatter ...') nor Campbell (1983) 75 (κυδαίνων helps stress the 'unadulterated pleasure at this supreme compliment') deal with the sense of *contrast* in these two terms.

[51] A question answered in different ways by the critics: 'The Hellene is shown glozing the foreign girl with his sweet speech', Clausen (1977) 220; 'his competence in beguiling the inexperienced Medea is beyond praise', Carspecken (1952) 101; 'knowledgeable and uniquely resourceful actor', Lawall (1966) 151; 'traditional values of heroism, honor and integrity are jettisoned, as Jason puts into motion the machinery of success', Lawall (1966) 168; 'a practised courtier', Beye (1982) 139.

becoming embroiled in a highly self-reflexive discourse. So, I have been varying my general points and passages of examples. Extracting critics' remarks as examples of method. Taking passages of the *Argonautica* to frame an argument. Which is to say that reading and exemplification both rely on gestures of selectivity and framing (which may be naive but can never be innocent). Part of my desire to discuss exemplarity here is because it involves procedures basic to critical reading; part of my interest in the *Argonautica* is the way its self-reflexive writing pre-figures its own critical reading.

I want briefly to turn to two particular and interrelated formal aspects of epic composition, both of which involve an articulation of the general and the specific, and both of which depend on a strong sense of framing, namely, the simile and the *ekphrasis*. Both offer instructive insights into the process of exemplification in the *Argonautica*. Now the epic simile has in recent years been the subject of extensive analysis, specifically with regard both to the interplay of similarity and difference – that is, the relation between the simile and the framing narrative – and also to the importance of a literary tradition. Apollonius' use of similes is a key area for the discussion of exemplarity, the literary past and the exemplarity of the past.[52] This is not the place for a full-length discussion of Apollonius' similes, but I do wish to point towards one important aspect of what is a complex set of issues by looking at two particular similes. As Jason approaches the meeting with Medea that I have been discussing, he is described as follows (956–61):

> Not long afterwards, he appeared where she waited,
> springing up high like Sirius from the Ocean,
> a star which rises, beautiful and awe-inspiring to see,
> but which brings unspeakable grief to the flocks.
> So, to her, Jason approached, beautiful to see;
> but his appearance gave rise to the toil of miserable desire.

The simile is, as usual, formally framed by an introductory term (ἅ τε, 'like') and a conclusion, marking the point of the comparison, (ὥς, 'so'). The comparison is based on the double import of the rising of Sirius: beautiful to see, but heralding the harsh heat of the summer. Jason brings to Medea, in his beautiful appearance, the heat of passion – a toil (κάματον) that is the sign and symptom of desire that leads to misery (δυσίμερον). Yet, as has been noted by many commentators, the simile also

---

[52] On Apollonius' similes see in particular Fusillo (1985) 327–41 with extensive bibliography. (Faerber (1932) deserves to be singled out among the earlier treatments.)

recalls first his approach to Hypsipyle, where he was likened to a star, whose 'beautiful blushing light enchants (*thelgei*) and gives pleasure to the virgin who awaits her absent young man' (1.777–9). The prefigurement on Lemnos of the erotic scenario in Colchis is signalled by the links between the two similes at the two moments of Jason's approach to a young and waiting woman. But second, the use of Sirius in particular recalls the famous and murderous rampage of Achilles across the plain of Troy towards the destruction of Hector in the *Iliad* (22.25–32). It is worth remarking how this commonly noted allusion adds a further set of implications to the interplay of likeness and difference in the simile: 'Jason is like Sirius as Achilles is like Sirius ...' – which poses the question of the similarity and difference between the hero of the *Iliad* and the hero of the *Argonautica*. The exemplarity of the simile is fragmented – or supplemented – by the allusive presence of another paradigm that allows difference to echo from within the affirmation of similarity. To seek to express what Jason is like, is (inevitably) to return to the texts of the past (and) to articulate his otherness.

The simile quoted above from Book 1 indicates how Apollonius is prepared to experiment with the construction of a relation between tenor and vehicle: as Jason approaches, watched by the women of Lemnos, the star to which he is likened is watched by young brides, one of whom rejoices, despite the absence of her prospective husband. It is not hard to see how overdetermined this extended image is, not least in the highlighting of one young girl from the many young women, as Hypsipyle's affair with Jason is to be singled out in the following narrative. Yet there is one remarkable passage in Book 4 which – typically enough – shows a willingness explicitly and self-reflexively to mark this manipulation of the exemplarity of the simile (4.1337–42):

> Jason leapt up and shouted loudly to the crew.
> He was burnt dry with dust, like a lion, who howls as he seeks
> his mate through the woods. The copses throughout the mountain roar
> with the deep sound from afar, and the oxen in the field and their
>   herdsmen
> tremble greatly with fear. But, to the crew, Jason's voice was not at all
> chilling, since it was a companion calling to friends.

The development of the simile to the point where it no longer applies and has to be withdrawn, ironically comments both on the expansiveness of Homer's epic similes and on the poet's turn here to the most typical of *topoi* for his intricately allusive simile, the lion and the herd. If the image seems at first sight to be the literary development of a literary *topos*,[53] the poet's final witty mask of irrelevancy erased, like the rhetoric of *praeteritio*, focuses in a self-reflexive manner on the principles of inclusion with which Hellenistic epic works – and on the literary tradition of extended lion similes within and against which it is set. As Apollonius denies the allusive exemplarity he has developed, one could have few better demonstrations of how Apollonius' voice explicitly places the past '*sous rature*' – with all the irony and self-reflexiveness such a practice implies.

The paradigms of the past, then, inform and fracture the exemplification of the simile in the *Argonautica*. At the same time as the simile (in the present tense) – however specific – draws the preterite narrative into the framework of the general, so the repeated echoes of the voices of the past draw the simile into the specifics of literary allusion – and a sense of conflicting paradigms integral to Apollonius' depiction of the heroic world.

If there is one passage, however, where the question of exemplarity and relevance has been debated with intensity by critics, it is the *ekphrasis* of Jason's cloak (which immediately precedes his approach to Hypsipyle and the simile of the seductive starlight that I have just been discussing). I have already considered, especially in the previous chapter, how the *ekphrasis*, particularly in epic, is regularly taken as a significant paradigm for the framing narrative. Here, it is not hard in general terms to agree with the many critics who have argued that the choice of a cloak – an ornament and something to sleep on – makes a significant contrast with the shields of Homer and Hesiod, a contrast which has important implications for the sort of figure Jason is and the sort of narrative we are engaged in.[54] So, too, that the Ram whose fleece is the object of Jason's quest appears in the final scene on the cloak, links the *ekphrasis* to the narrative in a direct way that contrasts markedly with the generalizing technique of Homer. Yet each of the seven individual scenes depicted on the cloak and especially the sequence of scenes have prompted considerable disagreement about the precise functioning of the *ekphrasis* in the narrative. For Lawall, the *ekphrasis* is a didactic model: each of the scenes and the sequence of scenes together project a message.[55] The scenes

---

[53] So Livrea (1973) ad 1338.
[54] See Rose, A. (1985); Shapiro (1980); Lawall (1966) 154ff; George (1972) 48ff; Levin (1977); Beye (1982) 91–3; Zanker (1987) 44–50, 69–70, 75–6, 203; Fusillo (1985) 300–6; Fränkel (1968) 100–2.
[55] Lawall (1966) 154–8.

demonstrate in turn a reliance on the gods, especially Aphrodite; the pathos of war; the need for *mētis*; a warning not to behave insolently. The sequence through positive and negative images promotes the need to have the gods' support and to behave within proper human limits – a message that Jason's maturation through his adventures is to express. For Shapiro, however, 'each of the scenes wrought on the cloak reflects an aspect of contemporary doctrines of aesthetics'.[56] Yet, depite – or because of – the fact that each scene reflects a particular aesthetic interest, 'among the seven scenes ... there are no connections, no obvious contrasts ... no meaningful transitions'.[57] (Yet even Shapiro cannot hold to this apparent subscription to a lack of any significant order in a narrative: 'The order of the scenes on the cloak appears to be random, *except that* ...'[58] (my emphasis).) For Shapiro, it is the aesthetics of the *Argonautica* that is figured in the *ekphrasis*. For Bulloch, the model of the catalogue of women in the *Odyssey* provides a key: which leads to Hypsipyle's significant association with Ariadne, a connection we have seen to be important in Jason's meeting with Medea also.[59] The concealed literary narrative structures the *ekphrasis*. Beye sees each scene in different ways to be allusively significant – and indeed the central image of Aphrodite, looking at herself reflected in the shield of Ares, is not hard to see as significant for both the erotic narrative and for Apollonius' self-reflexive technique – but he rejects reading the whole sequence as equally allegorical.[60] The fragmentation into scenes can be seen as part of the Hellenistic commitment to a poetics of discontinuity. As the poet puts it (729), the cloak is ἐν ... διακριδὸν εὖ ἐπέπαστο, 'well traced in separate sections'. The ancient scholia, however, read the cloak as a full cosmological allegory – a holistic Weltanschauung comparable to the shield of Achilles.[61] These views and variations on them can be multiplied, and such critical disagreements about (degrees of) coherence are to be seen in part at least as the product of the problematic tension we also saw with the series of scenes on the cup in Theocritus' first *Idyll*: how can there be a reading of such a sequence of images that does not attempt a structuring, an intimation of order, a narrative? But how can there be a structuring that is sufficient to the continuing production of meaning in reading the interplay of differences such a sequence constitutes? Yet I do not wish here to view the critical crux of the *ekphrasis* of Jason's cloak simply as another demonstration of how the openness of the literary text

---

[56] (1980) 266.   [57] (1980) 275.   [58] (1980) 276.   [59] (1985a) 594–5.
[60] (1982) 91–2, especially n. 20.   [61] Σ ad 763.

inevitably produces a multiplicity of critical readings (important though
this is for what we mean by 'the meaning' of a text). Rather, I intend to
look at some of the ways that Apollonius thematizes the concern with
coherence and fragmentation in the description itself. For not only does
Apollonius himself, in a way largely overlooked by critics, point towards
the difficulty of comprehending the cloak, but also this analysis will help
show how the *ekphrasis* may be paradigmatic for the narrative of the
Argonautica.

George in a stimulating article observes that in this *ekphrasis* in comparison with Homer's shield 'there is a subtle de-emphasis on the manufacture of the art-work by the deity . . . and corresponding emphasis on
its viewing'.[62] I mentioned above how the response to a work of art
becomes an important *topos* of Hellenistic writing, and, indeed, the
opening description of the form and the manufacture of the cloak (720–
29) includes this striking image of looking at it (725–6):

> You could cast your eyes more easily on the rising sun
> than you could stare at that crimson.

The brightness of the cloak is dazzling. Its depiction is introduced by an
image of the *difficulty* of looking at it. So, the final image on the cloak
suggests a similar barrier to a clear, critical gaze (763–7):

> On it too was Phrixus the Minyan, as if truly
> listening to the Ram, and the Ram looked like he was speaking.
> You would keep silent watching them, and beguile your heart,
> hoping to hear some canny utterance from them,
> although you would wait a long time in expectation.

The aesthetic of realism – that art's beguilement is centred in its ability
to imitate the form of the world – here stresses the viewer's beguilement
into the expectation of a message (*pukinēn baxin*) beyond the image,
words from the silent picture. George argues that this expression of the
enchantment of art provides a model for the following scene: 'the poet
warns the reader that he is liable to be charmed (765ff); the subsequent
narrative tells us that the women *are* charmed. The reader's experience
becomes his reference-point for understanding the women's experience.'[63] Yet the promise of enchantment is also the promise of deception:
ψεύδοιό τε θυμόν, 'you would beguile', 'lie to your heart'. If the viewer
could stare at the dazzling cloth, and see the image of Phrixus and the

---

[62] (1972) 49.   [63] (1972) 50.

Ram, s/he would be destined to look long, beguiled into a false hope of more to be said.

The introduction to the *ekphrasis* and its final scene both emphasize, then, the difficulty of seeing the cloak distinctly, of not being dazzled by its purple (passages), of not being deceived by its appearance. This is not to replace other allegorical readings with the suggestion that the cloak is an allegory of its own unreadability. It is rather to stress once more how Apollonius as he offers the allusive structures of allegory, prefigurement, a modelling of the narrative, interlaces his offer with the imagery of illusion, of misreading. The *ekphrasis*, like the simile whose similarity is erased, retracted, places its exemplarity 'sous rature'.

So far, I have been concerned with certain formal aspects of exemplarity: the mythological exemplum, the simile, the *ekphrasis*. In each case, it is precisely the formal aspects of exemplarity that are placed in question – as the interplays of difference are explored and exploited in the proclamation of similarity. Figuration disfigured. Yet as we saw with Homer, the exemplarity of epic is also and perhaps most importantly to be located in the models of behaviour provided by the heroes and the paradigmatic representation of divinity. Both areas have been extensively discussed for Apollonius, though as Richard Hunter has recently and persuasively argued, many of the modern clichés about Jason as Hellenistic anti-hero need further and more careful consideration, particularly with regard to the way the representation of Jason works through the texts of the past.[64] I shall begin with a very brief comment on the representation of the divine, and conclude this section on exemplarity with a consideration of some aspects of heroism in the *Argonautica*.

Now it is evident that in the representation of the divine and heroic figures of the expedition Apollonius writes through the past – a turn to the past that depends on a deformation of past texts, past narratives. Yet this rewriting of the past turns out to be extremely difficult to analyse. When Athene is at a loss for a plan to help Jason (3.19–21) – she cannot find specifically a *dolos* – or when Athene indicates her awkwardness, as a virgin, in erotic matters (3.32–5), it is easy to see that the humour stems from the subversive contrast of Apollonius' figure with Homeric and other literary and cultural models of Athene as the schemer *par excellence*,

---

[64] (1988). Although Hunter states (1989) 31–2: 'the nature of "heroism", as a particular form of behaviour, is not A.'s central concern', he also notes (1988) 452–3, 'Apollonius' constant concern with the experimental, with testing the limits and possibilities of the epic form and with exploring what it has seemed to take for granted' – which includes the norms and patterns of (heroic) behaviour.

a figure of assured awareness. Yet the implications of such a paradigm of the divine for the recognition of the humanity and mortality of the heroes is more difficult to determine. It is often stated – by 'even normally sober critics', as Hunter amusingly puts it[65] – that the divine figures are reduced to the level of human models, 'ladies of the court' and the like. Indeed, in the famous opening scenes of Book 3, part of the humour of the representation of Aphrodite and Eros is precisely that the goddess of desire is incongruously depicted with a host of domestic details in the role of the parent of an unruly child. So Zanker writes 'the grand ladies of Olympus look "just like us" ... Aphrodite appears like any beautiful woman disturbed while preening herself.'[66] Yet what makes Zanker's view so insufficient here is first that in this scene as elsewhere we see full evidence of divine majesty and the force of their appearance in the human world. The juxtaposition of domestic detail and grandeur of epiphany is already a major element in Homer's depiction of Olympus, and Apollonius emphasizes this disjunction to maximize the possible incongruities of representation. Athene, the embarrassed virgin, also lifts the Argo through the clashing rocks with one hand (2.598–9). It is not so much a desire for realism as a heightened interplay between models of reality that produces Apollonius' figuration of the divine. Second, even as Aphrodite is discovered engaged in the everyday activity of her toilet, it is quite inadequate to say she 'appears like any beautiful woman'. For, as Lennox (1980) has shown in detail, the narrator, through a series of careful allusions to Homer, builds up an expectation that Aphrodite will be discovered with her lover Ares – an expectation that is amusingly overturned when she is found alone combing her hair (preparation for/ after her lover?). The depiction of Aphrodite as mother is set up by the suggestion she will be caught as lover. So, too, as several critics have pointed out, the modelling of this scene on Thetis' trip to Hephaestus establishes a significant contrast between that request for a shield for Achilles and Hera's and Athene's search for erotic assistance. This depiction of the 'vie quotidienne' of the goddesses is elaborately informed with a set of literary expectations and manipulations: the difference from earlier representations of the divine is articulated through the appropriation and deformation of the language and narratives of the past.

The domestication of the divine, then – a repeated comic device not only in Apollonius – is conjoined with extraordinary invasions and manipulations of the human world from the security of Olympus and the

[65] (1989) 25 n. 107.   [66] (1987) 70.

gods' immortality, and with a highly articulated allusive reconstruction of an inherited representation of the divine world. The contrast between the *divina commedia* of Olympus and the human struggles and tragedy is intense – as, say, with Medea's extended torments that follow from Eros' carefree arrow – but the tension is constantly refracted through the appropriation and manipulation of the different voices of Homer and Euripides in particular (different structures of contrast and similarity) and through the highly stressed disjunctions within the portrayal of the divine figures themselves.

The difficulty of determining the interplay of distance from and dependence on the past is especially marked in the depiction of the Argonauts and has prompted much recent criticism.[67] Some general points to begin. First, in the Homeric texts, as we have seen, there is no single and simple model of heroism: not only does the *Odyssey* differ in many respects from the *Iliad*, but also within each epic there are disagreements, contestations about the limits of action, the logic of commitment. It will not do to construct an oversimplified idea of heroism from Homer and then use it to call Apollonius a 'radical rewriter' of the past. Zanker, for example, compares Jason's approach to the Lemnian city – where, as we have seen, his beauty is especially stressed – with the Iliadic Hector's hectoring of Paris as 'beautiful in form but lacking force and prowess' (*Il.* 3.43–5), and concludes that in his depiction of Jason as hero 'Apollonius is turning the values of traditional heroism upside down'.[68] Yet, what Hector is complaining about is the disjunction between beauty and strength – that Paris' appearance belies his qualities. For being *kalos* is without doubt an essential attribute of the aristocratic hero and deeply inscribed in the value system of the epics (and fifth-century culture and beyond). Hector himself is marvelled at for being *kalos* by the Greeks and Achilles demands such recognition for himself.[69] So, too, Odysseus steps forth from various baths and similar transformations beautified and sexually attractive. And the *Odyssey* certainly sets up *mētis* as a quality against *biē*, force. The Alexandrian Jason *cannot* be a Homeric heroic figure – but it is not his beauty or his sexual allure or his turn to *mētis* that sufficiently distinguishes him from the heroes of the past.

---

[67] In particular, see Carspecken (1952); Fränkel (1960); Lawall (1966); Beye (1969) (with Zanker (1979)); Levin (1971b); George (1972); Vian (1978); Beye (1982) especially 77–144; Klein (1983) with extensive bibliography 116 n. 7; Hunter (1988).

[68] (1987) 203.

[69] *Il.* 21.108; 22.370–1. Thersites as counter to Achilles is, of course, also expressed precisely in terms of physical beauty/ugliness.

Second, it has become a modern critical *credo* that Apollonius sets up Heracles and Idas as figures of an old style heroism to be rejected. Heracles, who will not go to the Lemnians, who pulls up trees by the roots, who tries to row the Argo by himself, is left behind – an act of wilful narrative manipulation that not only shows Apollonius working with a mythic tradition which offers contrasting versions of the make-up of the crew of the Argo, but also marks Heracles' 'deficiency', has 'impossible anachronism' for this 'new epic'.[70] Idas, as a foil for Jason, rejects the blandishments of Eros for the power of the sword, wheedling for the boast, and is regularly depicted as having an insufficient comprehension of events.[71] There are, then, different responses to the toils of the journey, different models of behaviour among the Argonauts. Yet, it is often forgotten that on the one hand in the literary tradition Idas is a notorious blasphemer.[72] He is a very strange figure to take as representative of a heroic ethos since he explicitly transgresses the very terms of that model even before the *Argonautica*. Idas may provide a foil to the representation of Jason, but it is not simply in terms of 'old heroism' versus 'new ethos'. On the other hand, Heracles is a deeply polyvalent exemplary figure. Not only are there strongly contrasting representations in, say, comedy and tragedy, but also he is in Pindar and elsewhere the supreme hero, the one figure whose final access to divinity provides a limit case for mortal activity: an unfollowable model. And so, indeed, the final image of Heracles in the *Argonautica* is of him seen or half-seen by Lynceus 'bestial and god-like ... striding off alone across the desert towards divinity'[73] – an uncatchable hero, a figure apart. For certain Stoic and Cynic philosophers, however, Heracles becomes a paradigm, a figure through which to debate man's intellectual and physical attainments.[74] Heracles' road to virtue dramatizes every man's search for excellence. It must not be forgotten that in constructing Heracles as a figure to be left behind, Apollonius is actively creating a particular representation that itself must be understood in and against a tradition of the representations of Heracles. So, when Heracles refuses to join the crew in Lemnos, it is

---

[70] Beye (1982) 93; see also Lawall (1966) 124–31; Levin (1971b); Galinsky (1972) 108–12, who writes paradigmatically (109) 'Herakles appears among the Hellenistic citizen-heroes of the *Argonautica* like a solitary mastodon left over from the palaeolithic world.'

[71] See in particular Fränkel (1960).

[72] A point made (with testimonia) by Hunter (1989) ad 515–20.

[73] Feeney (1986) 66 – a good discussion of Heracles, that I am following here.

[74] See for a general picture Galinsky (1972) 101–25; and specifically on the philosophical tradition from Prodicus to the Cynics, Höistad (1948) 22–73; Feeney (1986) 52–3.

not enough simply to call this heroic – or even aristocratically homosexual – restraint, as, for example, Beye does.[75] To any reader of, say, the *Trachiniae*, Heracles' sexual restraint is itself a reversal of expected behaviour, a marked *move* towards Heracles of the philosophers, the exponent of wisdom and self-control. Indeed, Denis Feeney has demonstrated how the second book of the *Argonautica* in particular 'shows the Argonauts, in various ways, coming close to Heracles, or falling short of him. Polydeuces comes closest of all; in the use of brains, the crew approximate him; but in his invulnerability and isolated self-sufficiency Heracles remains unique.'[76] Heracles may be disposed of, removed from the voyage, but as a model he continues to echo throughout the adventures, not merely in difference but also in similarity with the crew's heroics, as his portrayal in the epic itself veers between comic over-achiever, philosophical saint, savage slayer of savage monsters etc. The paradoxical and polyvalent representation of Heracles cannot be reduced to the simple apotheosis of outdated heroic values. The limits he provides for the other heroes, the limits he transgresses, are far more complexly formulated.

Third, the contestation of the heroic values of Homeric epic is itself part of a tradition. In particular, Athenian tragedy of the fifth century constitutes a powerful rewriting of the texts of the past for the contemporary city.[77] So, too, as discussed in chapter 2, the Pindaric lyric reformulates a set of heroic concerns with a new aristocratic and civic framework. Nor is it by chance that I single out tragedy and Pindar, since Euripides' *Medea* and Pindar's fourth *Pythian* are two of the most important texts against which the *Argonautica* resounds. This background is all too often forgotten in one of the most important areas of difference between the *Argonautica* and the *Odyssey*, namely, the relation between Jason and the crew. As Richard Hunter in his careful reappraisal of the problem writes, 'the hierarchical organization of the two voyages is certainly quite different': for Jason, unlike Odysseus, 'it is better to rely on πολέων μῆτις (4.1336) [the *mētis* of many] than on one πολύμητις [*polumētis*] individual'[78] – an emphasis on collectivity and its values that is stressed from the opening line of the epic to the joint return of crew and leader (an aim that eludes Odysseus and his companions). Yet, this shift must also be seen against the fifth- and fourth-century reworking

[75] Beye (1969).   [76] Feeney (1986) 61.
[77] See for discussion and bibliography Goldhill (1986a) 138–67.
[78] (1988) 441, 442.

of the Homeric consideration of the relations between an individual and a collective enterprise in the new context of the *polis* and its ideology. The popular acclamation by which Heracles is elected leader, only to defer to Jason, is to be understood not only through the contest of values in the quarrel in the opening book of the *Iliad*,[79] but also through the very different narratives of expeditions and leadership in, say, Xenophon,[80] and also through the different sense of commitment to collectivity developed through fifth- and fourth-century discourse.

Fourth, as with the representation of the divine, Apollonius regularly emphasizes contrasting traits present in earlier depictions of heroic behaviour to maximize the disjunctions with bold and startling effect. This has been particularly well discussed for Medea, where the juxtaposition of *parthenos*, racked by desire, and witch, locked into a narrative of violence and magic, produce a figure hard to comprehend within Romantic notions of 'unity and consistency of character'.[81] Yet, for all the modern claims of the need to go beyond such Romantic ideology in reading Hellenistic poetry in particular, the presupposition of a need to examine the epic for a central character and a psychology has proved hard to escape. The extensive depiction of Medea's psychological torment – often excerpted – has reinforced this tendency. The category 'character' itself, however (which scarcely translates the Greek terms *ēthos* or *prosōpon* or *charactēr*) and its instantiation in narrative need further attention, if Apollonius' characters are not merely to be appropriated as examples of modern psychological concerns.[82]

Now, within these general provisos, it can be said that the protocols of heroic behaviour and the *exempla* they provide are subject to Apollonius' questing experimentation. I have already indicated briefly how different models of behaviour are instantiated within the epic, and how Heracles – the heroic *exemplum* par excellence – is both displaced in the epic and yet plays an exemplary role throughout as an absent/present model, drawing on a range of earlier paradigmatic configurations. I want to conclude this section by looking at a fascinating passage that links these various concerns and raises also a difficult question for the idea of heroization itself. The passage is the episode of the Doliones in Book 1, and in particular the final battle.

---

[79] So Hunter (1988) 442–3 *contra* Beye and Vian.
[80] See the suggestive analysis of Tatum (1989) especially 139–239.
[81] See above n. 48.
[82] I have discussed this with bibliography in Goldhill (1986) 168–74.

The Argonauts, after a friendly reception from the Doliones and their newly married king Cyzicus (and after defeating some less friendly giants), set sail, but are driven back by a storm at night. The Doliones assume that they are raiders, arm for battle, but are routed by the Argonauts. Jason kills the king, whose wife commits suicide, and the Doliones' grief-struck refusal even to cook their food results in a ritual of communal corn-milling still performed today. There are few violent clashes for the Argonauts and this is the only armed military encounter between humans in the epic that can be called a battle. Its pathos has often struck critics. Cyzicus is described as 'like Jason, a young man with down still on his cheeks' (972), and so recently married that his attendance at the feast for the Argonauts is described as 'deserting the bedroom and the bed of his bride' (977). His bride's subsequent suicide prompts even the Nymphs to such mourning that a fountain, named after the queen, comes into being (1065–9). That it is Jason who kills Cyzicus suggests the common narrative pattern of Killing the Double; or, more precisely, the mistaken killing of someone assumed to be an enemy who turns out to be closely connected. The tragic error is particularly emphasized in comparison with Odysseus' experience with the Cicones in the *Odyssey*: after sacking a city, Odysseus' fleet is also blown back by a storm to be attacked by other inhabitants of the land and he loses several men before escaping. For Jason, by contrast, it is a battle with those linked by the ties of *xeinosune*, a battle that destroys a king and queen, poised on the threshold of maturity, and that thus wipes out their dynasty, their *oikos*, to the grief of all concerned.[83] The military endeavour that is crucial to the exemplarity of the heroes of the *Iliad* – the route to excellence, the reason for memorial – becomes for Apollonius a site of tragic error and failed aspirations.

Yet the description of the battle itself – emphasizing this difference – forcefully parodies a Homeric narrative (1040–7):

> And Heracles slaughtered Telecles
> and Megabrontes. Acastus destroyed Sphodris.
> Peleus took Zelys and Gephyrus, swift in war.
> But Telamon with the fine lance killed Basileus.
> Idas slew Promeus, Clytius Hyacinthus,
> and the two Tyndaridae Megalosaces and Phlogius.
> The son of Oeneus in addition to these triumphed over bold Itymoneus
> and also Artaces, leader of men.

[83] See Rose, A. (1984).

This passage is modelled on the summaries of battles in the *Iliad* (and in particular perhaps *Il.* 14.511–22) though there is no passage in Homer (or elsewhere in Apollonius) that lists quite so barely a catalogue of victors and vanquished (for all the typically aware variation of verbs of killing (ἐνήρατο, ἐνάριξεν, εἷλεν, κατέκτα, ἔπεφνεν, ἕλεν). It is a surprising narrative that parodies Homer's *effets du réel* by such a *reductio*: here we have a list of the names of otherwise unmentioned Doliones, with occasional but very general epithets, without the patronymics, brief histories or descriptions of manners of death that structure Homeric battle scenes. Since the scholia, indeed, it has been debated whether the names are 'real' – that is, taken from a source that claims knowledge of the honoured war dead of Cyzicus (as the kingdom is known after this king) – or fabricated by Apollonius ('mere names').[84] I will return in the final section of this chapter to the way that this continuing discussion raises interesting questions about the categories of 'realism', 'science', 'objectivity' in Apollonius. For the moment what I wish to stress is that the suspicion of fabrication – of a mask, a fiction, of scholarship – is raised in particular here because this catalogue of war dead moves (with the customary turn to the apparatus of historical explanation) from a parody of Homer's battles to a narrative of heroization (1047–8):

> All of whom still
> the inhabitants worship with the honours of hero cult.

The barely listed victims of the heroes of this epic turn out to be the heroes for the Doliones. Hero cult is unknown in Homer; in the fifth century, as we have seen, the status – and cult – of hero may be awarded to those who die for the state in war, as, for example, with the Marathonomachoi for Athenians. If this battle scene casts a tragic and ironic gaze at the heroes' military success, the defeated Doliones none the less achieve the status of hero, the honours and prayers of cult. The shift from Homeric parody to aetiological tale of the hero cults of this area of the Propontis is, then, not merely a scholarly addition to the narrative but sets in tension two sets of heroes, two sorts of heroization. And the tragic error which joins the Argonauts' martial prowess with the Doliones' doomed bravery makes this tension highly ironic.

Indeed, the killers of Cyzicus go on to hold a funeral with games for their victim, together with the Doliones ('as is right', ἣ θέμις 1061, as if

---

[84] See e.g. Hasluck (1910); Fitch (1912); Wendel (1932) 106; Hurst (1964); Vian (1976) 99 n. 1. This material is discussed in detail below.

there were a model for the proper or usual behaviour in such circumstances) and 'to this day' (ἔτι νῦν περ 1061) 'this barrow (*sēma*) is there to be seen by future generations also', τόδε σῆμα καὶ ὀψογόνοισιν ἴδεσθαι (1062). The echo of the funerals of Patroclus and of Hector, and of Hector's hope for immortality – to have 'a barrow (*sēma*) for future people also to enquire of', σῆμα καὶ ἐσσομένοισι πύθεσθαι – serves to stress the difficult nuances of memorial that the barrow of the hero Cyzicus, killed at night by mistake, by a guest-friend, before he had produced children, offers to the sight of posterity. How is that *sēma* to be read?

The paradigmatic activities of warfare and dying for the state, then, that found heroic status are here carefully manipulated both by the allusive reworking of the Homeric texts and by the ironic juxtapositions of the mistaken battle. The language of memorial with which the scene is composed only ironizes further its exemplary value.

So, too, marriage, that cornerstone of Odysseus' and Penelope's *kleos*, becomes in the *Argonautica* for Jason and Medea an act of strategic necessity: the lovers are prompted to consummate their relationship by the decision of Alcinous that if Medea is already married she should stay with her husband, but if she is unmarried she should return to her father. Apollonius stresses that the marriage is not desired at this time by either partner (4.1161–4):

> οὐ μὲν ἐν Ἀλκινόοιο γάμον μενέαινε τελέσσαι
> ἥρως Αἰσονίδης, μεγάροις δ' ἐνὶ πατρὸς ἑοῖο,
> νόστησας ἐς Ἰωλκὸν ὑπότροπος· ὡς δὲ καὶ αὐτὴ
> Μήδεια φρονέεσκε· τότ' αὖ χρεὼ ἦγε μιγῆναι.

> The hero Jason did not desire to consummate
> the marriage in Alcinous' home, but in the halls of his own father,
> when he had returned home to Iolcus. So, too, Medea herself
> was intending. But necessity led them to be joined together then.

The normative vocabulary of marital consummation within the social order of the house of the father, and the echoes of Odysseus' desire for *nostos* as a return to (his) marriage, stress the distortion of the ideal *oikos* that necessity here enjoins. The final verb μιγῆναι, translated 'to be joined together', implies both the tie of marriage and the sexual act: it is important that the erotic narrative of tryst and elopement has led to this moment of disaffected union, where as they are 'warmed by sweet love' they are 'gripped by fear' (1168–9). And if there is symbolism in Penelope and Odysseus returning to their bed rooted around an olive tree in the centre of the *oikos*, then what is to be made of the consummation of

Jason's and Medea's marriage on the Golden Fleece itself, the princess and the object of the quest together (not forgetting the sinister echo of the cloak on which Ariadne and Dionysus lay)? What sort of *telos* is this? What is more, the spreading of the Golden Fleece is in order to make the marriage (1143) τιμήεις τε καὶ ἀοίδιμος, 'honoured and the subject of song'. While 'the subject of song' may imply the Hymenaeal (referred to at 1160), it also recalls (at this precise juncture of consummation) the tragedy of marriage to come, as, inevitably and with wonderful precision, the echo of Homer's one use of the term emphasizes: Helen at *Il.* 6 353 tells Hector that the evil fate of her marriage to Paris is sent by Zeus so that the couple should be 'the subject of song' (ἀοίδιμοι) 'for future generations of men'. Where Odysseus' erotic encounters are structured towards the confirmation of the ideal he lauds to Nausicaa, Jason's and Medea's narrative is constantly mined by the inevitability of the violent tragedy to come.

The marriage of Jason and Medea, then, resounds against the exemplarities of heroic marriage in Homer. It is none the less for Apollonius a paradigm (1165–7):

> ἀλλὰ γὰρ οὔποτε φῦλα δυηπαθέων ἀνθρώπων
> τερπωλῆς ἐπέβημεν ὅλῳ ποδί, σὺν δέ τις ἀιεὶ
> πικρὴ παρμέμβλωκεν ἐυφροσύνῃσιν ἀνίη.

> For, however, never do we tribes of woe-stricken men
> tread the path of pleasure with a sure foot. Always some
> bitter anguish walks alongside joy.

The consummated marriage of hero and princess proves the paradigm of the uncertainty of success, the fragility of pleasure. In Apollonius' text, the narrator's voice – with how secure a tone? – claims the exemplarity of his hero(in)es as and when they demonstrate the lack of security all humans share. Models of a uniform certainty of the ambiguity of success.

Exemplarity is integral to epic, its turn to the past. Apollonius fractures that exemplarity. Not only does he explore and recompose the paradigm of the past in his rewriting of the language and narratives of the past to tell his tale of 'men born long ago', but also he opens to question the selectivity and manipulation of arguments from *exempla*; he offers and retracts – places 'sous rature' – the language of exemplification; ironically and self-reflexively plays with the structures of epic memorialization and praise. As the logic of similarity and difference is explored in this allusive engagement with the paradigms of the past, it is the secure position of the reader vis-à-vis the past and its exemplarity that is set at risk. What we make of the past, how we make the past exemplary, how we say what the past is like ... this is Apollonius' terrain, his archaeology.

THE EXPLANATION OF THE PAST: AETIOLOGY AND THE HUMAN
SCIENCES

That Callimachus' central work, the *Aetia*, consists in a series of obscure narratives, formally linked by the repeated device of aetiology, has become seen as emblematic for Hellenistic poetics. Although aetiology plays an important part in, say, Euripidean tragedy or in Pindaric narrative – and is presumably the very basis of such genres as the tales of the foundations of cities (*ktiseis*)[85] – the pervasiveness of aetiology in Callimachus and Apollonius in particular has been repeatedly termed a defining characteristic of Alexandrian poetry – a fundamental element in its turn to scholarship. Aetiology is inherently a way of articulating a relation between present and past and thus is integral to any discussion of the paradigms of the past in the *Argonautica*; I wish to end this chapter with a brief consideration of this important area.

Now although aetiology is inherently a way of articulating a relation between past and present, the precise nature of this articulation has prompted considerable discussion by modern critics. For Fränkel, aetiology in the epic's tale of long ago is primarily a way of mutually binding past and present: 'auf diese Weise wird der Zug der Argonauten mit der Gegenwart des Dichters und Lesers fast verbunden; und zwar wirkt sich die gegenseitige Verspannung and Verankerung in beiden Richtungen aus';[86] aetiology is the embodiment of continuing tradition. For Bing, however, a sense of rupture persists in the search for origins: he describes Callimachus' *Aetia*, for example, as 'a compendium of tales attempting to explain the peculiarities of the present by reference to their "causes" in the distant past, the very need for which bespeaks at once an awareness of the enormous gulf separating past and present, and the desire to bridge it'.[87] Zanker subsumes the sense of rupture and the desire to bridge it to his argument for 'realism' as a dominant concern of the Alexandrians. For him, the desire to bridge the gap with the past means a desire 'to confer immediacy and credibility on poetic subject matter, in particular on myth' – and thus 'aetiological evidence' is brought to bear in order 'to prove the truth of particular myths', 'to prove the historicity of his tale'.[88] Aetiology is an attempt to control the otherness of the past with

[85] See Pfeiffer (1968) 144.   [86] Fränkel (1957) 5.
[87] (1988) 71.   [88] (1987) 113, 123.

the apparatus of contemporary knowledge. For Hutchinson, however, aetiology works not to place poetic subject matter under the control of 'immediacy and credibility', but rather to alienate the reader from a secure and consistent emotional involvement with the narrative: aetiologies 'are handled in such a way as to distance us from the story, and to obtrude on our attention with recondite lore ... The reader is apt to be made suddenly and sharply aware of the scholarly narrator.'[89] For Hutchinson, then, aetiology as a structural device – and the scholarly apparatus of the *Argonautica* in general – is part of an aesthetics of discontinuity.

The apparent tension between seeing aetiology as the embodiment of continuing tradition, and as the demonstration of an aesthetics of discontinuity, is, as Fusillo shows in the most extensive recent discussion of aetiology, integral to its functioning in Apollonius' epic.[90] Fusillo analyses first how the use of aetiology has to be seen in the light of the epic's experimental temporal framework – the structuring of expansion and contraction, continuity and disjunction, within the co-ordinates of the round-trip, that I have already briefly discussed. For aetiology, like the narrator's *praeteritio*, breaks into the epic's preterite narrative, changes the relation to the past that Homer's epic constructs, brings the epic towards the moment of reading – ἔτι νῦν περ, 'still now today ...' It is a 'tradimento' of tradition by its insistence on the incompleteness of the past. In Homer, explicit projections into the future, argues Fusillo, occur only in the direct speech of the characters – promises of future fame, tombs that are to be seen etc. In Apollonius, however, *aitia* are introduced exclusively by the narrator – thus blurring the boundary between the otherness of the epic world of the past and the present world of the narrator: 'l'eziologia provoca dunque un "tradimento" dell'epos tradizionale, in quanto mina alla base la funzione del "completamente passato", immettendovi di continuo dati tratti del presente dell'autore ed interrompendo in tal modo il fluso perpetuo del conto che proviene direttamente dalla Musa: il raconto si tramuta così, per un attimo, in "discorso"'.[91] This move is also to be seen in generic terms. Adopting a phrase of Klein, Fusillo describes the turn to aetiology as a 'counter-genre within the genre'[92] – a modern, contemporary genre, aetiology, grafted onto the traditional structures of epic. This melding of forms is

---

[89] (1988) 93.   [90] (1985) 116–58.   [91] (1985) 139.
[92] Klein (1974) – who sees (230) an 'interrogation and refutation of the concept of epic *within the epic itself*'.

to be seen, Fusillo contends, not so much as 'avant-garde rupture' with the past, as a 'subtle intellectual ideology' of transformation 'from within', that is the condition of possibility for the inclusion of, say, the erotic narrative of Jason and Medea and in particular the representation of Medea ('tutta intima e solipsistica') within epic.[93] That is, aetiology is a constitutive and enabling element of the discourse of the *Argonautica* and needs to be read as such.

The way in which aetiology is part of a rewriting of epic discourse and epic temporality can be well seen if we return to the idea of *kleos*, the instantiation of fame. With Jason's seduction of Medea, we saw how *kleos* as the object of traditional epic becomes a sign of deception, a counter in the game of persuasion, which is, ironically, also a mark of the future history of Jason – the *kleos* of the hero in the literary tradition against and within which the scene of seduction is composed. The opening and closing of the epic promise and reaffirm *kleos* as the production of epic, but also in the gesture of *praeteritio* refuse to recite the songs of the past. And, of course, as several critics have pointed out, both Jason's fight with the bulls and his manipulation of Medea are described in ways that draw on Homeric narratives of excellence, *aristeiai*. Yet it is in the repeated aetiologies that the language of continuing memory and renown is also and importantly evidenced. Consider first the example of Idmon, a seer, whose prophetic powers do not enable him to avoid being killed by a wild boar. He dies – pathetically – in the arms of his companions, and a grand funeral takes place, with the proper sacrifices. The narrative continues (2.841–50):

> And so there was raised for this man in that land
> a barrow. There is a sign on it for posterity to see,
> a ship's roller of wild olive. It flourishes with leaves,
> a little beneath the Acherousian headland. But if I must
> declare this too, forthrightly, impelled by the Muses –
> Apollo indicated directly to the Boeotians and Nisaeans
> to propitiate this hero as guardian of the city,
> and to build the town around this roller
> of ancient olive. But they, instead of god-fearing Idmon,
> the Aeolid, still to this day worship Agamestor.

The funeral ends with the preparation of a tomb (*tumbos*), and on the tomb a sign, a *sēma*. (*Sēma* in Homer means both 'omen' and 'tomb' itself, and 'tomb as sign' – here it means specifically the distinguishing feature

[93] (1985) 142.

of this grave.) It is a memorial for future generations to see, like the tomb of Cyzicus, like the barrow promised to a dead Homeric warrior. Yet this narrative of *kleos* achieved – physically in the *sēma* and poetically in this account – is immediately effaced by the narrator's interruption. The inspiration of the Muses is the mask of compulsion for the narrator to turn to a more polemical aetiology. Despite Apollo's direct oracle, the Boeotians and Nisaeans pay honours not to Idmon but to Agamestor. As Fränkel notes, the repeated deictic pronouns, '*this* man', '*this* hero', '*this* roller', are to emphasize the mistaken identity of the figure in the tomb and the necessary connection between the ship's roller and the Argo.[94] Yet this corrective turn is not merely Apollonius marking his active selection amid mythic variants, authorized by the appeal to the Muses, as Händel would have it.[95] Nor, as Fusillo more subtly suggests, is the intervention of the narrator only an ironic apology for breaking the traditional 'impersonal flow of the epic past' with this erudite archaeology of 'the stratification of myth left in the names and the cults of his time'.[96] For while there is an uncovering of discrepancies between different narratives of the history and ritual of the area, it is to be seen – as the appeal to the Muses also suggests – within the poetic claims of memorial. For the memorial of Idmon, his *kleos*, is concealed in the cults of honour for Agamestor. The εἴσετι νῦν, the 'still today', of this account is the continuation of an error in naming, a misreading of the *sēma*. The poet's scholarly reordering of ritual and mythic narrative, then, is to rediscover the memorial of Idmon in this monument. The narrative tells of Idmon's renown, only to veil it in the local inhabitants' ignorance, and to rediscover it by scholarly intervention (impelled by the now authoritative Muses). The aetiology here, together with the discourse of erudite precision, is to reaffirm the *kleos* buried in the confused history of names and memorial.

So, in a neatly self-reflexive aetiology, the name of the island Anaphe (4.1717) is revealed to come from the moment when it was revealed (*anephēnen* 4.1718) by the gleaming bow of Apollo (the god of poetry to whom the poem is first addressed) as the Argonauts languished in the dark (4.1710–18).[97] The Argonauts in response make 'a sanctuary in a shaded grove and a shady altar' (ἄλσει ἐνὶ σκιερῷ τέμενος σκιόεντά τε

---

[94] (1968) 236–7.   [95] (1954) 72–3.   [96] (1985) 370.

[97] This story is also told by Callimachus in the *Aetia* (fr. 9–21 Pf. with 250 *SH*), although the fragmentary state of Callimachus' version makes it difficult to make anything more than the type of very general comments offered by Zanker (1987) 123.

βωμόν 4.1715) to call on 'Apollo Aigletes' because of his shining (*aiglē*) that is seen from afar (*euskopou*). The repetition and variation in 'shaded ... shady', σκιερῷ ... σκιόεντα, emphasizes the play on light and dark, revealing and shading, that also underlies the pun in the term *euskopou*, which I translated as 'seen from afar', but which also means 'of good aim' (and is applied, for example, to Apollo himself in Herodotus (5.61) and to bows in Aeschylus (*Cho.* 694)). There is a revealing here also of the double sense of *euskopos* in the double use of Apollo's bow. Aetiology's discovery of veiled significance is here focused on the enlightenment sent by the riddling god Apollo himself.

Indeed, the many aetiologies of the *Argonautica* repeatedly produce a picture of a sedimented world, where each object, cult, ritual, name, may be opened, like Odysseus' scar, into a narrative of origination, and where each narrative, each event, may lead to a cult, ritual, name, monument. Even what might be termed 'natural phenomena' are part of this sedi-mentation. So, as the Argonauts are forcibly delayed by the Etesian winds, the narrative turns to explain at length the origin of the winds in Zeus's response to the petitions of Aristaeus against the heat of the Dog Star (2.500–27) – a story introduced with a disarming πέφαταί τις (2.500), 'someone has said ...', 'the story goes ...' This, the longest *aition* in the *Argonautica*, is called by Beye 'no more than description for description's sake',[98] but thereby he both misses the joke of self-reflexively delaying the narrative journey with such a lengthy description of the origin of the delay; and misunderstands the role of epic in producing a valorized depiction of the world, which means that description can be called 'for description's sake' only by an impoverished view of the power of language to order the world: here, indeed, the retelling of a famous Pindaric narrative (*Pyth.* 9.1–70), itself a rewriting of Hesiod (fr. 215–17 M–W) ('someone has said' ...) marks the appropriation of literary tradition in this Alexandrian explanation of the history of a delaying wind.

So, too, the colour of the stones on Elba is directly related to the Argonauts' having scraped themselves clean on the beach (4.654–8), an *aition* that uses an everyday event – cleaning oneself – to explain a phenomenon in the natural world, the colour of stones, by an unexplained and totally strange process of transformation (an example that is difficult to fit into Zanker's model of aetiology investing myth with credibility through realism). In such examples – as with Orpheus' song in Book 1 – the cosmogonies of traditional hexameter verse become part of an explan-

[98] (1982) 99.

atory archaeology of the natural world, part of the Alexandrian discourse of knowledge that combines *divina commedia* and natural history
as analytic modes. The scholarly apparatus of etymology, history, anthropology, physics etc., both enables the collection of the multiform
material that informs this sedimented view of things, and also provides
the framework for its ordering, its analysis – an analysis that, as the all
too brief examples above have shown, interweaves authoritative demonstration with ironic and varied treatments of the power and scope of
aetiological explanation: the narrative of the *Argonautica* explores the
possibilities of (causal) connection, both in its telling of the sequence of
events and in the implication of such events in a continuing history of
the terrain mapped by the narrative's journey.

The interrelations of 'science' – as Apollonius' interconnected interests
in anthropology, physics, language etc. are often termed – and literature have been extensively discussed in recent years, in particular for
the writing of the eighteenth, nineteenth and twentieth centuries. For
Barthes, 'the voice of science' in what he calls the classic texts of the
bourgeois novel functions as the law that (like myth) naturalizes and
validates a particular set of cultural values.[99] The voice of science appears
as the product and mainstay of a self-legitimating educational system (in
the widest sense) – as literature is read as a cultural product invested in
a discourse of knowledge, an *epistēmē*.[100] Yet, as Beer writes, when
revolutionary scientific theory is first advanced, it 'is at its most fictive':
'it can tax, affront, exhilarate'.[101] As the paradigm shifts of science in-
augurate a need 'to look at nature in a different way'[102] – and make
possible such a shift in recognition – the disruptions of science constitute
a disruption of the discourse of knowledge. (Science (in literature) can
contest as well as validate.) And as the radical realignments of Darwinian
or Freudian theory, say, become part of the voice of science, so their
legitimating role within a cultural discourse has developed and
changed.[103] (It is, as ever, in periods of most rapid change, most acute
conflict, that discourses of legitimation are hardest to evaluate.)

These detailed cultural and literary studies of modern European writing, however, cannot be translated simply into a model for approaching
Apollonius. First, as so often in the ancient world, the quantity and
quality of the material for engaging in such studies is simply not available.

[99] (1975) 205–6.
[100] The term *epistēmē* is taken from Foucault (1970) and (1972).
[101] (1985) 3. See also Shuttleworth (1984).   [102] Kuhn (1962) 52.
[103] See e.g. the essays collected in Jordanova (1986).

The voluminous writings of the Hellenistic period are known to us primarily as titles or brief citations. The importance of a changing sociology of knowledge for Hellenistic Alexandria can be more easily divined than it can be described or analysed. Second, the modern categories of 'science' and 'literature' have all too often been used in an uncontested and distorting way to approach Hellenistic writing. (It is not hard to see the categories of Romanticism εἴσετι νῦν, 'still today', in, for example, Hutchinson's description of aetiology as erudition dispelling and frustrating emotional investment in what should be the 'delicious' experience of poetry.) Although the institutionalization and demarcation of disciplines is a crucial part of the Hellenistic intellectual enterprise, it is far from clear that *sophia* is usefully to be divided into an opposition of 'science' and 'literature', at least in terms formulated by a (post-)Romantic discourse. Philosophy may to a large degree have taken over the privileged voice of poetry in archaic society, but the Alexandrian *philologi* demonstrate an engagement in the complete range of critical writing across modern disciplinary boundaries.[104] Third, many of the valorized associations of 'science' in the modern opposition of science and literature – objective critical method, precision of measurement, cataloguing and categorizing the phenomena of the natural world – are disseminated, as far as one can tell, throughout the intellectual discourse of Hellenistic culture, and play an important role in the aesthetics as well as the physics of the period.[105]

Yet there are two points that I think can be made in the light of these discussions and which bear emphasis. First, it is quite insufficient to regard the scholarly apparatus of the *Argonautica* as a supplement to its poetry, aesthetics or narrative. For this turn to scholarship informs the

---

[104] An interesting case of such problems of categorization can be seen in the scholia to Aratus (ad *Phain.* 30), where Aratus is said to deal with material proper (ἴδιον) to a poet, that is, *muthos*, but to do so in a persuasive and controlled manner (κατὰ καιρὸν μέντοι οὐκ ἀπιθάνως). As poet he introduces such material, the scholiast writes, but as someone talking about physics (περὶ φυσικῶν διαλεγόμενος) he has to distance himself from *muthos*, and so he introduces the qualification εἰ ἔτεον δή as an indication of his doubt (ὅπερ ἐστὶν ἀμφιβάλλοντος). As Stinton (1976) 63 points out (*contra* Heinze) 'Alexandrian didacticism does not in general eschew myth' (and, of course, the *Phainomena* is a poem about astronomy). What this scholion indicates most clearly is the insufficiency of simple and opposed categories of 'poet(ry)' and 'scholar(ship)' or 'scientist'.

[105] 'There is a complete unity of the creative poet and the reflective scholar in Callimachus', writes Pfeiffer (1968) 124, whose study of the polymathic aims of Alexandrian intellectual life remains the most useful.

strategies of representation within the epic: it constitutes an integral alignment of recognition, a condition of possibility for the descriptive authority to which epic lays claim. Apollonius' practice of uncovering sedimented history, as with his constant reworkings of the paradigms of the past, is a constitutive element in a discourse of knowledge – a recognition of the world, of man's place in it, man's possibilities of understanding. The different modes of representation – of recognizing, describing, commenting on reality; the different ways of ordering and explaining events, together make up the complexly polyphonous and disjunctive narrative of the *Argonautica*, and the voice of scholarship is an integral part of this polyphony.

Yet – and this is my second point – the interplay of allusion and collusion that we saw to be so important in the reworking of the paradigms of the past, is also crucial to the instantiation of this (authoritative) archaeology of the past. For Apollonius takes his narrative to the margins of the known world (in all senses) and with its combination of scholarship, fantasy, scholarly fantasy, scholarship about fantasy (etc.) explores (the boundaries of) representing the real. Indeed, the more arcane the details are that Apollonius alludes to, the more difficult it is for the reader to distinguish between the author's access to authoritative knowledge and the suspicion of fabrication – the fiction of scholarship. Let us return here to the battle-list of dead Doliones. The scholia, it will be remembered, report a difference of opinion, and modern scholars have continued the attempt to determine levels of 'fiction' and 'history' in this passage. Lucillus of Tarrha, it is attested, states directly that there is fiction in this list. This scholion is attached to two names in particular, Telecles and Megabrontes, and specifies that these names are not 'from historical research',[106] and so Hasluck, for example, assumes that these two names are, for whatever reason, fictional additions to the list.[107] A second scholion reports that Sophocleios says that Apollonius has culled the names of those killed from Deiochus, an obscure historian of Cyzicus, who is mentioned several times in the scholia as the source that Apollonius follows or differs from in his account of Cyzicus.[108] So Vian[109] – assuming

---

[106] Σ ad 1040–41: Τηλεκλῆα ἠδὲ Μεγαβρόντην · πέπλακε τὰ ὀνόματα ταῦτα Ἀπολλώνιος, οὐκ ἀπὸ ἱστορίας ἔλαβεν · οὕτω Ταρραῖος.

[107] (1910) 239–40.

[108] μνημονεύει Δηίοχος τῶν ἀναιρεθέντων, ὥς φησι Σοφόκλειος. Even the precise spelling of the historian's name is uncertain. Sometimes it is given as Deilochos. See Jacoby *FGrH* 471.

[109] (1976) 99 n. 1.

first that the earlier scholion refers not to two specific names but to all of them – claims that this second scholion must be right – assuming, that is, that the scholion accurately reports Sophocleios' accurate report of Deiochus' authoritative account which Lucillus had no access to or ignored;[110] thus these names represent a scholarly awareness of otherwise unknown eponymous heroes of Cyzicus – assuming that the list in Deiochus of the 'many' who died is not significantly altered or reduced for this aetiology of hero cult.

Now it is difficult to see how a modern reader, faced by such a recession of citations, can hope finally and certainly to remove the suspicion of Apollonius' fabrication of detail here, except by making the sort of sweeping and unprovable assumptions Vian uses. Yet – as the contrasting reports in the scholia may suggest – this insecurity is not produced merely because of the different possibilities of authentication or verification with which modern scholars work, hamstrung by a necessarily lacunose knowledge of the Alexandrian archive and Alexandrian culture. For, as the Hellenistic investment in recondite scholarly precision also turns back on the reader the requirement of critical reading, critical knowledge – and it is a commonplace that Apollonius' text requires a reader of sophisticated critical acumen – so Apollonius' testing of the boundaries of the real, amid his multiple frames of reference, also teases the reader with the difficulty of securely determining the voice of fiction, the voice of scholarly accuracy. Are these names in the battle-list signs of language's power to order and to record, a result of obscure but researched knowledge? Or are they signs of language's power to invent, to fictionalize? The *Argonautica*'s constant deployment of details of fiction, details of uncovered history, details of fantasy, details of physics, implicates the reader – collusively – in the search,to order, to explain, to determine the stratifications and accretions within the *muthoi* of the epic.

This teasing of the reader's control on the boundaries of authoritative knowledge is nowhere more evident than when Apollonius places his own certainty at stake. When Lynceus is introduced in the catalogue of heroes as a figure of so keen a faculty of vision that he can see into the earth, the story is introduced by (1.154) εἰ ἐτεόν γε πέλει κλέος ..., 'if this *kleos* is indeed true'. Stinton comments that this expression 'could indicate that this faculty of Lynkeus is mere hyperbole, or voice a disclaimer absolving the poet from responsibility for the truth. Or again it could be, or

---

[110] Wendel (1932) 106 asserts that there cannot have been a quarrel between Sophocleios and Lucillus, despite the scholia's recognition of different accounts.

anticipate in others, an expression of incredulity. But it may just as well be a way of underlining the bizarre or supernatural character of this detail: Lynkeus is no ordinary mortal. It may also be that Apollonius is drawing attention to a variation of a standard legend.'[111] Stinton's scrupulous teasing out of the possibilities of this expression of doubt testifies to the teasing manipulation of the rhetoric of plausibility here, the difficulty of pinning down the narrator's or the author's commitment to the fact of the story he weaves into this catalogue under the sign of uncertainty. In the *Argonautica*, the discourse of scholarship with its concomitant language of critical evaluation does not merely construct an authoritative and (self-)legitimating language of order and explanation; it does not merely 'enhance the objective tone proper to this kind of poetry'.[112] The author also ironically plays with the reader's commitment to and involvement in the determination of authoritative knowledge. The apparatus of scholarly control is part of the play of masks through which the poet's voice is disseminated, through which the reader is manipulated and implicated in the voyage of the *Argonautica*.

I wish to conclude with one further aetiological narrative that both brings together some of the aspects I have been discussing and shows also how closely and intricately aetiology in the *Argonautica* is tied to a sense of the paradigm of the past. The brutal killing of Apsyrtus, Medea's brother – the only human apart from Cyzicus to be killed by the hero Jason – has been completed; the blood spurts over Medea's delicate robes and veil, as she averts her eyes from the deceitful murder. The narrative continues (4.475–81):

> With a piercing, side-long glance, the pitiless Erinys
> saw the destructive deed that they had done.
> The hero, Aeson's son, cut off the extremities of the dead man;
> three times he licked the gore, three times he spat the pollution from
>   his mouth,
> as is right for a murderer to atone for a treacherous death.
> He hid the damp body in the earth, where still now today
> those bones lie among the Apsyrtian men.

The phrase 'still now today', ἔτι νῦν περ, indicates the aetiological conclusion to the story: the damp corpse still abides in the earth, though now as bones, so that the significance of the name of the local inhabitants, the Apsyrteis, (named after Apsyrtus) can be understood. This connection

[111] (1976) 63.   [112] Stinton (1976) 64.

of the death and burial of Apsyrtus with the name of the Apsyrteis can be set in contrast with a variety of alternative explanations of the precise relation between the voyage of the Argo and the names of this part of the world.[113] Apollonius' aetiology is also an affirmation of the (proper) sense of the name through its history. The phrase ὑγρὸν νέκυν (translated 'damp body') is splendidly evocative. It implies the blood that covers the victim; the cold sweat of death; the looseness of the recently killed body; and, Livrea adds,[114] since *hugros* is also used to indicate 'life', 'suppleness' as opposed to the dry dust of death, it may suggest that 'the burial of Apsyrtus is so rapid that the last pulse of life has not been extinguished'. The move from 'damp body' to 'those bones', Hutchinson comments,[115] heightens the horror of the murder by emphasizing the abiding effect of the deed. There is certainly a contrast here between the funeral and barrow of, say, Cyzicus or Idmon, and this ritual of desecration and unmarked grave. In each of these three deaths, memorial follows, yet in each case, not only is the form of the memorial – or lack of it – different, but also the relation between the burial and the memorial forms an ironic gloss on the Homeric Hector's promise of a *sēma* for posterity. Where Cyzicus offers a memorial to a mistaken death, and Idmon an unrecognized *kleos*, despite the permanence of his monument, here the lack of a *sēma* does not prevent the continuation of the name.

The hero Jason's act is a deceit and a desecration of the body (and the contrast with, say, even Achilles' treatment of Hector is marked). The rituals of *maschalismos* (the cutting off of the extremities) and of purification are both found in the texts of tragedy, but there is a finely nuanced irony in the narrator's ἣ θέμις, translated 'as is right'. The phrase in Homer normally means 'as is customary', but in later Greek has the strongly normative sense of 'as is right', 'as is the law'. The phrase is not 'mecanicamente ripresa', as Livrea puts it,[116] but manipulates the tension between the two senses to question the moral status of the hero's actions here (as, with the burial of Cyzicus, the same phrase is used to suggest the far from 'usual' or 'proper' situation).[117] The ritual attempt to control

---

[113] For testimonia see Livrea (1973) ad loc.; Vian (1981) 20–46.
[114] (1973) ad loc. Vian (1981) 167 is unnecessarily restrictive here.
[115] (1988) 95–6.   [116] Livrea (1973) ad 1129.
[117] Hunter (1989) 32 may be right to note the sense of 'grim necessity' behind this murder, but it does not follow that it is 'not to be examined in a fine ethical calculus'. Both the description of the death as (450) *kakos*, 'evil', and the apostrophe of Eros (445ff) as the root cause of the murder prompt questions of evaluation both of the action itself and of its causation.

the implications of this murder is held up to scrutiny by the narrator's distancing irony.

Yet both the aetiology of the name of the Apsyrteis and the representation of Jason's ritual are introduced by the intervention of the divine figure of the Erinys (coming between the splattering of Medea's clothes with blood and Jason's licking and spitting of the defiling gore). Vian sees the Erinys, together with the particularly Aeschylean language of slaughter, as another demonstration of Apollonius' combination of tragedy and epic.[118] The 'piercing, side-long' glance of the Erinys may indeed recall tragedy's preoccupation with both the necessity and the surprising twists of punishment for wrong-doing. Even the verb *erexan*, 'they had done', which often is used absolutely to mean 'to complete a sacrifice', may carry undertones of the dominant ritual imagery of killing in tragedy. Yet there is more to be said of this appearance of the Erinys. For, as Hurst notes (but does not develop), the hostile gaze of the Erinys and the aetiology are linked in the projection of the future implication of the murder.[119] The Erinys indeed here looks forward first to another intervention from the world of the divine. At 4.552, the Muses are invoked to tell of the route of the Argo, and of the 'necessity and constraint' (ἀνάγκη καὶ χρειώ) that drove them on; and the force behind this part of the voyage is then said to be Zeus, who is 'angered by the death of Apsyrtus' (558–9). Zeus and the Erinys, connected as so often in Greek literature, provide an explanatory framework for the route of the Argonauts. But the influence of the Erinys may not stop there. For the imagery of dismemberment in the *maschalismos* – a variation on the common tale of the *sparagmos* of Apsyrtus – looks 'forward' to Jason regaining the throne, through another trick of dismemberment, and, finally, to Euripides' Medea, where her infanticide is explicitly related to her earlier acts of violence, and where Medea's actions are seen by the chorus as the embodiment of an Erinys.[120] Apsyrtus' slaughter is also a founding moment in a history of dismemberment to come. The Erinys' 'piercing, side-long glance' also directs attention to the tradition in which Jason and Medea are inscribed, that both undermines the ritual of propitiation – destined to fail – and sets the aetiology from the name of Apsyrtus against other projections into the future. Apollonius interweaves the apparent demonstration of his authoritative control over the past's future

---

[118] (1981) 20–3.
[119] Hurst (1967) 112–13. See also Fusillo (1985) 134; Hutchinson (1988) 96.
[120] Eur. *Med.* 1260. See also 1389 for the wish for more Erinys-influenced violence!

in the archaeology of the name of the buried Apsyrtus with images of his figures' misplaced attempts at controlling their own narratives.

In this passage, then, we see how the language of aetiology is an integral strand of the discourse of the epic: aetiology may offer a paradigm of how the past may be seen in the present – but it is a paradigm that is subject to Apollonius' ceaseless irony and constant testing of the connections between events in a narrative.

In Apollonius, then, we have seen a series of responses to the past as example, and a complex articulation of the influence of the past as a controlling, even determining example for the present. The chronological framework of the epic, set before the time of the privileged literature to which it constantly alludes; the repeated turn to aetiology and the archaeology of the past; the exploration of the process of exemplification, how one might say what the past is like; the rupture and revival of rewriting the language of the past; the conflicting and contrasting models of explanation and description; together these form an interrelated set of concerns that explore – in an ironic and self-reflexive manner – the paradigms of the past and the past as paradigm.

For this book that on the one hand has emphasized the interrelated problems of self-reflexivity, intertextuality and representation, and on the other has read the poetry of the past from the necessary vantage of the present, it will, I hope, be clear enough why Apollonius' exploration of such concerns is a suitable and proper place to conclude these analyses of the poet's voice.

Bibliography

Adkins, A. (1960) *Merit and Responsibility*, Oxford.

  (1963) '"Friendship" and "self-sufficiency" in Homer and Aristotle', *CQ* 13, 30–45.

  (1982) 'Values, goals, and emotions in the *Iliad*', *CP* 77, 292–326.

Adrados, F. (1975) *Festival, Comedy and Tragedy*, trans. C. Holme, Leiden.

Ahl, F. (1984) 'The art of safe criticism in Greece and Rome', *AJP* 103, 174–208.

Alpers, P. (1979) *The Singer of the Eclogues: a Study of Virgilian Pastoral*, Berkeley.

Ameis, K. and Hentze, C. (1900) *Homers Odyssee*, Leipzig and Berlin.

Amory, A. (1963) 'The reunion of Penelope and Odysseus', in Taylor (1963).

  (1966) 'The gates of horn and ivory', *YCS* 20, 1–58.

Andersen, O. (1977) 'Odysseus and the wooden horse', *SO* 52, 5–18.

  (1978) *Die Diomedesgestalt in der Ilias, SO suppl. 25*, Oslo.

Anderson, G. (1981) 'ΛΗΚΥΘΙΟΝ and ΑΥΤΟΛΗΚΥΘΟΣ', *JHS* 101, 130–2.

Apthorp, M. (1969) *The Manuscript Evidence for Interpolation in Homer*, Heidelberg.

  (1980) 'The obstacles to Telemachus' return', *CQ* 30, 1–22.

Ardizzoni, A. (1965) 'Echi Pitagorici in Apollonio Rhodio', *RFIC* 93, 257–67.

Armstrong J. (1958a) 'The marriage song – Odyssey 23', *TAPA* 89, 38–43.

  (1958b) 'The arming motif in the *Iliad*', *AJP* 79, 337–54.

Arnott, G. (1979) 'The mound of Brasilas and Theocritus' seventh Idyll', *QUCC* 32, 99–105.

Arthur, M. (1973) 'Early Greece: the origins of Western attitudes towards women', *Arethusa* 6, 7–58.

Aubriot, D. (1984) 'Les *Litai* d'Homère et la *dikè* d'Hésiode', *REG* 97, 1–25.

Auerbach, E. (1953) *Mimesis: the Representation of Reality in Western Literature*, trans. W. Trask, New York.

Auger, D. (1979) 'Le théâtre d' Aristophane: le mythe, l'utopie et les femmes', in *Aristophanes: Les Femmes et la cité, Les Cahiers de Fontenay* 17, Paris.

Austin, J. (1962) *How To Do Things with Words*, Oxford.

Austin, N. (1966) 'The function of digressions in the *Iliad*', *GRBS* 7, 295–312.

(1967) 'Theocritus and Simonides', *TAPA* 98, 1–21.

(1969) 'Telemachus polymechanos', *CSCA* 2, 45–63.

(1972) 'Name magic in the *Odyssey*', *CSCA* 5, 1–19.

(1975) *Archery at the Dark of the Moon*, Berkeley.

Aycock, W. and Klein, T. edd. (1980) *Classical Mythology in Twentieth-Century Thought and Literature*, Lubbock, Texas.

Babcock, B. (1978) 'Introduction', in Babcock ed. (1978).

ed. (1978) *The Reversible World*, Ithaca.

Bader, F. (1976) 'L'art de fugue dans l'*Odyssée*', *REG* 89, 18–39.

Bain, D. (1985) 'ΛΗΚΥΘΙΟΝ ΑΠΩΛΕΣΕΝ: some reservations', *CQ* 35, 31–7.

Bakhtin, M. (1968) *Rabelais and his World*, trans. H. Iswolsky, Cambridge, Mass.

(1973) *The Problems of Dostoevsky's Poetics*, trans. R. Rotsel, Ann Arbor.

(1981) *The Dialogic Imagination*, trans. C. Emerson and M. Holquist, Austin and London.

Balandier, G. (1970) *Political Anthropology*, trans. A Sheridan-Smith, London.

Barber, C. (1959) *Shakespeare's Festive Comedies*, Princeton.

Barish, J. (1981) *The Antitheatrical Prejudice*, Berkeley.

Barkhuizen, J. (1979) 'The psychological characterization of Medea in Apollonius of Rhodes *Argonautica* 3 744–824', *A Class* 22, 33–48.

Barkhuizen, J. and Els, A. (1983) 'On Sappho fr. 16 (L–P)', *A Class* 26, 23–32.

Barnes, J. (1973) 'Genetrix:genitor::nature:culture', in Goody (1973).

Barrell, J. (1988) *Poetry, Language and Politics*, Manchester.

Barrett, W. (1964) *Euripides Hippolytos*, Oxford.

Barron, J. (1964) 'The sixth-century tyranny at Samos', *CQ* 14, 210–29.

(1969) 'Ibycus: *To Polycrates*', *BICS* 16, 119–49.

Barthes, R. (1970) 'L'ancienne rhétorique, aide-mémoire', *Communications* 16, 172–237.

(1975) *S/Z*, trans. R. Miller, London.

(1978) *A Lover's Discourse: Fragments*, trans. R. Howard, New York.

(1984) *The Rustle of Language*, trans. R. Howard, New York.

Basset, S. (1923) 'The proems of the *Iliad* and the *Odyssey*', *AJP* 44, 339–48.

Bate, W. (1970) *The Burden of the Past and the English Poet*, London.

Baxandall, M. (1971) *Giotto and the Orators*, Oxford.

Beaujour, M. (1981) 'Some paradoxes of description', *YFS* 61, 27–59.

Beer, G. (1985) *Darwin's Plots: Evolutionary Narrative in Darwin, George Eliot and Nineteenth-Century Fiction*, London.

Bekker, I. (1863) *Homerische Blätter*, Bonn.

Bell, J. (1984) 'God, man and animal in Pindar's second Pythian', in Gerber ed. (1984).

Ben-Porat, Z. (1979) 'Method in *Mad*ness: notes on the structure of parody, based on MAD TV satires', *Poetics Today* 1, 245–72.

Benveniste, E. (1969)   *Le Vocabulaire des institutions indo-européennes*, 2 vols., Paris.

(1973)   *Indo-European Language and Society*, trans. E. Palmer, London.

Berger, H. jnr. (1984)   'The origins of bucolic representation: disenchantment and revision in Theocritus' seventh *Idyll*', *Classical Antiquity* 3, 1–39.

Bergren, A. (1979)   'Helen's web: time and tableau in the *Iliad*', *Helios* 7, 19–34.

(1981)   'Helen's "good drug": Odyssey IV 1–305', in Kresic (1981).

(1983)   'Odyssean temporality: many (re)turns', in Rubino and Shelmerdine (1983).

Bernadini, A. (1983)   *Mito e Attualità nelle Odi di Pindaro*, Rome.

Berry, P. (1989)   *Of Chastity and Power: Elizabethan Literature and the Unmarried Queen*, London.

Besslich, S. (1966)   *Schweigen, Verschweigen, Übergehen*, Heidelberg.

Beye, C. (1968)   *The Iliad, the Odyssey and the Epic Tradition*, London.

(1969)   'Jason as love-hero in Apollonius' *Argonautica*', *GRBS* 10, 31–55.

(1982)   *Epic and Romance in the Argonautica of Apollonius*, Carbondale-Edwardsville.

Bing, P. (1988)   *The Well-Read Muse. Present and Past in Callimachus and the Hellenistic Poets*, Göttingen.

Bloch, E. (1982)   'The narrator speaks: apostrophe in Homer and Vergil', *TAPA* 112, 7–22.

Bloom, H. (1973)   *The Anxiety of Influence. A Theory of Poetry*, London.

(1982)   *Agon*, Oxford.

Blum, H. (1969)   *Die Antike Mnemotechnik*, Spudasmata 15.

Blumenthal, H. (1984)   'The order of Aeschylus' *Choephoroi* 1–9', *LCM* 9, 134–5.

Boas, M. (1905)   *De Epigrammatis Simonideis*, Groningen.

de Bolla, P. (1988)   *Harold Bloom: Towards Historical Rhetorics*, London and New York.

Bond, G. (1981)   *Euripides: Herakles*, Oxford.

Bonelli, G. (1987)   *Il Mondo Poetico di Pindaro*, Turin.

Bourdieu, P. (1977)   *Outline of a Theory of Practice*, trans. R. Nice, Cambridge.

Bowie, A. (1982)   'The parabasis in Aristophanes: prolegomena, *Acharnians*', *CQ* 27–40.

Bowie, E. (1985)   'Theocritus' seventh Idyll, Philetas and Longus', *CQ* 35, 67–91.

(1988)   'Who is Dicaeopolis?', *JHS* 108, 183–5.

Bowra, M. (1938)   *Early Greek Elegists*, Cambridge, Mass.

(1961)   *Greek Lyric Poetry*, Oxford.

(1964)   *Pindar*, Oxford.

Braswell, B. (1971)   'Mythological innovation in the *Iliad*', *CQ* 21, 16–26.

(1982)   'The song of Ares and Aphrodite: theme and relevance to *Odyssey* 8', *Hermes* 90, 129–37.

Brelich, A. (1969)   *Paides e parthenoi*, Rome.

Bremer, J. (forthcoming)   'Patronage in Greek Literature'.

Bresson, A. (1982)   *Mythe et contradiction*, Paris.

Bristol, M. (1985)   *Carnival and Theatre: Plebeian Culture and the Structure of Authority in Renaissance England*, London.

Brommer, F. (1977)   *Der Parthenonfries*, 2 vols., Mainz.

Brooke, A. (1971)   'Theocritus' *Idyll* 11: a study in pastoral', *Arethusa* 4, 73–81.

Brooks, P. (1984)   *Reading for the Plot: Design and Intention in Narrative*, New York.

Brown, C. (1966)   'Odysseus and Polyphemus. The name and the curse', *Comp. Lit.* 18, 193–202.

Brown, E. (1981)   'The Lycidas of Theocritus' *Idyll* 7', *HSCP* 86, 59–100.

(1984)   'The bridegroom and the athlete. The proem to Pindar's seventh Olympian', in Gerber ed. (1984).

Bryson, N. (1981)   *Word and Image: French Painting of the Ancien Régime*, Cambridge.

Bulloch, A. (1985a)   *Callimachus: the Fifth Hymn*, Cambridge.

(1985b)   'Apollonius Rhodius', in *The Cambridge History of Classical Literature*, vol. I, *Greek Literature*, edd. P. Easterling, and B. Knox, Cambridge.

Bundy, E. (1986)   *Studia Pindarica*, Berkeley.

Burke, P. (1978)   *Popular Culture in Early Modern Europe*, London.

Burkert, W. (1960)   'Das Lied von Ares und Aphrodite', *RhM* 103, 130–44.

(1985)   *Greek Religion*, trans. J. Raffan, Oxford.

Burton, R. (1962)   *Pindar's Pythian Odes*, Oxford.

Butor, M. (1968)   *La Critique et l'invention*, Paris.

Buxton, R. (1982)   *Persuasion in Greek Tragedy: a Study in Peitho*, Cambridge.

Byl, S. (1980)   'Parodie d'une initiation dans les Nuées d'Aristophane', *Revue Belge de Philologie et d'Histoire* 58, 5–21.

Byre, C. (1988)   'Penelope and the suitors before Odysseus', *AJP* 109, 159–73.

Cairns, F. (1972)   *Generic Composition in Greek and Roman Poetry*, Edinburgh.

(1976)   'The Distaff of Theugenis: Theocritus *Idyll* 28', *PLLS*, 293–305.

(1979)   *Tibullus: a Hellenistic Poet at Rome*, Cambridge.

(1984a)   'Theocritus' first Idyll: the literary programme', *WS* 97, 89–113.

(1984b)   'Propertius and the Battle of Actium (4.6)', in *Poetry and Politics in the Age of Augustus*, edd. T. Woodman and D. West, Cambridge.

Calame, C. (1976)   'Mythe grec et structures narratives: le mythe des Cyclopes dans l'*Odyssée*', *ZAnt* 26, 311–28.

(1977)   *Les Choeurs de jeunes filles en Grèce archaique*, 2 vols., Rome.

Cameron, A. (1963)   'The form of the "Thalysia"', in *Miscellanea di studi alessandrini in memoria di Augusto Rostagni*, Turin.

(1965)   'Wandering poets: a literary movement in Byzantine Egypt', *Historia* 14, 470–509.

Campagner, R. (1988)   'Reciprocità economica in Pindaro', *QUCC* 29, 77–93.

Campbell, D. (1967)   *Greek Lyric Poetry*, London.

Campbell, M. (1983)   *Studies in the Third Book of Apollonius Rhodius' Argonautica*, Hildersheim, Zurich, New York.

Carey, C. (1976)   'Pindar's eighth Nemean ode', *PCPS* 22, 26–42.

(1981)   *A Commentary on Five Odes of Pindar*, New York.

Carne-Ross, D. (1976)   'Weaving with points of gold: Pindar's sixth Olympian', *Arion* 6, 5–44.

Carpenter, R. (1946)   *Folktale, Fiction and Saga in the Homeric Epics*, Berkeley and Los Angeles.

Carrière, J. (1948a)   *Théognis: poèmes élégiaques*, Paris.

(1948b)   *Théognis de Mégare*, Paris.

(1979)   *Le Carnaval et la politique*, Paris.

Carson, A. (1986)   *Eros the Bittersweet*, Princeton.

Carspecken, J. (1952)   'Apollonius Rhodius and the Homeric tradition', *YCS* 13, 35–143.

Cartledge, P. (1981)   'The politics of Spartan pederasty', *PCPS* 27, 17–36.

Cassio, A. (1982)   'Arte compositiva e politica in Aristofane: il discorso di Ermete nella *Pace*', *RFIC* 110, 22–44.

Castle, T. (1986)   *Masquerade and Civilization*, London.

Cataudella, Q. (1955)   'Lycidas' in *Studi in onore di U.E. Paoli*, Florence.

Cave, T. (1988)   *Recognitions. A Study in Poetics*, Oxford.

Caws, M. (1985)   *Reading Frames in Modern Fiction*, Princeton.

Chantraine, P. (1948–53)   *Grammaire Homérique*, 2 vols., Paris.

(1956)   *Études sur le vocabulaire grec*, Paris.

(1974)   *Dictionnaire etymologique de la langue grecque*, vol. 3, Paris.

Chapman, G. (1978)   'Aristophanes and history', *A Class* 21, 59–70.

Chatzis, A. (1914)   *Der Philosoph und Grammatiker Ptolemaios Chennos*, Paderborn.

Clack, J. (1972/3)   'The Medea similes of Apollonius Rhodius', *CJ* 68, 310–15.

Clairmont, C. (1983)   *Patrios Nomos: Public Burial in Athens during the Fifth and Fourth Centuries* B.C., London.

Clapp, E. (1913)   'Two Pindaric poems of Theocritus', *CP* 8, 310–16.

Clarke, W. (1981)   *Homer's Readers*, East Brunswick.

Claus, D. (1975)   '*Aidos* in the language of Achilles', *TAPA* 105, 13–28.

Clausen, W. (1977)   'Ariadne's leave-taking. Catullus 64 116–20', *ICS* 2, 219–23.

Clay, D. (1982)   'Unspeakable words in Greek tragedy', *AJP* 103, 277–98.

Clay, J. S. (1974)   '*Demas* and *Aude*: the nature of divine transformation in Homer', *Hermes* 102, 129–36.

(1976)   'The beginning of the *Odyssey*', *AJP* 97, 313–26.

(1983)   *The Wrath of Athena: Gods and Men in the Odyssey*, Princeton.

Cobb-Stevens, V. (1985)   'Opposites, reversals, and ambiguities: the unsettled world of Theognis', in Figuera and Nagy (1985).

Coffey, M. (1957)   'The function of the Homeric simile', *AJP* 78, 113–32.

Collins, L. (1988)   *Studies in Characterization in the Iliad,* Frankfurt am Main.

Combellack, F. (1973)   'Three Odyssean problems', *CSCA* 6, 17–46.

   (1981)   'The wish without desire', *AJP* 102, 115–19.

Compagnon, A. (1979)   *La seconde main ou le travail de la citation,* Paris.

Conte, G. B. (1986)   *The Rhetoric of Imitation: Genre and Poetic Memory in Virgil and other Latin poets,* ed. C. Segal, Ithaca and London.

Couat, A. (1883)   *Le second livre d'Élégies attribué à Théognis,* Paris.

Coward, R. (1983)   *Patriarchal Precedents,* London.

Coward, R. and Ellis, J. (1977)   *Language and Materialism,* London.

Crane, G. (1986)   'Tithonus and the prologue to Callimachus' *Aetia', ZPE* 66, 269–78.

   (1988)   *Calypso: Background and Conventions of the Odyssey,* Frankfurt am Main.

Crotty, K. (1980)   '*Pythian* 2 and conventional language in the Epinicians', *Hermes* 108, 1–12.

   (1982)   *Song and Action: the Victory Odes of Pindar,* Baltimore.

Culler, J. (1975)   *Structuralist Poetics,* Ithaca.

Cunningham, I. (1971)   *Herodas. Mimiambi,* Oxford.

Dale, A. T. (1982)   'Homeric ἐπητής/ἐπητύς: meaning and etymology', *Glotta* 60, 205–14.

Dällenbach, L. (1977)   *Le Récit spéculaire: essai sur la mise en abŷme,* Paris.

Davis, N. (1987)   *Society and Culture in Early Modern France,* Cambridge and Oxford.

Davision, J. (1958)   'Note on the Panathenaea', *JHS* 78, 23–42.

Dawe, R. (1988)   Review of G. Kirk (1985), *CJ* 84, 69–74.

Del Corno, D. (1985)   *Aristofane, Le Rane,* Naples.

de Man, P. (1971)   *Blindness and Insight,* New York.

Derrida, J. (1975)   'The purveyor of truth', *YFS* 52, 31–113.

   (1976)   *Of Grammatology,* trans. G. Spivak, Baltimore.

   (1978)   *La Vérité en peinture,* Paris.

   (1981)   *Dissemination,* trans. B. Johnson, Chicago.

Descat, R. (1979)   'L'idéologie homérique du pouvoir', *REA* 81, 229–40.

Des Places, E. (1947)   *Le Pronom chez Pindare,* Paris.

Detienne, M. (1963)   *Crise agraire et attitude religieuse chez Hésiode,* Brussels.

   (1967)   *Les Maîtres de vérité dans la Grèce archaique,* Paris.

   (1977)   *Dionysos mis à mort,* Paris.

Detienne, M. and Vernant, J-P. (1978)   *Cunning Intelligence in Greek Culture and Society,* trans. J. Lloyd, Brighton.

Diano, C. (1963)   'La poetica dei Feaci', *Belfagor* 18, 403–24.

Dick, B. (1968)   'Ancient pastoral and the pathetic fallacy', *Comp. Lit.* 20, 27–44.

Dimock, G. (1956)   'The name of Odysseus', *Hudson Review* 9.1, 52–70.

Donaldson, I. (1970)   *The World Upside Down: Comedy from Jonson to Fielding,* Oxford.

Donlan, W. (1969)   'Simonides fr. 4d and *P. Oxy.* 2432', *TAPA* 100, 71–95.

(1979)   'The structure of authority in the *Iliad*', *Arethusa* 12, 51–70.

(1982)   'Reciprocities in Homer', *CW* 75, 137–75.

(1985)   '*Pistos philos hetairos*', in Figuera and Nagy (1985).

Douglas, M. (1966)   *Purity and Danger,* London.

Dover, K. (1959)   'Pindar *Olympian Odes* 6.82–6', *CR* 9, 194–6.

(1963)   'Notes on Aristophanes' *Acharnians*', *Maia* 15, 6–21.

(1970)   'Comedy (Greek), Old', in *Oxford Classical Dictionary,* edd. N. Hammond and H. Scullard 2nd edn, Oxford.

(1971)   *Theocritus. Select Poems,* London.

(1972)   *Aristophanic Comedy,* Berkeley and Los Angeles.

(1975)   'Portrait-masks in Aristophanes', in Newiger (1975).

DuBois, P. (1978)   'Sappho and Helen', *Arethusa* 11, 89–99.

(1982)   *History, Rhetorical Description and the Epic. From Homer to Spenser,* Totowa, New Jersey.

Duckworth, G. (1933)   *Foreshadowing and Suspense in the Epics of Homer, Apollonius, and Vergil,* Princeton.

Dupont-Roc, R. and Le Boulluec, A. (1976)   'Le charme du récit (Odyssée IV 1–305)', in *Écriture et théorie poétiques. Lectures d'Homère, Éschyle, Platon, Aristote,* Paris.

DuQuesnay, I. (1979)   'From Polyphemus to Corydon: Virgil *Eclogue* 2 and the *Idylls* of Theocritus', in *Creative Imitation and Latin Literature,* edd. D. West and T. Woodman, Cambridge.

Eagleton, T. (1981)   *Walter Benjamin: Towards a Revolutionary Criticism,* London.

Easterling, P. (1982)   *Sophocles: Trachiniae,* Cambridge.

Eckart, C. (1963)   'Initiatory motifs in the story of Telemachus', *CJ* 59, 49–57.

Edmunds, L. (1980)   'Aristophanes' *Acharnians*', *YCS* 26, 1–41.

(1985)   'The genre of Theognidean poetry', in Figuera and Nagy (1985).

(1987)   'The Aristophanic Cleon's "disturbance" of Athens', *AJP* 108, 233–63.

Edquist, H. (1974)   'Aspects of Theocritean otium', *Ramus* 4, 104–14.

Edwards, A. (1984)   '*Aristos Achaion*: heroic death and dramatic structure in the *Iliad*', *QUCC* 46, 61–80.

(1985)   *Achilles in the Odyssey. Ideologies of Heroism in the Homeric Epic,* Königsten.

Edwards, M. (1975)   'Type scenes and Homeric hospitality', *TAPA* 105, 51–72.

(1987)   *Homer: Poet of the Iliad,* Stanford.

Ehrenberg, V. (1951)   *The People of Aristophanes: a Sociology of Attic Old Comedy,* Oxford.

Eichholz, D. (1953)   'The propitiation of Achilles', *AJP* 74, 137–48.

Eichorn, F. (1965) *Homers Odyssee*, Göttingen.

Eitrem, S. (1953) 'The Pindaric phthonos', in *Studies Presented to D. M. Robinson* vol. II, ed. G. Mylonas, St Louis.

Ellman, M. (1982) 'Polytropic man: paternity, identity and naming in *The Odyssey* and *A Portrait of the Artist as a Young Man*', in *James Joyce: New Perspectives*, ed. C. MacCabe, Brighton and Bloomington.

Emlyn-Jones, C. (1986) 'The reunion of Penelope and Odysseus', *G&R* 31, 1–18.

Empson, W. (1960) *Some Versions of Pastoral*, New York.

Erbse, H. (1965) 'Dichtkunst und Medizin in Theokrits' 11 Idyl', *MH* 22, 232–6.

(1972) *Beiträge zum Verständnis der Odyssee*, Berlin.

(1975) 'Dionysos' Schiedsspruch in den *Fröschen* des Aristophanes', in *ΔΩΡΗΜΑ Hans Diller zum 70. Geburtstag*, Athens.

Ettin, A. (1984) *Literature and the Pastoral*, New Haven and London.

Fabiano, G. (1971) 'Fluctuation in Theocritus' style', *GRBS* 12, 517–37.

Faerber, H. (1932) *Zur Dichterkunst in Apollonios Rhodios Argonautika*, Berlin.

Fantuzzi, M. (1985) *Bionis Smyrnaei Adonidis Epitaphium*, Liverpool.

Farnell, L. (1930) *The Works of Pindar*, 3 vols., London.

Feeney, D. (1986) 'Following after Hercules: in Virgil and Apollonius', *PVS* 18, 47–83.

Felman, S. (1985) *Writing and Madness. (Literature/Philosophy/Psychoanalysis)*, Ithaca, N.Y.

Fenik, B. (1968) *Typical Battle Scenes in the Iliad*, Hermes Einzelschriften 21.

(1974) *Studies in the Odyssey*, Hermes Einzelschriften 30.

Fennell, C. (1879) *Pindar: the Olympian and Pythian Odes*, Cambridge.

Fernandez-Galliano, M. and Heubeck, A. (1986) *Omero: Odissea Libri xxi–xxiv*, Verona.

Ferrari, G. (1988) 'Hesiod's mimetic Muses and the strategies of deconstruction', in *Post-Structuralist Classics*, ed. A. Benjamin, London and New York.

(forthcoming) 'Poetry as performance: the example of Ion'.

Figuera, T. (1984) 'The ten *archontes* of 579/8 at Athens', *Hesperia* 53, 447–73.

(1985) 'The Theognidea and Megaran society', in Figuera and Nagy (1985).

Figuera, T. and Nagy, G. edd. (1985) *Theognis of Megara: Poetry and the Polis*, Baltimore and London.

Finley, J. (1978) *Homer's Odyssey*, Cambridge, Mass.

Finley, M. (1954) *The World of Odysseus*, London.

Fitch, E. (1912) 'Apollonius Rhodius and Cyzicus', *AJP* 33, 43–56.

Floyd, E. (1980) 'Kleos aphthiton: an Indo-European perspective on early Greek poetry', *Glotta* 58, 133–57.

Fluck, H. (1931) *Skurrile Riten in griechischen Kulten*, Endingen.

Fogelmark, S. (1972) *Studies in Pindar*, Lund.

Foley, H. (1978)   ' "Reverse similes" and sex roles in the *Odyssey*', *Arethusa* 11, 7–26.

(1982)   'The "female intruder" reconsidered: women in Aristophanes' *Lysistrata* and *Ecclesiazusae*', *CP* 77, 1–21.

(1988)   'Tragedy and politics in Aristophanes' *Acharnians*', *JHS* 108, 33–47.

ed. (1982)   *Reflections of Women in Antiquity*, London, Paris, New York.

Ford, A. (1985)   'The seal of Theognis: the politics of authorship in Archaic Greece', in Figuera and Nagy (1985).

Fornara, C. (1971)   'Evidence for the data of Herodotus' publication', *JHS* 91, 25–34.

Forrest, W. (1963)   'Aristophanes' *Acharnians*', *Phoenix* 17, 1–12.

Forsyth, N. (1979)   'The allurement scene in Greek Oral Epic', *CSCA* 12, 107–20.

Foss, M. (1971)   *The Age of Patronage: the Arts in England 1660–1750*, Ithaca, N.Y.

Foucault, M. (1970)   *The Order of Things: an Archaeology of the Human Sciences*, London.

(1972)   *The Archaeology of Knowledge*, London.

(1984a)   *L'Usage des plaisirs*, Paris.

(1984b)   *Le Souci de soi*, Paris.

Fraenkel, E. (1950)   *Aeschylus Agamemnon*, 3 vols., Oxford.

(1975)   'Die Parabasenlieder', in Newiger (1975).

Fränkel, H. (1957)   'Das Argonautenepos des Apollonios', *MH* 14, 1–19.

(1960)   'Ein Don Qijote unter den Argonauten des Apollonios', *MH* 19, 1–20.

(1968)   *Noten zu den Argonautika des Apollonios*, Munich.

(1975)   *Early Greek Philosophy and Literature*, trans. M. Hadas and J. Willis, Oxford.

Frame, D. (1978)   *The Myth of Return in Early Greek Epic*, New Haven.

Friedrich, P. and Redfield, J. (1978)   'Speech as a personality symbol: the case of Achilles', *Language* 54, 263–88.

Friedrich, R. (1987)   'Heroic man and *polymetis* Odysseus in the *Cyclopeia*', *GRBS* 28, 121–34.

Frontisi-Ducroux, F. (1976)   'Homère et le temps retrouvé', *Critique* 32, 538–48.

(1986)   *Le Cithare d'Achille*, Rome.

Fusillo, M. (1985)   *Il tempo delle Aronautiche*, Rome.

Gaisser, J. (1969)   'Adaptation of traditional material in the Glaucus-Diomedes episode', *TAPA* 100, 165–76.

Galinsky, K. (1972)   *The Herakles Theme: the Adaptations of the Hero in Literature from Homer to the Twentieth Century*, Oxford.

Gallop, J. (1982)   *Feminism and Psychoanalysis: the Daughter's Seduction*, London.

(1985)   *Reading Lacan*, Ithaca, N.Y.

Garvie, A. (1986)   *Aeschylus Choephoroi*, Oxford.

Gaunt, D. (1972) 'Argo and the gods in Apollonius Rhodius', *G&R* 19, 117–26.

Geertz, C. (1972) 'Deep play: notes on a Balinese cockfight', *Daedalus* 101, 1–38.

Genette, G. (1966) *Figures I*, Paris.

(1969) *Figures II*, Paris.

(1972) *Figures III*, Paris.

(1980) *Narrative Discourse*, trans. J. Lewin, Oxford.

(1982a) *Palimpsestes*, Paris.

(1982b) *Figures of Literary Discourse*, trans. A. Sheridan, Oxford.

Gentili, B. (1977) '*Addendum*. A proposito dei vv. 253–4 di Teognide', QUCC 26, 115–6.

(1978) 'Poeta-Committente-Pubblico', in *Studi in onore di Anthos Ardizzoni*, Rome.

(1983) 'Poeta e musico in Grecia', in *Oralità, Scrittura, Spettacolo*, ed. M. Vegetti, Turin.

(1984) *Poesia e Pubblico nella Grecia Antiqua, da Omero al V secolo*, Bari.

George, E. (1972) 'Poet and characters in Apollonius Rhodius' Lemnian episode', *Hermes* 100, 47–63.

(1977) 'Apollonius, *Argonautica* 4.984–5: apology for a shameful tale', *Riv. di Stud. Class.* 25, 360–4.

Gerber, D. (1970) *Euterpe*, Amsterdam.

ed. (1984) *Greek Poetry and Philosophy: Studies in Honor of Leonard Woodbury*, Chico.

Giangrande, G. (1963) 'The origins of Attic comedy', *Eranos* 61, 9–24.

(1967) '"Arte Allusiva" and Alexandrian epic poetry', *CQ* 17, 85–97.

(1968) 'Théocrite, Simichidas, et les *Thalysies*', *AC* 37, 491–533.

(1970) 'Hellenistic Poetry and Homer', *AC* 39, 46–77.

(1973) *Zu Sprachgebraucht Technik und Text des Apollonios Rhodios*, Amsterdam.

(1976) 'Aspects of Apollonius Rhodius' Language', *PLLS*, 271–91.

Gianotti, G. (1973) 'Mito ed encomio: il carme di Ibico in onore di Policrate', *RFIC* 101, 401–10.

(1975) *Per una Poetica Pindarica*, Turin.

Gildersleeve, B. (1979) *Pindar: the Olympian and Pythian Odes*, Harbour View, N.Y. (First published 1885).

Glenn, J. (1971) 'The Polyphemus folktale and Homer's *Kyklopeia*', *TAPA* 102, 133–81.

Gluckman, M. ed. (1962) *The Ritual of Social Relations*, Manchester.

(1963) *Order and Rebellion in Tribal Africa*, London.

(1965) *Custom and Conflict in Africa*, Oxford.

Gnoli, G and Vernant, J-P. (1982) *La mort, les morts dans les sociétés anciennes*, Cambridge and Paris.

Goffman, E. (1974) *Frame Analysis*, New York.

Goldhill, S. (1984)   *Language, Sexuality, Narrative: the Oresteia*, Cambridge.
  (1986a)   *Reading Greek Tragedy*, Cambridge.
  (1986b)   'Framing and polyphony: readings in Hellenistic poetry', *PCPS* 32,
      25–52.
  (1987a)   'An unnoticed allusion in Theocritus and Callimachus', *ICS* 12, 1–6.
  (1987b)   'The dance of the veils: reading five fragments of Anacreon', *Eranos*
      85, 9–18.
  (1987c)   'The Great Dionysia and civic ideology', *JHS* 107, 58–76.
  (1988a)   'Desire and the figure of fun: glossing Theocritus 11', in *Post-
      Structuralist Classics*, ed. A. Benjamin, London and New York.
  (1988b)   'A footnote in the history of Greek epitaphs: Simonides 146 Bergk',
      Phoenix 42, 189–97.
  (1988c)   'Reading differences: juxtaposition and the *Odyssey*', *Ramus* 17.1,
      1–31.
  (1990)   'Supplication and authorial comment in the *Iliad*: *Iliad* z.61–2', *Hermes*
      166, forthcoming.
Gomme, A. (1938)   'Aristophanes and politics', *CR* 52, 97–109.
Goody, J. ed. (1973)   *The Character of Kinship*, Cambridge.
Gordon, R. ed. (1981)   *Myth, Religion and Society*, Cambridge.
Gould, J. (1973)   'Hiketeia', *JHS* 93, 74–103.
  (1983)   'Homeric epic and the tragic moment' in *Aspects of the Epic*, edd. T.
      Winnifrith, P. Murray and K. Gransden, London.
Gouldner, A. (1965)   *Enter Plato*, London and New York.
Gow, A. (1950)   *Theocritus*, 2. vols., Cambridge.
Greenblatt, S. (1975)   *Sir Walter Ralegh: the Renaissance Man and His Roles*,
      New Haven and London.
Greengard, C. (1980)   *The Structure of Pindar's Epinicean Odes*, Amsterdam.
Griffin, J. (1980)   *Homer on Life and Death*, Oxford.
Griffith, J. (1970)   'ΛΗΚΥΘΙΟΝ ΑΠΩΛΕΣΕΝ: a postscript', *HSCP* 74, 43–4.
Griffiths, F. (1979a)   *Theocritus at Court*, Leiden.
  (1979b)   'Poetry as *pharmakon* in Theocritus *Idyll* 2', in *Arktouros: Hellenic
      Studies presented to Bernard M. W. Knox on the occasion of his 65th birthday*,
      Berlin.
  (1981)   'Home before lunch: the emancipated woman in Theocritus', in *Re-
      flections of Women in Antiquity*, ed. H. Foley, New York.
Grillo, A. (1988)   *Tra filologia e narratologia*, Rome.
van Groningen, B. (1946)   'The proems of the *Iliad* and the *Odyssey*', *Meded.
      Ned. Ak., Afd. Letterk.* 9.8, 279–94.
  (1958)   *La Composition littéraire archaïque grecque*, Amsterdam.
  (1959)   'Quelques problèmes de la poésie bucolique grecque', *Mnemosyne* 12,
      24–53.
  (1966)   *Théognis. Le premier livre*, Amsterdam.

Gross, N. (1976) 'Nausikaa: a feminine threat', *CW* 69, 311–17.

Gundert, H. (1935) *Pindar und sein Dichterberuf*, Frankfurt am Main.

Gunn, D. (1971) 'Thematic composition and Homeric authorship', *HSCP* 75, 1–31.

Guthrie, W. (1969) *A History of Greek Philosophy*, vol. III, Cambridge.

Gutzwiller, K. (1983) 'Charites or Hiero: Theocritus *Idyll* 16', *RhM* 126, 212–38.

Gzella, S. (1971) 'The fee in ancient Greek literature', *Eos* 49, 189–202.

Haft, A. (1984) 'Odysseus, Idomeneus, and Meriones: the Cretan lies of *Odyssey* 13–9', *CJ* 79, 289–306.

Hagstrum, J. (1958) *The Sister Arts: The Tradition of Literary Pictorialism and English Poetry from Dryden to Gray*, Chicago.

Hall, E. (1989) *Inventing the Barbarian*, Oxford.

Halliwell, S. (1982) 'Notes on some Aristophanic jokes (*Ach.* 854–9; *Kn.* 608–10; *Peace* 695–9; *Thesmo.* 605; *Frogs* 1039)', *LCM* 7.10, 153–4.

  (1984a) 'Ancient interpretations of ὀνομαστὶ κωμῳδεῖν in Aristophanes', *CQ* 34, 83–8.

  (1984b) 'Aristophanic satire', in *English Satire and the Satiric Tradition*, ed. C. Rawson, Oxford.

  (1986) *Aristotle's Poetics*, London.

Halperin, D. (1983) *Before Pastoral: Theocritus and the Ancient Tradition of Bucolic Poetry*, New Haven.

Hamilton, R. (1974) *Epinikion. General Form in the Odes of Pindar*, The Hague.

Hamon, P. (1981) 'Rhetorical status of the descriptive', *YFS* 61, 1–26.

Händel, P. (1954) *Beobachtungen zur epischen Technik des Apollonios*, Munich.

Hansen, W. (1972) *The Conference Sequence. Patterned Narration and Narrative Inconsistency in the Odyssey*, Berkeley.

Hardie, A. (1983) *Statius and the Silvae: Poets, Patrons and Epideixis in the Graeco-Roman World*, Liverpool.

Hardison, O. (1962) *The Enduring Monument: a Study of the Idea of Praise in Renaissance Literary Theory and Practice*, Chapel Hill.

Harriot, R. (1969) *Poetry and Criticism before Plato*, London.

  (1982) 'The function of the Euripides scene in Aristophanes' *Acharnians*', *G&R* 29, 35–41.

  (1986) *Aristophanes: Poet and Dramatist*, London and Sydney.

Harrison, E. (1902) *Studies in Theognis*, Cambridge.

Harsh, P. (1950) 'Penelope and Odysseus in *Odyssey* XIX', *AJP* 71, 1–21.

Hasluck, F. (1910) *Cyzicus*, Cambridge.

Hatzantonis, E. (1974) 'La resa omerica della feminilità di Circe', *AC* 43, 38–56.

Hatzikosta, S. (1982) *A Stylistic Commentary on Theocritus' Idyll VII*, Amsterdam.

Hauvette, A. (1896) *De l'authenticité des épigrammes de Simonide*, Paris.

Haynes, J. (1984) 'Festivity and the dramatic economy of Jonson's *Bartholomew Fair*', *English Literary History* 51.4, 645–68.

Heath, M. (1987a) *Aristophanes' Political Comedy*, Göttingen.

(1987b) *The Poetics of Greek Tragedy*, London.

(1988) 'Receiving the κῶμος: the context and performance of epinician', *AJP* 109, 180–95.

Helgerson, R. (1983) *Self-Crowned Laureates: Spenser, Jonson. Milton and the Literary System*, Berkeley.

Henderson, J. (1972) 'The lekythos and *Frogs* 1200–48', *HSCP* 76, 133–43.

(1974) 'ΚΩΔΑΡΙΟΝ: a reply', *Mnemosyne* 27, 293–5.

(1975) *The Maculate Muse*, New Haven and London.

(1980) '*Lysistrate*: the play and its themes', *YCS* 26, 153–218.

Henderson, J. G. (1986) 'Becoming a heroine (1st): Penelope's Ovid . . .', *LCM* 11, 7–10; 25–8; 37–40; 67–70; 82–5; 114–21.

Henrichs, A. (1980) 'Human sacrifice in Greek religion; three case studies', in *Sacrifice dans l'antiquité, Entretiens sur l'antiquité classique* 27.

Herman, G. (1987) *Ritualized Friendship and the Greek City*, Cambridge.

Herter, H. (1947) *Vom dionysischen Tanz zum komischen Spiel*, Iserlohn.

Heubeck, A. (1954) *Der Odyssee-Dichter und die Ilias*, Erlangen.

(1984) *Kleineschriften*, Erlangen.

Hinds, S. (1985) 'Booking the return trip: Ovid and *Tristia* 1', *PCPS* 31, 13–32.

(1987) *The Metamorphosis of Persephone: Ovid and the Self-Conscious Muse*, Cambridge.

Hirschkop, K. (1989) 'Bibliographical Essay' in Hirschkop and Shepherd (1989).

Hirschkop, K. and Shepherd, D. edd. (1989) *Bakhtin and Cultural Theory*, Manchester.

Hogan, J. (1976) 'The temptation of Odysseus', *TAPA* 106, 187–210.

Höistad, R. (1948) *Cynic King and Cynic Hero: Studies in the Cynic Conception of Man*, Upsala.

Hölscher, U. (1967) 'Die Atridensage in der Odyssee', in *Festschrift für Richard Alewyn*, edd. H. Singer, and B. von Wiese, Cologne.

Holtsmark, E. (1966) 'Poetry as self-enlightenment: Theocritus 11', *TAPA* 97, 253–9.

Hooker, J. (1970) 'Lekythion', *RhM* 113, 162–4.

(1987) 'Homeric φίλος', *Glotta* 65, 44–65.

Hopkins, K. (1980) 'Brother-sister marriage in Roman Egypt', *CSSH* 20, 303–54.

Hopkinson, N. (1984) *Callimachus: Hymn to Demeter*, Cambridge.

(1988) *A Hellenistic Anthology*, Cambridge.

Hopper, R. (1971) *The Acropolis*, London.

Horstman, A. (1976) *Ironie und Humor bei Theokrit*, Meisenheim am Glan.

Householder, F. (1944) 'ΠΑΡΩΔΙΑ', *CP* 39, 1–9.

Hubbard, T. (1981) 'Antithetical simile pairs in Homer', *GB* 10, 59–67.

(1985) *The Pindaric Mind: a Study of Logical Structure in Early Greek Poetry*, Leiden.

(1986) 'Parabatic self-criticism and the two versions of Aristophanes' *Clouds*', *Cl. Ant.* 5, 182–97.

Hudson-Williams, T. (1910) *The Elegies of Theognis*, London.

Hunter, R. (1983) *A Study of Daphnis and Chloe*, Cambridge.

(1986) 'Apollo and the Argonauts: two notes on Ap. Rhod. 2, 669–719', *MH* 43, 50–60.

(1987) 'Medea's flight: the fourth book of the *Argonautica*', *CQ* 37, 129–39.

(1988) '"Short on heroics": Jason in the *Argonautica*', *CQ* 38, 436–53.

(1989) *Apollonius of Rhodes: Argonautica Book III*, Cambridge.

Hurst, A. (1964) 'La Retour nocturne des Argonauts', *MH* 21, 232–7.

(1967) *Apollonios de Rhodes, manière et cohérence*, Rome.

(1984) 'Aspects du temps chez Pindare' in *Pindare, Entretiens sur l'antiquité classique* 31, Geneva.

Hurwit, J. (1985) *The Art and Culture of Early Greece 1100–480 B.C.*, Ithaca and London.

Hutcheon, L. (1985) *A Theory of Parody*, New York and London.

Hutchinson, G. (1988) *Hellenistic Poetry*, Oxford.

Huxley, G. (1975) *Pindar's Vision of the Past*, Belfast.

Iser, W. (1974) *The Implied Reader: Patterns of Communication from Bunyan to Beckett*, Baltimore.

Jaeger, W. (1966) 'Tyrtaeus on the true virtue', in *Five Essays*, trans. A. Fiske, Montreal.

Jameson, F. (1981) *The Political Unconscious: Narrative as a Socially Symbolic Act*, Ithaca.

Javitch, D. (1978) *Poetry and Courtliness in Renaissance England*, Princeton.

Jeanmaire, H. (1939) *Couroi et couretes*, Lille.

Jenkins, I. (1985) 'The ambiguity of Greek textiles', *Arethusa* 18, 109–32.

Johnson, B. (1980) *The Critical Difference*, Baltimore.

Jones, P. (1988) 'The κλέος of Telemachus: *Odyssey* 1.95', *AJP* 109, 496–506.

de Jong, I. (1987) *Narrators and Focalizers: The Presentation of the Story in the Iliad*, Amsterdam.

Jost, F. ed. (1966) *Proceedings of the IVth Congress of the International Comparative Literature Association*, The Hague.

Jouan, F. (1978) 'Nomen-omen chez Eschyle', in *Problèmes du mythe et son interprétation*, ed. J. Hani, Paris.

Kahn, L. (1978) *Hermès passe; ou les ambiguités de la communication*, Paris.

Kaibel, G. (1873) 'Quaestiones Simonideae', *RhM* 28, 436–60.

Kakridis, J. (1949) *Homeric Researches*, Lund.

(1971)   *Homer Revisited,* Lund.

Kambylis, A. (1965)   *Die Dichterweihe und ihr Symbolik,* Heidelberg.

Kearns, E. (1982)   'The return of Odysseus. A Homeric theoxeny', *CQ* 32, 2–8.

Kennedy, G. (1986)   'Helen's web unraveled', *Arethusa* 19, 5–14.

Ketterer, R. (1980)   'Stripping in the parabasis of the *Acharnians*', *GRBS* 21, 217–21.

King, H. (1986)   'Tithonos and the tettix', *Arethusa* 19, 15–35.

King, K. (1987)   *Achilles: Paradigms of the War Hero from Homer to the Middle Ages,* Berkeley.

Kirk, G. (1962)   *The Songs of Homer,* Cambridge.

(1970)   *Myth: its Meaning and Function in Ancient and Other Cultures,* Berkeley.

(1985)   *The Iliad: a Commentary,* vol. 1, Cambridge.

Kirkwood, G. (1981)   'Pythian 5, 72–6, 9, 90–2, and the voice of Pindar', *ICS* 6, 12–23.

(1982)   *Selections from Pindar,* Chico.

(1984)   'Blame and envy in the Pindaric epinicean', in Gerber ed. (1984).

Klein, T. (1974)   'The role of Callimachus in the development of the concept of the counter-genre', *Latomus* 33, 217–31.

(1983)   'Apollonius' Jason: hero and scoundrel', *QUCC* 42, 115–26.

Koch, K-D. (1965)   *Kritische Idee und komisches Thema: Untersuchungen zur Dramaturgie und zum Ethos der Aristophanischen Komödie,* Bremen.

Köhnken, A. (1971)   *Die Funktion des Mythos bei Pindar,* Berlin.

(1976)   'Die Narbe des Odysseus', *A&A* 22, 101–14.

Koller, H. (1965)   'ΘΕΣΠΙΣ ΑΟΙΔΟΣ', *Glotta* 43, 277–85.

Komornicka, A. (1964)   *Métaphores, personnifications et comparisons dans l'oeuvre d'Aristophane,* (Wroclaw, Warsaw, Cracow).

Konstan, D. (1985)   'The politics of Aristophanes' *Wasps*', *TAPA* 115, 27–46.

(1986)   'Politique et rituel dans les *Grenouilles*', *METIS,* 1, 291–308.

Konstan, D. and Dillon, M. (1981)   'The ideology of Aristophanes' *Wealth*', *AJP* 102, 371–94.

Kowzan, T. (1983)   'Les comédies d'Aristophane, véhicule de la critique drama-tique', *Dioniso* 54, 83–100.

Kranz, W. (1961)   'Sphragis: Ichform und Namensiegel als Eingangs-und Schlussmotiv antiker Dichtung', *RhM* 104, 3–46.

Kraus, W. (1955)   'Die Auffassung des Dichterberufs im frühen Griechentum', *WS* 68, 65–87.

Kresic, S. ed. (1981)   *Contemporary Literary Hermeneutics and the Interpretation of Classical Texts,* Ottawa.

Krevans, N. (1983)   'Geography and literary tradition in Theocritus 7', *TAPA* 113, 201–20.

Kristeva, J. (1980)   *Desire in Language,* trans. and ed. L. Roudiez, Oxford.

Kroll, J. (1936)   *Theognis-Interpretationen,* Leipzig.

Kühn, J-H. (1958) 'Die Thalysien Theokrits', *Hermes* 86, 40–79.

(1978) *Der Adressatenwechsel in Theokrits Hieron-Gedicht: Das id. 16 ein Wechselrahmengedicht?*, Waldkirch.

Kuhn, T. (1962) *The Structure of Scientific Revolutions*, Chicago.

Lanata, G. (1963) *Poetica Preplatonica*, Florence.

Landfester, M. (1979) 'Geschichte der griechischen Komödie', in Seeck (1979).

Lasserre, F. (1959) 'Aux origines de l'Anthologie II: les Thalysies de Théocrite', *RhM* 102, 307–30.

Lavagnini, B. (1947) *Aglaia*, Turin.

Lawall, G. (1966) 'Apollonius' *Argonautica*; Jason as anti-hero', *YCS* 19, 119–69.

(1967) *Theocritus' Coan Pastorals. A Poetry Book*, Cambridge, Mass.

Leach, E. (1961) 'Time and false noses', in *Rethinking Anthropology*, ed. E. Leach, London.

(1964) 'Anthropological aspects of language: animal categories and verbal abuse', in *New Directions in the Study of Language*, ed. E. Lenneberg, New York.

Lee, D. (1964) *The Similes of the Iliad and the Odyssey Compared*, Melbourne.

Lee, H. (1978/9) 'The "historical" Bundy and encomiastic relevance in Pindar', *CW* 72, 65–70.

Lee, R. (1967) *Ut Pictura Poiesis: the Humanistic Theory of Painting*, New York.

Lefkowitz, M. (1963) 'ΤΩ ΚΑΙ ΕΓΩ: the first person in Pindar', *HSCP* 67, 177–253.

(1975) 'The influential fictions in the scholia to Pindar's Pythian 8', *CP* 70, 173–85.

(1976) *The Victory Ode*, Park Ridge.

(1979) 'Pindar's *Nemean* XI', *JHS* 99, 49–56.

(1980) 'Autobiographical fiction in Pindar', *HSCP* 84, 29–49.

(1984) 'The poet as athlete', *SIFC* n.s. 2, 5–12.

(1988) 'Who sang Pindar's victory odes?', *AJP* 109, 1–11.

Legrand, P. (1898) *Étude sur Théocrite*, Paris.

Lehnus, L. (1981) *Pindaro. Olympiche*, Milan.

Lennox, P. (1980) 'Apollonius' *Argonautica* 3, 1ff and Homer', *Hermes* 108, 45–73.

Lenz, L. (1980) 'Komik und Kritik in Aristophanes' *Wespen*', *Hermes* 108, 15–44.

Le Roy Ladurie, E. (1979) *Carnival in Romans*, trans. M. Feeney, Harmondsworth.

Lesker, J. (1981) 'Perceiving and knowing in the *Iliad* and *Odyssey*', *Phronesis* 26, 2–24.

Letoublon, F. (1983) 'Défi et combat dans l'*Iliade*', *REG* 96, 27–48.

Levin, D. (1971a) *Apollonius' Argonautica re-examined: the neglected first and second books*, Leiden.

(1971b)   'Apollonius' Hercules', *CJ* 67, 22–8.

(1977)   'ΔΙΠΛΑΞ ΠΟΡΦΥΡΕΗ', *RFIC* 98, 17–36.

Levine, D. (1985) 'Symposium and the *polis*', in Figuera and Nagy (1985).

Lévi-Strauss, C. (1966)   *The Savage Mind*, Chicago.

Lewalski, B. (1973)   *Donne's Aniversaries and the Poetry of Praise: the Creation of a Symbolic Mode*, Princeton.

Lewis, J. (1985) 'Eros and the *polis* in Theognis Book II', in Figuera and Nagy (1985).

Lilja, S. (1976)   *Dogs in Ancient Greek Poetry*, Helsinki.

Livrea, E. (1973)   *Apollonio Rodio IV*, Florence.

Lloyd-Jones, H. (1971)   *The Justice of Zeus*, Berkeley.

(1973)   'Modern interpretations of Pindar: the second Pythian and seventh Nemean odes', *JHS* 93, 109–37.

Lohmann, D. (1970)   *Die Komposition der Reden in der Ilias*, Berlin.

Long, A. (1970) 'Morals and values in Homer', *JHS* 90, 121–39.

Loraux, N. (1981a)   *L'Invention d'Athènes*, Paris.

(1981b)   *Les Enfants d'Athéna*, Paris.

(1982)   'Mourir devant Troie, tomber pour Athènes: de la gloire du héros à l'idée de la cité', in Gnoli and Vernant (1982).

(1986)   *The Invention of Athens*, trans. A. Sheridan, Cambridge, Mass. (translation of Loraux 1981a).

Luck, G. (1966) 'Zur Deutung von Thalysien Theokrits', *MH* 23, 186–9.

Luther, W. (1966) 'Wahrheit, Licht and Erkenntnis', *Archiv für Begriffsgeschichte* 10.

Lynn-George, M. (1983) '*Epos*: word, narrative and the *Iliad*', unpublished dissertation, Cambridge.

(1988)   *Epos: word, narrative and the Iliad*, Atlantic Highlands.

Lytle, G. and Orgel, S. edd. (1981)   *Patronage in the Renaissance*, Princeton.

MacCaffery, W. (1961) 'Place and patronage in Elizabethan politics', in *Elizabethan Government and Society, Essays presented to Sir John Neale*, edd. S. Bindoff, J. Hurstfield, C. Williams, London.

McCanles, M. (1977) 'Festival in Jonsonian comedy', *Renaissance Drama* 8, 203–19.

McDiarmid, J. (1987) 'Pindar Olympian 6.82–3: the doxa, the whetstone, and the tongue', *AJP* 108, 368–77.

MacDowell, D. (1975) 'Aristophanes *Frogs* 1407–67', in Newiger (1975).

(1978)   *The Law in Classical Athens*, Ithaca, N.Y.

(1983)   'The nature of Aristophanes' *Acharnians*', *G&R* 30, 143–62.

Macleod, C. (1982)   *Homer: Iliad XXIV*, Cambridge.

Maehler, H. (1963)   *Die Auffassung des Dichterberufs im frühen Griechentum bis zur Zeit Pindars*, Göttingen.

Marg, W. (1956) 'Das erste Lied des Demodokos', in *Navicula Chiloensis*, Leiden.

(1957) *Homer über die Dichtung*, Münster.

(1976) 'Kampf und Tod in der Ilias', *WJ* 2, 7–19.

Maronitis, D. (1981) 'Die erste Trugrede des Odysseus in der *Odyssee*: Vorbild und Variationen', in *Gnomosyne. Festschrift für Walter Marg*, Berlin.

Marrou, H. (1956) *A History of Education in Antiquity*, trans. G. Lamb, London.

Martin, R. (1990) *The Language of Heroes: Speech and Performance in the Iliad*, Ithaca, N.Y.

Marx, K. (1978) *The Marx – Engels Reader*, ed. R. Tucker, New York.

Mastromarco, G. (1984) *The Public of Herondas*, Amsterdam.

Mastronarde, D. (1968) 'Theocritus' Idyll 13: love and the hero', *TAPA* 99, 273–9.

Mattes, W. (1958) *Odysseus bei den Phäaken*, Würzburg.

Meincke, W. (1965) *Untersuchungen zu den enkomiastischen Gedichten Theokrits*, Kiel.

Meyerhoff, B. (1978) 'Return to Wirikuta: ritual reversal and symbolic continuity on the Peyote Hunt of the Huichol Indians', in Babcock ed. (1978).

Miles, G. (1977) 'Characterization and the ideal of innocence in Theocritus' *Idylls*', *Ramus* 6, 139–74.

Miller, D. (1982) *Improvisation, Typology, Culture and the 'New Orthodoxy'. How Oral is Homer?*, Washington.

Miller, H. (1979) 'The critic as host', in *Deconstruction and Criticism*, edd. H. Bloom, P. de Man, G. Hartman, London.

Millett, P. (1984) 'Hesiod and his world', *PCPS* 30, 84–115.

Mondi, R. (1983) 'The Homeric Cyclopes: folktale, tradition and theme', *TAPA* 113, 17–38.

Monsacré, H. (1984) *Les Larmes d'Achilles: l'héros, la femme, et la souffrance dans la poésie d'Homère*, Paris.

Montrose, L. (1977) 'Celebration and insinuation: Sir Philip Sidney and the motives of Elizabethan courtship', *Renaissance Drama* 8, 3–35.

Most, G. (1981) 'Sappho fr. 16.6–7 (L – P)', *CQ* 31, 11–17.

(1985) *The Measures of Praise: Structure and Function in Pindar's Second Pythian and Seventh Nemean Odes*, Göttingen.

Motzkus, D. (1964) *Untersuchungen zum 9. Buch der Ilias unter besonderer Berücksichtigung der Phoenixgestalt*, Hamburg.

Moulton, C. (1974) 'The end of the *Odyssey*', *GRBS* 15, 139–52.

(1977) *Similes in the Homeric Poems*, Göttingen.

(1981) *Aristophanic Poetry*, Göttingen.

Muecke, F. (1977) 'Playing with the play: theatrical self-consciousness in Aristophanes', *Antichthon* 11, 52–67.

(1982) 'A portrait of the artist as a young woman', *CQ* 32, 41–55.

Mueller, M. (1978) 'Knowledge and delusion in the *Iliad*', in *Essays on the Iliad: Selected Modern Criticism*, ed. J. Wright, Bloomington and London.

(1984)   *The Iliad*, London.

Mullen, W. (1982)   *Choreia: Pindar and Dance*, Princeton.

Murnaghan, S. (1987)   *Disguise and Recognition in the Odyssey*, Princeton.

Murray, P. (1981)   'Poetic inspiration in early Greece', *JHS* 101, 87–100.

(1983)   'Homer and the bard', in *Aspects of the Epic*, edd. T. Winnifrith, P. Murray, K. Gransden, London.

Nagler, M. (1974)   *Spontaneity and Tradition: a Study of the Oral Art of Homer*, Berkeley.

Nagy, G. (1974)   *Comparative Studies in Greek and Indic Meter*, Cambridge, Mass.

(1979)   *The Best of the Achaeans. Concepts of the Hero in Archaic Greek Poetry*, Baltimore.

(1981)   'Another look at *kleos aphthiton*', *WJA* 7, 113–16.

(1984)   'On the range of an idiom in Homeric dialogue', in *Studies Presented to Stirling Dow on his Eightieth Birthday* edd. A. Boegehold, W. Calder, J. Camp, et al., Durham, N.C.

(1985)   'Theognis and Megara: a poet's vision of his city', in Figuera and Nagy (1985).

Nannini, S. (1982)   'Lirica greca arcaica e *recusatio* augustea', *QUCC* 10, 71–88.

Nash, L. (1975)   '*Olympian* 6: *Alibaton* and Iamos' emergence into light', *AJP* 96, 110–16.

Neitzel, H. (1979)   'ΦΕΡΕΙ ΦΕΡΟΝΤ': ein aischyleisches Orakel, *Aga.* 1562', *Hermes* 107, 133–46.

Newiger, H-J. (1957)   *Metaphor und Allegorie. Studien zu Aristophanes*, Munich.

ed. (1975)   *Aristophanes und die alte Komödie*, Darmstadt.

(1980)   'War and peace in the comedy of Aristophanes', *YCS* 26, 219–317.

Newton, R. (1983)   'Poor Polyphemus: emotional ambivalence in *Odyssey* 9 and 17', *CW* 76, 137–42.

Niles, J. (1978)   'Patterning in the wanderings of Odysseus', *Ramus* 7, 46–60.

Nimis, S. (1987)   *Narrative Semiotics in the Epic Tradition. The Simile*, Bloomington.

Nisetich, F. (1980)   *Pindar's Victory Songs*, Baltimore.

Northrup, M. (1980)   'Homer's catalogue of women', *Ramus* 11, 150–9.

Norwood, G. (1930)   'The *Babylonians* of Aristophanes', *CP* 25, 1–10.

(1941)   'Pindar *Olympian* VI 82–8', *CP* 36, 394–6.

(1945)   *Pindar*, Berkeley.

Notopoulos, J. (1949)   'Parataxis in Homer', *TAPA* 80, 1–23.

(1951)   'Continuity and interconnexion in Homeric oral composition', *TAPA* 82, 81–101.

Nussbaum, M. (1980)   'Aristophanes and Socrates on learning practical wisdom', *YCS* 26, 43–97.

(1986)   *The Fragility of Goodness*, Cambridge.

Ober, J. (1989)   *Mass and Elite in Democratic Athens*, Princeton.

Ogilvie, R. (1962) 'The song of Thyrsis', *JHS* 82, 106–10.

Orgel, S. (1975) *The Illusion of Power: Political Theater in the English Renaissance*, Berkeley.

Osborne, R. (1985) 'The erection and mutilation of the Hermai', *PCPS* 31, 47–73.

(1987) 'The viewing and obscuring of the Parthenon frieze', *JHS* 107, 98–105.

O'Sullivan, J. (1984) 'The sign of the bed: *Odyssey* 23. 137ff', *GRBS* 25, 21–5.

Ott, U. (1969) *Die Kunst des Gegensatzes in Theokrits Hirtengedichten*, Heidelberg.

Pade, M. (1983) 'Homer's catalogue of women', *C&M* 34, 7–15.

Paduano, G. (1970) 'L'inversione del rapporto Poeta-Musa nella cultura ellenistica', *ASNP* 39, 378–86.

(1972) *Studi su Apollonio Rodio*, Rome.

Page, D. (1951) 'Ibycus' poem in honour of Polycrates', *Aegyptus* 31, 158–72.

(1955) *The Homeric Odyssey*, Oxford.

(1959) *History and the Homeric Iliad*, Berkeley.

Parke, H. (1977) *Festivals of the Athenians*, Ithaca.

Parker, R. (1983) *Miasma: Pollution and Purification in Early Greek Religion*, Oxford.

Parry, A. (1956) 'The language of Achilles', *TAPA* 87, 1–7.

Parry, H. (1988) 'Magic and the songstress: Theocritus *Idyll* 2', *ICS* 13, 43–56.

Parry, M. (1971) *The Making of Homeric Verse*, ed A. Parry, Oxford.

Pavese, C. (1964) 'Pindarica', *Maia* 16, 307–13.

Pearce, T. (1988) 'The function of the *locus amoenus* in Theocritus' seventh poem', *RhM* 131, 276–304.

Pedrick, V. (1982) 'Supplication in the *Iliad* and the *Odyssey*', *TAPA* 112, 125–40.

Peek, W. (1955) *Griechische Vers-Inschriften*, Berlin.

Penella, R. (1973) 'κῳδάριον in Aristophanes' *Frogs*', *Mnemosyne* 26, 337–41.

(1974) 'κῳδάριον: a comment', *Mnemosyne* 27, 295–7.

Peradotto, J. (1974) '*Odyssey* 8.564–571. Verisimilitude, narrative analysis and bricolage', *Texas Studies in Language and Literature* 15.5, 803–32.

Péron, J. (1974) *Les Images maritimes de Pindar*, Paris.

(1982) 'La poéme à Polycrate: une "palinodie" d'Ibycus', *Rev. Phil.* 56, 33–56.

Perotta, G. (1925) 'Studi di Poesia Ellenistica', *SIFC* 4, 5–68.

Petre, Z. (1983) 'Homère archaïsant – Homère archaique', *Stud. Class.* 21, 7–14.

Pfeiffer, R. (1949) *Callimachus*, 2 vols., Oxford.

(1968) *History of Classical Scholarship*, Oxford.

Phinney, E. (1967) 'Narrative unity in the *Argonautica*; the Medea – Jason romance', *TAPA* 98, 327–41.

Pickard-Cambridge, A. (1962)   *Dithyramb, Tragedy, Comedy*, rev. T. Webster, Oxford.

(1968)   *The Dramatic Festivals of Athens*, 2nd edn, rev. J. Gould and D. Lewis, Oxford.

Podlecki, A. (1961)   'Guest-gifts and nobodies in *Odyssey* 9', *Phoenix* 15, 125–33.

(1968)   'Simonides 480', *Historia* 17, 257–75.

Poggioli, R. (1974)   *The Oaten Flute*, Cambridge, Mass.

Poliakoff, M. (1980)   'Nectar, springs, and the sea: critical terminology in Pindar and Theocritus', *ZPE* 39, 41–7.

Pomeroy, S. (1975)   'Andromache and the question of matriarchy', *REG* 89, 16–19.

(1984)   *Women in Hellenistic Egypt from Alexander to Cleopatra*, New York.

Powell, B. (1977)   *Composition by Theme in the Odyssey*, Meisenheim am Glan.

Prato, C. (1968)   *Tyrtaeus*, Rome.

Praz, M. (1970)   *Mnemosyne: the Parallel between Literature and the Visual Arts*, Washington.

Pucci, P. (1977)   *Hesiod and the Language of Poetry*, Baltimore.

(1979)   'The song of the sirens', *Arethusa* 12, 121–32.

(1980)   'The language of the Muses', in Aycock and Klein (1980).

(1982)   'The proem of the *Odyssey*', *Arethusa* 15, 39–62.

(1986)   'Les figures de la métis dans l'*Odyssée*', *METIS* 1, 7–28.

(1987)   *Odysseus Polytropos. Intertextual Readings in the Odyssey and the Iliad*, Ithaca.

(1988)   'Banter and banquets for heroic death', in *Post-Structuralist Classics*, ed. A Benjamin, London and New York.

Puelma, M. (1960)   'Die Dichterbegegnung in Theokrits "Thalysien"', *MH* 17, 144–64.

Radin, M. (1927)   'Freedom of speech in ancient Athens', *AJP* 48, 215–30.

Rau, P. (1967)   *Paratragödia*, Munich.

Reckford, K. (1987)   *Aristophanes' Old-and-New Comedy*, Chapel Hill.

Redfield, J. (1973)   'The making of the *Odyssey*', in *Parnassus Revisited*, ed. A. Yu, Chicago.

(1975)   *Nature and Culture in the Iliad. The Tragedy of Hector*, Chicago.

Reeve, M. (1973)   'The language of Achilles', *CQ* 23, 93–5.

Reinhardt, K. (1961)   *Die Ilias und ihr Dichter*, Göttingen.

Reinhardt, T. (1988)   *Die Darstellung der Bereiche Stadt und Land bei Theokrit*, Bonn.

Reinsch-Werner, H. (1976)   *Callimachus Hesiodicus*, Berlin.

Richardson, N. (1974)   *The Homeric Hymn to Demeter*, Oxford.

(1975)   'Homeric professors in the age of the sophists', *PCPS* 21, 65–81.

Riginos, A. (1976)   *Platonica*, Leiden.

Rissman, L. (1983)   *Love as War: Homeric Allusion in the poetry of Sappho*, Königsten.

Robbins, E. (1975) 'Jason and Chiron: the myth of Pindar's Fourth Pythian', *Phoenix* 29, 205–13.

Rohde, E. (1925)² *Psyche: Seelencult and Unterblichkeitsglaube der Griechen*, New York.

Rohdich, H. (1980) 'Die Hund Argos und die Anfänge bürgerliches Selbstbewusstseins', *A&A* 26, 33–50.

Rose, A. (1984) 'Three narrative patterns in Apollonius' Berbrycian episode (*Argonautica* 2, 1–163)', *WS* 18, 115–35.

(1985) 'Clothing imagery in Apollonius' *Argonautica*', *QUCC* 50, 29–44.

Rose, G. (1979) 'Odysseus' barking heart', *TAPA* 109, 216–20.

(1980) 'The swineherd and the beggar', *Phoenix* 34, 285–97.

Rose, M. (1979) *Parody//Metafiction*, London.

Rose, P. (1974) 'The myth of Pindar's first Nemean: sportsmen, poetry and paideia', *HSCP* 78, 145–75.

(1975) 'Class ambivalence in the *Odyssey*', *Historia* 24, 129–49.

Rosellini, M. (1979) '*Lysistrata*: une mise en scène de la fémininité', in *Aristophane: Les Femmes et la cité, Les Cahiers de Fontenay* 17, Paris.

Rosenmeyer, P. *The Poetics of Imitation: Anacreon and the Anacreontic Poets* (forthcoming)

Rosenmeyer, T. (1969) *The Green Cabinet: Theocritus and the European Pastoral Lyric*, Berkeley.

Rösler, W. (1980) *Dichter und Gruppe*, Munich.

(1985) 'Persona reale o persona poetica? 'L'interpretazione dell' "io" nella lirica greca arcaica', *QUCC* 19, 131–44.

(1986) 'Michail Bachtin und die Karnevalekultur in antiken Griechenland', *QUCC* 23, 25–44.

Rosner, J. (1976) 'The speech of Phoenix: *Iliad* 9.434–605', *Phoenix* 30, 314–27.

Rubin, N. (1980a) 'Pindar's creation of epinician symbols', *CW* 74, 67–87.

(1980b) '*Olympian* 7: the toast and the future prayer', *Hermes* 108, 248–52.

Rubino, C. and Shelmerdine, C. edd. (1983) *Approaches to Homer*, Austin.

Ruck, C. (1968) 'Marginalia Pindarica', *Hermes* 96, 129–42.

(1976) 'On the sacred names of Iamus and Ion: ethnobotanical referents in the hero's parentage', *CJ* 71, 235–52.

Russell, D. (1981) *Criticism in Antiquity*, London.

Russo, J. (1974) 'The inner man in Archilochus and the *Odyssey*', *GRBS* 15, 139–52.

(1982) 'Interview and aftermath: dream, fantasy and intuition in *Odyssey* 19 and 20', *AJP* 103, 4–18.

(1985) *Omero: Odissea Libri xvii–xx*, Verona.

Rusten, J. (1983) 'ΓΕΙΤΩΝ ΗΡΩΣ. Pindar's prayer to Heracles (N. 7.86–101)', *HSPh* 87, 289–97.

Rüter, K. (1969) *Odysseeinterpretationen*, Göttingen.

Rutherford, R. (1982) 'Tragic form and feeling in the *Iliad*', *JHS* 102, 145–60.

(1985) 'At home and abroad: aspects of structure of the *Odyssey*', *PCPS* 31, 133–50.

Sacks, R. (1987) *The Traditional Phrase in Homer: Two Studies in Form, Meaning, and Interpretation*, Leiden.

Saïd, S. (1979) '*L'Assemblée des Femmes*: les femmes, l'économie et la politique', in *Aristophane: Les Femmes et la cité, Les Cahiers de Fontenay* 17, Paris.

de Ste Croix, G. (1972) *The Origins of the Peloponnesian War*, London.

Salingar, L. (1979) 'Crowd and public in *Bartholomew Fair*', *Renaissance Drama* 10, 141–59.

Saunders, J. (1951) 'The stigma of print: a note on the social bases of Tudor poetry', *Essays in Criticism* 1, 139–64.

Schadewaldt, W. (1928) *Die Aufbau des pindarischen Epinikion*, Halle an der Salle.

(1938) *Iliasstudien*, Leipzig.

(1965) *Von Homers Welt und Werk*, Stuttgart.

Schaps, D. (1977) 'The woman least mentioned: etiquette and women's names', *CQ* 27, 323–30.

Schein, S. (1970) 'Odysseus and Polyphemus in the *Odyssey*', *GRBS* 11, 73–83.

(1980) 'On Achilles' speech to Odysseus. *Iliad* 9.308–429', *Eranos* 78, 125–31.

(1984) *The Mortal Hero. An Introduction to the Iliad*, Berkeley.

Schenkeveld, D. (1976) 'Strabo on Homer', *Mnemosyne* 29, 52–64.

Schlegel, A. (1966) *Vorlesungen über dramatische Kunst und Literatur*, Mainz.

Schlesinger, A. (1936) 'Indications of parody in Aristophanes', *TAPA* 67, 296–314.

(1937) 'Identification of parodies in Aristophanes', *AJP* 58, 294–305.

Schmiel, R. (1987) 'Achilles in Hades', *CP* 82, 35–7.

Schmitt, R. (1967) *Dichtung und Dichtersprache in indogermanischer Zeit*, Wiesbaden.

Schnapp-Gourbeillon, A. (1982) 'Les funérailles de Patrocle', in Gnoli and Vernant (1982).

Scholes, R. and Kellogg, R. (1966) *The Nature of Narrative*, New York.

Schwinge, E-R (1975) 'Kritik und Komik: Gedanken zu Aristophanes' *Wespen*', in *Dialogos: für Harald Patzer zum 65. Geburtstag*, edd. J. Cobet, R. Leimback, A. Neschke-Heutschke, Wiesbaden.

Scodel, R. (1982) 'The autobiography of Phoenix: *Iliad* 9.444–95', *AJP* 103, 128–36.

(1983) 'Timocreon's encomium of Aristides', *CA* 2, 102–7.

Scott, M. (1982) '*Philos, philotes*, and *xenia*', *A Class* 25, 1–19.

Scott, W. (1974) *The Oral Nature of the Homeric Simile*, Leiden.

Scully, S. (1981a) 'The polis in Homer. A definition and interpretation', *Ramus* 11, 1–34.

(1981b) 'The bard as custodian of Homeric society', *QUCC* 37, 67–83.

Searle, J. (1969)   *Speech Acts*, Cambridge.

Seeck, G. (1975)   'Dichterische Technik in Theokrits "Thalysien" und die Theorie der Hirtendichtung', in *ΔΩPHMA Hans Diller*, Athens.

(1979)   *Das griechische Drama*, Darmstadt.

Seelbach, W. (1964)   *Die Epigramme des Msalkes von Sikyon und des Theodoridas von Syrakus*, Wiesbaden.

Segal, C. (1961)   'The character and cults of Dionysus and the unity of the *Frogs*', *HSCP* 65, 207–42.

(1962)   'The Phaeacians and the symbolism of Odysseus' return', *Arion* 1, 17–64.

(1967)   'Transition and ritual in Odysseus' return', *PP* 22, 321–42.

(1970a)   '"The myth was saved": reflections on Homer and the mythology of Plato's *Republic*', *Hermes* 106, 315–36.

(1970b)   'Protagoras' *orthoepeia* in Aristophanes' "Battle of the Prologues"', *RhM* 113, 158–62.

(1971)   *The Theme of the Mutilation of the Corpse in the Iliad*, Leiden.

(1974)   'Time and the hero: the myth of *Nemean* 1', *RhM* 108, 29–39.

(1981)   *Poetry and Myth in Ancient Pastoral: Essays on Theocritus and Virgil*, Princeton.

(1983)   '*Kleos* and its ironies in the *Odyssey*', *AC* 52, 22–47.

(1984)   'Underreading and intertextuality: Sappho, Simaetha and Odysseus in Theocritus' second Idyll', *Arethusa* 17, 201–9.

(1985)   'Space, time and imagination in Theocritus' Second Idyll', *CSCA* 16, 103–19.

(1986a)   'Tithonus and the Homeric *Hymn to Aphrodite*: a comment', *Arethusa* 19, 37–47.

(1986b)   *Pindar's Mythmaking: the Fourth Pythian Ode*, Princeton.

Serrao, G. (1971)   *Problemi di Poesia Allesandrina: 1, Studi su Teocrito*, Rome.

Serres, M. (1979)   'The algebra of literature: the wolf's game', in *Textual Strategies: Perspectives in Post-Structuralist Criticism*, ed. J. Harari, Ithaca.

Severyns, A. (1928)   *Le Cycle épique dans l'école d'Aristarque*, Liège.

Shannon, R. (1975)   *The Arms of Achilles and Homeric Compositional Technique*, Leiden.

Shapiro, H. (1980)   'Jason's cloak', *TAPA* 110, 263–86.

Shaw, P. (1981)   *American Patriots and the Rituals of Revolution*, Cambridge, Mass.

Shey, H. (1976)   'Tyrtaeus and the art of propaganda', *Arethusa* 9, 5–28.

Shipp, G. (1972)²   *Studies in the Language of Homer*, Cambridge.

Shlonsky, T. (1966)   'Literary parody: remarks on its method and function', in Jost (1966).

Shuttleworth, S. (1984)   *George Eliot and Nineteenth-Century Science: the Make-Believe of a Beginning*, Cambridge.

Sifakis, G. (1971)   *Parabasis and Animal Choruses*, London.

Silk, M. (1974)   *Interaction in Poetic Imagery*, Cambridge.

(1983)   'LSJ and the problem of poetic archaism: from meaning to iconyms', *CQ* 33, 303–30.

Silverman, K. (1982)   *The Subject of Semiotics*, New York.

Simon, E. (1983)   *Festivals of Attica*, Madison.

Sinfield, A. (1983)   *Literature in Protestant England 1560–1660*, London.

Sinos, D. (1980)   *Achilles, Patroklos and the meaning of Philos*, Innsbruck.

Sisti, F. (1966)   'Ibico e Policrate', *QUCC* 2, 91–102.

(1967)   'L'ode a Policrate: un caso di recusatio in Ibico', *QUCC* 4, 59–79.

Slater, W. (1972)   'Simonides' house', *Phoenix* 26, 232–40.

(1977)   'Doubts about Pindaric interpretation', *CJ* 73, 193–208.

(1984)   '*Nemean* One: the victor's return in poetry and politics', in Gerber ed. (1984).

Snell, B. (1944)   'Ibykos' Gedicht auf Polykrates', *Philologus* 96, 290–2.

(1953)   *The Discovery of the Mind*, trans. T. Rosenmeyer, Cambridge, Mass.

(1961)   *Poetry and Society*, Bloomington.

(1979)   'Lekythion', *Hermes* 107, 129–33.

Snodgrass, A. (1974)   'An historical Homeric society?', *JHS* 94, 114–25.

Snyder, T. (1974)   'Aristophanes' Agathon as Anacreon', *Hermes* 102, 244–6.

(1981)   'The web of song: weaving imagery in Homer and the lyric poets', *CJ* 76, 193–6.

Sommerstein, A. (1974)   'Aristophanes' *Frogs*', *CQ* 24, 24–7.

(1980)   *Acharnians*, Warminster, Wilts.

(1986)   'The decree of Syrakosios', *CQ* 36, 101–8.

Sourvinou-Inwood, C (1986)   'Crime and punishment: Tityos, Tantalus, and Sisyphos in *Odyssey* 11', *BICS* 33, 37–58.

Spofford, A. (1969)   'Theocritus and Polyphemus', *AJP* 90, 22–35.

Stagakis, G. (1975)   *Studies in Homeric Society. Hermes Einzelschr.* 25.

Stallybrass, P. and White, A. (1986)   *The Politics and Poetics of Transgression*, London.

Stanford, W. (1959)²   *The Odyssey of Homer*, 2 vols., London.

(1963)   *Aristophanes. The Frogs*, London.

Steiner, W. (1986)   *The Crown of Song: Metaphor in Pindar*, London.

Stern, J. (1970)   'The myth of Pindar's *Olympian* 6', *AJP* 91, 332–40.

(1978)   'Theocritus' *Epithalamium for Helen*', *RBPh* 66, 29–37.

Stern, J. and Calder, W. (1970)   *Pindaros und Bakchylides*, Darmstadt.

Stewart, D. (1976)   *The Disguised Guest: Rank, Role and Identity in the Odyssey*, Lewisburg.

Stewart, S. (1978)   *Nonsense: Aspects of Intertextuality in Folklore and Literature*, Baltimore and London.

Stinton, T. (1976)   '"Si credere dignum est": some expressions of disbelief in Euripides and others', *PCPS* 22, 60–89.

Stone, L. (1965)   *The Crisis of the Aristocracy 1558–1641*, London.

Suerbaum, W. (1968) 'Die Ich-Erzählung des Odysseus', *Poetica* 2, 108–77.

Suleiman, S. and Crossman, I. edd. (1980) *The Reader in the Text*: *Essays on Audience and Interpretation*, Princeton.

Sulzberger, M. (1926) 'ONOMA ΕΠΩΝΥΜΟΝ: les noms propres chez Homère', *REG* 39, 381–447.

Svenbro, J. (1976) *La Parole et le Marbre*, Lund.

Tanner, T. (1979) *Adultery in the Novel*, Baltimore.

Taplin, O. (1980) 'The shield of Achilles within the *Iliad*', *G&R* 27, 1–21.

(1983) 'Tragedy and trugedy', *CQ* 33, 331–33.

(1990) 'Agamemnon in the *Iliad*', in *Character and Individuality in Greek Literature*, ed. C. Pelling, Oxford.

Tarkow, T. (1977) 'Theognis 237–54: a re-examination', *QUCC* 26, 99–114.

(1983) 'Tyrtaeus 9D: the role of poetry in the new Sparta', *AC* 52, 48–69.

Tarrant, D. (1955) 'Plato as dramatist', *JHS* 75, 81–9.

Tatum, J. (1989) *Xenophon's Imperial Fiction*: *on The Education of Cyrus*, Princeton.

Taylor, C. (1961) 'The obstacles to Odysseus' return', *Yale Review* 50, 569–80.

ed. (1963) *Essays on the Odyssey*: *Selected Modern Criticism*, Bloomington.

Tennenhouse, L. (1981) 'Sir Walter Ralegh and the literature of clientage', in Lytle and Orgel (1981).

(1986) *Power on Display*: *the Politics of Shakespeare's Genres*, New York and London.

Thalmann, G. (1984) *Conventions of Form and Thought in Early Greek Epic Poetry*, Baltimore.

Theyer, C. (1963) *Ben Jonson*: *Studies in the Plays*, Norman, Oklahoma.

Thiercy, P. (1986) *Aristophane*: *fiction et dramaturgie*, Paris.

Thompson, E. (1972) '"Rough music": le charivari Anglais', *Annales ESC* 27, 285–312.

Thornton, A. (1976) *People and Themes in Homer's Odyssey*, London and Dunedin.

(1984) *Homer's Iliad*: *its Composition and the Motif of Supplication*, Göttingen.

Thorsen, S. (1978) 'The interpretation of Sappho's fr. 16 L–P', *SO* 53, 5–23.

Thummer, E. (1968) *Die Isthmischen Gedichte*, 2 vols., Heidelberg.

Todorov, T. (1977) *The Poetics of Prose*, trans. R. Howard, Ithaca.

(1982) *Theories of the Symbol*, trans. C. Porter, Oxford.

Tompkins, J. ed. (1980) *Reader-Response Criticism*: *from Formalism to Post-Structuralism*, Baltimore and London.

Trahman, C. (1952) 'Odysseus' lies', *Phoenix* 6, 31–43.

Treu, M. (1955) *Von Homer zur Lyrik*, Munich.

(1963) 'Selbstzeugnisse alexandrinischer Dichter', in *Miscellanea di studi alessandrini in memoria di Augusto Rostagni*, Turin.

(1965) 'Von der Weisheit der Dichter', *Gymnasium* 72, 434–49.

Turner, V. (1967)   *The Forest of Symbols*, Ithaca.
  (1969)   *The Ritual Process*, Chicago.
  (1978)   'Conclusion', in Babcock ed. (1978).
Ulmer, G. (1984)   *Applied Grammatology*, Baltimore.
Usener, H. (1902)   'Milch und Honig', *RhM* 57, 177–95.
Vaio, J. (1971)   'Aristophanes' *Wasps*: the relevance of the final scenes', *GRBS* 12, 335–51.
Van Dam, H. (1988)   Review of Hardie (1983), *Gnomon* 60, 704–12.
Van Gennep, A. (1960) (1908)   *The Rites of Passage*, trans. M. Vizedom and G. Caffee, Chicago.
Van Nortwick, T. (1979)   'Penelope and Nausikaa', *TAPA* 109, 269–76.
Van Sickle, J. (1976)   'Theocritus and the development of the conception of bucolic genre', *Ramus* 5, 18–44.
Verdenius, W. (1970)   'Homer the educator of the Greeks', *Meded. Akad. van Wet. Afd. Letterk.* 33, 207–31.
  (1979)   'Pindar's fourteenth Olympian ode', *Mnemosyne* 32, 12–38.
Vernant, J-P. (1965)   *Mythe et pensée chez les Grecs*, Paris.
  (1979)   'ΠΑΝΤΑ ΚΑΛΑ d'Homère à Simonide', *Annali della Scuola Normale di Pisa* 9, 1365–74.
  (1980)   *Myth and Society in Ancient Greece*, trans. J. Lloyd, London.
  (1982)   'La belle mort et le cadavre outragé', in Gnoli and Vernant (1982).
Vetta, M. (1980)   *Theognis. Elegiarum liber secundus*, Rome.
Vian, F. (1976)   *Apollonius de Rhodes: Argonautiques. Tome 1*, Paris.
  (1978)   'ΙΗΣΩΝ ΑΜΗΧΑΝΟΣ', in Livrea and Privitera edd. 1978.
  (1980)   *Apollonius de Rhodes: Argonautiques. Tome 2*, Paris.
  (1981)   *Apollonius de Rhodes: Argonautiques. Tome 3*, Paris.
Vidal-Naquet, P. (1981)   *Le chasseur noir: formes de pensée et formes de société dans le monde grec*, Paris.
  (1981 (1970))   'Valeurs religieuses et mythiques de la terre et du sacrifice dans l'*Odyssée*', in Vidal-Naquet (1981), first published *Annales ESC* 25 (1970) 1278–97, translated with corrections in Gordon ed. (1981)
Vivante, P. (1972)   'On time in Pindar', *Arethusa* 5, 107–31.
Voigt, C. (1972)   *Überlegung und Entscheidung: Studien zur Selbstauffassung des Menschen bei Homer*, Meisenheim am Glan.
de Vries, G. (1973)   'Mystery terminology in Aristophanes and Plato', *Mnemosyne* 26, 1–8.
Walcot, P. (1977)   'Odysseus and the art of lying', *Ancient Society* 8, 1–19.
Walker, S. (1980)   *Theocritus*, Boston.
Walsh, G. (1984)   *The Varieties of Enchantment: Early Greek Views of the Nature and Function of Poetry*, Chapel Hill.
  (1985)   'Seeing and feeling: representation in two poems of Theocritus', *CP* 80, 1–19.
Waszink, J. (1974)   *Biene und Honig als Symbol des Dichters und Dichtung in der griech. -Röm. Antike*, Opladen.

Weber, C. (1983) 'Two chronological difficulties in Catullus 64', *TAPA* 113, 263–71.

Wellein, L. (1959–60) 'Duality in Ibycus 3', *CB* 36, 40–1.

Wendel, C. (1932) *Die Uberlieferung der Scholien zu Apollonios von Rhodos*, Berlin.

Wender, D. (1978) *The Last Scenes of the Odyssey*, Leiden.

West, M. (1966) *Hesiod. Theogony*, Oxford.

   (1970) 'Melica', *CQ* 20, 205–15.

   (1974) *Studies in Greek Elegy and Iambus*, Berlin.

   (1978) *Hesiod. Works and Days*, Oxford.

   (1985) 'The lost opening of the *Choephoroi*', *LCM* 10, 130–1.

White, M. (1954) 'The duration of the Samian tyranny', *JHS* 74 (1954) 36–43.

Whitehead, O. (1984) 'The funeral of Achilles. An epilogue to the *Iliad* in Book 24 of the *Odyssey*', *G&R* 31, 119–25.

Whitman, C. (1958) *Homer and the Heroic Tradition*, Cambridge, Mass.

   (1964) *Aristophanes and the Comic Hero*, Cambridge, Mass.

   (1969) 'ΛΗΚΥΘΙΟΝ ΑΠΩΛΕΣΕΝ', *HSCP* 73, 109–12.

Wilamowitz-Moellendorff, U. (1884) *Homerische Untersuchungen*, Berlin.

   (1886) *Isyllos von Epidauros*, Berlin.

   (1913) *Sappho und Simonides*, Berlin.

   (1922) *Pindaros*, Berlin.

   (1924) *Hellenistische Dichtung II*, Berlin.

Wilden, A. (1968) *The Language of the Self*, Baltimore.

Wilkerson, K. (1982) 'From hero to citizen: persuasion in early Greece', *Ph and Rh* 15, 104–25.

Will, Ed. (1957) 'Aux origines du régime foncier grec', *REA* 59, 5–50.

Will, Er. (1965) 'Hésiode: crise agraire ou recul de l'aristocracie', *REG* 78, 542–6.

Willcock, M. (1964) 'Mythological paradeigma in the *Iliad*', *CQ* 14, 141–54.

Williams, F. (1971) 'A theophany in Theocritus', *CQ* 21, 137–45.

   (1986) 'Odysseus' homecoming as a parody of Homeric formal welcomes', *CW* 79, 395–7.

Wills, G. (1969) 'Aeschylus' victory in the *Frogs*', *AJP* 90, 48–57.

Wilson, J. (1974) 'The wedding gifts of Peleus', *Phoenix* 28, 385–9.

Winkler, J. (1990) *The Constraints of Desire*, New York.

Woodbury, L. (1952) 'The seal of Theognis', in *Studies in Honour of Gilbert Norwood*, Toronto.

   (1953) 'Simonides on ἀρετή', *TAPA* 84, 135–63.

   (1955) 'The tongue and the whetstone: Pindar *Ol.* 6.82–3', *TAPA* 86, 31–9.

   (1968) 'Pindar and the mercenary muse: *Isth.* 2.1–13', *TAPA* 99, 527–42.

   (1985) 'Ibycus and Polycrates', *Phoenix* 39, 193–220.

Wright, E. (1984) *Psychoanalytic Criticism*, London.

Wycherley, R. (1946) 'Aristophanes and Euripides', *G&R* 15, 98–107.

Young, D. (1968) *Three Odes of Pindar*, Leiden.

(1970a) 'Pindaric criticism', in Stern and Calder (1970).

(1970b) 'Pindar *Nemean* 7: some preliminary remarks (vv. 1–20)', *TAPA* 101, 633–43.

(1971) *Pindar Isthmian 7. Myth and Exempla*, Leiden.

(1979) 'Pindar's style at *Pythian* 9.87f', *GRBS* 20, 133–43.

Zagagi, N. (1984) 'Self-recognition in Theocritus' seventh Idyll', *Hermes* 112, 427–38.

Zanker, G. (1979) 'The love theme in Apollonius Rhodius' *Argonautica*', *WS* 13, 52–73.

(1983) 'The nature and origin of realism in Alexandrian poetry', *A&A* 29, 125–45.

(1987) *Realism in Alexandrian Poetry: a Literature and its Audience*, London.

Zeitlin, F. (1982a) 'Travesties of gender and genre in Aristophanes' *Thesmophoriazusae*', in Foley ed. (1982).

(1982b) *Under the Sign of the Shield: Semiotics and Aeschylus' Seven against Thebes*, Rome.

Index